AMERICAN LABOR

FROM CONSPIRACY
TO
COLLECTIVE BARGAINING

THE LABORER

A Remedy for His Wrongs

William Dealtry

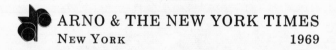

ARNO & THE NEW YORK TIMES

NEW YORK   1969

Reprint edition 1969 by Arno Press, Inc.

Library of Congress Catalog Card No. 76-89729

Reprinted from a copy in the
U. S. Department of Labor Library

Manufactured in the United States of America

THE LABORER

A Remedy for His Wrongs

My aim is to teach that all governments are usurpations on the rights of laboring people. They corrupt and plunder mankind. For laborers to delegate power to rich men to make laws, is to create enemies and plunderers of the toiling people. Modern civilization, with its train of luxury, sacrifices human beings, consigns them to sorrow, and engulfs them almost in living tombs.

Wm. Dealtry.

The Laborer:

A Remedy for His Wrongs;

OR,

A DISQUISITION ON THE USAGES OF SOCIETY.

BY WILLIAM DEALTRY,

(Cabinet Maker,)

Author of "The History of Money; its Evils and Remedy."

"Oh mankind, what noble creatures you ought to be! You have keys to all sciences, arts, and mysteries, but one! You can not frame a tolerable law for the life and soul of you. You lay down rules it is impossible to comprehend, much less to obey. You call each other monsters because you can not conquer the impossibility! You invent all sorts of vices, under pretense of making laws for promoting virtue. You make yourselves as uncomfortable as you can by all sorts of galling, vexatious institutions."—Bulwer's Paul Clifford.

CINCINNATI.

Wm. Dealtry, *Compositor;* R. Allison & Co., *Stereotypers.*

MDCCCLXIX.

STEREOTYPED AT THE FRANKLIN TYPE FOUNDRY, CINCINNATI, O.

This
collection of
opinions and his-
torical facts are affec-
tionately dedicated to the

Honorable B. F. Wade,

and those Senators who "can not solve
the labor question," and also to those who
believe the hours of labor can be shortened by industry, frugality, and the
use of machinery; to those parents who wish their chil-
dren saved from un-
necessary labor;
to those American youths
who wish to become acquainted with
their duties as citizens of the GREAT REPUBLIC.
This book is kindly given by an humble laborer,
with the earnest hope that it may teach them this.

The author is indebted to these and others for his facts.

Raynal's History of the East and West Indies, six volumes.

Encyclopedia Britannica, Edinburgh edition of 1780.

Abbott's French Revolution.

Mildmay's Financial History of England.

Smith's Wealth of Nations.

Wade's History of the Middle and Working-classes.

Giddings' Exiles of Florida.

Chambers' Repository and Papers for the People.

Godwin's Political Justice and Inquirer.

Rev. Sidney Smith's Works.

Knight's Biographical Dictionary, six volumes.

Hume's History of England.

Randle's Life of Jefferson, three volumes.

Glimpses of the Dark Ages.

Carey's Social Science, three volumes.

Bulwer's England and the English, two volumes.

Stanton's Sketches of Reforms and Reformers.

De Toqueville's Old Regime and the French Revolution.

Ramsey's History of the United States and South Carolina.

Hildreth's History of the United States, four volumes.

Disraeli's Curiosities of Literature.

Turner's Sacred History of the World.

Miller's Schools and Schoolmasters.

Lord Kame's History of Man, four volumes.

Wesley's Works, thirty volumes, edition of 1780.

Kay's Social condition of England.

Pridden's History and present condition of Australia.

Howitt's Rural Life in England.

Abbott's life of William the Conqueror.

Winterbottom's, Rochefoucalt's, De Warville's, Weld's, Melish's, Volney's and Peto's Travels in the United States.

PREFACE.

WEALTH or fame is not the author's motive for writing this book; it is to encourage the working-man to persevere in his efforts to shorten the hours of labor and ameliorate his condition. The laborer who does so much for the happiness of mankind —who accomplishes such mighty works—ought to have the greatest reward; he deserves it.

It has been said, if the laborers were educated, none would be found to black the boots or curry the horses of those who were above the laborer. Learning will, in time, level all inequalities of life. In boyhood, the writer read one of the American Tract Society's reprints, called the "Shepherd of Salisbury Plain." A gentleman on horseback entered into a conversation about the weather. Said he, "Do you live where I see yonder smoke?" Said the shepherd, "No, I have not much firing, and sometimes *nothing to eat*." This narration moved the writer to tears, to think that there was one in this world so destitute. The writer's reflections on reading this were, the earth was full of abundance, and it needed labor to bring it out.

This gentleman had a habit of taking a walk "to con-

template the goodness of God." It occurred to the mind
of the writer, if this man would contemplate the goodness of
God on the plow handles, it would be better for mankind.
It is idleness on the part of others, and robbery caused by
governments, that caused the shepherd's misery. This employment could not be any better. This shepherd would
not drink ale with the gentleman. He was very industrious.
His earnings were a shilling a day. He had a wife and six
children; their food was mostly potatoes. This gentleman paid the family a visit, and overheard one of the children say, having salt to their food, they should be contented.
Religion is not given us to make us contented with misery.
This gentleman gave to the family blankets, which, perhaps,
had been taken from a starved tenantry, in the shape of rent
or profits on the labor of others. This shepherd was made
a parson's clerk. On Sunday he wore a white robe and said
"Amen" to the Church of England's prayers. The scanty
pittance he got for this from the congregation only lessened
their comforts of life.

This tract led to this reflection, if all the kings, nobles,
priests, soldiers, lawyers, custom-house officers, and many
others would do something of utility, there would be no
poverty in the world. Hannah More wrote books to cure
French infidelity. They got the name of " Village Chips."
France was so full of philosophers, priests, nobles, kings, and
courtiers, that the common people had not a sufficiency of
food; this led to their destruction

Miss More by her village chips and other writings, gain-

ed $150,000. This amount was left to build a church as
a monument. If Miss More had not been a Christian, she
would have left this money at interest, it would have given
$9,000; this sum would have kept in idleness 960 *persons*,
or 120 families on potatoes. This interest at the time of
this lady's death, [1833] would keep in idleness thirty mechanics' families in comfort and happiness.

It is the duty of every one to resolve to work at useful,
laborious toil. It is the duty of every one who labors thus
to keep himself only. The misery of the world arises from
one man's keeping another doing nothing, and whose claim
for support is not founded on nature. That rich men should
leave their families to be clothed and fed, by the industrious, by interest, life insurance or otherwise, is absurd, and
a more enlightened age will sweep them away.

The apology for intruding this book upon the laborers'
notice, is that the writer has had access to large, and costly
libraries, and his reading has been of that nature, so that he
may set his own class to reasoning correctly on political
subjects. The facts in this book have been acquired when
the day's labor was done, most of them during the last two
years. This book has its literary faults. The writer quit
school at ten years of age.

The writer can get no one to print this book. He has
purchased type and sets them up. He is a cabinet-maker,
not a printer; and this will account for typographical faults.

It is a pleasing thought this book can be printed without
asking permission. Greater changes are to be made in

men's condition. The thunders of the Vatican have tried to strike out of the hands of men, the writings of Wickliff, Huss, and Luther. At Rome a body of literary despots make out a catalogue of books, that are forbidden to be read. In Spain a book goes through half a dozen courts before it is published. Queen Elizabeth punished an author for an offending book. King James compelled books to be examined "and purged of offensive matter." Milton's Paradise Lost was altered, after a few years it was printed as written. Sir Mathew Hale did not want his books printed after his death, he was afraid the "Licensers of the Press" might change them.

This book will show what others have suffered for to ameliorate the condition of those who toil. Sir Thomas More lost his head on the block; his Utopia would offend many. Fenelon was banished from the French court. In prison Voltaire wrote his "Henriade" and "Toleration;" Cobbett his "Paper against Gold;" and Montgomery some of his poems. Brissot De Warville, after his visit to this country, with thirteen others suffered on the guillotine. Byron only went three times to the House of Lords; he told them they were robbers of the people. Bulwer says the writings of the social philosophers of last century are not generally known. If this collection of opinions and historical facts shall teach the young, to think, and save them from unpaid toil; the writer's labor has not been in vain.

CIN. UNION BLOCK. 3rd ST.   W. DEALTRY.

CONTENTS.

CHAPTER X.

MERCHANTS AND LAWYERS.

MERCHANTS are the Founders of Cities—A Cause of the Overthrow of Slavery—Merchants are too Numerous—The Causes why Lawyers Exist—They are too numerous—An injury to Society............217

CHAPTER XI.

PHYSICIANS AND MINISTERS.

JOHN WESLEY'S Remedies for Sickness—Opinions of the Democratic Review—Jefferson—Priessnitz—Bulwer—Havelock--Volney--The Early Christians—St. Chrysostom—Tertullian—The Moravians.241

CHAPTER XII.

FARMERS AND MECHANICS.

THE Farmer's Burdens are too Heavy—It is his duty to make them Lighter—How to Educate his Children—To Fertilize the Soil—How the Mechanic may Shorten his Labor—How to Obtain a Home.......265

CHAPTER XIII.

THE AMERICAN GOVERNMENT.

THE American Government has not Ameliorated the Condition of the Working People—It Should be Changed—It Benefits the Rich, not the Poor—Opinions of Brissot de Warville—Marquis de Chastellux...289

CHAPTER XIV.

THE FRENCH REVOLUTION.

ITS Causes, Cruelties, and Benefits—A Contest between Nobles and People—The Number of its Victims—The Edict of Nantes—The Profligacy of the Kings of France—Death of Louis the Fourteenth....313

CHAPTER XV.

STATESMEN AND POLITICAL ECONOMISTS.

CHAPTER XVI.

SOCIAL AND MORAL INNOVATORS.

CHAPTER XVII.

REASONS FOR REFORMS.

CHAPTER XVIII.

CONCLUSION.

NOTE.

PAGE twenty-four, line nineteen, and page two-hundred and ninety, line two, the writer quotes from memory. The proper books can not at this time be obtained.

THE LABORER,

&c.

CHAPTER I.

REFORMS ARE NECESSARY.

HUMAN SOCIETY IS FULL OF MISERY--THERE IS A COMPLETE REMEDY--THE HOURS OF TOIL CAN BE SHORTENED--OPINIONS OF GOOD MEN.

"The history of the past is to enlighten men."--SWIFT.

THE minds of the good and benevolent are continually pained by the sight of human sorrow, caused by want. This comes from man's ignorance; from one man oppressing another, and blinding his reason. The Creator of the Universe has done his part well; nothing is lacking to complete man's happiness. If a poor man spends his time sculpturing a stone, and calls it Apollo or Diana, he will want bread. If the man parts with his statue, some one else suffers want. The peasant of Ireland, for the use of the soil, which ought to be his own, is compelled to give three-fourths of his food to another. If the landlord gives this food to painters and sculptors, their concentrated labor is at the expense of the peasant's comforts. How abject and mean are the inhabitants of Bavaria. Its ruler is guilty of the madness of impoverishing his subjects. He has built two large and costly temples, of the finest style of architecture. These temples are filled with paintings and statuary. The Bavarians are poor; if the labor on these temples, statues, and paintings had been put on the homes of the Bavarians, they would be happy. "The introduction of the fine arts into America may be regarded as a national calamity."*

Men work on luxuries, and want necessaries. Men work on stone carvings for a mansion front, and go to a home destitute of comfort, or even ornament.† Nature designed that men should work more for themselves and less for others. The poverty of many of the Americans arises from keeping many doing nothing. Their Legislators, in trying to put down evil, do a great deal of wrong; while doing it they consume large quantites of labor.

If the laborers lived in the palaces they build and adorn, it would be more rational. History is silent how those who built the Pyramids lived; their labor made them wretched: much of modern labor does the same. We need earnest-hearted men to turn labor into other channels. It is the duty of the good to do something for those who suffer. These cases call for a reform.

The "Methodist Book Concern" has a book called "Aunt Effie." Her husband was killed while making a fine cornice; the scaffold fell. Her nice home passed away. At No. 6 Court street she put out this sign: "Washing done

---

* BRISSOT DE WARVILLE's Travels in North America, in 1787.

† The writer knows a good, temperate, marble cutter, who sleeps in an alley. Others work on tombstones worth forty thousand dollars, they have no homes. These men do themselves and society an injustice. It is a wrong.

here:" none came to give her work, and she was reduced to her last crust. After trying to beg she returned to her home—to die! Her thoughts were that she would fill a pauper's grave. She was thirty-six hours without food. Some benevolent ladies, at last, found her out, when ready to faint with hunger.

Near Louisville two women lived in a hollow tree; their bed was corn shucks, which they sold in the market; they did washing. They were found by a hunter, who saw their tracks in the snow. The Cincinnati Commercial tells us of Stewart, the New York merchant, living in a mansion worth $2,000,000, and of news boys sleeping in boxes and barrels. It also tells us of a steam plow, that plowed in England four hundred acres of land. Another paragraph, by way of contrast, tells us of a dozen persons found frozen in the streets of London; besides those who were frozen in their dens.

Monarchy and Republicanism are the same. They both divide into two classes; one to create labor, the other to destroy; into rich idlers and poor workers, one part possessing all, the other nothing. A life of toil and labor is binding on us all; from it there is no escape. If a man escapes toil, it is at the expense of some one else. When a man will not work, he does an injustice to those who will work. It is the duty of those who work to throw off this burden.

There have in every age and clime of the world, appeared men who could see clearly into the social ills of life. The ancient philosophers, as soon as symbolical writing had passed away, and letters were used, then taught that agriculture and pastoral pursuits, were for the happiness of men. Among the greatest who have tried to banish poverty, is Jesus. He would not allow his followers to possess riches. His command was sell all that thou hast, and give

it to the poor.　Excessive riches are made by speculation.
Many will buy a piece of ground, suitable for a home, for
$100 and sell it for $200.　Does not this seller do an injustice to the buyer?　If the seller makes many such sales,
he lives without laboring.　He is guilty of a breach of this
command, "Thou shalt not covet or desire other men's
goods."　Jesus saw that riches gave birth to idleness, and
that they impoverished the industrious and increased their
toils.　Even Paul said "If any man will not work neither
shall he eat."　He was a true reformer, and a rule for us
all.　For three centuries the early Christians despised
riches and lived together doing good.

St. Basil, who died A. D. 378, perceiving that many
Christians were in trouble from the wars, advised them to
unite in colleges.　He taught them that the Scriptural
doctrines led to the reformation of life, and men had something to practice.　St. Basil had seen religious societies in
Egypt.　He built a house large enough for his friends,
to share his retirement.　The place had near it a river,
that rolled over a rock, and it was full of fish, the woods
contained deer and wild goats.　They were constantly
employed at such labors, as gave them occupation without
anxiety.　Those arts were preferred which combined cheapness and simplicity, not requiring costly materials, or ministering to vanity.　Their pursuits were building, weaving,
and shoe making.　Others attended the flocks and soil.
Their house was a school for orphans, whom they clothed
and fed.　Pious people have not always lived this natural
life,—a life of labor and self denial.

The followers of John Huss became Moravians, Tunkers, and Mennonists.　Count Zinzendorf helped the Moravians to lands, which they worked with ingenuity, industry, and economy.　The Tunkers and Mennonists were

sects of Christians, who settled in Pennsylvania last century, having sprung from the Hussites; their principles were not to go to law, fight, or take interest for the loan of their money. They subsisted by attending lands, flour, oil, and paper mills, and other useful pursuits.

John Wesley paid a visit to Hernhutt, and Count Zinzendorf set him to work in his garden.* He did not like this, though he inculcated a life of plainness to his followers, and forbid ornaments in dress, houses, or equipages. His mind saw that luxury deprived some of the comforts of life. It may not appear very clear to some, as it does to Christians, how luxury is productive of evil; take this example: three girls in England each worked sixteen weeks on a scarf, for Queen Victoria; it was flowers worked on thin cloth with a needle. These girls ought to have been making flannels and stockings for themselves. There is no difficulty in proving, that those who do this work are poor. The pay of these girls was taken from others, by taxation. Nature designed that queens and ladies should make their own scarfs.

Archbishop Fenelon, in his Telemachus, plainly shews the causes of human misery, and the virtues of useful industry. Sir Thomas More, in his Utopia, where he describes the happy islanders, gives us plain, good advice, and how useful labors make men happy. The satires of these men on human society are very keen.

Lord Bolingbroke, in the time of Queen Anne, said, if every man would work one year, it would maintain him twenty years. Franklin tells us "If every one would labor four hours a day, at something useful, poverty and want would be unknown." Robert Owen spun the first bale of

* Chambers' Miscellany—The Moravians.

2

Sea Island cotton that was sent to England, into thread of very fine, even, and smooth texture. His earnings at nineteen were three thousand dollars a year. At twenty seven he purchased a factory worth $400,000. He saw a boy of sixteen years in chains, to be sent to a penal colony for his faults. This scene led Owen to reflect that, if other circumstances had been thrown around this boy, he would have been a better member of society. It led him to devote his wealth to improve his fellow-men. His workmen rented his cottages at the lowest price. He got for them the necessaries of life at first cost; and distributed them for the same. He introduced infant schools among the working people.

Robert Dale Owen says, in his writings: "My father had access to documents that others had not. His extensive experience as a manufacturer convinced him that England's labor-saving machinery, was equal to 400,000,000 of working men. Nineteen-twentieths of this power has been created in the last century. In the making of cotton goods, 3,000,000 of persons do the labor of 36,000,000. The labor-saving machinery of Great Britain, is the same as if every workman had forty slaves working for him, from morn to night without food or clothing. One-fortieth part of the present wealth of England, formerly afforded her population subsistence and comfort. A great number of these laborers, have not at this moment sufficient to subsist on in comfort. Great Britain has learned to produce wealth, and she does produce it most abundantly; but she has not learned to distribute it, to help her present distress. Now it is self-evident that if every person produced for himself every article of wealth that he required, no possible injustice could happen in its distribution; for each producer would retain and consume his own produce. It is also evident that if such a state of things could exist, labor-saving machinery must necessarily increase man's comforts, or diminish the hours of labor; for instance, if a man's powers of production increased forty-fold, and he was still content with the same quantity of wealth that satisfied his wants before the increase, he would only have to labor *eighteen minutes a day* instead of twelve hours, or he ought to have forty times as much wealth."

Lord Brougham has, in his writings on the nature of labor-saving machinery, declared: "That after the most careful investigation of the subject in England, with its present advantages in labor-saving machinery, but *twenty minutes* daily toil, by each individual would be required to furnish all with abundance."

Richard Cobden, in his political writings, says: "The effects of labor-saving machinery must ultimately reduce the hours of labor, as it already has mitigated its severity. The work of day will be crowded into a smaller space, so soon as our good people can learn that gold is not the highest good, and that man is something better than a beast of burden. We shall throw off the shackles which now make our callings our masters, and which reduce our life to one long unmitigated bondage to work. There is abundant evidence of approaching *emancipation* to the tillers of the soil, the artisan and operative."

If human labor is so productive, why are the feelings of good men pained, "with every day's report, of wrongs and outrages." These have appeared. "William Feidler, who killed himself in St. Louis, on account of poverty, and lack of employment, was the son of a wealthy merchant in Leipsic, Saxony."* "Last December, a mother and two

---

* Cincinnati Com. of Jan. 9th, 1868.

children perished with severe cold."* The same night, in Brooklyn, John Durant died with cold and hunger. On the first of Jan. 1866, a man died with hunger in Chicago, where there is food enough to support a province, and men often get smothered in wheat. Many will say intemperance causes much of this; it is not the cause of all the misery, which may be inferred from these two cases. A girl, of the name of Cooley, came to Covington from the country to work; and failed to get it. She was soon without money to get a night's lodging. After wandering about in a state of mind bordering on to distraction, the poor girl went on the Main Street ferry boat, and asked if the water was deep enough to drown. Upon being answered that it was, and before any one was aware, she jumped over board. The swift current swept her down the stream. She was saved and cared for.† Mary Wheeler was found sleeping out of doors. She was a woman of about fifty years, poorly clothed, but respectable in appearance, with a countenance indicative of honesty, and pinched with want. She said she had no home, no place to sleep, nothing to eat. She was alone in the world and friendless. A paralytic stroke had deprived her of the use of her right arm. The husband of this woman, twenty-five years ago, was one of the wealthiest in Chicago. He was a sober and industrious builder, and the father of an interesting family, and the owner of ten acres of land, on the north side of Kenzie Street.

The husband was drowned, the widow married again. In a few years she was deserted and robbed of her possessions. Her family died, except a daughter, who married unfortunately, and cannot give her mother a home. The

*Cincinnati Times, Dec. 1865. † Cincinnati Times of July, 1866.

poor, friendless, homeless and heart-broken woman is left to depend on public charity.—Times."

At the present time [winter of 1868] 50,000 mechanics are out of employment in the city of New York. If these persons go to work at toy-making, street-cleaning, and sewer-building their wants are relieved at some others' expense. Franklin says: " If the women will go behind the counter, and the men go to the workshop and the plow, the hardness of the times will cease."

Sir Morton Peto, in his Resources of America, says: "The annual value of the products of the farmers and mechanics are $2,000,000,000. And when the great Pacific Railroad is completed, the amount of gold added to the country will be yearly $150,000,000." If this amount is divided into the products of labor the product will be thirteen. These gold seekers destroy a thirteenth of the hats, shoes, clothes, and houses that are created. The man who earns a $1,000 in a year contributes $75 to the support of the gold seekers. The meaning of this language is this, the labor that is spent seeking for gold, would, in ten years' give every ten persons a home worth $500. We should think it a great hardship if a conqueror was to come and carry away annually one-thirteenth of our labor. The gold finders do this. We can not see the injury they do us.

If the laborer would relieve himself of care and anxiety, he must believe and act in a different manner from what he does. Human society may be likened to a column, the base is the farmers and mechanics, who have resting on them lawyers, doctors, soldiers, custom- house officers, merchants, bankers, landlords, and those who govern us. These get two-thirds of the laborer's toil. Many of these can be dispensed with. These classes have arisen through the corruptions of ages, and were necessary to eat up the subsistence of the people—to make, them poor. This poverty quickens the inventions of men. It is necessary. It was poverty that made Watt improve the steam-engine and Arkwright invent spinning machinery. Mankind, some time or other, will have a sufficiency of machinery and these unproductive classes will be swept away.

Says Bishop Clark: "In how many homes does poverty, care-consuming, pinching poverty—make its permanent abode! Daily toil scarcely suffices to provide for daily wants. The humblest and coarsest fare is all that is craved, and that, alas! is often craved in vain. How often does the very image of poverty, thinly clad, shivering in the winter's cold, with hasty step and averted eye, glide past us upon all our streets! Go to the desolate, cheerless home of want; mark its nakedness of all that is essential to home comfort; think how hard these parents toil, and how little they earn; how much these children need, and how little they have. And as you stand there, amid that scene of poverty and want, as you feel the pressure of their necessities, and your heart yearns towards them, ask thyself who hath made us to differ."

How painful is this description of sorrow. Many of these were once in affluence; childhood to them was full of toys, sunshine and flowers; they entered the learned professions and became briefless lawyers, doctors without patients, and ministers with thread-bare coats. Many of these did not think with Douglas Jerrold, that "The dignity of human life consisted in knowing how to handle a spade, and if we cultivate mother earth it will never cheat us, and we need not tell thumping lies, as they do on 'Change."

A young man in Indiana, said: He had cultivated sixty acres of corn, with machinery, and that he had 2,700 bu· shels of corn. One bushel of corn fattens twelve pounds of pork. This farmer raised also 500 bushels of wheat. This quantity lasts eighty years, allowing soldiers'rations. One bushel of wheat makes fifty pounds of flour. A pound of flour is a soldier's daily ration, with three-fourths of a pound of pork. The farmer had six barrels of molasses. This is the calculation:

60 acres$\times$45 bu.=2,700 bu. of corn.
2,700 bu.$\times$12 lbs.=32,400 lbs. of pork.
500 bu. of wheat$\times$50 lbs.=25,000 lbs. of flour.
32,400 lbs.$\div$273 lbs.=119 years, time to consume the pork.
25,000 lbs. of flour$\div$365 days=60 years, time to consume the flour.
119+60$\div$2=89 years, the average time to consume this food.

This is a paper demonstration and not very easily proved. This one is: A city laborer earns $500 in a year, working ten hours a day; he spends out of this sum $100 for tobacco, drinks and trifles; and $100 for house rent. By cutting off the trifles, in five years, this laborer will have saved sufficient for a country home, with a large garden. This laborer can now live with six hours labor in a day. Much of the laborer's earnings go to the market for vegetables, bacon, butter, eggs, and fruit. A country home cuts off all this expense. This life will reduce the hours of toil to four. In the days of Franklin there was a large commons, for the use of all; where cattle and hogs could graze. De Warville tells us in 1787: "The people on the banks of the Ohio did not labor more than two hours in a day." The people were not divided into hair-dressers, boot-blacks, cigar-makers, and milliners. There were no merchants to take away the food, and bring back silks and satins, silver and gold. The clothing of this period was home-spun and durable, not shoddy, which is old, filthy, woollen rags, ground into dust, one-third of which is mixed with long wool. This cloth is soon worn out.

There is nothing that makes the laborer so sick at heart, as being repulsed when begging work; and living in fear of being turned away for one who can work faster. There is misery among the higher classes. Many a father has spent his money, to put his son among the learned, or trading classes and failed. It often happens that he who was raised in affluence, descends to the lowest walks of human life; to be the drudge of others; to spend a life in wretchedness, penury, and want. There is a remedy.

Men are misled by writers on Political Science. This is an extract from M. Say, a Frenchman, whose book was used in American colleges for many years: " What is necessary subsistence, depends, therefore, partly on the habits of the nation, to which the laborer belongs. In proportion to the value he consumes his wages may be small, and the product of his labor cheap. If his condition be improved, and his wages raised, either his product becomes dearer to the consumer, or the share of his fellow-producers is diminished. The disadvantages of their position are an effectual barrier against any great extension of the consumption of the laboring classes. *Humanity, indeed, would rejoice to see them and their families dressed in warm clothing suitable to the climate and season; with houses roomy, warm, airy, in healthy situations, and fed with wholesome and plentiful diet, with an occasional delicacy*. But there are few countries where wants, apparently so moderate, are not considered beyond the limits of strict necessity, and therefore not to be gratified by the customary wages of the working classes."

The books of Wayland and Say have been the text books of the American Colleges for nearly half a century, and they have never given the laborer a champion. These books have not prevented want which is constantly growing in our large cities. Political Economists do not favor the humble classes; Mills and Carey are exceptions. From their teachings, and the practices of governments, come many of the inequalities of life. Their teachings are of the same nature as Dame Lobkins' advice to Paul Clifford, a stealer in one of Bulwer's novels; which reads thus:

"Mind thy kittychism, child, and reverence old age. Never steal, 'specially when any body be in the way. Never go snacks with them as be older than you,—'cause why? The older a cove be, the more he cares for hisself, and less for his partner. Read your Bible, and talk like a pious 'un. People goes more by your words, than your actions. If you wants what is not your own, try and do without it; and, if you can't do without it, take it by insinivation, not bluster. 'Cause they as only swindles, *does more* and *risks less* than those who rob outright. Now go and play; but here, take some money in your pocket, and don't play for nothing; it's loss of time; but mind, always play with them as be less than yourself, and then, if they says you go for to cheat, you go for to beat 'em."

In the city of New York, there is one person worth $60,000,000. A laborer would have to toil 120,000 years to get this amount, at the rate of $500 a year. A person to count this at the rate of $20,000 a day will be six years doing it. The annual income of this person is $6,000,000. A sum equal to the average yearly earnings of 10,000 mechanics. This yearly income will purchase 5,000,000 of acres of wild lands. This will make a province eighty miles square; and capable of supporting 1,500,000 persons, whose offspring can support twenty families in splendor for ages to come. For this man of wealth, seas must be crossed, dangers endured; the whole world must be ransacked, for costly food and clothing. Dozens of cringing

3

idle servants wait to do his bidding, and spend more time to prepare and ornament his food, than it does the farmer to create it. Often this man of money has no appetite, his food, which ought to nourish useful laborers, is often wasted. From his mansion comes the sounds of revelry and mirth, which mingles with the plaintive cry of the news-boy, whose voice may be heard sixteen hours in a day, his appetite is sharp, and he has often no food; then his gnawing stomach—tells him to steal! This needs reform.

In the city of New York 100 persons possess $200,000,000; this would give to every five persons in that city a home worth $1,000. Three-fourths of its people have no homes. Such a state of things makes these scenes. This is told by Solon Robinson, how a widow and four children lived on a dime a day. She got two cents' worth of coke, three cents' worth of salt pork, four cents' worth of white beans, and one cent's worth of corn-meal. This was boiled two hours; the soup was divided into three parts for the day. The next day's food was four cents' worth of oat-meal, one cents' worth of potatoes, and same amount of pork. The next day's food was five cents' worth of beef, with meal and potatoes. This woman could only make two pair of drawers in a day, at five cents a pair. She could not beg. This is taken from "Economy of Food."

Says Wm. Godwin: "There is no real wealth but the labor of man. Were the mountains of gold and the valleys of silver, the world would not be one grain of corn the richer; not one comfort would be added to the human race. In consequence of our consideration for the precious metals, one man is enabled to heap to himself luxuries at the expense of the necessaries of his neighborhood; a system admirably fitted to produce all the varieties of disease and crime, which never fail to characterize the two extremes of opulence and penury. A speculator takes pride to himself as the promoter of his country's prosperity, who employs a number of hands in the manufacture of articles avowedly destitute of use, or subservient only to the unhallowed cravings of luxury and ostentation. The nobleman who employs the peasants of his neighborhood in building his palaces, flatters himself that he has gained the title of a patriot by yielding to the impulses of vanity. The show and pomp of courts adduces the same apology for its continuance; and many a fete has been given, many a woman has eclipsed her beauty by her dress, to benefit the laboring poor and to encourage trade. Who does not see that this is a remedy which aggravates, whilst it palliates, the countless diseases of society? The poor are set to labor,—for what? Not the food for which they famish; not the blankets for want of which their babes are frozen by the cold of their miserable hovels; not those comforts of civilization without which civilized man is far more miserable than the meanest savage; oppressed as he is by all its insidious evils, within the daily and taunting prospect of its innumerable benefits assiduously exhibited before him: no; for the pride of power, for the miserable isolation of pride, for the false pleasures of the hundredth part of society. No greater evidence is afforded of the wide extended and radical mistakes of civilized man than this fact; those arts which are essential to his very being are held in the greatest contempt; employments are lucrative in an inverse ratio to their usefulness: the jeweler, the toyman, the actor gains fame and wealth by the exericse of his useless and ridiculous art; whilst the cultivator of the earth, he without whom society must cease to exist, struggles through contempt and penury, and perishes by that famine which, but for his unceasing exertions, would annihilate the rest of mankind.

"I will not insult common sense by insisting on the doctrine of the natural equality of man. The question is not concerning its desirableness, but its practicability; so far as it is practicable, it is desirable. That state of human society which approaches nearer to an equal partition of its benefits should be preferred; but so long as we conceive that a wanton expenditure of human labor, not for necessities, not even for the luxuries of the mass of society, but for the egotism and ostentation of a few of its members, is defensible, on the ground of public justice, so long we neglect to approximate to the redemption of the human race.

"Labor is required for physical, and leisure for moral improvement: from the former of these advantages the rich, and from the latter the poor, by the inevitable conditions of their respective situations, are precluded. A state which should combine the advantages of both, would be subjected to the evils of neither. He that is deficient in firm health, or vigorous intellect is but half a man; hence it follows, that, to subject the laboring classes to unnecessary labor, is wantonly depriving them of any opportunities of intellectual improvement; and that the rich are heaping up for their own mischief the disease, lassitude, and *ennui*, by which their existence is rendered an intolerable burden.

"Wealth is a power usurped by the few, to compel the many to labor for their benefit. The laws which support this system derive their force from the ignorance of its victims: they are the result of a conspiracy of the few against the many, who are obliged to purchase this pre-eminence by the loss of all real comfort.

"The commodities that substantially contribute to the subsistence of the human species form a very short catalogue; *they demand from us a very slender portion of our indus-*

try. If these only were produced, and sufficiently produced, the species of man would be continued. If the labor necessarily required to produce them were equitably divided among the poor, and, still more, if it were equitably divided among all, each man's share of labor would be light, and his portion of leisure would be ample. There was a time when this leisure would have been of small comparative value, and it is to be hoped the time will come, when it will be applied to the most important purposes. Those hours which are not required for the production of the necessaries of life, may be devoted to the cultivation of the understanding, the enlarging of our knowledge. * * * * * It was, perhaps, necessary that a period of monopoly and oppression should subsist, before a period of cultivated equality could exist. Savages perhaps would never have been excited to the discovery of truth and the invention of art, but by the narrow motives which such a period affords. But, surely, after the savage state has ceased, and men have set out in the glorious career of discovery and invention, monopoly and oppression can not be necessary to prevent them from returning to a state of barbarism."—*Godwin's Enquirer, Essay II. Pol. Jus., book* viii, *chap.* 11.

It is a calculation of this admirable author, that all the conveniences of civilized life might be produced if society would divide the labor equally among its members, by each individual being employed in labor two hours during the day.

Gov. Hammond, of South Carolina, in the House of Representatives, in 1858, says : "In all social systems there must be a class to do the mean duties, to perform the drudgery of life—a class requiring but a low order of intellect and but little skill. Such a class you must have, or you would not have that other class which leads to progress, refinement, and civilization. It constitutes the very mud-sills of society. The man who lives by daily labor, and scarcely lives at that, and who has to put his labor in the market, and take the best he can get for it—in short, your whole class of manual laborers and operatives, as you call them, are slaves. They are hired by the day, not cared for, and scantily compensated; which may be proved, in the most deplorable manner, at any hour, in any street in any of your large towns. Your slaves are white, of your own race—you are brothers of one blood; they are equals in natural endowment, and they feel galled by their degradation; your slaves vote, and, being in the majority, are the depositories of all your political power. If they knew the tremendous *secret* that the ballot-box is stronger than an army with bayonets, and could combine—where would you be? Your society and government would be reconstructed by the quiet process of the ballot-box. How would you like us to send lecturers or agitators North to teach the people this, to aid and assist in combining and leading them?"

When this language was known among the monarchs of Europe what feelings they must have had. The great Republic had existed three-fourths of a century and no freedom for its laborers. Can this be true? The New York Tribune gives us this: "Last week a single soup-house gave out a ton of meal, 2,000 loaves of bread, 1,400 pints of soup; supplying daily 2,500 persons. Twenty cellars are near, where, for a penny a head, all colors lie down promiscuously, in bunks at night. Two pennies will get some straw. When morning breaks, though it be cold, and snow is on the pavement, they are driven out sick and shivering, hungry and unrefreshed, into the dreary streets to obtain, by beggary and theft subsistence for the day."

Intemperance has much to do with this, it can be bettered. Men are not wicked before they are born. Make society better and this vice will cease. Drunkenness is often caused by sorrow. Bulwer puts this language into the mouth of the sorrow stricken woman, "Drink! drink! drink! there's nothing like drink for the poor, for then we fancy oursels what we wish." Her husband was the giant of his tribe, a soldier once, he died with hunger "from frequent famines that are the scourge of Ireland." It is this scene that makes Bulwer exclaim: "When will those hideous disparities be banished from the world? How many noble natures—how many glorious hopes—how much of the seraph's intellect, have been crushed into the mire, and blasted into guilt by the mere force of physical want! What are the temptations of the rich to those of the poor? Yet how lenient we are to the crimes of the one—how relentless to those of the other! It is a bad world; it makes a man's heart sick to look around him. The consciousness of how little genius can do to relieve the mass, grinds out as with a stone, all that is generous in ambition; and to aspire above the level of life is to be more graspingly selfish?"

"Can legislators, or the moralists that instruct legislators, do so little toward universal good?" said Lester, doubtingly.

"Why, what can they do but forward civilization? And what is civilization but an increase of human disparities? The more the luxury of the few, the more startling the wants and the more galling the sense of poverty. Even the dreams of the philanthropist only tend toward equality; and where is equality to be found but in the state of the savage? No; I thought otherwise once; but I now regard the vast Lazar-house around us without any hope of relief: Death is the sole physician!"

The remedy for this is universal labor. Intemperance is

caused much of it by extremes of wealth and poverty. The
sons of the rich, by having no occupation, learn vice. The
poor in cities with their small, cheerless homes, with no attainments in learning, are many of them ensnared in the de-
corated saloons. A remedy for intemperance is rural life.
Land-speculators put a check on this. This class are the
bane of society; they, with whisky makers and sellers, poison human society. Many a family has been pushed among
the Indians, and fallen a sacrifice to those human parasites.
These make many parts of this land neither savage nor
civilized—a wilderness. A concentrated people have better
roads, school-houses, and churches. Why should a laborer give $400 for forty acres of wild land, that only cost
fifty; and has no labor on it. Land speculators have no
moral right to lands they can not cultivate; they have no
benevolence, or moral feelings! Why should laborers go
without comforts that others may have luxuries? If lands
held for speculation were ordered to be cultivated, population would increase to pay a nation's debts. National lands:

Improved lands.........................163,210,720 acres.
Unimproved lands inclosed....................244,101,808 "
Uncultivated territory.......................1,466,969,862 "
25,500 farms exceed.....................................500 "
One-fifth of the farms only exceed...................100 "

The quantity of improved land for each inhabitant is
fifty acres, and also 600 acres of wild land. Eighty years
must pass away before this will come into cultivation. It
would be a great benefit to this country if wild lands were
not sold to any one. The Cin. Gazette, of Jan. 28th, 1868,
says: "Somebody has introduced a bill, to grant a million
of acres, to the District of Columbia, for educational purposes. No one thinks the public lands of any use but to
squander. This has been transferred into the hands of

speculators, to the injury of settlers, until it will fetch, perhaps, twenty times the cost. This is the most costly way
Congress can devise for school purposes. The system, of
granting public lands to corporations, is the worst system of
internal improvements that was ever invented." This
same paper tells us Congress has given to railroads lands
to the amount of 305,000,000 of acres. Words can not tell
how wicked is this gift, to the present and to future generations.

Capital has been defined an accumulation of labor. A
laborer wants a house, he creates food and clothes to consume while building it. This builder says to another, if you
will help me, I will give you half of the food and clothes.
The builder has a right to his home, he paid for it with toil.
Those who fed and clothed the workmen, of the Illinois
Central Railroad, ought to possess it. It is said the Roths-
childs have built this road, at a cost of $20,000,000. Did
these men and their partners make clothes and food with
their own hands? No, they have got others to do it. The
printing of $20,000,000 costs $40,000, this is all the cost
put forth to get this road. It takes 34,000 laborers one
year to build the road. It will take a printer two years to
print this amount. This company had from government
3,500,000 acres of land. What has been sold has brought
nearly $30,000,000. The State authorities could have is-
sued $20,000,000, and would have had yearly $2,000,000
for school purposes. These lands, towns, and road will
in twenty years give an annual income of $10,000,000;
when this amount is squandered, its recipients will smile at
the simplicity of the common people. This company has
seventy towns that give revenues from lots.

We are often told that wars with England have been the
means of introducing manufactures among us, to our ad-

vantage. The \$30,000,000, that has been spent in Ill nois for railroads, would have put linen and woolen factories all over the State. A people who send their wool 1,000 miles to be spun, wear costly clothing. Greeley says "Why should 500 men be the carriers between 500 farmers and 500 mechanics." A plea is made that giving away lands to railroads promotes public good; it is not so. Franklin, in 1739, printed paper money for the authorities of the colony of Pennsylvania. By means of five loan commissioners this colony paid nearly all the public expenses. This money lasted till 1774; it was always good, and uniform in amount. The colony of South Carolina loaned paper money on silver plate and lands in 1750. The interest was used for fighting Indians. Franklin's money was loaned on lands. This money rendered bankers, carriers, and railroad builders not necessary; these eat up food, and have the most luxuries.

What the colonies did with paper money, could have been done in Illinois; had the State printed the money, hired the laborers, the people would have a circulating medium and a revenue. This tells how happy were the colonies: " The economy which is so particularly attended to in Pennsylvania does not prevent both sexes from being well clothed; there is a constant plenty, and a universal appearance of easy circumstances. The pleasing view of this abundance is never disturbed by the melancholy appearance of poverty. *There are no poor in all Pennsylvania.* A traveler is welcome to stop in any place, without uneasy sensations, except regret at departure."* The giving away of the wild lands should be to those who will cultivate them.

Toussaint Breda, a slave, in the island of St. Domingo, in the latter part of last century, was taught to read by a slave who had learned of the Jesuits. Toussaint got from his

*Abbe Raynal's E. and W. Indies, vol. 6th, page 17. Strahan, London, 1798

overseer the writings of Abbe Raynal, he read these words: "What shall be done to overthrow slavery. Self-interest alone governs nations and kings. We must look elsewhere. These are so many indications of the impending storm, and the negroes only want a courageous chief to lead them on to vengeance and slaughter.

"Where is the great man whom nature owes to her vexed, oppressed, and tormented children? Where is he? He will undoubtedly appear, he will show himself, he will lift up the sacred standard of liberty. This venerable signal will collect around him the companions of his misfortunes. They will rush on with more impetuosity than torrents; they will leave behind them traces of their resentment."

In 1787, the island contained 30,000 whites, 20,000 free mulattoes, the children of planters, and 500,000 slaves. The Assembly of the French, at the beginning of the Revolution proclaimed, that slavery should cease. The free blacks sent deputies to the Assembly, with $1,000,000 and offered to mortgage a fifth of their property for the debts of France, for the privilege of being equal with the whites in law. This led to fighting between the two classes. The English invaded the island under Gen. Maitland. Toussaint and his fellow slaves drove them out of the island. Slavery was ended through the teachings of a slave, who had been taught to read; he remembered the teachings of the good Abbe Raynal. Will some one deliver us.

We have misery around us which may be seen. "A laborer has to put forth incessant toil to keep his head above the rising waters of indigence; at the first trifling accident these close around and overwhelm him. For the thousand casualties of life there is not the scantiest provision. The indisposition of a day curtails the amount of food that is dealt out the next day. A week's sickness threatens with starva tion his wife and little ones."*   Strange confession is this.

Relief will come, it is to be inferred from this: "Doubtless, there are great statesmen; wizards in bullion and bank-paper; thinkers profound in cotton, and every turn and variation of the markets abroad and at home.   But there are *statesmen yet to come; statesmen of nobler aims—of more heroic action*; teachers of the people; vindicators of the universal dignity of man; apostles of the great social truth that knowledge, which is the spiritual light of God, like his material light was made to bless and comfort all men.   And when these men arise—and it is worse than weak, it is sinful, to despair of them—the youngling poor will not be bound upon the very threshold of human life, and made, by want and ignorance, life's shame and curse.   There is not a babe lying in the public street on its mother's lap—the unconscious mendicant to ripen into the criminal—that is not a reproach to the state; a scandal and a crying shame upon men who study all politics, save the politics of the human heart." †

The reader can learn from "The Rights of Man," some of the causes of human woe: "There is a family of five persons, the farmer becomes king, the family have no food; the weaver becomes a gold seeker, the family have no clothes; the hatter becomes a custom-house officer, the family have no hats; the shoemaker becomes a banker, the family have no shoes.   Society is a large family, and they must be useful."

* Speech before Cin. Mercantile Library, 1848, by R. D. Owen.   † D. Jerrold.

CHAPTER II.

ANCIENT AND MODERN SLAVERY.

SLAVERY IN GREECE AND ROME—IN NORTHERN AFRICA—IN AMERICA—
SLAVERY NECESSARY TO IMPROVE THE CONDITION OF MEN—SLAVERY
NOT NECESSARY WHEN NATIONS ARE IMPROVED.

"Mankind is always consuming men for luxury and civilization." COUNTESS IDA.

HISTORY is a long record of wars and slavery. How painful is the contemplation of slavery! the separation of its victims from friends and home, to spend a life in unmitigated toil; without reward, kindness, or sympathy; to be treated in life and death like brutes. We might inquire, why does the Father of us all permit a part of his helpless creatures to be thus tormented? None to defend or vindicate them! We can not answer.

When man was first placed on this earth, it was in a part where the climate was warm; where the fruits were perpetual, and only needed gathering. In a country like this invention would not be very rapid, or have no existence. As men increased they would have to migrate to climates that changed, from heat to cold; where the fruits perished, and only prevailed a part of the year. This would quicken invention, and improve the intellect. Trees or caves would not do for habitations. Clothing has to be comfortable, the houses durable. The people of the new colony are superior to those they left. The flesh of animals would be used as food. This would call for instru-

(25)

ments to bring down the game, and which can be used for the destruction of men. When this colony increased migration again took place, either to ruder climes or back to the starting point. If these were not received kindly force can be used with effect. This invaded people fall an easy prey to the ferocious hunters. Failure of crops produces a war. Hunger makes men savage and fearless, and they go where there is food. From war comes the sparing of the lives of prisoners, on condition of becoming slaves.

It was no doubt hunger that compelled the Northmen to conquer Normandy and Britain. England was barbarous before the advent of the Romans. The various conquests she has undergone has given refinement, learning, and abundance to a few; which sometime or other will belong to the many.

These painful facts will throw some light on the motives for conquest: "The failure of crops for seven successive years in Swedish Nordland, has brought some 300,000 persons to starvation, and many of them to death, and now their miserable bread, made of bark and straw, has given out. They sit in their cheerless huts and die."*

This suffering described here is calculated to make men ingenious and frugal. "Indeed it is a fortunate thing that the people are not more numerous, for bad harvests are very frequent in this rude climate; it is impossible to provide against occasional scarcity of food, and one would not wish there should be a greater number of poor to suffer from it. A large population is commonly considered a sign of prosperity, but it is only where they are certain of having bread to eat. The earth will not complain, if she is left uncultivated, but man will complain bitterly if he must suffer the cravings of hunger. When population once begins to

* W. W. Thomas representative to Sweden.—Cin. Com. of Mar. 6th, 1868.

advance, it increases rapidly, in a ratio far exceeding that in which the earth's fertility can be increased, so that in a very short time all equality ceases between the demand and supply. Then want begins and advances with the increasing population, offering this strange problem: 'The less bread the more children.' * As for the poor old earth, I hope she is quite insensible to a great deal that passes upon her, or her emotions must be of a most painful kind. Oh God! her hardest rocks might be softened by the torrents of tears, blood, and sweat, which have poured on her in an increased shower. No, no! the earth is hard and firm, and sympathizes neither with our sorrow or our joys. Mankind is always consuming men for its own luxury and civilization, sometimes by war, maufactures, hunger, sorrow, and care. Why should we give it any more to consume? When a man is born we would wish him to have a little happiness. Yet it is upon the classes that are the most numerous—the hard-working, industrious classes, that misery is sure to fall. It is in a strange world we live in. God mend it! But it seems to me so much warped on one side, that it will by and by turn itself quite over on the other." †

The spirit of conquest is not ended. The occupation of India will in time fill it with steam engines, and clear its jungles of tigers. Many parts of Algiers abound with lions; that take a fourth of the cattle. The French will destroy these, as they have conquered this land.

One hundred and fifty years ago, some voyagers visited Patagonia; they tell us the natives wore no clothing, and the snow beat on their bodies, and they eat snails, and shell fish. The deer were in the distance, and they had no power

---

* This lady has feelings for working people. She has not learned that three-fourths of the earth is a wilderness, and it is the duty of the rich to work.
† Travels in Sweden, by Bahn Bahn—Countess Ida.

to strike them down. A nation too full some will have to leave. If the country of these savages will sustain more, it is the duty of the poor Northmen to go there, and use kindness to the natives. Persuading them to learn better ways may have no effect. It will not be wrong to use force to make them improve. "The punishment of nature, hunger and want," is not any more severe than slavery. Indian slavery can only be accomplished if there are no means of escape. England after it was left by the Romans, from whom many arts were obtained, was invaded from Scotland. The Britons wrote to Rome for help, saying: "The barbarians are driving us into the sea." No help came the inhabitants submitted, and learned the ways of the conquerors.

For civilization the Indian has no wish; there he sees the laborer have no homes, living in cellars and garrets, going about begging work, often used with contumely. The Indian burns trees down for want of an ax; his hut is made of peeled bark. In 1621, two of the Pilgrims visited the Indians, they could give them nothing to eat; two small fish were divided among forty, the visitors came away while they had strength. Savage life is precarious in subsistence, so is civilization, we need something better. *

These extracts will show what changes and cruelties, have been used to make man what he is. Slavery existed in Greece from her earliest history; it prevailed in the days of Homer; in all the Grecian states a majority were slaves. In Athens there were three slaves to one freeman; in Sparta the proportion was greater. The Spartans treated slaves with humanity, the Athenians were the opposite. The introduction of agriculture led to the sparing of the lives of prisoners to cultivate the earth. The commerce of the

* THOMAS RABOLD, a tailor hanged himself eight miles from Louisville. Poverty and failure to obtain employment the cause.—Com. Mar 25th, 1868.

Chians, the early Greeks, led them to visit parts of Asia Minor, and the Southern coasts of the Black Sea, where they purchased slaves. The yoke of bondage was galling; the slaves took refuge in the mountains. These bondmen chose a leader. The Chians could not conquer them, but suffered defeat. The bondmen made these terms, if their necessities required it, they should be supplied out of the Chian stores in an orderly manner. The ruler of the slaves punished the unruly, and would not allow them to waste the country. In process of time the Chians were subjugated by Mithridates, who gave them to their own slaves, to be carried into captivity. The Athenians considered this a just punishment, for introducing the slave-trade into Greece.

In Athens slaves could indict their masters for assault. The temples were to them places of refuge for safety. In times of war the Grecians were good to their slaves, as *flogged slaves go over to the enemy*. Slaves were sold at auction, on tables. Owners hired them out. In Athens slaves were public and private; clerks and messengers of public works; they were educated, and accompanied the generals and treasurers of the army, and kept an account of the expenditures. Slaves, in the dwellings of the wealthy and luxurious, fanned their masters and mistresses, and drove away the flies. Slave bakers had gloves on while making bread, and wore gauze over their mouths, so as they could not eat what they made. They turned mills, carried water, and cut wood.

The Helots were named from the town Helos, from it they were taken 1,000 B. C. They were the property of the state, who had the disposal of their freedom and servitude, and gave them to different masters. Lycurgus prohibited the Spartans from laboring. If these Helots increased too fast, the young Spartans, it is said, were sent out to

4

assassinate them. Their number was estimated at 500,000.
They several times rose against their masters, but without
any success. Plutarch tells us, "Youths distinguished for
ability were sent forth, armed with daggers and furnished
with provisions, to scour the country at night, to slaughter
all the Helots found abroad. Sometimes they fell on them
while they were at their labors in the fields." Sometimes
they were offered the gift of freedom, crowned with garlands, conducted to the temples—then they disappeared;
their fate was unknown.

The Helots were a source of terror; they revolted when
they could, and joined an enemy when he appeared. Sparta
often stipulated for aid from foreign states. The serfs of
the Syracusans were so exceeding numerous, that it gave
them courage, and they drove out their masters, and retained Syracuse.

The Sicilians treated their slaves with rigor, branded
them like cattle, and gave them incessant toil. Ennius excited them to a revolution. Houses were pillaged, the inhabitants slaughtered, and infants dashed on the ground.
At one time 60,000 insurgents were armed with axes and
clubs, and they defeated several armies.

The people of Rome were nobles, plebeians, and slaves.
As Rome extended her dominions, the nobles acquired
large estates, which were cultivated with the labor of slaves.
Their numbers were so great, that the poor freeman were
unemployed. It was to remedy this evil that some of the
Roman rulers, were for limiting the quantity of land. The
elder Gracchus saw that slavery impoverished the people
and that the nation needed little farms nursing an independent race, and the plow in their hands, and not in the hands
of slaves. Some of the nobles possessed 10,000 slaves, some
20,000. The constant wars of Rome increased slaves.

Spartacus was compelled to serve in the Roman army, he was a Thracian by birth, he deserted and at the head of his companions carried on a partisan war. He was taken prisoner and sold as a slave, to be reserved as a gladiator. He formed a conspiracy among the slaves and escaped. He was joined by 10,000 slaves. Spartacus plundered several of the cities in Italy. He had 60,000 followers, and defeated the legions many times that were sent against him. The various classes of slaves of this period, became the serfs of the middle ages. Slaves trained to be gladiators show how wicked is man. These had to fight each other with short swords, and sometimes engage with wild beasts. At other times a gladiator would throw a net over another, if he failed he retreated, the other pursued to kill him. A hook was fastened into those who were slain, and they were dragged out of the arena. These scenes were forbidden by Christian emperors.

Accounts of the wealth and splendor of the first classes, in Rome, almost exceed belief. A writer of this period, describing the state of Rome under Honorius, relates that several of the senators received from their estates an annual sum of $800,000. Provisions of corn and wine, which, if sold would have realized one-third of that sum. The estates of these patricians spread over distant provinces, and, as early as the time of Seneca, " Rivers which had divided hostile nations flowed through lands of private citizens." With such resources at their command, there were no bounds to their extravagances. " Many of their mansions might excuse the exaggeration of the poet, that Rome contained a multitude of palaces, and that each palace was equal to a city; since it included within its precincts every thing which could be subservient to the use of luxury—markets, hippodromes, temples, fountains, baths, porticoes, groves, and

aviaries." * The house of Scaurus was valued at the sum
$3,603,000. The lower apartments were occupied by at-
tendants. The upper apartments were filled with tables
and couches, and adorned with curtains. Garlands en-
twined with ivy divided the walls into compartments, which
were bordered by fanciful ornaments. Bronze lamps suspended from the ceiling shed a brilliant light. The tables
were of citron-wood more precious than gold, and rested
on ivory feet. The couches were overlaid with silver, gold,
and tortoise shell; the mattresses were of Gallic wool, dyed
purple ; the cushions of silk embroidered with gold, cost
$150,000. The pavement was mosaic and represented the
fragments of a feast not swept away. Young slaves strew-
ed over the pavement saw-dust dyed with vermillion.

In the fourth century the Roman nobility carried out luxury to the greatest excess. They adorned their houses with
magnificent statues of themselves, their robes were of the
most costly kind, and became a burden to the wearer on
account of the weight of embroidery. When they traveled any distance, so large was their retinue that it was like
the march of an army. Their tables were covered with
the rarest delicacies, and the pleasures of the feast occupied
much of the time. Concerts, visiting, baths, theaters, and
other amusements took the rest of the time. Roman simplicity had been succeeded by oriental magnificence. Services of plate set with precious stones, furniture of costly
materials and most elaborate workmanship, banqueting halls
of florid architecture, baths of marble, and villas surrounded
with enchanting gardens, were now signs of greatness instead of valor in the field, or wisdom in the cabinet.

Many of the plebeians forsook all industrious employments, lived upon the public distribution of bread, bacon,

* Gibbon, vol. iv. page 94.

oil, and wine, which, from the time of Augustus, had been made for the relief of the indigent. These idlers spent some of their time in baths and taverns, which great men with the emperor provided, so as to be popular. "Some passed the nights in taverns, and under the awnings of the theaters, they played dice, and went to the circus, and discussed the merits of the horses and charioteers."*

Slaves formed a large portion of the population of Rome. They were artisans and devoted to the professions. They were physicians, librarians, and secretaries. At one time the possessors of slaves scourged and put them to death at pleasure. Under the emperors Adrian and the Antonines, the shield of legal protection was thrown over this oppressed portion of society. Some amelioration was secured, no doubt, during the last age of the empire; but the wrongs inseparable from slavery were still endured, and a disposition to be avenged on their oppressors was still nourished; for amid the scenes of violence which marked the taking of Rome by Alaric, when 40,000 slaves joined the Goths in shedding Roman blood, and in trampling into dust the remains of Roman greatness. That the servile part of the Roman population, ministering as they did to the luxury, the extravagance, and the vices of their masters, partook of the prevalent moral corruption of the times is certain.†

It was self-interest that induced the rulers of Europe to put an end to the sale of men with estates. Slavery was to those who used it troublesome and painful. The owners of lands knew that rents would give the same results that slavery did, splendor and magnificence, without whipping or feigned sickness, or the care of feeble childhood and helpless age. The lords of Britain knew that, being surrounded with water, the laborers could not escape, and that they

---

* Ammianus Marcellinus, lib., xiv. c. 25.   † See Gibbon's Roman Empire.

would still contribute to their idleness and luxury. The
nicety of legislation, wherever used, is to give the laborer
sufficient to keep him alive, and not enough to make him
independent. How much has the laborer gained? Splendor and magnificence meet the eye every-where! The laborer lives in a humble manner, under the fear of want, and
others having more ability are unceasingly, and unobserved,
consuming his labor. Religion and learning are often used
to favor the rich man. Light and knowledge sometime
or other will descend on the humble man, and this home
will be a model of his.

A Rothschild's Home.—You go up a flight of marble
steps, a vestibule opens on one of the most spacious halls
in Europe furnished as a reception room, and lighted from
the roof which is muffled glass. At night an arrangement
of gas illuminates the vast space. A gallery runs around
the upper part of the hall, into which party rooms open.
The lower floor contains the family apartments.

Purple velvet *portiers* have an admirable effect at each end
of the *salle*, which has been constructed on the most perfect accoustic principles. The effect of music here is marvelous. Ordinary paper hangings are banished, and each
room is hung with tapestry, velvet or silk. Every visitor
has a splendid drawing-room, boudoir, bedroom, and dressing-room. In every dressing-room is a gorgeous dressing-
case—ivory brushes surmounted with the Baron's coronet;
silver boxes containing *cosmetique poudre de ris*, exquisite hand
mirrors, mounted in sculptured ivory, silver, and sandal
wood. A scent bottle of costly workmanship contained a
jeweled watch, a fair lady using the perfume was informed
of the time of the day. Hot and .cold water supply each
dressing-room. To describe the thrones taken from the
summer palace at Pekin, the jeweled cup from Cellina's

chisel, the crystal beakers from Venice, the hangings of green-broidered satin, in the Baron's own bedroom, is beyond description. Menemo's queen would be puzzled to tell what are the half of all the treasures of art in each room. It is a positive relief to go on the grounds, where the power of attention has fewer calls. These grounds are reached through a series of conservatories and hot-houses, filled with Flora's choicest gifts, and the rarest specimens of the sculptor's art, and enlivened by the brightest-winged birds of the tropics. The grounds are diversified by sheets of water, on which are fairy boats. A number of gazelles, elands, and all the foreign animals, of the harmless species, enjoy this Eden. In the Baron's absence the visitors get princely food; the cellar contributes to their enjoyment the finest Madeira in Europe.

This description should awaken a feeling of indignation. Hundreds must be employed to beautify and adorn this place, at the expense of the most deserving part of the community. Many say this gives employment. Men should do work only for themselves, they will have more. The robber takes your money in disguise. Does it atone for his crime to purchase your goods, or set you to work? No!

The sophisms men of wealth have started are the same as the robber's plea. The means put forth to get this extreme wealth is, "interest," "rent," and "profit." The time is coming when toilers will be more intelligent, and not so selfish as they are now, and will keep the fruits of labor.

"It is said there are in the city of New York, not less than a dozen houses, that cost $1,000,000 to $1,500,000, each rivaling the royal palaces of Europe, only inferior in point of magnitude. The most elegant residence in the city cost $250,000. Another residence has fitted up five rooms at a cost of $54,000. A single room has been fitted up at a cost of $30,000. Side by side with these palaces is misery worthy of the old world."*

Servants are only removed a few degrees from the slave. Many of them by frugality may rise above their condition. It is not their duty to invest their earnings, so as to get the earnings of others, or be the dupes of those who are wiser. The Romans called their slaves *servi*, from *servare*, to "keep or save," those who were not killed in battle, and made to yield money by sale or work. Slaves were taken from Britain and sold in the market-place at Rome. The word slave comes from Sclavus, the name of a Sythian people, whom Charlemagne condemmed to imprisonment. The Italians and Germans used to buy those Sclavonians to make drudges of them. The proper name of a nation in time became the name of a condition of life.

A long strip of land, on the northern coast of Africa, the Mediterranean washing its shores, was to be the scene of great events. To the Greeks it was the land of mystery and fable, filled with giants and monsters. The Phœnicians founded Carthage, which became a ruler of the seas, and a founder of trading depots as far as the Niger and the Baltic. The Carthaginians became the rivals of Rome and were conquered by them. The spoils of Carthage adorned the proud city of Rome. After the decay of the Roman power, the Vandals ruled for one hundred years. The Greeks then took this land, to be followed by an irruption of Saracens. Swarms of Arabs came out of Egypt till it was ruled by the Caliphs. These were driven out by Musa. These new conquerors crossed over the narrow straits, and laid the foundation of Arabian dominion in Spain. These conquerors of Spain, enriched by a fertile soil and prosperous commerce, have blended intellectual culture with

* N. Y. Journal.

Arabian luxury and magnificence. The palaces of their princes were splendid, their colleges famous for learning, their libraries were filled with books, their agriculture and manufactures produced abundance, when all the rest of Europe was buried in darkness. These enjoyed peace for three centuries; then arose conflicts between the Moors and Spaniards for four centuries. The Moor was compelled to abandon Spain.

After the fall of Grenada, in 1492, about 100,000 Spanish Moors crossed over to Africa, and took possession of some deserted Roman towns. They spoke the same language as the people to whom they went. These new emigrants taught navigation, and turned their attention to naval affairs. These Moors built row boats, and crossed the channel, and plundered the Spaniards at night, and made them slaves. From this sprung a system of piracy, that compelled the nations of Europe to pay tribute and buy the freedom of the captives. The order of the Redemption Brothers was, in 1188, founded by Jean Matha. These went begging over Europe for money to redeem captives; they took a procession of redeemed captives, wearing red Moorish caps, white bornouces, and chains. Banners, wax-candles, music, and silver covered *angels* were in the procession. These, on approaching a place, were met by the chief men, who collected for them. In 1551, Brother Sebastian established a hospital, and it became the residence of the Brothers, who were the mediums of exchanges. These Christian slaves became carpenters, blacksmiths, masons, rope-makers, and ship-builders. They received one-third of their earnings for their own use.

Says a narrative of 1720, the Redemptionists offered for a surgeon, a father, and son $3,000, the Dey added a Lutheran for $3,500, the reluctant Fathers were compelled to
5

take him. The British Parliament appropriated money, in 1646, to buy 750 captives at an average of $190 each. In 1631, from the town of Baltimore, Ireland, 237 persons were taken by these pirates.

England, in 1621, made an attempt to release the captives by force, but failed. In 1682, the French tried to stop the piracies by sending a fleet with a newly invented mortar, it proved as destructive to the French as to their enemies. A French fleet, in 1688, threw 10,000 bombs into the city of Algiers and burnt it. Piracy was resumed in a few years. In 1816, Lord Exmouth, with a fleet, destroyed the city, released 3,000 captives, and destroyed Christian slavery forever. The Tripolitans declared war against the United States. Gen. Eaton, the American commander, went to an exiled bashaw, and got his assistance to take Tripoli. This chief, with his wild tribes, attacked the city in the rear, and Gen. Eaton in the front with warships, which resulted in a treaty, to make no more slaves of American seamen. The Americans also paid tribute. Thos. Jefferson writes from Paris to John Jay, in 1786. He says: "It will take to make peace, with the Barbary States, £250,000."

These States have been conquered by the Turks. The Viceroys sent there have usurped the government into their own hands. Algiers has, by conquest, become a colony of France. It is to be hoped that justice and natural kindness will prevail after so many conquests.

The ancients called that part of Africa, lying along the Mediterranean, Libya; the interior, Ethiopia. It has been a land from which slaves have been taken in all ages. The Briton and the African have been fellow-slaves at Rome. The first were easily obtained, the latter were kept as novelties. The Portuguese were the first to steal negroes, and become acquainted with Africa. No part of Africa was known except the countries on the Mediterranean and the Red Sea. In the year 1412, the Portuguese began to sail south, along the western coast. Each navigator got bolder and went farther. Vasco de Gama, in 1497, rounded the great cape, and sailed through the Mozambique Channel, into the open ocean for India. In 1434, Antonia Gonzales carried away some Guinea coast blacks, and sold them to some Moorish families in the south of Spain. It became customary for captains to take from Guinea a few young blacks of both sexes. Their labor was found valuable on the ships and ports at home. These blacks were sold to others. From this it became a regular traffic, and thousands were carried away annually. The villages along the African coast obtained them, and exchanged them for beads, cloths, and knives.

America was discovered in 1492. The islands, between the north and south part, were first colonized by the Spaniards, who made the Indians dig for gold, and carry burdens; they soon died. Labor, ill usage, and sickness carried them off by thousands. In 1508, the natives numbered in St. Domingo 60,000. In 1515, the number was 14,000. The Dominicans denied the right of the Spaniards to make slaves of Indians. As early as 1503, negroes were carried across the Atlantic. In 1510, the king of Spain sent fifty slaves to work gold mines. Charles V gave one of his favorites a right to ship 4,000 blacks. His monopoly was sold for 25,000 ducats, to some Genoese merchants, who, when they got started, carried more than that number. In Venezuela there was an insurrection—so numerous were the slaves—in which six Spaniards were killed.

In 1562, Elizabeth legalized the slave-trade. In 1620, a Dutch ship let some Virginia planters have some negroes. On trial they proved good, and it led the English to engage in the traffic of slaves. In the middle of the seventeenth century all Europe was engaged in buying and selling men. Companies of men would build forts, on some part of the coast, and mount them with cannon, to protect from the natives within, and Europeans without. Soldiers, gunners, factors, clerks, and mechanics, resided in the fort. The stores had all kinds of fancy goods, to supply the traders. Factors would go into the interior, and set the tribes against each other. A looking glass, a string of beads, or a few yards of red cloth, to possess these was the motive of an African for setting fire to the villages of joining tribes, and pursuing the fleeing inhabitants, to be carried into bondage. Black slave-merchants tied the hands of the captives to a long rope. Ivory and other merchandise is fastened on the slave to be carried hundreds of miles to the ships. Beaten, famished, sick, and feeble, many lay down to die. On the coast many died broken-hearted.

Life in these forts was ease, indolence, and licentiousness. Smoking and gambling passed away the time, of those who engaged in this shameful traffic. On the arrival of traders with gold dust and ivory, they were supplied with wine and brandy; under its influence these products did not sell for much. "These slaves were obtained partly by the sword and other means, and exchanged in Hispaniola for hides, ginger, and sugar. Prosperous were the voyages, and brought great profit to the adventurers." *

The middle passage of the African was horrible. Between the decks of a vessel were ten feet: a scaffold was between the two floors. Slaves could not stand upright; and were compelled to lie as close as if they were in their coffins. Revolts were prevented by chaining them together. It often happened that a living and dead person were chained

* HAKLUYT, historian of SIR JOHN HAWKINS' slave voyage. 1562.

together, death taking one away. At times they were taken on the decks, and made to dance with a whip. Some were lost by suffocation. The acting of the slaves was often like that of animals, when put into an exhausted air receiver; they gasped for breath, exclaiming, "We are dying." The slaves took every method to commit suicide. Often half of them died during the passage.

The brutality that was shown to slaves, was often felt by the seamen. In parts of the West Indies might be seen emaciated and starving seamen, without hope or comfort, fearful examples of wrong doing. If a cabin boy broke a glass, or a seaman was untidy, lashes, blows, and kicks were applied. Sailors have often destroyed themselves.

The beautiful islands, that stretch along the joining parts of North and South America, have been the scenes of great cruelty. Human pen can not describe the miseries that Africans have endured for two centuries. Acclimation, melancholy, fevers, and cruelty took them away. They were divided into mechanics, house, field, and dock hands. If the task was not done the slaves were flogged. Sugar boiling caused the slave to work eighteen hours out of twenty four. Slaves had land given them to work Sundays and Saturday afternoons. This labor was to give them food for the week. The whip was applied to the bare skin, which made scars and pools of blood. How cruel is man!

This system of cruelty, by means of the printer's skill was made known over England. Rev. Morgan Godwin was the first to write against slavery. Richard Baxter protested against the trade, and denounced as pirates those who sold men. Dr. Primate wrote on the "Duty of Mercy, and the Sin of Cruelty." In 1735, Atkins, in a voyage to Brazil and Guinea, exposes the cruelty of slavery. In 1750, Rev. Griffith Hughes, of Barbadoes, showed the wickedness of slavery. In 1787, Adam Smith wrote his "Theory of Moral Sentiments." Said he: "Fortune never exerted more cruelly her empire over mankind, than when she subjected those nations of heroes to the refuse of the jails of Europe, to wretches who possess the virtues neither of the countries they came from, nor of those they go to, and whose levity, brutality, and baseness so justly expose them to the contempt of the vanquished." In 1774, John Wesley wrote his "Thoughts on Slavery."

Planters, last century, were in the habit of taking their slaves to England. These ran away, were baptized, thinking that baptism made them free. In 1729, some masters went to the Solicitor-General for his opinion. He said: "Baptism did not change the condition of slaves." At this period the papers began to advertise the sale of slaves, and offer rewards for their arrest when they ran away.

In 1765, David Lyle brought over Jonathan Strong from Barbadoes, as his servant. His master struck him on the head with a pistol, which caused fever, lameness, and partial blindness. This slave applied to Wm. Sharp, a surgeon, who healed the poor gratuitously, for relief and was healed. Granville Sharp, a brother of the surgeon, gave the slave some money, and got him a place as a messenger to a druggist. The master determined to possess again his now robust slave. He was sent for to a public house, here he was seized upon, and two officers took him to prison. He was there sold for thirty pounds. Mr. Sharp caused the Mayor of London to liberate Strong, as he was in prison without a warrant. Captain Laird took hold of Strong to take him to his ship. Mr Sharp said: "I charge you with an assault on the person of Jonathan Strong." This frightened the Captain, and he let his slave go free.

Mr. Sharp was affected by this case, and thought it time

something should be done for slaves. This slave would
have died; he was saved by a benevolent man. To return
him to slavery again, was abhorrent to the feelings of Granville Sharp. Mr. Sharp devoted three years to the study of
English law, so that he could advocate the cause of this
unhappy people. In 1769, he gave the world this book,
"The Injustice and Dangerous Tendency of Tolerating
Slavery in England."

James Somerset, a slave, was brought to England, in
1769. He left his master, who recovered him, and sent
him to Jamaica to be sold. This question was carried to a
court: "Whether a slave, by coming to England, became
free." This question was debated for three months. The
eloquence displayed in it by those who were engaged on the
side of liberty was, perhaps, never exceeded on any occasion.
The decision was, as soon as ever any slave set his foot on
English territory, he was free. In 1772, this trial occurred.

Dr. Peckard, of Cambridge University, in 1785, gave to
Mr. Thomas Clarkson the prize for the best essay on this
theme: "Is it right to make any one a slave against their
will?" Mr. Clarkson, in the twenty-fourth year of his age,
resolved to try and put an end to slavery. He lived to the
28th of August, 1833. On that day slavery was abolished
throughout the British Colonies. He spent his time getting
knowledge and writing books; these he gave to the members of Parliament, to show them the evils of slavery. Mr.
Clarkson called on Wm. Pitt, and showed him how the
slave-trade destroyed the seamen. In the year 1787, 3170
sailors left Liverpool to engage in the slave-trade; only 1428
returned. Mr. Clarkson showed the muster-roll of every
ship and the names of seamen who had died. African cotton cloth, leather, and iron were also shewn. Mr. Pitt promised to do something for the African slaves. On the 9th

of May, 1788, in the House of Commons, Mr. Pitt said: "He intended to move a resolution of more importance than any which had ever been agitated in the house."

The amiable poet, Cowper, wrote fifty-six lines, called the " Negro's Complaint." This did much good.

> " Forced from home and all its pleasures,
>   Africa's coast I left forlorn,
> To increase a stranger's treasures,
>   O'er the raging billows borne ;
> Why did all-creating Nature
>   Make the plant, for which we toil ?
> Sighs must fan it, tears must water,
>   Sweat of ours must dress the soil.
> Think, ye masters, iron hearted,
>   Lolling at your jovial boards,
> Think, how many backs have smarted
>   For the sweets your cane affords."

This plaintive song was printed on hot-pressed paper, [a new invention at that time,] and sent in letters to the nobility and others. It was set to music. Street ballad singers sung and sold it all over England. Appropriate notes were attached, to arouse the popular mind against slavery.

Mr. Wedgewood, the great improver of earthen ware, made a cameo of delicate white. In the center was a negro, in relief and in his own color. He was in an imploring attitude, saying: "Am I not a man and a brother?" These were sent all over England, and were inserted into snuff boxes, bracelets, and hair-pins, to serve humanity's cause.

For seven years Mr. Clarkson corresponded with 400 persons, and traveled in that time 35,000 miles. In Pennsylvania, the Quakers became the opponents of slavery as early as 1688. Anthony Benezet, in 1762, wrote against slavery. He became a school-teacher, so that he could serve the cause of humanity. In 1772, the House of Burgesses, of Virginia, presented a petition to the king to

remove restraints on his governors of that colony, which in-
hibited their assent to such laws as might check the slave-
trade. It was, afterward, made a reason for separating
from the mother country.

Dr. Benjamin Rush, in 1772, wrote against slavery. His
publications were written in a polished style, and showed
learning and benevolence. In 1787, a society was formed
for abolishing slavery. Dr. Franklin was the President.

The Revolution opened the eyes of the American people
to the evil effects of slavery. David Ramsey wrote the
history of this country, from 1776 to 1812. He says:
"Among the many circumstances which induced the rulers
of Great Britain to count on an easy conquest of America,
the great number of slaves had a considerable weight. On
the sea-coast of the five more southern provinces, the number of slaves exceeded those of the freemen. It was supposed that the offer of freedom would detach them from
their masters' interests, and bind them by strong ties to support the royal standard.

" The mischievous effects of slavery in facilitating the
conquest of the country, now became apparent. As the
slaves had no interest at stake, the subjugation of the State
was of no consequence to them. Instead of aiding in its
defense, they, by a variety of means, threw the weight of
their little influence into the opposite scale.

"Slavery was particularly hostile to the education of
youth. Slavery also led to the monopoly of lands in the
hands of the few. It impeded the introduction of laboring
freemen; and at the same time endangered internal tranquillity, by multiplying a kind of inhabitants who had no interest
in the soil. The sea-coast, which, from necessity, could
only be cultivated by the labor of black men, was deficient
in many of the enjoyments of life, and lay *at the mercy of*

every bold invader. The western country, where cultivation was more generally carried on by freemen, sooner attained the means of self-defense and the comforts of life.

"They were not ignorant that their slaves might be worked on, by the insidious *offers of freedom* to slay their masters in the peaceful hour of domestic security. The hopeless Africans, allured with the hopes of freedom, forsook their owners and repaired in great numbers *to the royal army*. They endeavored to recommend themselves to their new masters, by discovering where their owners had concealed their property, and assisted to carry it away." *

Gen. P. Horry, in his life of Marion, says: "Now it is generally believed the British, after the loss of Burgoyne and their fine northern army, would soon have given up the contest, had it not been for the foothold they got in Carolina, which protracted the war at least two years.

"When the war broke out you heard of no division in New England; no toryism, nor any of its horrid effects; no houses in flames kindled by the hands of fellow-citizens; no neighbors way-laying their neighbors and shooting them and carrying off their stock, and in aiding the British in their work of American murder and subjugation."

Hildreth, the historian, says: "The policy of Dunmore, at the beginning of the contest, of arming slaves against their masters, had not been persevered in by the British. Neither in Virginia nor the Carolinas had the negro been regarded in any other light than as property and plunder. The slaves carried off, from Virginia alone, were estimated at 30,000. Had they been treated, not as property, *but as men*, and the king's subjects, and converted into soldiers, the conquest of the Southern States would almost have been inevitable." South Carolina was not able to furnish

* See RAMSEY's Transactions in Virginia, and History of South Carolina.

her share of men for public defense, "by reason of the
great number of citizens necessary to remain at *home*, to prevent insurrection among the negroes, and their desertion to
the enemy." Virginia had 105,000 slaves during the Revolution; 25,000 were seduced from their masters. South
Carolina lost the same number, and Georgia 4,000. Lord
Dunmore, with slave soldiers that he trained, burned Norfolk in Virginia, to ashes, Jan. 1st, 1776. Arnold was sent
by the British against Richmond, in Virginia, which he took
with 900 men, and destroyed the public stores. 200,000
people in Virginia were made helpless by slaves. The
Governor could only get 200 persons to attack this bold invader. The excuse was, slaves had to be watched. Slaves
fortified Savannah, and made it impregnable against the attacks of Count D'Estaing and Gen. Lincoln. Hundreds
of Americans were slain in ditches dug by slaves.*

An article in Harper's Magazine, 1864, "The burning of
Washington, in 1814," says: "The 5,000 men that burned
the city were composed of infantry, marines, and *negroes*,
who were bribed by promises, and forced by threats, to
enter the British army."

The "great Democratic party" has ever been the bul-
wark of slavery; the advocate of a system of cruelty that
has made this government the derision of the world. Had
there been no slaves, the United States would have had no
wars. It was 500,000 slaves, in 1776, that invited a foreign army to these shores. It was to enable the South to
sell cotton, rice, tobacco, and sugar in Europe, that caused
the war of 1812. It was to recover 1,500 runaway slaves
that the Florida Indians were fought. The Florida war
cost this nation $40,000,000, and the lives of 4,500 soldiers.
The Mexican war was to favor slavery, and took thousands

* See "History of Slavery" p. 833. By W. O. BLAKE, Columbus, O. 1857.

of lives and cost $60,000,000. This war, and the repeal of the "Missouri Compromise," has led to the late unhappy war, the evil effects of which will be felt for a generation.

If this country had been without wars, there would have been twice as many cities, houses, and farms. There can be no apology for African slavery. The importation of African slaves degenerates the people who receive them, their manners become like those of the slave. Slavery, brutalizes master and slaves, makes a people feeble in intellect and resources, and incapable of self-defense from internal and foreign invasion.

Look at the condition of the savage; he is always on the verge of famine. In civilized society there is an abundance; it is very unequally distributed. Slavery may have been a cause of this abundance. Queen Anne, in N. Y. State gave Van Rensselaer, the right to take a piece of land containing 5,000 square miles, and has now more than 300,000 persons on it. Fulton had a conception of a steamboat, and was too poor to build it. Had he asked any of the farmers who inhabit this wide domain, for assistance he would have got none. He asked for help of one of the "lords of a manor," and with it gave the world a steamboat. The sight of wealth is a stimulant to invention and toil. As slavery has passed away, the laborer should try and get more of earth's comforts. There is nothing in nature why the laborer, who does quadruple work, should only get single pay.

CHAPTER III.

HISTORY OF THE LABORING CLASSES.

"Man is born free, yet he is everywhere in fetters."—ROUSSEAU.

IT must be self-evident to those who will reason—human society needs reconstructing. This can be proved by the many scenes of suffering around us. A poor mother was found in the railroad station, at Dayton, with a dead child in her arms; it had died with hunger. The parents and other children were in a starving condition for want of food. In London a woman went in the street to sell flowers; her child died in her arms for want of nourishment. It is true there is public relief, but doled out in small quantities, and grudgingly given; those who apply for it are often rudely repulsed. In a state of nature all things are common. The Australian native does not suffer like those who live in ruder climes. The bill of fare to these natives is not very scanty. The whale, when cast on the shore, opens in the heart of the discoverer feelings of hospitality; he kindles a fire on the beach, which is the signal for his companions to come and have a feast. Pieces of whale are toasted on sticks before the fire. Eating and sleeping, singing and dancing, for days now take place. A hunter in civilized countries is often a gentleman, and cares

49

nothing for what he kills; it is the sport, the appetite to eat up other's food that is wanted. It is with an Australian a more serious affair. Hunting quickens his sight and hearing. With skill and patience he throws a spear at an animal, whose hind legs are twice as long as his fore ones. If killed, wife and children prepare and cook it. A hole is heated in the sand. When hot the animal with his skin on, is put in. A fire on the top cooks it. The women dig and bake roots for this feast. Seals are sometimes surprised. The wife and children witness the skill and activity of the father; he plays and romps with his children till the seal is cooked. The Australian is very dextrous in feeling with his toes for turtles in the ponds, and he is skillful at fishing; these are wrapped in grass and baked in hot sand.

The civilized man is often in want of food. Those who possess the soil can make all others obedient to their will. The Commercial inquires, "Why are there bread riots in England? The country is filled with gold, and the nation has an abundant harvest." The reason is plain, the country is filled with machines, that do the labor; the living laborer is not wanted. The abundance that is made, feeds men abroad seeking for diamonds, pearls, silver, and góld.

The twentieth annual report of the Board of Directors of Girard College, says: "That 500 pupils were educated. Difficulty is experienced in binding out pupils in accordance with Mr. Girard's will, in consequence of the breaking up of the old system of apprenticeship, and the introduction of machinery into trades. It is apprehended that in the future permanent situations can only be for a few." Sad news to be told there are no places for boys to work in. It is sadder still to know that 2,000,000 of persons in this land, have soil sufficient to keep 200,000,000 in food. Much of this land is for speculation, to the injury of poor boys who want homes. These boys, to get this land, will have to toil very hard. Blackstone says : "A few words on parchment does not give the dominion of land." It seems to be the will of Providence that a few should monopolize the soil, to improve the rest. The wide domains that Queen Anne gave to her favorites did not belong to her. The rich men will pass away when the laborer is intelligent.

For a long time after the conquest, the Anglo-Saxon divisions of society were maintained, and the inhabitants of England were divided into freemen and slaves. Except the great baronial proprietors and their free tenants, the rest of the nation was depressed in servitude, which was uniform in its principle. Those who had fallen into bondage could not acquire any right to any species of property.

One class of villains, or villagers, though bound to the most servile offices of rural industry, were permitted to occupy small portions of land to sustain themselves and families. Other ranks of men, equally servile, are noticed in the ancient records, particularly the bordars and the cottars. The former, in consideration of being allowed a small cottage, were required to provide poultry, eggs, and other articles of diet for the lord's table. The latter were employed as smiths, carpenters, and other handicrafts, in which they had been instructed, at the expense of the lord. Inferior to these were the thralls, or servi, employed in menial services around the mansion. Their lives were protected by law. With the consent of their owners these cottars could purchase their manumission. In other respects they were in the lowest degradation; and were to be considered as mere chattels and regular articles of commerce.

Giraldus says: "That so great was the number exported into Ireland, for sale, in the reign of Henry II, that the market was overstocked. From William I to the time of John, scarcely a cottage in Scotland but what possessed an English slave." In the details of the border wars, mention is frequently made of the number of slaves taken prisoners as forming a principal part of the booty.

It is not easy to ascertain from writers, the difference in the condition of the bondmen. It arose, probably, from the utility of their occupations. The servi, or serfs, were less valuable than cottars or bordars, who had been trained to useful arts. All, however, alike have been denied the attributes of freemen. The law recognised in none the uncontrolled right to property, or change of place, without the consent of the superior. The lord had the absolute disposal of their persons, they might be attached to the soil, or transferred from one owner to another; in short, they were slaves, in the strictest sense of the word—men under perpetual servitude, which the master only could dissolve.

Sharon Turner says: "The population of England, after the desolation of the Normans, amounted to 1,700,000, or near that number. It is supposed that 100,000 persons were swept away by the Conqueror, in laying waste the country betwixt the Humber and the Tees. Attempts have been made to class the population, at the close of the the Anglo-Saxon period, into the several proportions of nobles, freemen, and those of servile condition, but with no pretensions to accuracy. In thirty-four counties the citizens are made to amount to 17,100, the villains to 102,700; the bordars to 74,800; the cottars to 5,900; the thralls or serfs to 26,500. The remaining population consisted of freemen, ecclesiastics, knights, thanes, and land-owners."

Of the domestic comforts enjoyed by this class we know but little. It may be presumed that from motives of interest, the lord would supply his villain in infancy and manhood, with the essential necessaries of life. It creates in the

This full-fed man offers this little outcast, a street sweeper, some money to buy a new broom. It is to test his honesty, so that he can assist him to gain wealth and ease. Such objects would never pain our minds, in this wintry scene, if the children of the poor were sent to a school of industry, and taught to plant, build, spin, and weave, so that they can cultivate the earth, and produce their food and fleeces. The managers of "Girard College," in their report, say it is difficult for them to find places for their orphans to learn trades; and the cause of this is, labor is done by machinery. This fact proves that society should do something to promote the happiness of those poor and abject boys, whose labor is of no utility to any person.

2

master the same motives for rearing and preserving his thralls as his cattle—a tie dissolved by the laborer becoming independent, and left to his own prudence to make a provision for the vicissitudes of health and employment.

The work of mitigation and final extinction of English slavery, was a gradual and lengthened operation. The first blow the system received was the disuse of the practice of converting war prisoners into bondmen. The diffusion of Christianity, by teaching mankind that they were equal, early awakened men to a sense of the injustice of making one man the property of another. Frequently at the intercession of confessors, the feudal lords were induced to enfranchise their slaves. In the eleventh century, the Pope formally issued a bull for the emancipation of slaves. It was declared at the great council, in 1102, held at Westminster, unlawful to sell slaves in the open market.

It would be a mistake to suppose that slavery ceased in the land with this decree. In the Magna Charta, and the charter of Henry III, obtained in 1225, a class of men are mentioned, who appear to have been treated as chattel property. The prohibition to guardians from wasting the men or cattle, on the estates of minors, is a clear proof that villains were held by servile tenures.* Long after this period they were considered a salable commodity. Sir F. Eden cites these instances from ancient authorities: "In 1283, a slave and his family were sold by the abbot of Dunstable, for 13s. 1d. In 1333, a lord granted to a chantry several messuages, together with the bodies of eight natives dwelling there, with all their chattels and offspring. In 1339, is an instance of a gift of a *nief* [a female slave,] with all her family, and all that she might possess, and did then own. It was not till the reign of Charles II, that slavery was

---

*VILLAINS—those who lived in villages. BORDARS—cultivators of bordage lands.

6

wholly abolished by statute." So late even as 1775, the colliers in Scotland were bondmen. If they left the ground to which they belonged, and as pertaining to which their services were bought and sold, they were liable to be brought back by summary procedure before a magistrate. This slavery was ended by Act 15, Geo. III cap. 28.

Wm. Howitt, in his "Rural Life in England," says: "A person is struck, when he enters Durham, with the sight of bands of women working in fields, under the surveillance of a man. You inquire why such regular bands of female laborers. The answer is: 'Oh, they are the bondagers.' Bondagers? that is an odd sound in England. What! have we a rural serfdom still existing in England? Even so. It is a fact. As I cast my eyes on these female bands, I was reminded of the slave-gangs of the West Indies."

Wm. Cobbett says: "The single laborers are kept in this manner: about four of them are put in a shed; which shed, Dr. Jameson, in his Dictionary, calls a 'boothie' a place where laboring servants are lodged. A boothie is a little booth; and here these men live and sleep, having an allowance of oat, barley, and peameal, upon which they live, mixing it with milk or water. They are allowed some little matter of money to buy clothes with. They hire for the year, under very severe punishment in case of misbehavior or quitting service. A new place can not be had without a character from the last master, and also from the *minister*. Upon a steam-engine farm are the married laborers. These live in a long shed, with stone walls, and divided into boothies. Each boothie is twenty feet square. In this a man, his wife and family have to live. To make the most of the room, berths are erected, which they get up into when they go to bed; and here they are, a man, his wife, and a parcel of children, squeezed up in a miserable hole, with their

meal and washing-tackle, and other things.   It is a shame
that they are permitted to enjoy so small a portion of the
fruits of all their labors.   Their dwelling place is bad, their
food is worse, that upon which horses and hogs are fed.

"The married man receives about four pounds a year.
He also has sixty bushels of oats, thirty of barley, twelve of
peas, and three of potatoes, and also pasture for a cow.
The oatmeal is made into porridge.   The barley-meal and
pea-meal are mixed and baked into cakes.   These cultivators get no wheaten bread, beef, or mutton, though the land
is covered with wheat and cattle.   The laborer is wholly
at the mercy of the master, who, if he will not keep him
beyond the year, can totally ruin him, by refusing him a
character.   The necessity of a character from the last employer makes the man a *real slave*, worse off than the negro
by many degrees.   The master has no motive to attend to
his health or preserve his life.   From daylight to dark these
people work.   The cattle, sheep, and wheat are sold.   The
farmer gets a little of the money, almost the whole of it is
squandered, by the lord at London, Paris, and Rome, to
whom the laborers are slaves, and the farmers slave-drivers.
Farm-yards are factories for making corn and meat."

In the reign of Edward I the condition of the villains
was so far ameliorated, that they were not obliged to perform every mean and servile office that the will of the lord
required.   Tenures were acquired on lands on condition of
rendering certain services, such as reaping the lord's corn, or
cleaning his fish-ponds, harrowing lands for two days in the
year, or carting the lord's timber.   As early as 1257, a servile tenant, if employed before midsummer, received wages,
and he was permitted, instead of working himself, to provide a laborer for the lord; from which it is evident he possessed the means of hiring one.   At this period a class of la-

borers began to exist, who were at liberty to barter their services to the best bidder. These were important transactions, indicating the rise of a middle class and independent race of workers. By granting to the vassals a right to property, they received a stimulus to acquire more; and by giving to them a part of the immunities of freemen, they were raised one step in the social scale, and put in a state to contend and treat with their oppressors for the remainder.

While the people were in a state of slavery, it may be conjectured that their diet would be the mere offal and refuse of their master; and no more than necessary, to enable them to support their toil. At this period, the food of the laborer was principally fish, bread, and beer. Mutton and cheese were considered articles of luxury, which formed the harvest-home feast.

Wages were a penny a day at harvest, and a half-penny at other times. Their habitations were without chimneys, and their principal furniture consisted of a brass pot, valued at three shillings; and a bed at six shillings.

The variations in the prices of commodities were great, owing to the absence of middlemen. The trade of a corn-dealer was unknown; except at the Abbey-Granges. The natural consequence must have been, that the farmers had no capital, and disposed of their crops at moderate prices soon after the harvest. Purchasers who only looked to immediate use, and having corn cheap, were usually improvident. As the year advanced, the price frequently arose enormously before harvest. Stowe relates, that in 1317, before harvest the supply of wheat was nearly exhausted, the price was £4 the quarter. After harvest it was 6s. 8d. A reference to the table of wages and the price of food tells of the misery of the times.

The progress of manufacturing industry, and town pop-

ulation operated favorably on the condition of the working
classes.   The woolen manufacture had been known as
early as the Conquest, and, for greater security during a barbarous age, had been chiefly established in boroughs and
cities.   It was at first carried on by the Flemings.   The
privileges, conferred by the sovereign, on weavers, fullers,
and clothiers, in allowing them to carry on their trades in
walled towns, and form themselves into guilds and companies, governed by corporate laws, were not more intended
for the advancement of their art, than to protect their persons from popular outrage, and their property from depre-
dation.   Such was the want of police during the thirteenth
and fourteenth centuries, that robbers formed themselves
into bands, under powerful barons, who employed them in
acts of violence and plunder, and justified their conduct,
and partook of their booty.   The king's retinue was often
beset and pillaged by banditti.   Towns, during the fairs,
were assaulted and ransacked, and men of rank carried off
and confined in the castle of some lawless chieftain, till
their ransom was paid.   In so general a state of insecurity it
was impossible that the pursuits of agriculture should thrive
without special protection.   The immunities granted to
merchants and manufacturers, to make laws, to raise troops
for their own defense, enabled them to taste the blessings
of order and protection, and enrich themselves, while the
occupiers of land were languishing in poverty and servitude.
The superior comforts enjoyed in towns, no doubt, inspired
the dependents of a manor with ideas of emancipation
from a state in which they could scarcely obtain the comforts of life.*

If in the hands of a poor cultivator, oppressed with the
services of villainage, some little stock should accumulate,

*Sir F. Eden's State of the poor, vol. 1 p 18.

he would naturally conceal it from his master, by whom it would be claimed, and take the first opportunity to escape to a town. The law was indulgent to the inhabitants of towns, and so favorable to diminishing the authority of the lord, over those in the country, that if a vassal should conceal himself from the pursuit of his lord for one year he was free forever.

By the demand for manufactures, a large number of villains were converted into free laborers. The number was increased, during the long wars of Edward III, in France, which must have obliged him to give freedom to many of his villains, to recruit his exhausted armies. The legislation of 1350, gives us this fact, that those who worked at husbandry and the loom worked for hire.

In 1344, a terrible pestilence prevailed, labor became extremely dear. A proclamation was issued to fix the price of labor. "The Statute of Laborers" was enacted to enforce it, by fines. The statute says, since the pestilence no person would serve unless allowed double wages, to the detriment of the lords and commons. It provides that in future plowmen, carters, shepherds, swineherds, and other servants shall receive such liveries and wages as they received in the twentieth year of the king's reign. If paid in wheat it was to be tenpence a bushel. Hay-makers and weeders were to be paid a penny a day; mowers were to receive fivepence a day; reapers twopence a day, without diet. Laborers were enjoined to carry their implements of industry in their hands to the market towns, in a public place, to be hired.

This unjust interference with the freedom of industry was repeatedly confirmed by succeeding parliaments. A law of 1363, regulated the diet and apparel of laborers; and that of 1388, which prohibits servants from removing from one place to another; and finally, to conclude these oppressive enactments, justices of peace were to fix the price of labor every Easter. The statute of 1363, directs that artificers, servants, and laborers, shall be served once a day, with meat and fish, or the waste of other victuals, as milk and cheese, according to their station. The cloth of yeomen and tradesmen, was not to cost more than one shilling and sixpence a yard. Plowmen and other farm hands were to use only black russet, at twelve pence a yard. Clothiers were to make and keep a sufficiency on hand.

One important fact may be elicited: the laborers had extricated themselves from the grasp of their feudal masters, who were compelled to resort to acts of parliament to get power to compel servitude. Law was in place of arbitrary power. Before the end of the fourteenth century, freedom, order, and industry, had made considerable progress. The mass of the people, when contrasted with those of the Conquest, were rich and thriving. Historians are silent on many points—there is evidence that domestic happiness was greatly improved. The immunities granted to cities, the introduction of manufactures, the dawning of the polite arts, the humanizing tendency of Christianity, are causes which have ameliorated the condition of the community.

It is to these that we may ascribe the changes in the political opinions of the laboring classes. Wat Tyler, in the year 1381, required of the king abolition of slavery; freedom of commerce in market towns, without toll or impost, and a fixed rent on lands instead of services by villainage.

"These requests," says Mr. Hume, "though extremely reasonable in themselves, the nation was not prepared to receive, and which it were dangerous to have yielded to intimidations, were however complied with. Charters of manumission were granted, and although they were revoked after the rebellion was crushed—many hundreds of the insurgents were executed as traitors. The spirit that manifested itself during this period, prevented masters from imposing, and vassals from again submitting, to the oppressive service of bondage."

Various causes changed the villains into free laborers, and created tenantry, who were strengthened by manufactures and commerce. At the Conquest, most of the lands in England were parceled out among the Norman nobility. Earl Morton acquired no less than 193 manors; and Hugh de Alrinces received the whole palatinate of Chester. The extensive county of Norfolk had only sixty proprietors. The owners of such vast possessions lived on their estates. Earl Spencer, in the time of Edward II, possessed 1,000 oxen, 28,000 sheep, 1,200 cows, 500 cart horses, 2,000 hogs, and of salted provisions 600 bacons, 80 beef carcasses, 600 sheep, and also ten tuns of cider. This nobleman's estate was probably managed by stewards, and cultivated by the labor of villains or slaves. This was spent in rude and riotous hospitality. Commerce at length led to allurements of a different kind, and induced him, from motives of personal gratification, to lessen the number of his idle retainers and to grant a portion of his demesnes to a tenant, on condition of receiving a rent, which might enable him to extend his pursuits beyond gorgeous entertainments, field pleasures, or domestic warfare.

The progress of manufactures led to a revolution among land-owners and other ranks of community. Instead of fortunes being spent in supporting numerous idlers, it was expended in the production of art. Dr. Smith, the author of the "Wealth of Nations," says: "For a pair of diamond buckles, or something as frivolous, they exchanged the maintenance of a thousand men for a year." It is to more rational causes this change may be attributed. The desire of bettering our condition is the parent of many virtues; it would compel the lord to prefer comfort to barbaric splendor, and the villain to engage in the independence of trade. These changes produced advantages for the general good. A man, by dismissing half of his *useless* domestics, increases his enjoyments; he could clothe himself in woolen and fine linen instead of coarse canvass and a leathern jerkin. It would add the production of horticulture to his table, and would render a dreary castle more comfortable with warm hangings on the bare walls.

In 1406, we have evidence, competition commenced between rural and town industry. A statute had been passed compelling those who had been brought up to the plow till they were twelve years of age, to continue at husbandry all their lives. To evade this law agricultural laborers sent their children to the town, as apprentices under that age. It was enacted that no person, unless possessed of land of a rental of twenty shillings, should bind a child to any trade, except that of the parents.

In the reign of Henry VII, the race of villains was almost extinct. The useful arts had made a wonderful progress. In the statute of laborers for 1496, bricklayers are for the first time mentioned as artificers, and also glaziers. In 1567, glass was a rarity, only in castles. It was used for farm houses in the time of James I.

The diet of laborers at this period had become wholesome by the introduction of vegetables. Their dress was simple, the hat and hose were made of cloth, the coat was fastened on with a belt. Laws were in force regulating the quantity and quality of the wearing apparel. A statute of Richard III limited the price of a hat to twenty pence. In the reign of Henry VIII, it was enacted that no serving

7

man, under the degree of a gentleman, should wear a coat containing more than three broad yards, under forfeiture. The cloth was not to exceed twenty-pence a yard. The statute of 1496, fixed the rate of yearly wages. A shepherd was to receive £1. A common farm servant's wages was 16s. The yearly allowance for his clothing was 5s. A woman received for a year 10s, and 4s. for her clothing. Artificers received 6d., and a laborer 4d. a day, and no food. In harvest 1d. a day more was paid. The food was 2d. a day. Yearly laborers received food. If any person refused serving at these wages he might be imprisoned.

The statute said the hours of labor should be from five o'clock in the morning to seven at evening, from March to September. One hour shall be allowed for breakfast. An hour for dinner, and half an hour to sleep. In winter, the hours of labor were from "springing of day" till dark. The diet of the artisan was one-third of his income, and one-half of the laborer's. The rewards and relaxation from labor are the same to the English laborer now as they were in 1514.

Erasmus says: "The dwellings of the common people, had not yet attained to the convenience of a chimney, to let off the smoke, the flooring of their huts was nothing but the bare ground; their beds consisted of straw, with a block of wood for a pillow." Fortesque, who wrote in the reign of Henry VI says of the French peasantry, "Thay drink water, thay eate apples, with right brown bread made of rye; thay eate flesch, but it be seldom; a little larde, or of the entrails, or of the heds of beasts, sclayne for the nobles or merchaunts of the lond."

At the close of the reign of Henry VII, originated that class denominated the poor—those who are free, but without the means of supporting themselves by their industry.

Individuals in this unhappy condition are in a state of slavery. Those who can not live independently of the support of others can not, in the affairs of life, act the part of freemen. The great mass of English poor is nothing more than the continuance, under a mitigated form, of the race of villains, who have exchanged baronial for parochal servitude.

With the feudal system, a regular chain of subordination subsisted from the highest to the lowest. All thought of personal independence was precluded, and each individual looked for maintenance and protection to his next superior.

A cause may be assigned for the contrast presented between rural and civic industry. In the country, laborers are often hired by the year. They are guaranteed against all casualties. Their remuneration does not depend on wages—they have the produce of a garden. These are not exposed to those temptations of pleasure and irregular life, which are among the many causes of extreme wretchedness in towns.

The extension of commerce is one of the causes of the poor. It is an evil inseparable from commerce—that it augments population, without providing a permanent subsistence for the people. The employments that spring from commerce must always be liable to variations. The inventions of machinery, or the ever-changing fashions, often take away work. Unless there be some certain provision for the people, independent of these fluctuations, there must be great distress, and numbers must perish.

In the year 1376, we have evidence that there was a disposition to vagrancy among laborers. It was a complaint that masters were obliged to give their servants high wages, to prevent them from running away; that many of the runaways turn beggars, and lead idle lives in cities and boroughs, although they have sufficient bodily strength to gain a livelihood, if willing to work; that others become staff-strikers, wandering in parties from village to village, but that the chief part turn out sturdy rogues, infesting the kingdom with frequent robberies. To remedy these evils, the Commons proposed that no relief shall be given; that vagrants, beggars, and staff-strikers [*cudgel-players*], shall be imprisoned till they consent to return home to work, and whosoever harbors a runaway servant shall be liable to a penalty of ten pounds. This is the first time beggars are mentioned; it shows the earliest opinion of the Commons on mendicity. These persons were chiefly found in towns where, owing to commerce and the introduction of manufactures, the principal part of the wealth of the nation accumulated.

In 1388, it was enacted that those who, by lameness or sickness, could do no work, had a legal claim on the revenues of the clergy. In 1391, an act was passed that a part of the tithes for the support of monasteries should be set apart for the maintenance of the poor. These regulations laid the foundation of the English system of poor laws. For two centuries before the Reformation, the legislature struggled against the evil which accompanied the transition from slavery to free labor, and their policy was directed to objects similar to those which now engage the attention of law makers, to analyze the mass of vagabondage, imposture, and real destitution. To punish the former and relieve the latter, branding, whipping, imprisonment, and sitting in the stocks, were employed. *Scholars* were liable to these penalties, unless provided with written testimonials from the chancellor of their university. Sailors, soldiers, and travelers were also provided with passports to travel homeward by the shortest road. Artificers and laborers were forbidden to play at unlawful games, ex-

cept on Christmas. Two justices were empowered to restrain the common selling of ale in towns and places where
they should deem it expedient, and to take surety of the
ale-house keepers for their good behavior.

In 1530, beggars got license to beg within certain limits.
Their names were registered if found without license, or
beyond the assigned limits. The offender was fed on bread
and water in the stocks for two days. Able-bodied men
found begging, were flogged, and made go to labor.

An act in the time of Henry VIII made it obligatory on
the head officer and householder of every parish to maintain, by collection of voluntary and charitable alms, for the
poor of the parish in such a way, that "none of them of
very necessity be compelled to go openly on begging," the
alms to be collected Sundays, holidays and festivals. The
ministers in their sermons, collations, confessions, and at
the making of wills, are required to "exhort, move, stir, and
provoke the people to be liberal in their contributions toward the comfort and relief of the impotent, decrepid, and
needy poor." Some of the poor are directed to go round
twice a week, and collect from each householder his broken and refuse meat and drink, for equal distribution among
the indigent. Precautions were taken by fines and penalties to guard against embezzlement the parochial alms and
doles, from constables and churchwardens.

The Reformation affected property more than industry.
It was the transfer of a large portion of the English soil to
laymen from spiritual corporations. That there was a necessity for it may be inferred from the Mortmain Act, passed
in the reign of Henry II, "That government had become
fully sensible of the hurtful tendency of the vast accumulations of the religious houses." It was this transfer that
made England take the lead of the nations of Europe in

wealth and intelligence. Had the vast possessions of the
clergy remained in their hands, they must have formed an
obstacle to the productive power of the country. The revenue used by the priesthood can not clearly now be ascertained. The number of religious houses were 1,041, and
the revenues were near £273,106. Tithes are supposed to
be twice that sum. Upon good authority it is stated the
clergy owned seven-tenths of the whole kingdom. There
were four orders of mendicants to be maintained, against
whom no gate could be shut, to whom no provision could
be denied, or secret concealed.

Henry VIII, to obtain the consent of parliament to his
spoliations, declared that the revenues of the abbeys should
be applied to the expenses of the state, and no loans, subsidies, or other aids be asked. The chief portion of these ben-
efices were given to the nobility. Sir F. Eden doubts if
the monasteries gave themselves any trouble with the poor,
that did not belong to their own demesnes. The abbeys
were burdened with the rich more than the poor. Sheriffs
and other great men traveled from abbey to abbey, with
great retinues, regaling themselves at each and exacting
presents. Laws were made to make abbeys keep the poor.

It has been computed that 50,000 monks were thrown
on society during the Reformation. Edward VI punished
"idleness and vagabondries," by enacting "That any person who refuses to labor, and lives idly for three days, he
shall be branded with a redhot iron on the breast, with the
letter V, and be adjudged a slave for two years to the person who informed on him. And the master is directed to
find his slave with bread and water, in small drink, and refuse meat as he thinks proper; and to cause his slave to
work by beating or chaining him. If the slave absconds for
fourteen days he is a slave for life; and if he runs away a

second time he shall suffer death." These laws were found
too severe and abolished. The statute provided that certain
of the poor shall be employed by the town.

In pursuing the various occupations of industry, the
people had discovered the means of emancipating themselves
from feudal servitude; and the nobility, preferred the arts
to baronial splendor, which was the source of idleness and
disorder. Personal authority was exchanged for luxury and
comfort. Their influence over their dependants wasted
away, and was still made weaker by civil wars. So many
ancient families were sacrified in civil contest, that Henry
VII could only get twenty-eight peers to his first parliament.
The dissolution of monasteries destroyed ecclesiastical authority, and removed obstacles to progressive industry and
a middle rank, whose condition it is to be hoped will be
enjoyed by all. Hume says: "In the interval between
the fall of the nobles and the rise of this order, many of
the monarchs assumed an authority almost absolute."

The police of the country was defective, and did not attain to perfect order. Punishment was not lenient, it was
vigorous and unrelenting. Harrison says that Henry VIII
executed his laws with such severity, that 72,000 "great
and petty thieves were put to death." He adds, in Elizabeth's reign, "rogues were trussed up apace. Commonly
in one year, 300 or 400 of them were eaten up by the gallows in one place and another." These punishments did
not prevent robbers, sometimes as many as 300 together,
from plundering dwellings and sheepfolds. These outrages
are attributed to the changes in society, the uninstructed
condition of the laborer.

Schools were rare. Young men were taught in monasteries, the women in nunneries, in writing, drawing, confec-
tionery, and needle work. Domestic manners were se-

vere and formal; a haughty reserve was affected by the old, and an abject deference by the young. Some, when arrived at manhood, are represented as standing uncovered and silent in their father's presence; and daughters were not permitted to sit before their mothers, but must kneel till she retired. Omissions were punished with stripes and blows, to such an excess, that the daughters trembled at the sight of their mother, and the sons avoided their father.

The diet of the people appears not to have differed from the present time. In cities meat was consumed. The food of laborers, in time of Henry VIII, was a small quantity of bacon, and it is probable they lived much in the same manner as the husbandmen in Scotland, their food consisting of oat and rye bread, milk, and pottage. The substantial diet of the sixteenth century was limited to the tables of persons of rank. A maid of honor of Elizabeth's court perhaps breakfasted on beefsteak, but the plowman was compelled to regale himself on barley or rye bread and water gruel. Morrison says: "Husbandmen weare garments of coarce cloth made at home, and their wives weave gowns of the same cloth, kirtles of light stuffe with linnen aprons, and cover their heads with a felt hat, their linnen is coarce and made at home."

In 1597, Elizabeth directed that four overseers be chosen, to set poor children to work and others wanting it. The church wardens were to build houses on the waste, and put poor people in them. James of Scotland had an act passed, that "Hail inhabitants shall be taxed and *stented* on their substance, to keep poor people." These acts were passed in Elizabeth's reign. Profaneness and immorality, neglecting to go to church, and not wearing a woolen cap on Sunday, were finable offenses, and the money was given to the poor. A curious act was also passed: "No cottage shall be erected unless it had attached to it *four* acres of land." A special commission from Charles I, was issued to enforce this statute. In 1495, a laborer working a certain amount of time, could purchase with his wages 199 pints of wheat; in 1593, the same time and labor would only purchase 82 pints of wheat; in 1610 the same time and labor only purchased 46 pints. The increase of indigence increased crime. A magistrate, in Somersetshire, in 1596, affirms that "Forty persons were executed, thirty-three burnt in the hand, and thirty-seven were whipped in one year." James I enacted "That dangerous rogues shall be branded with the letter R with a redhot iron and placed to labor; if afterwards found begging they shall suffer death." In 1610, Parliament gave to magistrates the power of rating the wages of the working people. They were to take notice of those who "Goe in good clothes and fare well, and none knowes where they live; those that be night walkers." They were to enforce the laws that required poor children to learn trades. A wandering family were required to tell when married, and if the children had been christened; "For these people live like salvages, neither marry, nor christen; which licentious libertie, make so many delight to be rogues and wanderers."

At this time a proclamation came out to the nobility and gentry, to take no suppers on Fridays, fast days, Lent, or Ember week, and the meat that was saved was to be given to the poor. In 1697 John Locke expressed an opinion that many who got public relief could work, and that work-schools should be started for destitute children, the boys to have trades, and the girls to be prepared for service. In 1714, John Bellars proposed "The College of Industry," for the poor. This writer said: "The poor without employment were like rough diamonds, their worth is unknown." In 1723, at Hanslope it was found that if houses were pro-

vided, a poor person could be kept for 1s. 6d. per week.
In 1758, Mr. Massie said the poor were increased by taking away the "commons," by removing the people from
farming to the fluctuating demands of trade and manufacture.   In 1760, Dr. Adam Smith states that half of the
people of England do not eat wheat bread, they use as a
substitute rye, oats, and barley.   In 1768, it was enacted
that tailors should work, from six in the morning to seven
o'clock at night, one hour allowed for meals, their wages was
not to exceed 2s. 7½d. a day.   In 1796, Mr Whitbread in
Parliament said: "In most parts of the country the laborer
had been long struggling with increasing misery, till the
pressure was too great to be endured."   Mr. Pitt replied
"That the condition of the *poor* was. cruel, and, as such
could not be wished on any principle of humanity or policy."

In 1807, the population of England and Wales numbered
8,870,000; not less than 1,234,000 persons were partakers
of public relief.   In 1818 infant schools were established
by Brougham, Macauley, Sir T. Baring, Lord Dacre, and
the Marquis of Landsdown.   The motive for instruction
"was to keep them from vice and mischief and give them
the rudiments of virtue and knowledge."

Lord Brougham ascertained that one-third of the English
children had no learning.   In Parliament he exposed the
abuses of school endowments from good people.   A clergyman was at the head of a school, and received £900 and
had only one scholar.   Another school yielded £500, and
had no scholars; the school-room was rented for a sawpit.
This nobleman has been the means of millions of the poor,
obtaining an education.   He began the cause of universal
instruction in 1816.   In 1823, Parliament sent to the Cape
of Good Hope 350 persons, and 586 to Canada as an experiment for unemployed poor.   At this period Mechanic's

Institutions were established. In 1824, all the old statutes, from the time of Edward I, relating to the combinations of workmen, the rates of wages, and the hours of work, were repealed. The great injustice had long been felt of allowing masters in concert, to fix the rate of wages and the hours of work, and interdicting the workman to fix theirs.

In 1827, a number of men distinguished for literary and scientific attainments, established a society, "For the Diffusion of Knowledge among Men." The object of this society was: "The imparting of useful information to all classes of the community, particularly to such as are *unable* to avail themselves of experienced teachers, or may prefer teaching themselves." In this year, a Committee of the House of Commons, reported: "That in the United Kingdom, circumstances indicated a great deterioration among the people of the agricultural districts, where wages were so depressed by competition for employment, that the laborer is compelled to live chiefly on bread and potatoes, seldom tasting meat. Symptoms of an approaching servile war are discernable, which can only be averted by relieving the market. In Ireland it was ascertained that a part of the population were dependent on the precarious source of charity, or is compelled to resort to plunder and spoliation, for the actual means of support." The committee said colonization was the best remedy.

In 1831, the barbarities practiced in manufacturing districts, caused an act to be passed that a person under twenty one years of age shall not work at night. The hours of labor to be from half past five in the morning to half past eight in the evening. The hours of labor to those under eighteen shall be twelve. One hour and a half shall be allowed for meals. A parliamentary committee said: "The cruelty and cupidity of mill-owners in the pursuit of gain has hardly been exceeded by the Spaniards in the pursuit of gold." Fifteen boys went to a ragged school on Sunday evening. The clock struck eight, which caused them to start away. The master detained one and said: "The lesson is not over." The reply was: "We must go to business, and catch them as come out of the chapels." The boy had no remorse or shame, in making this avowal; because he believed he would die with starvation, if he did not go and steal. To another boy the master spoke of the terrors of after life. The boy said: "That may be so, but I don't think it can be any worse than this world is to me." There are in London alone 30,000 juvenile beggars and thieves, many of whom are not as moral as the brutes of the earth, and many have nothing but rags tied on them.

This chapter will teach what laborers have suffered. It is not legislation men want, it is more industry. Were the kings of the earth, with their horses, servants, and soldiers, made to do work, misery would cease. Those who have started governments by conquest were robbers, they are continued among men by violence, fraud, folly, and ignorance. When the wrongs that governments do shall cease, mankind will be happy. Men are made poor by those who govern them. Want makes crime, and it will ever be so while one man works, and another does nothing. Society contains many who do single work and get quadruple pay.

CHAPTER IV.

GOVERNMENTS AND FEUDALISM.

Patriarchal Governments—The Origin of Monarchies—Their Corruptions and Changes—William the Norman—His Advent into England—Feudalism its Origin and Necessity to Improve Men.

"Governments are caused by men's wickedness."—Paine.

ON the earth, at the present time, may be found nations and tribes of men who are a type of the past generations in every period of time. In Ceylon some of the interior natives live in trees, and have little or no language. The habitations of the Australians are made by the women, of branches, bark, and clay. The Patagonians, in the days of Columbus, had no conception of a fire.

Little did man know when he commenced his career on this earth, he had none to guide him. Nature provided spontaneous productions for all his wants. Those who lived longest had the most experience, and were the guides to others. In course of time there would be an insufficiency of room, which would cause some one to start into the wilderness. His family would increase, after awhile this man would be the patriarch of his tribe, who would obey him because he knew the most. His commands would be reasonable because he loved his people. Their wealth would be flocks, which would give them milk and fleeces. These would require pasturage, and in changing their pasturage, these shepherds would come in contact with other tribes, which would lead to a conflict. The conquered party would be willing to be slaves for the sake of having their lives spared. The two tribes would easily overcome another tribe. Has the leader of the successful party a right to adoration, or a greater share of the spoils, than the others? Has his posterity a right to honors and rewards forever? A leader of a battle is often at a distance. The leader has a feeling of satisfaction, and this should be his only reward. Hereditary honors, how costly they are to mankind! The family of England's Queen, with her own salary costs her nation annually $6,000,000. This enormous sum requires hundreds of tax-gatherers to collect it. To keep the people from revolting, a standing army of 24,000 persons are required; these consume a fourth of the laborer's earnings. After the war between those shepherds, was there any need of the chief living a life of idleness, or lessening the scanty stores of the others?

There can be no doubt the ancient Britons were once rude shepherds. It is commerce and being conquered that has made England great among the nations of the earth. The Conquest in England's history marks the line of that which is authentic from that which is doubtful. All the history antecedent to William the I contains much that is marvelous and improbable. The improvements in the arts were slow in one period, rapid in the other. What a contrast between the two periods of time! One is a long night of bondage, darkness, and error, with only gleams of social amelioration. The latter period shows what a favorable climate, and the discoveries of men of genius can accomplish.

The Teutonic invaders of England did much to make stronger those germs of art and science started by the Romans. These latter taught the Britons how to build stone

houses, to spin and weave cloth. The Anglo-Saxon institutions were analogous to all communities entering on the
early career of civilization. Such was their rudeness that
the marriage rites were not always observed. They held
in slavery two-thirds of the people. It was the introduction
of Christianity that did much to reclaim them. The code
of laws made by King Alfred show the progress of religion.
It was William the Norman that gave to us all the usages
and customs of modern society, and it may be profitable to
know something of his life.

He was the seventh Duke of Normandy. He was called
a duke from this fact; 150 years before William's time a
pirate of the name of Rolla, left his rude home on the Baltic, with some followers. He took possession of a part of
France, and it was called Normandy, from the Northmen
who conquered it. The King of France could not expel
this invader. He made a compromise: Rolla should rule as
a duke if he would do homage for his dukedom. The homage was, that he should kneel in the presence of all the po-
tentates and chieftains, and put his clasped hands into those
of the king, and then kiss an embroidered slipper on the
king's foot. This Rolla did not like to do. One of the nobility was called to do it. He lifted up the king's foot so as
to throw him off his seat. The king had been besieged in
his capital, and was too feeble to resent this insult. Another
condition of peace was that Rolla should be baptized; and
marry a daughter of the king. A long peace followed; the
resources of the fertile country were drawn out. William had abundant means for his invasion of England. The
conqueror of England was not of noble blood, on the side
of his mother. Robert, the father of William, saw a girl,
the daughter of a tanner, washing clothes at a stream. He
sent for her to live at his castle. It was not customary for

dukes and peasants to marry. It is strange that those who are the most useful should be held in contempt, while a pirate's descendants, who can overrun a province and make its people poor, are held in esteem. At the present time excessive riches are acquired by injustice, and their possessors are more regarded than those who keep men from dying by their useful toil. The offspring of Robert and Arlotte was William, a very beautiful boy. His father was proud of him. At his father's death, when thirteen years of age, homage and fealty was shown to him by the barons. The reason of this obedience, was that the king of France might recover again his province, which had been given up. By being united they could keep down the common people. Barons are often quarrelsome; a duke or a king can do very much toward reconciling them. A king is a judge as well as a leader. A nice analysis of the laws of civilized society show they favor the rich more than those who do the hard toil. There is a sufficiency of labor done to make every one rich. The labor is put in the wrong place. Inequality must ever exist where the rich make the laws. If riches were universal, crime would cease.

William's pretext for invading England was, he considered himself the legitimate successor to its crown. Ethelred, the Saxon king of England, married Emma, a sister of one of the dukes of Normandy. Edward, one of her sons, was much in Normandy, and was often in William's company. When Edward became king of England, William paid him a visit. Edward had no children, and William, it is said, obtained a promise from him, that he should in his will be named as his successor.

Edward the king had a quarrel with the Earl Godwin, which led to a cruel civil war. A compromise was made; Godwin was to retain his rank, and the government of a province, and he promised to dismiss his armies, and to make war upon the king no more. He bound himself to the faithful performance of this covenant by giving the king *hostages*. Godwin gave to King Edward a son and grandson. Edward sent these to William for safe keeping. It was those who were the best beloved that were given up. A non-fulfillment of the contract subjected the hostages to torture and death. These lived in continual fear among their enemies. Godwin died. Harold his son asked King Edward if he could go to Normandy for his brother and nephew, as there was no longer any reason for detaining them. Edward did not like to give them up, as Harold was ambitious. Harold went over the channel; a contrary wind wrecked him on the dominions of the Count of Ponthieu, who demanded a large ransom before he was released. William received Harold with a great deal of hospitality, he got up games, feasts, and military spectacles, and gave to the followers of Harold suits of armor, presents of horses, and banners. William went on an expedition, and took Harold with him; on the journey home William told Harold that King Edward was to adopt him as his successor. Harold had designs to secure the crown for himself. As he was the guest of William he consented to his plans. The most solemm oaths were administered to Harold to bind him to his word. William kept Harold's brother, promising to bring him over when he came to England. Harold did not consider his oath binding, as it was taken to prevent being made a prisoner. Harold collected munitions of war, made friends of the wealthy, and sought the favor of the king. Edward, on his death-bed, told his nobles to choose whom they liked for their king. Harold was made king with much splendor. Wolves destroy in packs; they have a leader. Nobles and wolves are alike.

8

William, on receiving the news that Harold was made king, made preparations to invade England. Every baron in his realm was bound, by the feudal conditions on which he held his lands, to furnish his quota of men for any enterprise the sovereign should see fit to engage in. The nobles found ships and money. On the English soil the battle of Hastings was fought. It was long and severe. Harold with 250 of his nobles were slain. This battle made William king. He fortified London and reduced the island to his sway. He confiscated the property of the nobles who had fought against him. This conquest was the means of introducing into England and America pernicious customs, the evils of which it will be as difficult to convince the people, as it will the Chinese women that it is wrong to wear tight shoes.

Nothing could exceed the terror of the English on the death of Harold. Stigand, the primate, made submission to the conqueror in the name of the clergy. The nobility made submission also to him. William accepted the crown upon the terms that he should govern according to the customs of the country. He could have made what terms he pleased; though a conqueror he wished to be thought an elected king. For this reason he was crowned at Westminster. He took the oath that he would observe the laws, defend the church, and govern the kingdom with impartiality. William did not find ruling very pleasant. His wife and son Robert governed Normandy in his absence. Robert used his influence to supplant his father. The King of France assisted Robert, which caused William to invade his country and burn his towns. He assaulted the town of Mantes, and set it on fire; while riding among the ruins his horse stepped on some fire concealed among ashes; the pain made the horse to throw his rider, which caused the death of William. Many, when they come to die, think they can atone for a life of avarice, legal plundering, and abstracting others' comforts, by religious charity, by sending clothing and missionaries to Africa, or building a fine church. Religion makes men moral and saving. Many invest their religious savings in wild lands and corner lots, for speculation, after consuming a generous portion of the gains, "an offering to the Lord" is made to soothe the conscience of those who know their *money* comes from those suffering painful anguish of mind and bitter self-denial.

Remorse of conscience troubled William for his deeds. He cried to God for forgiveness, and ordered the monks to pray for him. He gave his money to the poor, and ordered the churches that he had destroyed to be rebuilt. As soon as William was dead, his attendants carried his arms, plate, furniture, and dresses away. Monks came with crosses and tapers, to pray for the repose of his soul. The body was put in a cart to be buried in a monastery he had built. As the procession was moving along, a fire broke out, and those in the procession went to put it out. The body went on. At the grave a person forbid the burial, because the abbey lands had been taken without paying for them. A sum was paid for a grave. A stone coffin had been made, it was found too small, and in trying to put the body in, the coffin broke. The church was so offensive every body left except the workmen, to fill up the grave.

The English historians complain, of the most grievous oppressions of William and his Normans. Whether by his conduct the conqueror willingly gave the English opportunities of rebelling against him, in order to have a pretense for oppressing them afterward, is not easy to say; but it is certain that the beginning of his reign can not justly be blamed. The first disgust against his government was ex-

cited among the clergy. William could not avoid the re-
warding of those numerous adventurers, who had accompanied him in his expedition. He first divided the lands of
the English barons,* who had opposed him, among his
Norman barons; but as these were found insufficient, he
quartered the rest on the rich abbeys, of which there were
many in the kingdom, until some opportunity of providing
them offered itself.

The whole nation was soon disgusted, by seeing the
real power of the kingdom placed in the hands of the Normans. He disarmed the city of London, and other places
which appeared most warlike and populous, and quartered
Norman soldiers wherever he dreaded an insurrection.
This was indeed acting as a conqueror and not as an elected
king. The king having thus secured England as he imag-
ined from any danger of revolt, determined to pay a visit
to his Norman dominions. He appointed Otho his brother,
and William Fitz Osborne as regents in his absence; and to
secure himself yet further he took with him such of the nobility as he had no confidence in.

His absence produced most fatal consequences. Dis-
contents and murmurings were multiplied every-where;
conspiracies were entered into against the government; hostilities were commenced in many places; and every thing
seemed to threaten a speedy revolution. William of Poic-
tiers, a Norman historian, throws the blame on the English.
He calls them a fickle and mutinous race. The English

---

* BARON, a degree of nobility, a lord or peer, in rank below a viscount,
and above that of a knight or baronet. The barons were the feudatories of
princes, the proprietors of land held by honorable service, and members of the
parliament. Barons had courts on their domains, and were judges of the people.

VISCOUNT, an officer who supplied the place of earl or count—a sheriff.

FEUDATORY, a tenant or vassal who holds lands of a superior, and owes for
the use of them military service.

historians tell us, that these governors took all the opportunities of oppressing the people, either with a view of pro-
voking them to a rebellion, or, in case they submitted, to
grow rich by plundering them. A secret conspiracy was
formed among the English for a general massacre of the
Normans. The conspirators had already taken the resolution, and fixed the day for the massacre, which was to be
on Ash-Wednesday, during the time of divine service,
when the Normans were unarmed, as penitents, according
to the discipline of the times. The presence of William
disconcerted all their schemes. Some of the conspirators
consulted their safety by flight; and this served to confirm
the proofs against those who remained. From this time
the king not only lost all confidence in his English subjects,
but regarded them as inveterate and irreconcilable enemies.
He had already raised such a number of fortresses, that he
did not dread any of his discontented subjects. He determined to treat them as a conquered people. He revived
the tax of the Danegelt.* This produced insurrections.
Exeter and Cornwall revolted; they were soon subdued, and
began to implore the conqueror's mercy. Many fled into
Scotland and other places.

The English did not fail privately, in the woods and high-
ways, to assassinate the Normans, when there was no possibility of being brought to justice. The conquerors began
to wish for security; several of them desired to be dismissed
from service. William, to prevent it, increased their boun-
ties. The consequences were fresh exactions from the
English, and new insurrections to prevent it. The county
of Northumberland, which had been most active in revolt,

DANEGELT, an ancient tax to procure money to expel the Danes, or give it
to them to leave. It was at first a shilling for every hide of land, and afterward seven. The Danes, when masters, levied the same tax.

suffered the most. On this occasion 100,000 persons perished by sword and famine. The estates of all the English gentry were confiscated, and given to the Normans. All the ancient families were reduced to beggary, and the English excluded from preferment.

In order that William might have a hunting ground, he created New Forest, by destroying many villages and twenty-two parish churches. Manors* and chapels were destroyed within a circuit of thirty miles. Blount says: "It was attended with divers judgments on the posterity of William—one son Rufus was shot by an arrow, Richard met the same fate. Henry, nephew of the oldest son, was caught by the hair of the head in a tree, like Absalom."

William caused a survey of lands in thirty counties in England. This survey was made in 1078. The reason given for this survey is, "That every man should be satisfied with his own right, and not usurp with impunity what belongs to another." All those who held lands became vassals† of the king, and paid him, as a fee, money, homage, service, in proportion to the lands they held. For the execution of this survey, commissioners were sent into every county and shire. These were to be informed upon oath by the inhabitants, of the name of each manor, and that of its owner; the number of hides of land, ‡ the quantity of wood, pasture, and meadow lands; how many plows in the demesne, § how many fish-ponds, and mills belonged to it; with the value of the whole; also whether it was capable

---

* MANOR, a gentleman's country house, a district bounded with stones, from maen, a stone. This word means the house and lands of a lord for his own subsistence, and the right to hold court-baron [a court.]

† VASSAL, a servant to a prince for the use of lands, which are cultivated by persons in humble life, who become vassals to the lord.

‡ HIDE OF LAND, a quantity of land, supposed to be what one plow can do

§ DEMESNE, a manor house for the use of the family, with sufficient lands.

of improvement or being advanced in value. They were likewise directed to return the tenants of every degree, the quantity of lands then and formerly held by each of them, what was the number of villains or slaves, the number and kinds of their cattle. These inquisitions were sent to the king's exchequer. This survey gave great offense to the people; and occasioned a suspicion that it was intended for some new imposition. This survey, "The Great and Little Doomsday Book," is now in Westminster, written in Latin, highly wrought, on vellum. A part is thus translated:

"The king holds Bermundesey, rated at 12 hides of land; on one is a demesne, 25 villains, 33 bordars, a new church with 20 acres of meadow, and pasturage for five hogs." *

Dr. Stuart says: "The spirit of feudalism was national defense and domestic independence." Feudalism is a system so contrived that a conquering people can defend themselves from enemies without, and an outraged people within. Without a knowledge of feudalism it is impossible to understand the nature of civil governments, or the laws relating to the possession of land.

* VILLAINS, were annexed to the manor, attached to the person of the lord, and transferable to others. BORDARS, those who tilled land to supply the lord's table, which were pieces of bords or boards. BORD-LAND was to supply the table, or boards, with food, from which comes bordars. These letters are specimens of those used to record this survey, and it reads thus: The king holds BERMUNDESEY [in Brixistan Hundred], rated at twelve hides of land, etc.

The constitution of feuds* had its origin in the military policy of the Goths, Franks, Vandals and Lombards, who poured themselves in vast multitudes into all the nations of Europe at the declension of the Roman empire. It was brought by them from their own countries, and continued in their new colonies, as the most likely means to secure them their new acquisitions. Large parcels of land were allotted by the conquering general to the superior officers of the army, and by them dealt out again to the inferior officers, and most deserving soldiers. These allotments were called "feoda," "feuds," "fiefs," or "fees," † which appellation signifies a conditional reward; and the condition was, that the possessor should do service faithfully, both at home and abroad in the wars. He who received them took an oath of fidelity to him that granted them. If this oath was broken, the stipulated service not performed, or the lord forsaken in battle, the rewards were to revert again to him who granted them.

Allotments thus acquired, naturally engaged such as accepted them to defend them; as they all sprang from the same right of conquest, no part could subsist independent of the whole. All givers as well as receivers were bound to defend each others' possessions. This could not be done in a tumultuous, irregular way, some subordination was necessary. Every receiver of lands, was bound, when called on to defend the same, when called upon by his benefactor, for his feud or fee. The benefactor was under the command of the prince. Almost all the real property of England is by the policy of the laws, granted by the superior lord or king in consideration of certain services to be rendered by the tenant for this property. This lord becomes a ten-

---

* FEUD, a quarrel between families or parties in a state, a right to lands on certain conditions. † FEE, a loan of land, an estate in trust for services.

ant of the king or a chief tenant. This grant was called a *tenement*, the manner of the possession a *tenure*,* and the possessors *tenants*. By this reasoning all the lands in England is supposed to be holden by the king, who is the *lord paramount*. The tenures, by which the lords held their lands, were sometimes very frivolous. One lord had a grant of land given him for being the king's champion. His duty was to ride armed *cap-a-pie* † into Westminster Hall, and by the proclamation of an herald, make a challenge, "That if any man shall deny the king's title to the crown, he is there ready to defend it at single combat." When this is done the king sends him a gilt cup full of wine, which the champion drinks, and keeps the cup for his fee. This championship is in the family of Sir John Dymock, who holds the manor of Sinvelsey, in Lincolnshire. This manor has been held in this family since Richard II. At the coronation of Charles II and George III, a person of this name was their champion.

Some had "feofs" or grants of land for carrying the king's banner, his sword, or holding the stirrup when mounting his horse, or for being a butler; others, who lived on the borders, for sounding a horn on the approach of an enemy. Some had grants of lands for annual gifts of bows and arrows. Others for gifts of ships. The greatest number of these tenures were held for knight service. ‡ These grants of land were great in proportion to the services given.

---

* Tenure, the manner of holding lands and tenements of a superior. All the species of ancient tenures may be reduced to four, three of which subsist to this day. 1. Tenure by knight service, which is now abolished. 2. Tenures by fealty or paying rent. 3. Tenure by copy of court roll or written deed. 4. Tenure in ancient demain, or having improved and occupied the land.

† Cap-a pie, covered with armor from head to foot.

‡ Knight, a man admitted to military rank by imposing ceremonies. A privilege conferred on youths of rank. In modern times a title, which is Sir.

Those who understand heraldry* can tell, from *coats of arms*,† for what purposes these grants of lands were given. Heraldry is a kind of rude writing that tells of the deeds of the lords in battle. It was in use before printing. Its devices are placed on the persons, houses, and carriages, of those who are entitled to them. The size of the grants of land gave birth to the orders of aristocracy of various names.

The king had daily wants, these at first were no doubt supplied by the labor of villains from his own lands, which exceeded the lands of the nobility. The lords supplied their wants from the labors of vassals and slaves. The difference between the two is this: the vassal was a soldier on foot for a limited period, frequently for forty days, or the payment of an assessment in place of it, such as plowing the lord's land for three days. The villain's services were base in their nature, such as manuring the fields and making the hedges, while the other was honorable. Sir Wm. Temple speaks of them as "A sort of people in a condition of downright servitude, used and employed in the most servile works, belonging, both they and their children, and also their effects, to the lords of the soil, like the rest of the cattle or stock upon the land, to be removed at the lord's pleasure or will."

These villains, belonged principally to lords of manors, and were either *villains regardant*—that is, annexed to the manors—or *villains in gross*, that is, annexed to the person of the lord, and transferable from one owner to another. They could not leave their lords without his permission; if they ran away, or were purloined from him, they might be

---

* HERALDRY, is the art. or science, of recording genealogies, and blazoning arms or armorial ensigns. It teaches what relates to processions and ceremonies.

† COAT OF ARMS, a short dress on which was embroidered the deeds of the family in silver and gold. Its devices are now put on panels and shields.

claimed like other beasts or chattels. They held small portions of land by way of sustaining themselves and families. The lord could dispossess him at any time when he pleased. A villain could acquire no property either in lands or goods; if he purchased either, the lord of the manor* could seize them to his own advantage, unless he contrived to dispose of them again before the lord seized them.

In many places a fine was payable to the lord, if the villain presumed to marry his daughter, without his consent, to any one. The lord could bring an action against the husband for purloining his property. The children of the villains were also in the same state of bondage with their parents. The law, however, protected the persons of villains, as the king's subjects, against atrocious injuries from the lords. The lord could beat his villain with impunity, and there was no redress for him. The lord was amenable to the law only for maiming or killing his villain.

In process of time villains became manumitted, and gained considerable freedom from their lords, and came to have an interest in their estates—the good nature and benevolence of many lords of manors having, time out of mind, permitted their villains and their children to enjoy their possessions without interruption in a regular course of descent. In general, these persons held their estates at the will of the lord, and were tenants by copy of court-roll.†

It is an instructive lesson to mark the transitions of the

* The lord, in addition to his manor lands, had tenemental lands which he distributed among tenants who held them by different modes of tenure. These lands were called book or charter lands, held by deed, rents, and soldier services, from which have arisen freehold tenants under particular manors, and were called folklands, held by no writing, but distributed among the common people at the pleasure of the lord.

† Court-roll, a tenant's tenure, made from the rolls of the lord's court.

social condition of men. Ten centuries ago portions of Europe were occupied by men who possessed the soil in common, and were nearly equal in their condition. This same land is now full of mansions, the abodes of learning, refinement, and splendor. This is all at the expense of humble toil. For the use of a piece of land the laborer has to give one-half of his labor, and half of what he has left to the power that enforces these exactions. These rents at the first were very mild and only occasional, and were called *aids* and *reliefs* to be given by the vassals on extraordinary occasions of the son coming of age, his marriage, or when the lord died, and his son took the oath of fealty to the king. These contributions are called aids.*

When the lord was reduced to distress and captivity by public or private wars, when he was in embarrassment from prodigality or waste, when he required means to support his grandeur or advance his schemes of ambition, the vassal came forward to relieve him. The vassal, on entering his fief [grant of land] felt grateful, and, won with the kindness of the lord, made him *presents*. These acknowledgments natural and commendable, produced the incident of relief.†

While these grants of land were precarious, or for life, the superior chose to educate, in his hall, the expectants of his fiefs. As these fiefs or fees were to descend to the

---

* AID, the assistance a person gives to another. AID IN LAW, a tax paid by a tenant to his lord; at first a gift it became a right demandable by the lord and was chiefly of three kinds. 1. To ransom the lord when a prisoner. 2. To make the lord's eldest son a knight. 3. To marry the lord's eldest daughter with gifts. These modest aids, and reliefs have now become rents.

† RELIEF is to remove or lift, in law, is a fine payable to a lord by the heir of a tenant, (whose parent or ancestor held land by knight service,) for the privilege of taking up the estate, which, on strict feudal principles, had lapsed or fallen to the lord on the death of his tenant. This relief consisted of horses, arms, money and the like. The amount was at first arbitrary, but afterward fixed at a certain rate by law. This fine was payable when the heir was of age.

heir of his vassal, at his death the lord took charge of the
son and his estate. The lord protected his person, directed
his education, and watched over his concerns, and felt a
pride in observing his approach to manhood, and delivering
to him, on his majority, the lands of his ancestors. When
the heir became of age he could sue for his estate from his
guardians. When the heir had possession of his estate he
paid a fine to his lord equal to half a year's profit of his
land. If this guardianship was done in a proper spirit, its
incidents were devoted and affectionate friendship, and
pleasing intercourse. These cares were expressed by the
interests of wardship.*

Grateful for the past, and anxious for the future favor
of his chief, the vassal did not incline to ally himself with
a family that was hostile to his chief, who was ambitious
to add to his power and splendor by consulting the beneficial alliance of his vassal. They joined in finding out the
lady whose charms and connections might accord with the
passions of the one and the policy of the other.†

When the vassal gave way to violence or disorder, or
when, by cowardice or delinquency, he rendered himself unworthy of his fief—the sacred ties that bound him to his lord
were infringed—it was necessary to deprive him of his land
and give it to one more honorable. This is called escheat.‡

* WARDSHIP, in feudalism, one of the incidents of tenure by knight service.
The wardship of the infant was a consequence of the guardian having an
ownership in the soil. The infant vassal was to be the companion of the lord,
hence he was the most proper person to give his ward such an education as
would enable him to perform the services he was bound to render.

† Marriage, in ancient times, was a means used to strengthen the power of
kings and nobles. Marriage has often merged two kingdoms peacefully into
one. The lords, in past times, quarreled often with each other. Intermarriages
would promote peace. Each lord was to his subjects the same as a king. What
marriage does for the chief lord, it does the same to the inferior lord.

‡ ESCHEATS, lands that are forfeited to the lord by the death of his vassal.

To perpetuate the conquest made it necessary to have all the lands in England divided into what are called *knight's fees* [fees mean fiefs or grants of land.] They numbered 60,000; and for every fee a knight or soldier was bound to attend to the king in his wars, for forty days in a year; in which space of time the campaign was generally finished, and a kingdom either conquered or was lost. By this means the king had at his command 60,000 men without expense.

The knights or soldiers were of two kinds. Knights to the king, and knights to the lord—the one had honor, the other service. They were distinguished by the name of knighthood and knight-service. To become a knight of the higher class required much ceremony. The council of the district where he belonged was assembled. His age and qualifications were inquired into; and if deemed worthy of being admitted to the privilege of a knight, his father adorned him with the shield and lance. In consequence of this solemnity, he prepared to distinguish himself, and his mind was open to the cares of the public; the concerns of his family were no longer the objects of his attention.

Knighthood, known under the name of *chivalry*, is to be dated from the 11th century. All Europe being reduced to a state of anarchy and confusion by the decline of the house of Charlemagne, every proprietor of a manor became a sovereign; the mansion house became a castle, and was surrounded by a moat. The lord of a castle had often engagements with others. It frequently happened that castles were pillaged, the women and treasures carried off by the conquerors. During this state of universal hostility, there was no friendly mode of communication between the provinces, nor any high roads from one part of the kingdom to the other. The traders traveling from one part to

another with their merchandise and families were in danger;
the lord of every castle extorted something from them on
the road; and at last, some one more rapacious than the
rest, seized upon the whole cargo, and bore off the women
for his own use. Thus castles became warehouses of all
kinds of rich merchandise, and the prisons of distressed females, whose fathers or lovers had been slain or plundered.

Many good lords associated together to repress these
scenes of violence and rapine, to secure their property and
protect the ladies. The association received the sanction
of a religious vow and ceremony. The first knights were
men of the highest rank. The fraternity were regarded
with reverence. Admission into this order was deemed the
highest honor. The candidate fasted from sunrise, confessed himself, and received the sacrament. He was dressed
in a white tunic, and placed himself at a side table, where
he was neither to smile, speak, or eat; while the knights
and ladies, who were to perform the principal ceremony,
were eating, drinking, and making merry at the big table.
His armor was put on—he advanced with his sword hanging about his neck, and received the benediction of the
priest. From this time the knight devoted himself to the
redress of wrongs, to secure merchants from the rapacious
cruelty of banditti, and women from their ravishers, to
whose power they were exposed by the confusion of the
times.*

Valor, courtesy, justice, humanity, and honor, were
traits of character in the knight, and to these were added
religious duties; these were productive of improvement in
manners. War was carried on with less ferocity, humanity
was deemed an ornament of knighthood, and knighthood
a distinction superior to royalty. Gentle manners were in-

* The lords engaging in the Crusades made wars cease among themselves.

troduced, and courtesy was recommended as the most amiable of virtues, and every knight devoted himself to the services of a lady. Violence and oppression decreased, when it was accounted meritorious to check and punish them. A scrupulous adherence to truth, with the most religious attention to every engagement, were some of the benefits of chivalry.

During the prevalence of chivalry, the ardor of repressing wrongs seized powerfully many knights. Attended by their esquires * they wandered about in search of objects whose misfortunes and misery required assistance. To assist and relieve the ladies was an achievement they most courted. This was the rise of *knights-errant,* whose adventures have been the foundation of many romances.†

If we compare the amount that an Englishman pays now for the loan of an acre of soil, with the amount that the barons of William I received, we can see how aggressive and unjust are a few to the many. The English tenant has now to give one-half to two-thirds of his labor for rent. It was not so with the Norman tenant. What he paid was only occasionally, and under the modest name of *aids, reliefs, presents,* the exactions of *wardships* and marriage *presents.*

The ties that bound the barons and his soldiers together, were destined to undergo a change. The bond of union was the danger that surrounded them. When the baron did not fear the subjugated English, then he began to increase the burdens that his vassal should bear, which may be illus-

* ESQUIRE, once a shield-bearer and an attendant on a knight. Now a title given to the younger sons of the nobility, to the king's court officers, to counselors at law, justices of peace, sheriffs, and gentlemen. In the United States this title is given to officers of all degrees, from governors down to justices and attorneys. When used to others it is a mark of respect.

† KNIGHT-ERRANT, a knight who traveled in search of adventures, for the purpose of exhibiting his military skill, prowess, and generosity.

trated by a benevolent writer:* "The Arab trains his camel, from its birth, to all the exercises and hardships it is to undergo during the whole course of its life. He accustoms it to labor hard and eat but little. He teaches it to draw its legs up under its belly, while it suffers itself to be laden with burdens, that are insensibly increased as its strength is improved by age, and by the habit of bearing fatigue. This singular plan of education princes sometimes adopt, the more easily *to tame their subjects*."

The generous maxims of feudal association and the wildness of chivalry were to suffer with time. Property was to be unfolded in all its relations. It became a distinction more powerful than merit, and was to alter the condition of human society. By separating the interests of the lord and his vassals, it was to destroy forever the principles of their association; and the incidents, which, in a better age, had fostered their friendships, were to feed their rage. As their union had been attended with advantages, their disaffection was attended with debasement. Out of the sweets of love, a fatal bitterness was engendered. Oppression was to succeed freedom; society and governments were to be disorderly; diseases and infirmities were to threaten its decay.

In the prevalence of property and mercenary views the *ward* † of the infant vassal was to be regarded in no other light than a lucrative emolument. He committed spoils on the estate which of old it was his duty to improve. He neglected the education of his heir, and gave insults to his person. His relations were often compelled to buy from his superior the custody of his person and his lands. This

---

*ABBE RAYNAL's Hist. of Europeans in East and West Indies, vol I, p. 333.

† WARD, a guardian over a child. To charge for these services would open a wide field of avarice and peculation, and be a source of bitterness.

right of wardship was frequently let out to the rapacity of strangers. The treasury of princes* was to increase with this traffic; and subject superiors were to imitate the example of princes. The heir, on his joyless majority, received the lands of his ancestors with a melancholy feeling, his castle bore the marks of neglect, his fields were deformed with waste, grievances were to embitter his complaints and swell his passions, his woods decayed, houses fallen down, stock wasted, lands barren. The heir was also to pay half a year's profits of the lands for suing out his livery,† and also the price and valuation of his marriage.‡

If he refused such a wife as his guardian provided for him and married another the fine was twice as large. The expensive honor of *knighthood* made the poverty of the heir apparent, and the deductions from his fortune to which he had to submit often ruined him, and if obliged to sell his patrimony, he had not even the privilege allowed him of selling out by a *license* of alienation.§ A slavery so complicated and extensive called for a remedy.

The *relief*, which originally was no more than a *present*, at the pleasure of the vassal on entering his fief, was consolidated into a right. An expression of gratitude was converted into a burden. The superior, before the heir entered on his land, made an exaction of him, in which he had no rule but his rapacity. His demand was exorbitant. If the fine of redemption was unpaid or delayed,

---

* The king was the guardian of the orphan children of his nobles.

† LIVERY, the ceremony of delivering to an heir his estate, and releasing the lord from wardship; it is also the form and color of the dress of servants, to distinguish them from others.

‡ Charles I was the last monarch to exercise this custom of finding a partner in marriage for his ward.

§ LICENSE, in law is authority granted to do some act. ALIENATION, a transfer of lands and tenements to another.

the superior continued the possession of the estate.   This
produced discontent which was not regarded.

The marriage of the vassal was a ruinous perquisite, and
the superior could give his vassal to whom he pleased.   If
the vassal married without the consent of the superior, it
involved the forfeiture of the estate.   The vassal could
only purchase a right to marry whom he pleased.   It was
the rule that the heir should not be married to his dispar-
agement; but this rule was overlooked in the violence of
the times.   The vassal had no relief but in remonstrance.

When the lord exercised his authority over his *female
ward* he paid no heed to her affections and made her submit to embraces unsanctioned by love.   It was a means of
oppression and ferocious cruelty.   Her beauty was to lose
its sweetness, and her heart its enjoyment, to gratify avarice.
Her relations had to buy from the tyrant exemption from
his unfeeling exactions and base demands.

The *aid*, the vassal bestowed out of benevolence, to relieve the distress, to assist the grandeur of his lord, became
a burden, a tax, a misery, and enforced as a duty.   Aids
were required on the most frivolous pretenses.   When the
crown or lord was disposed to be oppressive, they could
find a reason for an aid, which was to affect every moment the subsistence of the vassal.

Cowardice, dishonor, treachery, or treason, were causes
for *escheat*.   With the progress of time lesser delinquencies,
disagreements, trespasses, and trifles, were to multiply and
be causes of forfeiture of the fief.   If the vassal refused to
attend the court of the superior, or take the oath of fealty;
or infringe the oath; or if he foresaw any act or misfortune
that was to befall his lord, and not inform him; if he should
make love to his wife or daughter, caress his unmarried sister; these and other reasons still more absurd, were to for-

feit the estate to the superior, and involve the ruin of the vassal and his family.

These causes were to destroy the cordiality that existed between the lord and his vassal. The conditions of the fief were still obligatory, and the vassal could not renounce his ties without forsaking his importance. His property and subsistence fastened him to an enemy, whom he was to reverence. The vassal had to do military duties. With a cold heart he buckled on his armor, to follow, with reluctance, the march of his chief. Of old, it had been the ambition to carry all his strength against an enemy, that he might display his own greatness, and add to the magnificence of his superior. He now furnished unwillingly the assistance that he was bound to give. The fervor that he once displayed in advancing the ambitious plans of his lord was to cease.

The contentions between the nobles and his vassals, was to work important changes in the structure of human society. The king had often designs of his own to carry out, it might be a new conquest, or to gratify splendor and magnificence, which would require *aids* from the nobles, the collection of which might be easier with disaffected vassals. The king, by favoring his nobles' vassals, strengthened his own power, and is the source no doubt of gaining uncontrolled power, and a cause of fiefs being hereditary to be held by annual rents and taxes, instead of *knightservice*.

CHAPTER V.

PARLIAMENTS AND COMMONS.

PARLIAMENTS A RESULT OF CONQUEST—THE DISPUTES OF KINGS AND NOBLES
A CAUSE OF PARLIAMENTS—ORIGIN OF THE HOUSE OF COMMONS—AN AS-
SEMBLY OF MEN TO SAVE THEMSELVES FROM BEING PLUNDERED.

"It is better to be a great statesman than a common thief."—JONATHAN WILD.

FEUDALISM has displaced barbarism or rude society. Before it was introduced into England the
rich and the great lived in stone houses, without
glass in the windows, or plaster on the walls. The sleeping place was a recess in the wall filled with straw. To
hide the naked walls, in the Middle Ages the ladies hung
up tapestry or embroidered cloth. The Bayeux Tapestry,
is over four hundred feet long. The web is linen while the
embroidery is woolen. It was worked with a needle, and
executed with labor and care. This work is attributed to
Matilda, the wife of William the Norman, and is a series of
designs, illustrating the events of William's life, and gives
us battle scenes, rural, and domestic life. Feudalism has
changed this scene, and given to a few magnificent palaces,
with papered walls, carpeted floors, frescoed ceilings, carved
furniture, costly food and wines, waiting servants, grassy
lawns, and sparkling fountains. These scenes are before
the worker, and he wishes to possess them; yet they might
never have existed had no force been employed, which is
hunger and want, caused by idlers eating up the food of the

(97)

workers.   Hunger and a sight of wealth are powerful motives to quicken the energies of man.

In sight of the glittering mansion are to be seen boys,
who tie on their rags with ropes, which are all they possess.
Some of these boys sleep in water pipes, the park roller, and
in trees.*   "A widow, residing in Robert Street, was
found by some of her neighbors in a starving condition.
She occupied a room to herself, and she was so far reduced
in strength, that she could not cook food if she had abundance."†   To remedy the ills of life, men must be taught
to practice useful labor.   Legislation can not abolish the
evils of life.   To prove this it is only necessary to know
something of the history of legislation, and for what purpose it was introduced into the world.   Many suppose that
governments are to protect the weak; they are contrivances
of men to enrich themselves at the expense of the toiler.

It was not to be expected that the blood-stained warriors of
the conqueror could agree among themselves, or they could
make a subjugated people submit to their unfeeling demands, hence the necessity of a parliament, which comes
from the Latin word parley—to talk.

The original or first institution of parliaments is one of
these matters that lie far hidden in the Dark Ages of antiquity.   Their tracing out is a thing difficult and uncertain.
It signifies a place where men meet to settle difficulties.
King Alfred ordained for a perpetual usage: "That these
councils should meet twice a year, to treat of the government of God's people; and how they should keep themselves from sin, and live in quiet, and do right."

There seems in early periods of time to have been a constant struggle between kings, lords, and the people to gain
the ascendancy.   This same disposition still exists.   In

* London paper.   † Cincinnati Commercial, of January 17th, 1867

many countries the king rules without assembling parliaments. His word is law, from which there can be no appeal. The nobles are turbulent, and think themselves as good as the king, and they do not submit willingly to his authority. They court the good-will of the people to match the king. The king, on the other hand, grants the people all the favors he can so as to be able to rule the nobles. Parliaments are only compromises between kings and nobles to plunder the people, aided by unprincipled men who desert from the class that keep the race from perishing by useful labors. It is the soldiers and policemen that keep the people from ruling and obtaining the happiness that is their due.

William at first tried to rule his people without parliaments. His wars in Normandy required money, and the tenure upon which land was held was not sufficient to furnish supplies. This compelled William to call a meeting of his barons to obtain money from them.

In America, the land of freedom, is to be seen and felt the spirit of feudalism, which makes men so unequal in their condition. Look at Astor, his income is $3,000 a day. A farm laborer has to work six years to earn this sum, and it will take him fifteen years to save this amount. Another evidence of the spirit of feudalism among us, is to see, in large cities men, wearing a *livery*, with clubs in their hands. Another evidence is to see a large stone jail with a victim suspended on a gallows, to atone for a fault that would not have happened had better circumstances been thrown in his pathway. The miseries of mankind arise from a few growing rich, doing nothing and lessening the clothing and food of others who are industrious. Had the Fathers of the Revolution given to those who were willing to settle the uncultivated lands, a hundred acres and no more, and only to the cultivators, the painful contrasts that we see in human society would not have been known or even felt.

This pleasing description of a colony shows that a community is better without ruling powers, who eat up the substance of the people and cause crime. "It was in 1604, that the French settled in Acadia, [opposite the state of Maine,] four years before they had built the smallest hut in Canada. Instead of fixing toward the east of the peninsula, where they could have had plenty of cod, they chose the Bay of Fundy. It is probable that the founders chose this situation on account of furs. At their first arrival in Acadia they found the peninsula peopled with savages, who were called Abenakies, and they were sociable in their manners, and became enthusiasts in religion. Whenever hostilities took place between England and France, the peninsula was attacked and ransacked by the New Englanders.

No magistrate was ever appointed to rule over them. *No rents or taxes were ever exacted from them.** Their lands yielded wheat, rye, oats, barley, maize, and potatoes. The meadows were covered with numerous flocks. Sixty thousand head of horned cattle were computed to be there; and most of the families had horses, though the tillage was carried on with oxen.

The habitations, built entirely of wood, were extremely convenient, and furnished as neatly as any farm-house in Europe. The people bred a great deal of poultry of all the kinds, which made a wholesome variety in their food, which was in general wholesome and abundant. Their common drink was beer and cider. Their clothing was, in general, the produce of their own flax and fleeces. With these they made common linens and coarse cloths. Articles of lux-

---

* This picture of happiness was universal over the colonies. Criminals, or poor people were hard to find; the change may be attributed to the introduction of the National Government.

ury they procured from Annapolis, in exchange for corn, cattle, or furs. The French had no articles to dispose of among their neighbors, and still fewer exchanges among themselves, because each separate family was able, and had been used to provide for its wants. They, therefore, knew nothing of paper currency, which was so common in the rest of North America. Even the small quantity of specie which had stolen into the colony, did not promote that circulation which is the greatest advantage that can be derived from it.

"Their manners were extremely simple. There never was a cause, either civil or criminal, of enough importance to be carried before the court of judicature* established at Annapolis. Whatever little differences arose from time to time among them, were amicably adjusted by their elders. All their public acts were drawn by their pastors, who had likewise the keeping of·their wills, for which, and their religious services, the inhabitants gave them a twenty-seventh part of their harvests.

"There was a sufficiency to fulfill every act of liberality. Real misery was entirely unknown, *and benevolence prevented the demands of poverty.* Every misfortune was relieved, as it were, before it could be felt; and good was universally dispensed, without ostentation on the part of the giver, and without humiliating the person who received it. These people were, in a word, a society of brethren, every individual of which was equally ready to give and receive what he thought the common right of mankind.

"So perfect a harmony naturally prevented all those connections of gallantry which are so often fatal to the peace of families. There never was an instance in this society

---

* This court was established by the English, to whom the French nation ceded Acadia. This virtuous people had no use for courts.

10

of an unlawful commerce between the two sexes. This
evil was prevented by early marriages; *for no one passed his
youth in a state of celibacy.* As soon as the young man came
to the proper age the community built him a house, broke
up the lands about it, sowed them, and supplied him with all
the necessaries of life for twelve months. Here he received
the partner he had chosen, and who brought him her portion in flocks. This new family grew and prospered like
the others. They all together numbered 18,000 souls.

"Who will not be affected with the innocent manners
and the tranquillity of this fortunate colony? Who will not
wish for the duration of its happiness? Who will not construct, in imagination, an impenetrable wall, that may separate these colonists from their unjust and turbulent neighbors? The calamities of the people may have no period;
but, on the contrary the end of their felicity is always at
hand. A long series of favorable events is necessary to
raise them from misery, while one instant is sufficient to
plunge them into it. May the Acadians be excepted from
this general curse! but, alas! it is to be feared that they
will not.

"Great Britain perceived, in 1749, of what consequence
the possession of Acadia might be to her commerce. The
peace furnished an opportunity by the disbanding of the
troops for cultivating a vast territory. The British ministry offered particular advantages to all who chose to go
over and settle in Acadia. Every soldier, sailor, and workman was to have fifty acres for himself and ten for each
of his family—the land to be tax free for ten years. The
government found a passage, built a house, gave implements of industry, and subsistence for a year. These en-
couragements determined 3,750 persons to go to America.
These new inhabitants founded Halifax, in 1749. Some

disturbances began to break out among the neutral French. These people, whose manners were so simple, and who enjoyed such liberty, had already perceived that their independence must necessarily suffer from encroachments from any power that should turn its views to the countries they inhabited. To this apprehension was added that of seeing their religion in danger. This determined the happy American colony to quit their habitations and remove to New France, where lands were offered them. This resolution many of them executed immediately; the rest prepared to follow as soon as they had provided for their safety.

"This the English government either from policy or caprice, determined to prevent by an act of treachery—a base and cruel course in those whose power gives them an opportunity of pursuing milder methods. Under a pretense of exacting a renewal of the oath which they had taken at the time of their becoming English subjects, they called together all the remaining inhabitants, and put them on board of a ship. They were conveyed to the other English colonies, where the greater part of them died of grief.

"Such are the effects of national jealousies, and the rapacity of *governments, to which men as well as their property*, becomes a prey. Can it be said after this, that policy and society were instituted for the happiness of mankind? They were instituted to *screen the wicked, and to secure the powerful*." *

Hume, in his History of England, says: "Feudalism was a huge fabric, which for several centuries preserved such a mixture of liberty and oppression, order and anarchy, stability and revolution as was never experienced before—a system to secure conquests against the revolt of numerous subjects and tribes. The prince was nothing but a great

ABBE RAYNAL's History of the Settlement of the West Indies, Vol. V, p.350.

chieftain, who derived his power on account of his nobility or valor, and from the attachment of other chiefs. He seized the conquered lands, and kept a large share for himself. To support his dignity he granted lands to his chiefs; these made a new partition among their retainers, under the name of fiefs, on condition they take the field in defense of the nation. The conquerors separated that they might enjoy their new acquisition. They soon became attached to their lands and made improvements. To lose their possession, to be expelled for not submitting to another's will, made them wish for a change, so as the family could not be left to want by death. Fiefs were made hereditary in families, and descended to sons, grandsons, brothers, and more distant relations. The idea of property stole gradually upon that of military pay; and each century made some additions to the stability of fiefs.

"In all these changes the chief was supported by his vassals—by constant intercourse and friendship, arising from dependence, they followed their leader against all his enemies. The authority of the sovereign gradually decayed; and each noble, assisted by his vassals in his own territory, became too powerful to be expelled by an order from the throne.

"The king, therefore, when he found it necessary to demand any service of his chief tenants or barons, beyond what was due by their tenures, was obliged to assemble them, in order to obtain their consent. The question was discussed and decided among them. In these two circumstances of consent and advice consisted chiefly the civil services of the ancient barons, and these implied all the considerable incidents of government. No momentous affairs could be transacted without their consent or advice, it gave security to their possessions and dignitaries.

"The barons had their courts, and presided like the king over the nobles.   It was requisite to assemble the vassals, in order to determine by their vote any question which regarded the barony; and they sat along with the chief in all his trials, whether civil or criminal, which occurred within the limits of their jurisdiction.   The vassals were bound to pay suit at the court of their baron; and as their tenure was considered honorable, because military, they were admitted into his society and shared his friendship.   Thus was a kingdom considered a great barony, and a barony as a small kingdom.   The barons were peers to each other in the national council, and in some degree companions to the king.   The vassals were peers to each other in the court of barony, and companions to their barons.

"The vassal fell under greater subordination to the baron than the baron under the sovereign, which tended to augment the power of the nobles.   The great chief fortifying his country seat, lost a part of his acquaintance with the prince, and added new force to his authority over the vassals of his barony.   They received a military education at his hand, hospitality in his hall, retainers on his person, and partakers of his sports and amusements.   Their ambition was gratified by a position in his train, his favor was their honor, his displeasure was ignominy, and he was their protection in controversies with other vassals, and in the daily inroads and injuries of other barons.

"The feudal government was destructive of the security and independence of other members of the state.   A great part were serfs and lived in a state of absolute villainage or slavery.   The other inhabitants of the country paid their rents in services, which were in a great measure arbitrary, and they could get no redress of injuries, in a court of barony, from men who had no right to tyrannize and oppress them. The barons lived in rustic plenty, and gave no encouragement to the arts or elaborate manufactories. Every profession was held in contempt but that of arms. The industrious and opulent merchant was often exposed to injury from the envy of the nobles.

"The great baron always was submissive to the prince, so that he might have resource to him if necessary in exacting submission from his own vassals. Adherence to the crown protected from injury and powerful neighbors, and promoted the execution of more general and equal laws. The people had a still stronger interest to desire the grandeur of the sovereign—the king being the legal magistrate, who suffered by every internal convulsion, and who regarded the great nobles as his immediate rivals. The king assumed the salutary office of general guardian, or protector of the commons. Besides the prerogatives with which the law invested him, his large demesnes and numerous retainers rendered him in one sense the greatest baron in the kingdom and the fountain of law and justice.

"What preserved the first Norman kings from the encroachments of the barons was, they were generals and had to secure themselves from the revolt of the numerous natives, whom they had bereaved of all their properties and privileges. William and his immediate successors were absolute; it was lost as soon as the Norman barons began to incorporate with the nation, to acquire a security in their possessions, and to fix their influence over their vassals, tenants, and slaves. The immense fortunes which the Conqueror had bestowed on his chief captains, served to support their independence, and to make them formidable to the sovereign.

"William gave to Hugh de Abrinces, the county of Chester, and rendered his grant almost independent of the

crown. The Earl of Montaigne had 937 manors; Earl of
Brittany 442; Odo Bishop of Bayieux 439; Bishop of
Constance 280; Earl of Buckingham 107; Earl of Warrenne 298. These are only a few who had princely revenues. It was difficult to retain them as subjects. Earl of
Warrenne, in a subsequent reign, was questioned on the
right to his lands, drew his sword, which he produced as his
title; adding that William did not conquer the kingdom
himself, but that the barons, and his ancestor among the
rest, were joint adventurers in the enterprise.

"The executive power of the government was in the
king. The stated meetings of the Council or Parliament
was at Christmas, Easter, and Whitsuntide. The king
could summon them together at any time, the whole judicial* power was in his hands, and was exercised by officers
and ministers of his appointment.

"The general plan of the Norman government was, that
the court of barony† was appointed to decide controversies
between vassals. The hundred or county court‡ could
judge subjects of different baronies—the king's court to
give sentence among the barons themselves. The king often sat in his court, heard causes, and gave decisions. The
various courts that now exist have sprung from these.

"From the two lower courts there could be appeals to
the king's court, and by that means the administration of
justice was brought into the hands of the sovereign. And,
lest the expense of the journey or trouble to court should
discourage suitors, and make them acquiesce in the decisions of the inferior judicatures, itinerating judges were ap-

* JUDICIAL, what pertains to a court of justice, or the distribution of justice.

† COURT-BARON, a baron's court, or manor court. The lord was the judge.

‡ COUNTYCOURT, a court limited to a county, and its powers are now the
statutes of the land. COUNTY, the territory of a count or earl. Now a particular part of a state or kingdom, set apart for the administration of justice.

pointed, who made circuits throughout the kingdom, and tried all causes brought before them. The lawyers gradually brought all business before the king's judges."*

The Norman kings made considerable progress in gradually getting revenues. There were *eighteen* sources of revenue, many of which have passed away, and the king is dependent for support on the people, through the Parliament. *First* source of revenue was the crown lands, which were very extensive. *Second* source of revenue was the charge of the temporalities of the bishops. *Third*, was a pension from every abbey founded by royal benevolence. *Fourth*, was the first-fruits and tenths of all spiritual preferments. *Fifth*, rents of manors. *Sixth*, purveying which means when the king went on a journey he sent out purveyors† to levy on provisions for himself and household. As this led to abuses. Charles I had it commuted to fifteen pence on every barrel of beer that was brewed in the kingdom, on him and his heirs forever. *Seventh*, on licenses for selling wine. This was commuted to £7,000 a year by statute of Geo. II. *Eighth*, was from timber in forests. *Ninth*, was from courts of justice. *Tenth*, the royal fish, which are the whale and sturgeon, thrown ashore or caught near the shore; this was granted on consideration of protecting the coast from robbers and pirates. The remaining sources of revenues were a right to mines, wrecked ships, forfeited goods, treasure-trove,‡ waifs, estrays, estates that have no heirs, the care of the estates of minor lords. The present sovereign gets £900,000 a year, which is collected by the House of Commons who, a century and a half ago, rented the crown lands, or rather gave them away on very easy

---

* See article Feudalism, Hume's History of England.

† PURVEYOR, an officer who used to exact, or provide the king with food.

‡ TREASURE-TROVE, money found hidden in the earth, the owner unknown.

This well-clad man is setting this poor feeble, boy to sweeping before his mansion to pay for his new broom. It is self-evident, if this boy's father was a builder on this stone-paneled, and finely-carved building, he would be poor, and leave his children bitter poverty. Reflection should teach laboring people that the division of society into poor and rich classes is oppression, and should cease. In becoming civilized we have forsaken the plain path of nature. Many of the pursuits of civilization are as uncertain as those of the savage, to yield food and clothing. The remedy is, each one should labor for himself, at something useful, and exchange equally and directly with other useful laborers. This ends the laborer's wrongs.

3

terms. The means used to collect the royal salary is now called the *extraordinary revenues*, and are raised by *aids*, *subsidies*,* *and supplies.*†

The king was never contented with the stated rents, but levied heavy talliages‡ at his pleasure, both on the inhabitants of the town and country. He pretended to exact tolls on goods sold in the market; he took two hogsheads of wine from every vessel that imported it—all goods paid to his customs a part of their value. A passage over a bridge or river was loaded with tolls. The king exacted money for the renewal of charters, and the people were held in perpetual dependence.

The barons were exposed to the inroads of power, against which they had no security. The Conqueror ordained that the barons should pay nothing beyond their stated services, except a reasonable aid to ransom his person if he were taken in war, to make his oldest son a knight, or to marry his eldest daughter. What should on these occasions be deemed a reasonable aid, was not determined, and the demands of the crown were discretionary.

The king could in war require the personal attendance of his vassals, and if they declined the service, they were obliged to pay him a composition in money, which was called a *scutage*.§ This sum, was during some reigns, precarious and uncertain; it was sometimes levied without allowing the vassal the usual liberty of personal service; and it was an artifice of the king to pretend to an expedition, that he might be entitled to levy the scutage from his military tenants. This tax was one, two, or three marks for every

---

* Subsidy, aid in money, a tax to assist a prince in place of personal service
† Supplies, money granted by English Parliaments for public expenditures.
‡ Talliage, to cut off, to share, a tax or toll on the people for the king.
§ Scutage, a contribution from the knights toward furnishing the army.

11

knight's fee [a mark is 13s. 4d.] Henry III, for his voyage to the Holy Land, had a scutage of three marks for every knight's fee. This word comes from scutum, a shield, and was a sum paid by the knight to the king so as he could hire soldiers to fill his place. Moneyage was a tax levied by the two first Norman kings on hearth-stones. It was a shilling each, and was given to the king to induce him not to use his prerogative to debase the money. These taxes were so heavy, that William of Malmesbury tells us the reign of William Rufus, the farmers abandoned tillage, and a famine ensued.

The escheats were a great source of profit, especially during the first reigns after the conquest. In default of posterity from the first baron, his land reverted to the crown, and continually augmented the king's possessions. The prince had the power of alienating these escheats. By this means he had opportunities of establishing the fortunes of his friends and servants, and thereby enlarging his authority. Sometimes he retained these estates in his own hands. If the vassal was summoned thrice to attend his superior's court; and refused obedience, he forfeited all title to his lands. Denying his tenure, refusing his services, selling his right to his fief without liberty, adhering to his lord's enemies, deserting him in battle, betraying his secrets, debauching his wife, being found guilty of rape, murder, and arson, he lost his fief. The king had the right to detain his possession, spoil and destroy it, till the baron paid a reasonable compensation. The vassal's possession was precarious.

When the baron died the king took possession of his estate; the heir made application for it, by doing homage and paying a fine. This practice was founded on the notion that the fief was a benefice, and the superior was to be paid out of it till the heir became of age. By this means landed property was continually in the hands of the prince, and noble families were dependent on him. He could enrich a favorite at another's expense. Simon de Monfort paid Henry III 10,000 marks, for the wardship of Gilbert de Umfreville. Geoffry de Mandeville paid 20,000 marks [$60,000,] that he might marry the Countess of Gloucester, and possess all her lands and knight's fees.

If the heir was a female, the king could offer her any husband he thought proper of her own rank; if she refused she forfeited her lands. Even a male heir could not marry without the royal consent; and it was usual to pay large sums for the privilege of making a choice. None could sell lands without the consent of the superior, who held it at will. In course of time these lands became allodial* or subject to an annual tax.

Fines were sources of royal revenues. Records are preserved giving an account of the fines levied in those days. The ancient kings of England were like the barbarous eastern princes, whom no man must approach without a present. Permission was purchased to carry on business, and also to extort money. Justice was bought and sold; the king's court was not open to those who did not bring presents. The county of Norfolk, and the borough† of Yarmouth paid money that they might be fairly dealt with. Richard, son of Gilbert, paid the king for helping him to recover his debts from the Jews; Serlo, son of Terlarston, paid that he might be permitted to make a defense, if he was accused of homicide. Robert de Essart, paid for an inquest to find out if Robert the butcher accused him of robbery out of envy.

* ALLODIUM, lands allotted or portioned off, and owned by the cultivator.

† BOROUGH, a hill, or fortified town. In Saxon times an association of ten men, who were pledged to the king for the good behavior of each other, and was called a tithing. Ten of these associations formed a hundred, or a county.

Sometimes litigants offered the king a half, or a fourth, out of debts,which he as the executor of justice might help to recover. Theophania de Westland agreed to pay the half of 212 marks that she might recover from James de Fughleston. Solomon the Jew gave one mark out of seven that he should recover out of Hugh de la Hose.

The king was paid for a permission to exercise any industry. Hugh Oisel paid 400 marks for liberty to trade in England. Nigel de Haven gave fifty marks for a partnership in merchandise with Gervase de Hanton. Some men of Worcester paid 100 shillings, that they might have the liberty of selling fine, dyed cloth. The whole kingdom was under the control of the king. He created guilds,* corporations,† and monoplies wherever he pleased, and levied sums for these exclusive privileges.

There was no profit so small as to be below the king's notice. Henry, son of Arthur, gave ten dogs, to have an acknowledgment from the Countess of Copland. Walter le Madine gave two Norman hawks that he might have leave to export a hundred weight of cheese out of the king's dominions. The wife of Hugh de Neville gave two hundred hens for a visit to her husband. It is supposed he was in prison. The abbot of Ruckford paid ten marks for leave to erect houses and place men on his land, to secure his wood from being stolen. Hugh, the archdeacon of Wells, gave a tun of wine for leave to carry 600 sums of corn wherever he would. Peter de Peraris gave twenty marks for leave to salt fishes.

The eldest son and widow of Hugh Bigond, a nobleman, came to the court of Henry II and offered him large pres-

---

* GUILDS, companies of men carrying on some pursuit particularly commerce. These were licensed by the king, and governed by their own laws and orders.

† CORPORATIONS, societies acting like one man in the transaction of buisness.

ents to obtain her inheritance. The king ordered the case to be tried by the great council; but, in the meantime, he seized all the treasure and money of the deceased. Fines were not limited by law, and the person on whom they were imposed was frequently ruined. The forest laws were a great source of oppression. The king possessed sixty-eight forests, thirteen chases, and seven hundred parks, in different parts of England, in which the people were allured to hunt, and then punished by having their eyes put out. This was Norman law.

The Jews were out of the protection of the law, they were abandoned to the rapacity of the king and his ministers. It appears they were all at once thrown into prison, and the sum of 60,000 marks was exacted for their liberty. Henry III borrowed 4,000 marks from the Earl of Cornwall; and for his repayment consigned to him all the Jews in England. There was a particular kind of Exchequer set apart for managing revenue derived from the Jews.

Sir Henry Spellman says: "During the reign of the first Norman kings, every edict that came from them, with the consent of their private council, had the full force of law." It appears that the constitution had not fixed any precise boundaries to the royal power; that the right to issue proclamations on any emergency, and of exacting obedience to them—a right which was always supposed inherent in the crown—is very difficult to be distinguished by legislative authority. The extreme imperfections of the ancient laws, and sudden exigencies that have often occurred in such turbulent governments, obliged the prince to exert frequently the latent powers of his prerogative—that he naturally proceeded from the acquiescence of the people, to assume in many particulars of moment, an authority from which he had excluded himself by express statutes, charters, or concessions, which was repugnant to the personal liberty of his subjects. It appears from the great Charter itself, that John, Richard, and Henry, were accustomed, from their sole authority, without process of law, to imprison, banish, and attaint* the freemen of the kingdom.

A great baron in ancient times considered himself as a kind of sovereign within his territory; and was attended by courtiers and dependents more zealously attached to him than ministers of state. He often maintained in his court the parade of royalty, by establishing courts over which he presided with constables,† marshals,‡ and chancellors.§ He was assiduous in his jurisdiction.|| Delighting in the image of sovereignty, it was necessary to restrain his activity, and keep him from holding his courts too frequently. The example of his prince in mercenary extortion was frequently copied, his justice and injustice was frequently put to sale. He had the power, with the king's consent to exact talliages even from the free citizens who lived in his barony; and his necessities made him rapacious; his authority was often found to be more oppressive and tyrannical than that of the sovereign. He was ever engaged in hereditary or personal animosities or confederacies with his

---

* ATTAINT, stained, blackened, a person in this condition was not considered fit to live, but to be exterminated from the earth. From the word attinctus.

† CONSTABLE, an officer of high rank in the middle ages, the seventh in rank to the crown. A judge in chivalry, of deeds of arms, combats, and blazonry.

‡ MARSHAL, the chief officer in arms, whose duty it is to regulate combats, rank and order at a feast, or assembly, directs the king's processions and feasts.

§ CHANCELLOR, the highest crown officer, he has judicial power, the keeping of the king's conscience, seal, charters, and writings of the crown. He is the private counselor of the House of Lords, appointer of all the justices of peace, visitor of all hospitals and colleges founded by the king, a guardian of the public charities, and a judge of the high Court of Chancery. Enough to do.

|| JURISDICTION, a power to hear complaints, execute laws, and distribute justice. Jurisdiction is limited to a particular place or territory, and persons.

neighbors, and often gave protection to desperate adventurers and criminals, who could be useful in serving his violent purposes. He was able alone in times of tranquillity,
to obstruct the execution of justice within his territories;
and, by combining with a few malcontent barons of high
rank and power, he could throw a state into convulsions.
Though the royal authority was confined within narrow
bounds, yet the check was often irregular and frequently
the scenes of great disorders; nor was it derived from the
liberty of the people, but from the military power of many
tyrants, who were equally dangerous and oppressive to the
subjects.

The concessions of the Great Charter gave birth, by
degrees, to a new species of government, and introduced
some order and justice into the administration. The Great
Charter contained no new establishment of new courts,
magistrates, senates, or abolition of the old. It introduced
no new distribution of the powers of the commonwealth,
and no innovation in the political or public law of the kingdom. It only guarded, and that merely by verbal clauses,
against such tyrannical practices as are incompatible with
civilized governments. The barbarous license of the kings,
and perhaps of the nobles, was thenceforth more restrained.
Men acquired more security for their property and liberties,
and governments approached a little nearer to the distribution of justice and the protection of citizens. Acts of violence and iniquity in the crown, which before were only
deemed injurious to individuals, and were hazardous chiefly
in proportion to the number, power, and dignity, of the persons affected by them, were now regarded as public injuries
in some degree, and as an infringement of a charter calculated for general security. The establishment of the Great
Charter was an improvement in the distribution of political

power, the source of a mighty change in the customs and usages of society, and in the constitution of England.

There was a struggle between the king and his barons for supreme power for one hundred and fifty years after the conquest. The introduction of the Magna Charta made the Parliament the source of power instead of the king. It is very doubtful if this change has been of any benefit to the toiling classes, except to introduce a more systematic method of plundering them. That a number of men in gay robes, with high sounding names, in a gorgeous room, sitting in stalls and on woolsacks—that these should do any thing to lessen the labor of working people is not to be expected. Many of the customs and usages of the conquest are still in existence.

The House of Commons comes from the lower classes, who lived in the boroughs and towns. These were told to send deputies to tell how much they were worth under an oath, and then grant *aids* to the king in his wars, and then go home and collect them. These were forced or summoned by the sheriffs* when they came with their aids, re-*liefs*, *presents*, *and benevolences*. They asked for relief from the wrongs they suffered at the hands of the barons.

Before the time of the Stuarts the House of Commons was summoned at the pleasure of the king, or when an aid was wanted. Deputies were to assess scutages and talliages, not to make laws, that was a branch of the royal prerogative, and exercised by the summary process of proclamation, not by illiterate burgesses, whom it was assumed might be adepts in the mysteries of trade, and not sufficiently learned for the high task of legislation. The first members went with reluctance, and received wages for their unpleasant

---

*SHERIFF, an officer appointed by the king, to execute the laws in an earldom or county; once a collector of the king's revenue—a shire-reeve.

duty. All sorts of evasions were practiced to avoid sending representatives to the Parliament; some pleaded poverty, others their insignificance, and the honorable members were often constrained by force to appear at Westminster or Oxford, or other places of royal residence. The whole proceeding was analogous to what takes place in a city taken by storm. The victorious general calls together the inhabitants not to make laws for the government of the town, *but to determine how great a sum they will give to save themselves from pillage.* And so it continued till the advent of Hampden, Pym, Hollis, Elliott, and other master minds, who claimed for the Commons a nobler and more independent vocation.

It is, however, a contrivance to get out of the toiling classes of Great Britain the annual sum of $400,000,000. It takes from him who labors the fruits of his labor, and gives it to him who will not labor.

To trace the gradual evolution of the several parts of the English constitution; to show how the executive, legislative, and judicial power were blended and clumsily executed, and how they became separated, defined, and secured in the exercise of their respective functions by ages of conflict and trial, is a curious and pleasing subject of study and inquiry. It is the progress of man from rudeness to an abundance of comforts in the hands of a few. The progress of society has been like the reclaiming of a waste country, by the embankment of its rivers, the draining of its morasses, the cleaning out of the beasts of prey, and other operations by which it is brought into a state of security and productiveness. Divesting ourselves of the illusions of antiquity, it is impossible to conceal that the government for a long period was a simple despotism, occasionally controlled by the interference of the nobility and clergy. The first regular approach to constitutional rule was the grant of the Magna Charta. Doubtless the concessions extorted by the barons at Runnymede were in their own favor; but it also contained provisions which were a guide and a sanction for future and more general claims of freedom. The adoption of such an instrument denotes a progression in human society. A division of political power between two orders in the state had been formally recognized, and the idea of prescribing their respective immunities by law shows the time may come when they will be dispensed with altogether.

Many parts of the great charter were pointed against the abuses of the power of the king as lord paramount. But it contains a few maxims of just governments, applicable to all places and times. For almost five centuries it was appealed to as decisive authority on the people's behalf, though commonly so far only as the necessities of the case required. This continued in fashion till within a few years; but the public taste has altered, and it is more common for *reformers* to refer to principles of *utility* than to constitutional authorities.*

From the time of King John to that of Charles I, the constitution of England underwent no change of importance, the power of the several parts of which it consisted was the subject of contention, but it was not fixed or materially altered by any public act. Important movements have taken place among the people, and the silent influence of the commonality had encroached on the acts of the nobility. Vassalage has been exterminated. Manufactures have extended and flourished. Domestic comforts and great luxuries are in the sight of all.†

What are the causes that made Gov. Hammond, on the Senate's floor of the "The Great Republic" say: "Your

* MACINTOSH's History of England, Vol. I, p. 22.   † See HUME's England.

daily laborers are at best but slaves." It is because the institutions of the land are so contrived that a few can obtain
from the many, unceasingly and unobserved, large quantities of human labor without an equivalent. The reason is,
we follow too much after the civil institutions of other
lands. These institutions have been brought about in this
manner: From the shores of the Baltic there came forth
a race of Sea Kings who lived in their ships, and went to
plundering wherever they could get a landing. They were
a very great terror to the sea-coast inhabitants of Europe.
Those who were in fear of invasion had to devise means of
self-defense, which was called a government. When the
invaders got possession of a country they instituted a government also, which has continued to this day. Those who
laid the foundations of a civil state were pirates by profession, pagans in religion, men of ferocity, and dauntless
courage. They made two agreements—one was we will
plunder the people. This has been faithfully observed, and is
still observed. The second part of the agreement was not to
plunder each other. Kings have laid gradually exactions
on the nobles, who have re-laid them on their vassals. The
various names that used to be given to the sources of revenue have become "rents" and "taxes." The villains
and vassals have become mechanics and laborers.

Changes have been made in the social condition of men
at first the king ruled absolute, then a part of his power was
taken away by the nobles. The priests exercised a sway
over the nobility. Their power was broken at the time of
Henry VIII. These were succeeded by courtiers and court
gallants, who have used an influence over the ruling powers.
From the time of William III to the present, England has
been influenced by policy rulers, or political economists.
The laborers of England are now associating themselves to-

gether to get the necessaries of life at cost price, without employing merchants. In many cases the workmen are partners in the workshops and mines in which they labor. These facts indicate that the laborer will soon displace the other classes and rule.

Lord Kames, in his History of Man says: "Had the Norwegians known agriculture in the tenth century, they would not have ventured their lives in frail vessels upon a tempestuous ocean, in order to distress nations who were not their enemies. But hunger is a cogent motive; and it gave to these pirates superiority in arms above every nation that enjoyed plenty at home. Luckily such depredations must have their intervals; as they necessarily occasion great havoc among the victors. Agriculture, fixes a people to a spot, is an obstacle to migration, puts an end to a scourge, more destructive than a pestilence. It gives occupation and subsistence at home; it affords plenty of food."

William Walker thought in Nicaragua "That society was worn out, and they needed a new organization, and it would furnish certain labor to the negro." He chartered a vessel in California, and left in May, 1856, with fifty-eight passengers. On landing he began to levy contributions, this led to a conflict—six were killed and twelve wounded. He would have succeeded if the English warships had let him alone. If he had become chief ruler he could have used this language: "Dear people, I will establish justice, maintain order among you, and give you splendor and magnificence."

CHAPTER VI.

CITIES AND TOWNS.

FEUDALISM THE CAUSE OF THE GROWTH OF CITIES—A PLACE FOR ESCAPING
SLAVES—CITIES ARE NECESSARY TO IMPROVE MEN—HANSEATIC TOWNS—
NORTH AMERICAN REVIEW ON CITIES—SUFFERING IN CITIES.

"When we are piled on each other in large cities, as they are in Europe, we
shall become corrupt, and go to eating each other."—THOMAS JEFFERSON.

AFTER the fall of the Roman Empire the inhabitants of cities and towns were not any more favored than those of the country. They were, indeed, of a very different order of people from the first inhabitants of the ancient republics of Greece and Italy. These last were composed chiefly of the proprietors of land, among whom the public land was *divided*, and who found it convenient to build their houses in the neighborhood of each other, and to surround themselves with a wall for defense. After the fall of the Roman Empire, the proprietors of land seem generally to have lived in fortified castles on their own estates, and in the midst of their own tenants and dependants. The towns were chiefly inhabited by tradesmen and mechanics, who seem to have been in a servile condition.

Britain, once a land of savage pagans, was, long after the Norman conquest, the abode of ignorance and superstition. For centuries past she has been steadily advancing in knowledge, civil and religious liberty. Her men of letters

(121)

have sent down to posterity noble works that shall live till science, philosophy, and poetry are known no more.   Her lawyers have gradually worn off the rugged features of the feudal system, till the common law of England has been adopted as the basis of the American code.   Her spiritual bastile, the State Church, has yielded to the attacks of non-conformity, and opened its gates to a qualified toleration. All that was dangerous in the maxim, " The king can do no wrong," fell with the head of Charles I, in 1649.   A class of innovators, called " Reformers " are still at work on the institutions of England.

Humanity will find ample materials for despair, when contemplating the toiling classes condition.   But philan-trophy will find abundant source of hope in studying the character and deeds of their radical reformers.   The past half century has seen an uprising, of the very substratum of society, in a peaceful struggle for inherent rights.   No force has been employed except the force of circumstan-ces ; and the result has been eminently successful.   This class discovered its strength during the revolution of Ham-den and Cromwell, and received an impulse which it has never lost.

The nobility and gentry have too often silenced the popular clamor by admitting its leaders to the privileges of the " higher orders."   Concessions were made to the mid-dle men, which strengthened them to demand more.   But a truth, destined to be all-powerful in the nineteenth cen-tury, remained to be discovered, that the condition of the lower classes should be ameliorated.   The lines which cus-tom and intolerance had drawn between men, was to grow fainter as the day approached for the full discovery of truth. The earthquake shock of the French Revolution overthrew a throne rooted to the soil by a growth of a thousand years.

Britain felt the crash. The people discovered they were clothed with divine rights as well as kings. This was not expressed in courtly language, or made grateful to royal ears. From the conquest of William the Norman, to Victoria the Saxon, there has been a gradual circumscribing of the power of the nobles and prerogatives of the crown.

Much of all this is to be attributed to the rise and growth of cities, which have been fostered by kings and nobles. These are often at enmity with each other, and to gain the favor of the towns enabled one or the other to gain the ascendancy. A borough is a town and not a city. In its original signification it means a company consisting of ten families who were pledged to each other. Afterward a borough came to signify a walled town, and a place for safety. Some of the towns were called *free-burghs* and the tradesmen *free-burgesses*, from a privilege they had to buy and sell without disturbance and be exempt from toll.

These seem to have been very poor people, traveling about with goods from one place to another, and from fair to fair, as hawkers and peddlers. They paid taxes when passing through some of the great lords' manors, going over bridges, and for erecting booths or stalls at the fairs. These different taxes were known by the names of passage,* lastage,† and stallage.‡ Sometimes the king or a great lord, upon some occasions, would grant to particular trades, or to such as lived on their own demesnes, a general exemption from such taxes. Such were called "free-

---

* The most celebrated passage in Europe is the Sound, or the narrow entrance into the Baltic Sea. Here the King of Denmark has the Castle of Elsinore, and collects tolls from all nations. The Americans refused to pay the tax, this was a source of embarrassment to Denmark. To remit to one nation it would have to be done to all. The writer can not tell how settled.

† LASTAGE, a duty paid for freight on transportation.

‡ STALLAGE, the right to erect a stall in a fair—the rent for a stall.

traders." They in return paid an annual poll-tax* for the protection they received. In those days protection was seldom granted without a valuable consideration, and the tax might be considered as a compensation for what their patrons might lose by their exemption.

The American people, at the beginning of their national career, declared "that taxation was tyranny." Their descendants have learned to submit to taxation very gracefully, for the cause of which they are indebted to the great "Democratic party." It is not improbable the American people at this time [1869], pay a fifth part of all they earn for taxation. Bodin, a writer in 1606, says: "That there can be no ground or foundation, with immunity, from subsidies and taxes." Many Americans think the same—no existence as a nation without taxes. A Roman consul, by levying a tax on *salt* during the Punic war, was nicknamed the *salinator*. The Arabs exacted *presents and gifts* from pilgrims who were going to Mecca. Louis XI of France, to purchase a peace of Edward IV, paid annually in London the sum of 50,000 crowns, and *pensions* to the English ministers. This brought into use the terms *pensions* and *tributes*.

A purveyor was an officer who was to furnish every sort of provisions for the royal people during their progresses or journeys. His oppressive office was to compel countrymen to bring their articles to market, and he fixed their price. The officer became odious; Edward IV changed the name to *acheteur* or buyer. Changing the name did not conceal its nature. Levies of money were long raised under the pathetic appeal of *benevolences*. Edward IV went to France with money obtained by this method. He rode about the land, and used the people in such a fair manner, that they were liberal in their gifts. Edward was courteous in his

§ Poll-tax, a tax on those who have heads. Poll, a person's head.

newly-invented style, and was, besides, the handsomest tax-
gatherer in the kingdom! His royal presence was very
dangerous to the purses of his loyal subjects, particularly
to those of the females. In his progress, having kissed a
widow for having contributed a larger sum than was expected from her estate, she was so overjoyed at the singular honor and delight that she doubled her benevolence,
and a second kiss ruined her! In the succeeding reign of
Richard III, the term had lost much of its innocence. In
a speech delivered by the Duke of Buckingham, he said:
"Under the plausible name of benevolences, your goods
were taken from you very much against your will, as if by
that name it was understood that every man should pay, not
what he pleased, but what the king would have him." A
benevolence was levied by Richard III. Henry VIII demanded one and did not get it. The people had got it into
their minds that taxes should not be raised without consent of parliament!

Charles the First had urgent wants. His appeals for benevolences were unregarded. The custom of voluntary gifts
was lost, and compulsory taxation was laid on the people.
James I tried to warm up the hearts of his benevolent
people. It is said "He got but little money and lost much
love." When benevolences had become grievances, more
inviting names were invented. The subject was informed
that the sums demanded were only *loans*, or he was honored
by a *privy seal*—a bond which the king engaged to repay at
a definite period; these were peddled and hawked about,
even to persons coming out of church. Says a manuscript
letter: " Privy seals are flying thick in sight of all the world,
which might surely have been better performed in delivering them to every man at home." The *general loan* was,
in fact, a forced loan, and one of the many grievances under
12

Charles I. It was very ingenious in the destruction of his own popularity. Commissioners were to find out who was able to bear the largest rates [amounts.] Lord Burleigh's advice to Elizabeth was—"win hearts, and you have their hands and purses."

The inhabitants of the towns arrived at liberty and independence quicker than the occupiers of land. These inhabitants got whole manors, the rent of which was jointly paid, and collected their own way, and paid into the king's exchequer by the hands of their own bailiff, and they were freed from the insolence of the king's officers—a circumstance, in those days, of the greatest importance. In process of time, however, it seems to have been the practice to grant it to them in fee—that is, forever.

Along with this grant of paying all their rent at once instead of detail, the burghers got the privilege of giving away their own daughters in marriage, and also the liberty of disposing of their effects to their children by will. The principal attributes of slavery and villainage were taken away and they really became free. They were generally at the same time erected into a corporation, with the privilege of electing their own magistrates, choosing a town council, making their own laws, creating means of safety, building walls, and training the inhabitants to the use of arms, for the defense of their city or town. These were generally exempted from suit to the hundred or county court Difficulties were left to the decision of their magistrates.

In those days the sovereign, perhaps, of no country in Europe was able to protect, throughout the whole extent of his dominions, the weaker part of his subjects from the oppression of the great lords. Those whom the law could not protect, and who were not strong enough to defend themselves, were obliged either to have resource to the protection of a great lord, and, in order to obtain it, to become either his vassals or slaves; or to enter into a league of mutual defense for the protection of one another. The inhabitants of cities and burghs, considered as single individuals, had no power to defend themselves. By entering into a league of mutual defense with their neighbors, they were capable of making a good resistance. The lords despised the burghers, whom they considered as a parcel of emancipated slaves. The wealth of the burghers never failed to provoke their envy and indignation, and they plundered them upon every occasion without mercy or remorse.

The burghers naturally hated and feared the lords. The king hated and feared the lords also; but though he might despise, he had no reason to fear or hate the burgher. Mutual interest, therefore, disposed them to support the king, and the king to support them against the lords. It was the king's interest to render the burghers as secure and independent as possible. By granting them magistrates of their own, the privilege of making their by-laws for their government, that of building walls for defense, and that of reducing the inhabitants into a sort of military discipline, he gave them independence and the means of security against the barons, which it was in his power to bestow. Without the establishment of some regular government of this kind, without some authority to compel the inhabitants to act according to some plan or system, no voluntary league of mutual defense could have either afforded them any permanent security, or have given the king any considerable support. By giving them the farm of their town in fee, he took away all ground of jealousy, so that he could never afterward oppress them, by raising the farm rent of their town, or by granting it to some other person.

The princes who lived on the worst terms with their

barons, seem to have been the most liberal in their grants of this kind to the burghs. King John, of England, appears to have been a munificent benefactor of his towns. Philip the First, of France, lost all authority over his barons. Toward the end of his reign his son Lewis consulted with his bishops of the royal demesnes, concerning the best method of restraining the violence of the great lords. His advice was to erect a new order of jurisdiction, by establishing a *town council* with *magistrates* in every considerable town of his demesnes, and to form a new militia, by making the inhabitants of those towns, under the command of their own magistrates, march out upon proper occasions to the assistance of the king. It is from this period, according to the French antiquarians, that we are to date the institution of magistrates and councils in the cities of France.

It was during the unprosperous reign of some of the German princes, that the greater part of the free towns of Germany received their first grants and privileges. The Hansesatic league was very formidable, it derived its name from Hanse, an ancient name for a society of merchants, and it also means a multitude—an alliance, an association. The towns of these merchants were called the Hanse-towns, and were a union of German cities for the protection of commerce. Bremen and Amsterdam were the two first cities that formed it; whose trade received such an advantage by fitting out two men-of-war in each city to convoy their ships. This was a cause of other cities entering into the league. Kings and princes made treaties with them, and were often glad of their assistance and protection; by this means they grew so powerful both by sea and land, that they raised armies as well as navies, made peace and war, and had countries in sovereignty.* All this was to increase

* SOVEREIGNTY, supreme power; the power to make laws.

their trade. In the year 1200 the cities and towns in the league numbered seventy-two. The alliance was so powerful, that their ships of war were often hired by princes to assist them against their enemies. This confederacy of cities not only awed, but often defeated, all who opposed their commerce. In 1358, the Danes interrupted their commerce—revenge was taken on them; and the Danes to purchase peace, gave up the dues from the passage of the Sound for sixteen years. Many privileges were bestowed on these towns by the kings of Europe for loans of money and other good services.

The reader can very easily form a conception how the towns would forward human liberty, when kings and nobles oppressed their slaves, they found a welcome in these cities to make cloths, stuffs, silks, and linens. These slaves made good soldiers, as they would not like to be returned again to their masters and slavery. Those who opposed these free cities, would have to be kind to their slaves to get them to fight against them, and prevent them from running away. Hungary was a dissatisfied province of Austria. The invasion of the first Napoleon compelled Austria to be generous to the Hungarians, and teach them to fight. This people, having learned their power and the use of arms, became clamorous for liberty. In 1853, this people revolted, and have now gained all they have asked for. The English were constantly at war with France up to the time of Queen Elizabeth. In order to get the villains to go to the wars they promised them their freedom; on their return from France, they settled in the towns and became smiths, weavers, and artificers.

The militia in the cities were not inferior to the militia of the country. The citizens were always together, which gave them some advantage over the lords. In Italy and

Switzerland the government could not control the distant cities, which became independent, and conquered the surrounding nobles, and obliged them to pull down their castles, and to live like civil people. This is the history of Berne, and many other cities in Switzerland. There were Italian republics that arose from the same causes, and perished at the beginning of the twelfth century, after existing for four hundred years.

In such countries as that of France and England, the rule of the king was often low, but never extinguished, the cities had no opportunities of becoming independent. The king, however, could impose no taxes upon them without their consent, besides the stated rent of the farm. Towns would gain considerable wealth by trading with the surrounding and far-off countries. They were called upon to send deputies to the general assembly of the kingdom, so that they might join with the clergy and the barons, on urgent occasions, and grant to the king extraordinary aids. These deputies have been employed by the king, as a counterbalance in the assemblies of the powerful lords; hence the representation of boroughs or towns in all the great monarchies of Europe.

Order and security of individuals were established in the cities, when the occupiers of land in the country were exposed to every sort of violence. Men in this defenseless state naturally content themselves with their necessary subsistence; because to acquire more might only tempt the injustice of their oppressors. When men are secure of enjoying the fruits of their industry, they naturally exert it to better their condition, and to acquire the comforts as well as the necessaries of life. That industry which aims at something more than necessary subsistence, was established in cities long before it was done by the occupiers of land.

A poor villain, oppressed with servitude, would generally conceal some of his labor from the eye of his master, who claimed all. He would naturally take the first opportunity to run away to a town. The law was indulgent to the inhabitants of towns, and it diminished the authority of the great lords over those who belonged to them in the country. If a slave could conceal himself for one year he was a freeman. The accumulated property in the hands of slaves was taken to a city as a place of refuge, as the only sanctuary in which it could be secured to the person who acquired it.

Even in France, a country which made more early advances in arts and civil policy than England, their first corporation was sixty years before William's conquest. The erecting of these communities was an invention of Lewis the Gross, in order to free the people from slavery under the lords, and to give them protection by means of certain privileges, and a separate jurisdiction. An ancient French writer calls them "A new and wicked device, to procure liberty to slaves, and to encourage them to shake off the dominion of their masters." The famous charter of the Conqueror to the city of London, though granted at a time when he assumed the appearance of lenity and gentleness, is nothing but a letter of protection, and a declaration that the citizens should not be slaves.

It is plain to the reader that kings and lords, to live in ease, must have slaves. Their contentions gave birth to cities. These have given an appearance of freedom to men, not a perfect freedom. This will be attained when men live again in the country. It can not be denied that cities are the abodes of refinement and luxury. The history of an old city opens many views into the realms of the past, crowded with the romantic and religious. Buildings, dilap-

idated and dingy, or tastelessly modernized, in which great
geniuses were born and died, whose tales of valor and suffering, of heroism and patience, of virtue and piety, of the
patriot's life and the martyr's death, crowd thickly on the
memory. Nor do the opposite reminiscences of crime and
vice, of evil passion and false principles, fail to give us ad-
monitions and warnings. The broad thoroughfare is a channel, within whose banks there has been rolling for centuries a river of human life.

These dwelling-places of man are proofs and expressions
of his ingenuity, skill, and toil, of his social instincts and
habits. Their varied architecture and style, the various
motives and diversified purposes that led to their erection,
are symbols and illustrations of the innumerable forms, the
strange gradations of men's wealth, condition, character,
tastes, and feelings. Each house has a history of its own.
What changeful scenes has the interior of many a dwelling
witnessed! Families have come and gone, people have
been born and died, obedient to the law that man must die.
In many a mansion has been seen the gay wedding and
gloomy funeral, the welcome meeting, and the sad parting.
A mansion catches the eye by its splendor; through its windows flash the light of patrician luxury, at whose door lines
of proud equipages drive up; on the steps are obsequious
footmen in gilded liveries, to receive the visitors. In those
mansions are hearts pining away with envy, fear, jealousy,
remorse, and agony. In that humble cottage abode, is con-
tentment and piety, which are better than rubies or gold.

Who can live in a large city without a feeling of pain in
seeing splendid wealth contrasted with squalid poverty. In
cities may be seen the marble-fronted, or exquisitely-carved
stone-fronted mansion; the floors are mosaic or covered
with velvet carpets; the walls are covered with beautiful,

gold paper. In this mansion are easy chairs, luxurious sofas, carved book-cases, Sevres-china, sparkling cut-glass,
exquisitely framed pictures, beautiful gems of art, full length
mirrors, sculptured marble fire-places, canopied bedsteads
with deep oak carvings, and every luxury money can purchase. A short distance from this, is a dark cellar; in it is
to be found a widow and her children, no chairs or table,
these were sold to buy food. A few pieces of rags to cover
them during the night—they can scarcely sleep for cold.
These children have the coarsest food, while the other family has every dainty. The one family does no labor at all,
the other labors incessantly, and may be on a piece of finery
of no utility.

This narration will show some of the causes why people
are poor: "In Padbury, Buckinghamshire, was executed a
scarf two yards and three-quarters long, and three-quarters
wide, surrounded by a wreath-like pattern of flowers and
foliage, in which the large passion flower adorning each
corner was particularly noticeable as a triumph of skill.
The center or ground was studded with separate flowers,
analogous to those on the border. This effective piece of
work was made in strips, and joined, so as to defy the most
critical eye. This was executed by three sisters—Maria,
Susan, and Ann Salmon. They were employed eighteen
weeks, and in consideration of their pre-eminent ability, and
the importance of the task intrusted to them, were each re-
munerated by their employers at the comparative high rate
of six shillings a week. This beautiful lace scarf was shown
to the Queen, who became its purchaser."*

These lace-makers are often very wretched; their clothing poor and scanty, their food meager and rough. These
lace-makers suffer by the changes of fashion, wars, bad

* Lace and Lace-making, CHAMBERS' Repository.

13

harvests, and hard times.   It must be self-evident that if these women had done something of more utility, their condition would have been better, and that of the community also.

If we apply this reasoning to cities, we can soon remove the causes of misery that exists there.   We must all labor at something useful.   The first thing that strikes the eye, in a large city, is the magnificence of some of the streets that are devoted to the sale of goods.   They have a great deal of useless labor on them.   If this labor were put on the homes of those who toil, it would make a home attractive, and keep many from the haunts of vice.   If the goods that are sold in these palace-like stores were sold in a plainer building, the goods could be sold cheaper.   The rents keep many from toil, who are well able to do it, who are maintained by the laborer because he has been mistaught.

In cities women spend a little time fixing up, to go to market; then she works hard to carry home a small load of potatoes, turnips, beets, carrots, and corn.   Were the same time that is spent in carrying and bargaining for these and other articles, spent in the garden, it would yield the same quantity of vegetables.   One hour in a day spent in a garden would give garden produce sufficient for a family of six persons.   After the soil is plowed, to labor with a hoe or rake is not very severe when done in a morning. The gardener has to spend much time in going and staying in the market.   The gardener first supplies himself with food, and sells what is left to buy clothing.   He can make much of his clothing in the time which he spent cultivating for others.   The city person has first to earn money and then take time to spend it.   A person having a garden will cut off the time that is spent in earning market money.   A large part of the laborer's wages is spent for strawberries, currants, gooseberries, blackberries, peaches, plums, apples, and grapes.   Without these fruits men will be sick.   A paper-maker wishes to whiten his rags, he uses chloride of lime, this rots them.   The human stomach is a repository for tough steak and other things, it is necessary to use these fruits; that the stomach may use the acids they contain to dissolve hard food.   These fruits derive their cost from the labor of saving and gathering.   If this labor were done by women and children, the cost of these fruits would be cut off.   It is to be hoped that the time will come, when every family will have its own fruit-trees, and sit under its own grape-vine.

Citizen Miles Greenwood, of Cincinnati, will make for those who wish to shorten labor a hand loom, which, by turning a crank, will make thirty yards of cloth in a day. Society has two large classes, farmers and mechanics, one part miserably live in the towns, paying high rents.   A return to the primitive occupations of making cloth and shoes in the family would bring a great deal of happiness to many. Even to this day, in the country villages in some parts of England, the mothers and daughters make the linen, laces, and fringes for their own use.   Every reasonable person, after sleeping eight hours, reading eight hours, should be willing to work eight hours to complete the day.   It is a beautiful sight to see a bed covered with snow-white linen, and the table and bureau having on it a nice flower-worked cover.   This is a sight far more beautiful than to see a fine painting, the owner of which has sold a building lot to a mechanic for a high sum, which only cost a small sum. The contemplation of this painting, must bring to the sensitive mind this thought: those from whom the money was taken, what painful self-denial they must have practiced, in turning their coats, patching their trowsers, eating butterless bread, drinking faintly sweetened coffee, innocent of milk. A woman can make a yard of linen in a day, which is three hundred yards in a year. In a city like Cincinnati are tens of thousands idle boys and girls, rich and poor, who can not be set to work for want of space.

In a large city is a long business street, the houses have carved fronts, and many are magnificent. At the back of the stores is an alley, in which runs a stream of putrid water, emiting a strong smell or mephitic air. In the back of the store is the counting room, in which is the owner and his book-keepers. These last are tender and delicate, whose career in life may be prematurely ended. Nature intended men should harden themselves with outdoor toil. This room is badly lighted, it is alway a dim light never sufficient to save the sight from dimness. While the front of the house is devoted to traffic, the back part is a work-shop. It frequently happens that over the counting room, is a room containing twenty or thirty milliners. Those who are the oldest and use glasses can sit near the windows. Some are twenty feet from the window, and are hastening on premature blindness. All this is to gratify pride, and a love of gay clothing. Many printers and tailors have their shop windows in narrow alleys nine feet wide.

George Stephenson, the great improver of the locomotive, said: "The time was coming when men could not afford to walk, they will ride on railways." Why should not the shops, where men have to spend one-third part of their time, be cheerful, roomy, and full of light on all sides? It will be so when men go to the country and surround their shops with walks and grassy lawns. The time is coming when cities will not be so crowded. Would it not promote the happiness of book-printers, binders, and pressmen, of Cincinnati if they were in a town by themselves, the

folders, stitchers, and press-feeders are women, these, with
the families of printers would, form a large society. Why
should not a printer have a home? A home like a manor
house, ornamental in its architecture, with grass lawns, and
fragrant flower beds. The other mechanics, too, should have
homes. Not one mechanic in ten owns a home; the reason
is, it costs $3,000 in a large city, some more, others less. La-
borers should form suburban towns. The wages of a married mechanic seems to be divided thus: for rent one-
fourth, for chickens, honey, fruit, vegetables, pigs, milk,
and butter another fourth of the wages is consumed. All
families, three-fourths of a century ago, produced abundantly
these things; then a house had stable, fruit and kitchen garden. The banks of the Clyde, from its mouth to the city
of Glasgow, a distance of thirty miles, is a continuous ship-
yard. The banks of the Thames contain a succession of industrial towns. Cities should be contrived so as those who
live in them will not have to labor so hard. This will be
done when railroads are used more.

The city of Paris has 2,000,000 inhabitants; to supply
their wants persons come with garden stuff forty miles.
What an army it must take to supply them with their food.
The lighting of a city takes an enormous amount, which
should be saved. In a large city thousands are employed
at street-cleaning, sewer-digging, and in watching the city.
In a city are many drinking saloons and tobacco shops.
These make an enormous drain of persons from society.
When these are returned to useful labors, society will find
some relief. It is not improbable that if all the book-
keepers and clerks that are in Cincinnati should go to raising wheat they could keep the inhabitants in bread all the
time. This is based on the calculation that there are
6000 clerks, each producing 500 bushels of wheat, which

gives a bushel a month to 250,000 people. If the street-sweepers, sewer-diggers, lamp-lighters, watchmen, and the Members of the City Council were to work on Mr Green-wood's hand-loom, they could make for each in Cincinnati thirty-six yards of cloth. This is based on the calculation that there are 1,000 of these persons to do the city work, and they work for a year. This loom, it is said, can make thirty yards in a day. It has been computed there are in Cincinnati 4,000 persons engaged in selling beer, whisky, and tobacco. These could make each in a year 1,000 bush-els of corn. This will give to every one in Cincinnati, 195 pounds of hams, bacon, and lard. The corn will make this quantity. It can be easily proved that 20,000 persons can clothe and feed the 250,000 persons who live in Cin-cinnati. This proves that if each person were to work for himself five-sixths of an hour in a day, directly at food and clothes, he would have abundance of food, and plenty of common clothing. It is by making many unnecessary pur-suits that men are poor. Unproductive labor makes men poor, and causes crime. A return to productive labor will banish poverty and crime.

Thomas Jefferson was of the opinion "That no place should be larger than the members of one's own family." The New York Tribune, previous to the war of 1861, says: "Many would hesitate to believe how small is the compensation received by women for their labors, and the amount of work exacted of them in return, if it were not capable of strong proof. Even the skilled work of the pro-fessed dressmaker, milliner, and tailoress, is very poorly re-munerated. The sum received by that large class who do plain sewing for a support is least of all, and it is often not sufficient, even with the greatest economy and manage-ment, to procure the commonest necessaries of life. We have now in our city women employed in making coarse shirts at fourteen cents each. Two of these are as much as they can possibly make in a day, sewing incessantly. In a week the amount earned was not much over one dollar and a half. Out of this they were to clothe, board, and lodge themselves. And this was their only resource for a livelihood, and a precarious one, too. A steady supply of this kind of work can not be looked for."

"What is the position of the needle woman? Far worse than that of the servant. It matters not if she faints from exhaustion and fatigue; Mrs —— wants her ball dress, and the poor slave must labor, so that the gay robe may deck the form of beauty. The hour of release has come at last. The wearied girl walks feebly through the streets; she meets some one of her own sex bedecked with finery, the thought flashes across the mind, they are better off than I am. This thought is too often the precursor of her ruin. We level the poor to the dust by our general policy, and take infinite credit to ourselves, for raising them up by the grace of charity." *

"Great cities grow to be the nursing mothers of ignorance, vice, and crime. The tendency in that direction, being, as every-where, in the direct ratio of the exhaustion of the soil. Every stage of this downward progress, is marked by a growing tendency toward appropriation, as a substitute for honest labor. As a consequence our American cities are rapidly sinking, in this respect, to a level with the worst of those in Europe. During the last two years the writer (Mr Brace) has had considerable opportunities of observing, the degradation of Europe; and to him it is sadly ominous of evil, that our future society rests on such a base of guilt. There is nothing in Europe worse than

* Fontablanque.

the back streets of New York. The lanes of Liverpool,
St. Giles, and Westminister, the faubourgs of the Seine, the
suburbs of Vienna do not, any of them, present such min-
gled poverty and vice as do our lowest wards." *

"In Boston there are 2,000 persons begging, or by fraud
getting their daily bread. In Cincinnati may be seen daily
600 persons during the winter asking for public relief. The
Federal Government has now adopted a system looking
toward the perpetual maintenance of an indirect tax. The
nation doubles the salaries of secretaries and ministers at a
time when the artisan finds a daily difficulty of obtaining
food and clothing for his children. Trading cities treble
their expenditures, and pauperism gaines with great strides.
The expenses of the city of New York have risen in seven
years, from $3,000,000 to $9,000,000, and the fees of the
city attorney have advanced, from a moderate amount to
the annual sum of $71,296." †

This description of the sorrows of those who live in cities,
is from Charles Lamb's "Essays of Elia:" "The physical condition of the working classes, is more wretched than
we can bear to consider. The agricultural laborers are
subject to violent diseases, proceeding from acute inflammation, medical assistance is very remote, and negligently administered; their robust frames feed the diseases that attack them; they are stricken down in the summer of their
days and die in the zenith of their vigorous health. Not
so with the mechanic; he has medical aid at hand; acute
disorders fall light on the yielding relaxations of his frame;
it is not that he dies sooner than the laborer; he lives more
painfully; he knows not what health is; his whole life is
that of a man nourished on slow poisons; disease sits at his
heart, and gnaws it at its cruel leisure. The incessant

* Rev. C. L. Brace.   † North American Review, No. 72 page 181.

labor in some manufactories, the small deleterious parti-
cles that float upon the atmosphere, engendering painful
and embittering maladies, afflict with evils, even more
dreadful than the heritage of literary application. It is not
the disease to which the operative is subject; he bears in
the fiber of his nerves, and in the marrow of his bones, the
terrible bequeathments of hereditary affliction. His parents
married under age, unfit for the cares, inadequate to the labors which a rash and hasty connection has forced upon
them—each, perhaps, having resort to ardent spirits in the
short intervals of rest. The mother engaged in the factory
during the period of child-bearing—every hour she was so
employed added the seeds of a new infirmity to her new-
born offspring.

" Observe the young mother how wan and worn are her
cheeks; how squalid her attire; how mean her home, yet
her wages and those of her partner are sufficient, perhaps,
to smooth, with decorous comforts, the hours of rest, and to
provide for all the sudden necessities of toiling life. A slat-
tern and thriftless waste converts what ought to be compe-
tence into poverty; and amid cheerless and unloving as-
pects the young victim is ushered into light.

"The innocent prattle of his children takes out the sting
of a man's poverty. The children of the very poor do not
prattle! It is none of the least frightful features in that
condition that there is no childishness in its dwelling. A
sensible old nurse once said: 'Poor people do not bring up
their children; they drag them up.' The little careless dar-
ling of the wealthier nursery, in their hovel is transformed
betimes into a premature reflecting person. No one has
time to dandle it, to toss it up and down, to coax it, to hu-
mor, to sooth it. There is none to kiss away its tears. If
it cries, it can only be beaten. It has been prettily said,

'that a babe is fed with milk and praise.' The aliment of this poor babe was thin and unnourishing. The return for its little baby tricks, and its efforts to gain attention, is bitter, ceaseless objurgation. It never had a toy, or knew what a coral meant, it grew up without the lullaby of nurses; it was a stranger to the patient fondle, the blushing caress, the attracting novelty, the costlier plaything, or the cheap off-hand contrivance to divert the child, the prattled nonsense (best sense to it), the wise impertinence, the wholesome lies, the apt story interposed, that puts a stop to its present sufferings, and awakens the passions of young wonder. It was never sung too, or told a nursery tale.

"It was dragged up to live or die as it happened. It had no young dreams. It broke at once into the iron realities of life. A child of the very poor is not an object of dalliance; it is only another mouth to be fed, a pair of little hands to be inured to toil. It is the rival for the food of the parents, till it becomes a co-operator with them. It is never given to mirth, has no diversion or solace, it never makes him young again, recalling his young times. It makes the very heart bleed to overhear the casual street talk between a poor woman and her little girl. It is not of toys, of nursery books, of summer holidays, of the promised sight, or of the praised sufficiency at school. It is on mangling and clear-starching, of the price of coal or of potatoes. The questions of the child, that should be the very outpourings of curiosity in idleness, are marked with forecast and melancholy providence.

"It has come to be a woman before it was a child. It has learned to go to market; it chaffers, it haggles, it envies, it murmurs; it is knowing, acute, and sharpened. It never prattles. Have we not reason to say, that the home of the very poor is no home."

One cause of the expense of living in large cities is the waste of food. Hired girls, not being of a philosophic turn of mind, cook too large a quantity, and then the excess is thrown away. This will come to an end when the lady of the house does her own cooking. In Cincinnati there are hundreds of carts that go around and collect this wasted food. Could the waste that is in a large city be put on land, it doubles its fertility. These scavengers, were they to cultivate land thus highly manured, would lessen the hard toils of other cultivators.

There are in a large city many peddlers of peanuts, apples, soaps, needles, tape, and thread. Many of these aspired to be splendid merchants and failed. Some have been clerks, their places were supplied by those younger than they were. These consume. Do they produce? Let the young man look on them and be warned, and resolve to be a mechanic and farmer, and he will have something. If he labors from twenty to sixty years of age, he will have done 12,000 days' work. At the close of life he may have 6,000 of these days' work around him, in the form of a beautiful garden, farm, and home.

The laborer, who is the foundation of society, should ask himself: Are all the classes in society useful? can not some be dispensed with? There are in large cities, eating up the substance of the people, a class of men called Life Insurance Companies. The managers say if a healthy person gives a stipulated and annual sum for life, they will give at his death, to surviving friends $1,000. The twenty-third annual report of "The Mutual Life Insurance Company" contains the names of 200 persons who died in 1865. A person paid to them $7.62, and his friends received $1,000. Another paid $193, his friends received $20,000. Another paid $3,071, his friends received $3,000. The receipts of the year 1865 were $2,998,130. The disbursements were $1,540,130, which left a gain of $1,448,000. This is supposed to be divided among the policy holders. The expenses for postage, advertising, medical examinations, salaries, stationery, and printing was $212,000. The motives in both parties is to make gain out of each other. The Commercial tells us that these companies owe those who have insured with them $800,000,000. These companies have received $44,000,000. One thing is very certain, the people who own and manage these institutions, must be paid for their work. For their share they probably receive $15,000,000. As $500 will supply a person's wants for a year, it follows that 30,000 persons are kept in idleness, who can make on the Miles Greenwood loom in a year 270,000,000 yards of cloth. Money obtained by life insurance is soon gone, and then the family are as helpless as ever. If the insurer had gone to the country, and made a farm, taught his family spinning and weaving, they would have a constant support.

Mary Wollstonecraft says: "Woman thus infallibly becomes the solace of men when they are so weak in body and mind that they can not exert themselves, unless to pursue some frothy pleasure or to invent some frivolous fashion. What a melancholy sight it is to see numerous carriages that drive in the cities full of pale-faced ladies!" Many evils will cease when laborers leave the cities. They are no longer places of refuge for fugitive slaves. Laborers living in cities are slaves to landlords and merchants.

CHAPTER VII.

COMMERCE AND TRADE.

COMMERCE, ITS ORIGIN—MANKIND NEEDED COMMERCE TO IMPROVE THEIR
CONDITION—ITS EVILS AND REMEDY—FRANKLIN'S OPINIONS OF COM-
MERCE—REV. SIDNEY SMITH'S OPINIONS OF COMMERCE.

"The decay of commerce is a nation's strength."—WILLIAM PITT.

KINGS and nobles have started legislation, which
may be defined, the art of keeping mankind poor.
Commerce will do this most effectually. Franklin defines commerce to be "The exchanging of the necessaries of life for superfluities. It is giving our victuals
and clothes to the islands for rum and sugar."

That kings and courtiers believed in keeping the people
poor may be inferred from some of their expressions. Cardinal Richelieu says: "If the people were well off, it
would be difficult to keep them within legal bounds." In
the play of "Jane Shore" is this language: "The restive
knaves are overrun with ease, as plenty is the nurse of faction." Robert Owen was traveling in Europe; a great dinner was made for the purpose of drawing him into a con-
troversy with M. Gentz, a famous politician, and a champion of a different school of reform. M. Gentz enjoyed
"the full confidence of the leading despots of Europe,"
and was secretary of the congress of sovereigns, then about
to assemble at Aix-la-Chapelle. Mr. Owen opened to the
company his scheme for the improvement of the human

(145)

race, and for arranging the social machinery, "so as to saturate society at all times with wealth sufficient to amply supply all its wants through life." M. Gentz was asked for a reply; and, to Mr. Owen's surprise, said: "We know very well what you say is true; but how can we govern the masses if they were wealthy and so independent of us." Mr. Owen had engraved a picture of what society might be if reformed. He showed this to Lord Lauderdale, who looked at it attentively, and then suddenly exclaimed, "Oh I see it all! Nothing could be more complete for the poor and working classes. But what is to become of us?"*

Bulwer, in his "England and the English," tells us of a savage chief, who looked for some time at a printing press in operation, and then said: "If that was among my people I could not rule them." Montesquieu, in his "Spirit of the Laws," tells us that the Turkish rulers plundered their subjects as close as possible, to keep them from revolting. A people must have some accumulations of food, when they go to war.

Gov. Hammond, when he said "that in all social systems there must be a class to do the mean duties of life," knew that there must be some custom or usage, or some acts of legislating, some carrying away of the people's food, or selling away the public lands to favorites and speculators, or granting them to railroads which introduce habits of luxury to the few at the expense of the many. These acts make drudges of a part of the people. This senator knew, and many of the others knew that a state of universal riches and equality would give them no needle drudges to prepare for their wives and daughters costly robes, or kitchen drudges to prepare highly-wrought and costly food. A system that makes senators do drudgery will not do.

* Life of ROBERT OWEN, by Ashmead and Evans, Philadelphia, 1865.

Says D'Israeli, in his "Curiosities of Literature:" "That
the Romans did not practice the art of printing can not but
excite our astonishment, since they really possessed the art,
and may be said to have enjoyed it, unconscious of their
rich possession. I have seen the Roman stereotypes, or
printing immovable types, with which they stamped their
pottery. How, in daily practicing the art, though confined
to this object, it did not occur to so ingenious a people to
print their literary works, is not easily accounted for. Did
the wise and grave senate dread those *inconveniences* which
attended its indiscriminate use?"

The Marquis D'Arginson says: "Trading centralization
tends to make the world a single kingdom, plundered by a
multitude of intendants" (superintendents.) From these
sentiments we may learn that legislation is a means to
keep the people poor and in ignorance, which commerce
can accomplish.

After the conquest of England the villains and vassals
of the nobility had only themselves and their masters to
support. The lord, to keep his people poor, had only to increase the number of his retainers. As soon as commerce,
or rather ships, were invented, then the food could be carried away. As seamen were wanted to navigate these ships,
they would be taken from the working classes, which would
lessen their number. The workers would have to feed and
clothe themselves, their masters, and the seamen. The
ship is laden with food and clothing, and it sails to Brazil.
The natives are engaged at those pursuits that are useful—
they are creating food and clothes. The captain says to
the natives, "Quit your useful labors, and go to seeking diamonds, for which we will give you food and clothes." The
poor working people of England have now to clothe and
feed these diamond seekers. Another ship is laden with

food and clothing, requiring more sailors to be taken from the industrious classes. The ship goes to Ceylon. The captain says to the natives, " Your labor produces food and clothes, if you will quit that labor and dive for pearls, we will give you food and clothes for your labor." Another ship is laden with food and clothing, requiring more sailors from the industrious classes. This freight is taken away to Mexico, and for it the people are set to work seeking for silver, gold, dye-stuffs, sandal-wood, and many other useless things. The scholars of America, the men with certificates of learning written on sheepskin, can not deny that sailors come from the working classes, and to feed and clothe these lessens the scanty stores of those who remain to do useful work. It can not be denied that those who seek for gold, silver, diamonds, and pearls, are clothed and fed at the expense of the poor workers of England. If all this useless commerce were to come to an end, what a relief it would bring. Those who produce the values that obtain the products of the mines and the sea, do not enjoy any part of them. To see a person bedecked with diamonds ought to fill the just mind with indignation and sorrow. To see so much labor wasted should give pain.

The Rev. Sidney Smith says : " Every rock in the ocean where a cormorant can perch is occupied by British troops, has a governor, deputy governor, store-keeper, and deputy store-keeper, and will soon have an archdeacon and a bishop; military college, with thirty-four professors, educating seventeen ensigns per annum—being half an ensign for each professor—with every species of nonsense, athletic, sartorial, aud plumigerous. 'A just and necessary war' costs this country above one hundred pounds per minute. A pension for a man who broke his head at the pole—to another who had his leg shot at the Equator; subsidies to

Persia; secret service money to Thibet; an annuity to Lady Henry Somebody, and her seven daughters, the husband having been shot at some place, where we ought never to have had any soldiers at all. Such a scene of extravagance, corruption, and expense, must paralyze industry, and mar the fortunes of the most industrious people that have ever existed."

The evils of commerce have been necessary to improve mankind. There are inventions made all over the earth. Visiting and intercourse with other nations gives us the opportunities of obtaining these inventions, and it would be the means of improveing navigation. No doubt the ancient inhabitants felt themselves injured and impoverished to see their numbers lessened, and their food and clothes taken to foreign countries, to be exchanged for very foolish things. Their sufferings were to confer a benefit on future generations—it was to give to over-crowded nations the means of going to other lands. Were commerce to be abolished the poor would find some relief.

"A Chinese emperor, of the family of Tangs, said: 'Our family held it as a maxim, that if there was a man who did not work, or a woman that was idle, some one must suffer cold or hunger in the empire.' On this principle he ordered a number of the monasteries of the bonzes (priests) to be destroyed.

"The third emperor of the twenty-first dynasty, to whom some precious stones were brought that they had found in a mine, he ordered it to be shut up, not choosing to fatigue his people, in working for a thing that could neither clothe nor feed them.

"In employing so many persons in making clothes for one person is the way to prevent a great many people from getting clothes. There are ten men who eat the fruits of

14

the earth to one employed in agriculture, and is the means to prevent numbers from getting nourishment." *

Franklin wrote a letter to Benjamin Vaughan, Esq., in 1784: "It is wonderful how the affairs of the world are managed. Naturally one would imagine that the interests of a few individuals would give way to general interest. But individuals manage their affairs with so much more application, industry, and address than the public do theirs. We assemble parliaments and councils, to have the benefit of their collective wisdom, but we necessarily have at the same time the inconvenience of their collective passions, prejudices, and private *interests*. By the help of these, artful men overpower wisdom and dupe its possessors; and if we may judge by the acts, arrets, and edicts, all the world over, for regulating commerce, an assembly of wise men is an assembly of the greatest *fools* on earth.

"I have not thought of a remedy for luxury. I am not sure that, in a great state, it is capable of a remedy, nor that it is so great an evil as represented. Suppose we include in the definition of luxury all unnecessary expense, then let us consider whether laws to prevent such expense are possible to be executed in a great country, and whether, if they could be executed, our people would be happier or even richer. Is not the hope of being one day able to purchase and enjoy luxuries a great spur to labor and industry? May not luxury produce more than it consumes, if, without such a spur, people would be, as they naturally are, inclined to be lazy and indolent? To this purpose I remember a circumstance: The skipper of a shallop, employed between Cape May and Philadelphia, had done us some small service, for which he refused to be paid. My wife, understanding he had a daughter, sent her as a present

* History of China, by Father Du HALDE, quoted in the "Spirit of the Laws."

a new-fashioned cap. Three years after, this skipper was at my house with an old farmer of Cape May, his passenger. He mentioned the cap, and how much his daughter had been pleased with it. Said he: 'It proved a dear cap to our congregation. When my daughter appeared with it at meeting it was so much admired that all the girls resolved to get such caps from Philadelphia; and my wife and I computed that they could not have cost less than one hundred pounds.' Said the farmer: 'True, but you do not tell the whole story. I think the cap was, nevertheless, an advantage to us; for it was the first thing that set our girls to knitting worsted mittens, for sale at Philadelphia, that they might have wherewithal to buy caps and ribbons there; and, do you know, the industry has continued ever since, and is likely to continue to increase in value, and answer better purposes. Upon the whole, I was more reconciled to this little piece of luxury, since not only the girls were made happier by having fine caps, but by supplying you with warm mittens.'

"In our commercial towns upon the sea coast fortunes will be made. Some who grow rich will be prudent, live within bounds, and preserve what they have gained for their posterity; others, fond of showing their wealth, will be extravagant and ruin themselves. Laws can not prevent this. In some cases, indeed, certain modes of luxury may be a public evil, in the same manner as it is a private one. If there be a nation, for instance, that exports its beef and mutton to pay for the importation of claret and porter, while a great part of its people live upon potatoes, and wear no shirts, wherein does it differ from the sot, who lets his family starve, and sells his clothes to buy drink?

"Our American commerce is, I confess, a little in this way, we sell our victuals to the islands for rum and sugar, the necessaries of life for superfluities. But we have plenty, and live well, nevertheless; though, by being the soberer, we might be richer.

"What occasions so much want and misery? It is the employment of men and women in works that produce neither the comforts and conveniences of life—who, with those who do nothing, consume the necessaries raised by the laborious.

"To explain this: The first elements of wealth are obtained by labor from the earth and waters. I have land and raise corn ; with this if I feed a family that does nothing ; my corn will be consumed, and at the end of the year I shall be no richer than I was at the beginning. But if while I feed them I employ them, some at spinning, others in making bricks for building, etc. I employ a man in fiddling for me ; the corn he eats is gone; I have no wealth or conveniences added to the family. I shall, therefore, be the poorer for this fiddling man, unless the rest of my family work more or eat less, to make up for the deficiency he occasions.

"Look round the world and see millions employed in doing nothing, or something that amounts to nothing, when the necessaries of life are in question. What is the bulk of commerce for which we fight and destroy each other but the toil of millions for superfluities, to the great hazard and loss of many lives, by the constant dangers of the sea? How much labor is spent in building and in fitting great ships, to go to China and Arabia for tea and coffee, to the West Indies for sugar, to America for tobacco? These things can not be called necessaries, as our ancestors did very well without them.

"A question might be asked: Could all these people now employed in raising, making, or carrying superfluities, be subsisted by raising necessaries? I think they might. The world is large and a great part of it is uncultivated. Many hundred millions of acres in Asia, Africa, and America are still in forests, and even a great deal in Europe. On a hundred acres of this forest, a man might become a substantial farmer.

"It is, however, some comfort to reflect that, upon the whole, the quantity of industry and prudence among mankind exceeds the quantity of idleness and folly; hence the increase of good buildings, cultivated farms, and populous cities, filled with wealth, all over Europe, which, a few ages since, were only to be found on the Mediterranean; and, notwithstanding the mad wars continually raging, by which are often destroyed in one year the works of many years of peace. So that the luxury of a few merchants on the sea-coasts will not be the ruin of America."

Merchants and lawyers rule this country. It is their interest to promote luxury and corruption. There are many who wish and desire that American cities may have millions living in them, so as they can live by the corruption and crime that cities cause. There have been many writers on Political Economy, and none make this subject as clear in a few words as our illustrious Franklin.

Commerce comes from the Latin word "commercicum." Its carrying gives excessive toil to many of the human family. It is the duty of mankind to do away with carrying as much as possible. Take the example of two men: one goes and settles on eighty acres of government land, in two years he has a quantity of land cleared sufficient to give support to himself and wife. This farmer keeps on clearing land. As his children grow up they begin to plow and plant. A hired man is set to work; this gives the farmer ease from his toils, and his riches begin to increase.

He lives like a prince, and has an appetite for his food. He has the finest white wheat flour, which his wife knows how to mix with milk, butter, and home-made yeast. * This is baked, when it becomes light and puffy. The farmer has for his breakfast sweet butter, new-laid eggs, young chickens, and delicious sugar-cured ham. No prince or nobles fare better than this, though they may be able to get some simple ones to leave the pleasures of home, to risk their lives, to ransack sea and earth for some strange luxury not worth eating, and it is only eaten because it has cost a large sum. The farmer's food is varied—his chickens are baked, boiled, and fried. To this is added fat, tender beef, lamb, turkeys, and a sucking pig. The plan among farmers is to kill by turns and then divide. The farmer's wife stews all kinds of fruits in their season, which makes quite a pleasing variety to the farmer's food. When strawberries are in season, the wife presses out their juices, or they are discharged by boiling. The juices are gently boiled down or concentrated. In this manner cherries, raspberries, blackberries, whortleberries, black, red, and white currants, plums, peaches, pears, apricots, and grapes are preserved, or rather the fine flavor they possess. These juices are preserved in little jars. The farmer's wives take much pride in showing their friends their closet-shelves covered with these jars. These fruits are dried and stored away to make future puddings and pies. The wife, prepares as a substitute for coffee, dried and burnt sweet potatoes, which when mixed with cream and sugar, can not be distinguished from the coffee of Rio de Janeiro, which is the nearest coffee mart to us. This coffee is paid for by giving in ex-

* This is a harmless compound, it is made from a fluid obtained by boiling hops in water, and mixing with boiled potatoes. City people use much soda and alum in their bread. The alum whitens bad flour, put in by bakers.

change cottons, shoes, hats, and other useful things. The Brazilians do not want gewgaws, or even money. This farmer is not often sick; a plentiful supply of fruit or their juices cures and prevents disease. This farmer does not get his life insured, thereby keeping a parcel of idle men to eat up what the industrious produce. This farmer is never gloomy, or thinks of taking away his life.*

A young man chooses to work for the carriers, the men who own railroads and live like princes. This man's business is to roll barrels, and lift boxes in and out of the cars. This work is hard, as hard as farming. This hard work is constant—the same throughout life. If this man marries he will live in a town and give half of his earnings to his landlord and merchant. The probabilities are that this man will be poor. At his death his daughters will have to go to servitude, or become milliners, working many together in an ill-lighted room.

The farmer is the only one who toils and has abundance. Has he a natural right to keep others poor and mean, that he may have fine clothing and luxuries? This compromise must be made; the farmer must work in the fields in the summer, and at mechanical pursuits in the winter, as

*When the writer was setting up the first part of Franklin's letter, an artist from the opposite room came to the door—having in his arms his pupil, saying, "Oh Dealtry! my partner has stabbed himself!" The wound was nearly fatal. This was the third attempt to take life, the first was an attempt to throw himself from a window six stories high, the second was to take laudanum. Both attempts were prevented. He is twenty-one, and has been seven years trying to be an artist. He was in a despondent state of mind; the future looked dark. His teacher read to him my description how the farmers live, and it pleased him. He inquired: "If he was to go and get a piece of land, could he sell paintings?" I replied, "That farmers liked to exchange labor, and would help him." I told him the story of the spendthrift in "Foster's Decision of Character." A man spent his patrimony; he resolved to be rich again; he asked if he could shovel some coals, for which he got some food and money. He accumulated $3,000,000 from small savings and a willingness to work.

was done eighty years ago. Clothing lasted four times as long then as it does now. It was hard twisted and hard woven. Cloth is now mixed with "shoddy." This vile stuff is put in flannels and blankets. If persons could see the bales of dirty clothing and blankets that go to shoddy mills, they would be dissatisfied with factory cloth.

William Arthur, A. M., a Wesleyan minister, says: "Have you ever seen a shoddy mill? It is a curious sight. You find a multitude of rags and tatters gathered from all the winds—here a patch of Irish frieze, there a shred of tartan; scraps of women's shawls, of men's pantaloons, of flannels, horse-rugs, stockings; threads, snips, and morsels; blue, black, green and all hues—English, Welsh, and German; a strange heap of the outcast and the defiled; hopeless things that no housewife could work up, that no shivering wretch would look to for comfort. Yet there they are for restoration. See how that teethed and terrible machine makes them look more hopeless still; rends up even rags, tears up small tatters; champs, wrests, slashes, and flings them out at last fibers and choking dust. But next comes the oil-can, and oil, abundant oil, with working and turning, till the heap begins to look like some caricature of wool. Then the spinning frame, and lo! the tatters form to yarn once more; then the loom, where the tatters turn to blankets, druggets, pilot cloth, and even what would pass under your eye as decent broad cloth. This shoddy covers many a respectable floor, flourishes in paletots of low caste, and goes out in blue blankets to New Zealand to clothe the Maories.

"Society has its shoddy, its offcast rags, its hopeless tatters, polluted and undesirable to touch. The respectable world passeth them by. The Gospel in men's hearts has set them to search for the refuse to work them into society."

Shoddy machines can not be defended, they are an out-rage on human society.   When shoddy is not mixed into cloth it will last five times longer.   We take men from the work-shop and the plow to be inspectors of whisky and flour, and other things.   No one seems to take any note, or give us any plan to save the wool from being destroyed. Shoddy is worked into all the low-priced woolens, and it is worn by the humble work people, who do so much for the happiness of men.   The Scientific American gave a draw-ing of the machine, in the year 1860, or near that time. In 1861, the writer purchased a pair of pantaloons; they were woven smooth and thick.   They proved very treacherous, and did not last while teaching a three-months' school.   A farmer said, "Why is it your pantaloons have to be patched so soon."   Having been in a shoddy mill I promptly re-plied, "They are made of shoddy, or *devils' dust*, which is the dust of old clothes woven into long wool, at the rate of one-third dust and two-thirds wool."   Said the farmer, "See, my pantaloons are not patched, they are home-spun, and have lasted three years.   I have chopped wood and harvested in them."

It is a problem worthy of discussion how ought wool to be spun and woven so as to be the most durable?   Good wool is often badly spun and woven.   The cloth is ill made into clothing.   Leather is often spoiled by a bad method of making.   The best method of making the most durable cloth will help to shorten toil.   This appeared in the Commercial paper: "James Ferguson, of Barnett, Vt., is now ninety-seven years old, is in vigorous intellect, and he works every day.   He wears a coat of cloth woven one-hundred and thirty years ago, in Bushlivat, Scotland."   The writer when a boy, was told by an aged Englishman, in the days of home-spun, that two suits lasted a laborer a lifetime.

15

It seems as if the time were coming round again when cloth will be spun and woven in the family. This is to be inferred from the many contrivances that we see in a State fair for family spinning.

Shakspeare puts this language into the mouth of one of his characters: "I am a true laborer; I raise my own fleeces, I spin them, I wear them." Happy man! may this again soon be the condition of every humble laborer! If the farmer sends his wool to be spun in New England, the cloth will be very high in price. The merchant has to send wheat to pay for spinning the wool. If a bushel of wheat is worth in Ohio one dollar a bushel, and the carriage to New England is fifty cents, which will make the bushel of wheat worth one dollar and fifty cents—if the spinner or weaver get one dollar and a half a day, they have each a bushel of wheat for their days' labor. These two persons have in a day worked up a certain quantity of wool. The carriage of this wool costs a dollar. The carriage of the cloth to Ohio costs a dollar. The merchant charges one dollar for his trouble in sending the wool to be spun and to bring back the cloth. The farmer, to get this cloth, has to give six bushels of wheat for it. One bushel of the wheat goes to feed those who carried it. Two bushels feed those who carried the wool and cloth. The merchant consumes one bushel. Had these two mechanics made the cloth in the vicinity of the farmer, and received the two bushels of wheat from him, the farmer would have saved the four bushels of wheat. If the farmer had made the cloth himself, he would have saved the six bushels of wheat.

Merchants rule the American people, to gratify their own selfish ends and acquire wealth. Merchants are to modern society what the barons were to the middle ages.

Judge Hall in an Address to the "Young Men's Mercantile Association of Cincinnati," delivered, April, 1846, says: "It will require but little reflection to satisfy us, that the resources of this country are controlled chiefly by that class, which, in our peculiar phraseology, we term 'the business community'—embracing all those who are engaged in the great occupation of buying and selling, exchanging, importing and exporting merchandise, and include the banker, the broker, and the underwriter. I have no hesitation in asserting that they employ more of the industry, the intellect, and the *wealth* of the American people, than all other employments and professions united.

" Commerce is limited only by the boundaries of civilized intercourse. It employs the highest energies of the human intellect, and is seen in the most magnificent displays of wealth and power. The vast navies that circumnavigate the globe are hers; great cities acknowledge her sway; her merchants are *Princes*; the revenues of great and mighty nations are under her control. She is the arbitress of war and peace."

Such are the arrogant claims and pretensions of the commercial or "business community," the money princes of the world. These claims are not just, and ought to be resisted. Those who produce all the wealth of the country set up no such arrogant claims for themselves, and are unwilling to allow them to those who only distribute what the industrious laborer produces.

Much of this misery described by Carlyle may be attributed to commerce, which takes away the people's comforts and exchanges them for unnecessary trifles. " Between our Black West Indies and our white Ireland, between those two extremes of lazy refusal to work, and famished inability to find any work, what a world we have made of it, with our fine mammon worship and our benevolent phi-

landerings, and idle godless nonsense of one kind or another;
Supply and demand. Leave-it-alone. Voluntary principle.
Time will mend it; till British industry and all existence
seem fast becoming one huge poison-swamp of reeking pestilence, physical and moral; a hideous, living golgotha of
souls and bodies burnt alive; such a Curtius gulph, communicating with the Nether Deeps as the sun never saw
till now. Thirty thousand out-cast needle women working themselves swiftly to death; three millions of paupers
rotting in forced idleness, helping said needle women to die:
these are but items in the sad ledger of despair. Thirty
thousand wretched women sunk in that putrefying well of
abominations: they have oozed in upon London from the
universal Stygian quagmire of British industrial life."

Shelley, when a boy of eighteen, wrote his Queen Mab.
He has a different opinion on commerce from Judge Hall.
Very few believe it opens the door to famine and disease.
It is the truth.

> " Hence commerce springs, the venal interchange
>   Of all that human art or nature yields
>   Which wealth should purchase not, but want demand,
>   And natural kindness hasten to supply
>   From the full fountain of its boundless love,
>   For ever stifled, drained, and tainted now.
>   Commerce! beneath whose poison breathing shade
>   No solitary virtue dares to spring,
>   But wealth and poverty with equal hand
>   Scatter their withering curses, and unfold
>   The doors of premature and violent death,
>   To pining famine and full-fed disease,
>   To all that shares the lot of human life,
>   Which poisoned soul and body, scarce drags the chain
>   That lengthens as it goes and clanks behind.
>   Commerce has set the mark of selfishness,
>   The signet of its all-enslaving power,
>   Upon a shining ore, and called it gold :

Before whose image bow the vulgar great,
The vainly rich, the miserable proud,
The mob of peasants, nobles, priests, and kings,
And with blind feelings reverence the power
That grinds them to the dust of misery.
But in the temple of their hireling hearts
Gold is a living god, and rules in scorn
All earthly things but virtue."

Abbe Mably, in the beginning of this nation's career, gave to the Americans this advice: "If not to exclude exterior commerce, at least to keep it within bounds. The ruin of republicanism in the United States can happen only from exterior commerce. It is by great quantities of articles of luxury, and a frivolous taste, that commerce will corrupt their morals, and without pure morals a republic can not exist."

Dr Price, in his observations, says: "Alas! what can the United States import from Europe, except it be infection; I tremble in thinking on the furor for exterior commerce that is going to turn the heads of the Americans. Every nation spreads nets around the United States, and caresses them in order to gain a preference; but self interest cautions them to beware of these seductions." *

The Cincinnati Commercial, of Jan. 27, 1868, in an article on revolutions, says: "Thiers refers the (French) revolution to the rationalistic movement of Luther. According to Louis Blanc, its causes sprung from the ancient movement of John Huss and Jerome of Prague. The principles of liberty and equality, scattered through the writings of the French philosophers, were practically established in the institutions of the United States, in 1783. To the work of the Abbe Mably on the American revolution, written while it was still in progress, may be attributed much

Quoted in Brissot de Warville Travels, in North America, in 1787.

influence on the public mind. The more extended work of the Abbe Raynal on America though suppressed by authority, was widely influential in spreading free thought in Europe. At the same time, those prolific writers Brissot de Warville, Claviere, and Turgot, were widely read, and all of them had much to say regarding the triumph of Republicanism in America, and the glorious future about to open for humanity under their auspices."

The American fathers were not guided by these men. Had their simple plans been carried out, misery would have been unknown, the condition of the people would now be more equal. Foreign commerce has been fostered, the land has been sold and given away for speculation. Lands now can not be had except in the regions where winters are very severe, or where there are dangerous Indians. There are unoccupied lands in the hands of speculators sufficient to keep 100,000,000 persons. In the year 1868, this language was used, in a fourth of July oration, in Cincinnati. Dr Lilienthal, in the Broadway Synagogue, said: "In the North a crushing stagnation of business; a want of food and employment drive honest but starving laborers into the fangs of despairing suicide; bankruptcy stares and peeps into the houses of well established merchants; and last, but not least, corruption and dishonesty are every-where. The success of the people has yielded its place to the wealth and success of the few."

Wm. M. Ramsey, at Lockland, said: "Unaccountably a large part of our people seem to be betaking themselves to suicide. Old and young, of both sexes and of every station in life, are flying to self-destruction. To my mind the present political situation of our country is full of peril; its social condition full of evil. Our partisan predilections lead to different conclusions on the same facts."

Archbishop Fenelon, in his Telemachus, tells us: "It is a detestable maxim that the security of a prince depends on the oppression of the people. If you place your people in a state of ease and plenty they will labor no more; they will become insolent, intractable, and factious; *weakness* and *distress* only can render them supple and obedient. By easing your people you will degrade the royal authority; nothing but keeping them in the lowest subjection can keep them from the restlessness of discontent and the turbulence of faction."

Fenelon had access to the king of France. He was the teacher of the king's son, and knew some of the court secrets, some of the causes that oppressed the people. This good, upright Catholic prelate was banished from the court; the king took away his son, and did not speak to Fenelon for four years. Kings and nobles know that commerce is a means of keeping the people poor. American statesmen know that commerce will make fortunes for their children, if they choose its pursuits. Commerce has a long train of evils, among them is war, the parent of hunger and want. All modern wars have their causes in commerce. The South wanted to sell their cotton in Europe, and bring back goods duty free. The North said no, and it was one of the causes of the late unhappy war.

Commerce is a means of obtaining great wealth, which is an injury to the humble classes. They have to be oppressed so as to give the rich the means of gratifying luxury. Lord Kames, in his "History of Man," says: "Between the years 1740 and 1770, six of the mayors of London died in office, a greater number than the 500 preceding years: such havoc does luxury make. Consider the quantity of animal and vegetable food that can be produced on land employed entirely in raising vines, barley, and other materials of fermented liquors. The existence of thousands is destroyed by this species of luxury. The indulging in soft beds, downy pillows, and easy seats is a species of luxury, because it tends to enervate the body, and to render it unfit for fatigue. Nations, where luxury is unknown, are troubled with few diseases, and have but few physicians by profession. In the early ages of Rome, women and slaves were the only physicians, because vegetables were the chief food of the people, who were constantly employed in war or in husbandry. When luxury prevailed their diseases multiplied, and physic became a liberal profession.

"Cookery and coaches have reduced the military spirit of the English nobility and gentry to a languid state; overloading the body has infected them with dispiriting ailments; ease and indolence has banished labor, the only antidote for such ailments. Too great indulgence in the fine arts consumes part of the time that ought to be employed on the important duties of life. A man who lives above his fortune or profits, and accustoms his children to luxury, abandons them to poverty when he dies. Luxury is an enemy to population, it enhances the expense of living, and confines many to the bachelor state. Luxury is, above all, pernicious in a commercial state. Luxury has been the ruin of every state where it prevailed. Great opulence opens a wide door to indolence, sensuality, corruption, prostitution and perdition."

Buffon says: "The sole glory of the rich man is to consume and destroy; and his grandeur consists in lavishing in one day upon the expense of his table what would procure subsistence for many families. He abuses equally animals and men, a great part of whom are a prey to famine, and pine in want and toil to satisfy his immoderate desires. He destroys himself by excess and others by want."

A Russian writer says: "Commerce excites luxury, corrupts manners. Universal dissipation has taken the lead, and profligacy of manners has followed. Great landlords grind their people to supply the incessant demands of luxury. The miserable peasant groans under his taxes."

Montesquieu, in his "Spirit of the Laws," says: "If Poland had no foreign trade its inhabitants would be more happy. The grandees, who have only their corn, would give it to their peasants for subsistence. As their too extensive estates would become burdensome, they would therefore *divide* with their peasants. Every one would obtain skins, or sacks of wool from their herds or flocks, so that they would no longer be at such an immense cost in providing clothes. The great, who are always fond of luxury, not being able to find it in their own country, would encourage the labor of the poor. This nation, I affirm, would then become more flourishing."

Great cities are great evils, and are created by commerce. They are places of suffering, and should be abolished. A few centuries ago they were thought an evil. In 1672, an edict came from Louis XIV, that asserted: "That by enlarging the city, the air would be rendered unwholesome; that cleaning the streets would prove a great additional labor; that adding to the number of inhabitants would raise the price of provisions, of labor, and of manufactures; that the ground would be covered with buildings instead of corn, which might hazard a scarcity; that the country would be depopulated by the desire that the people have to resort to the capital; and, lastly, that the difficulty of governing such numbers would be an encouragement to robbery and murder."

In 1602, Queen Elizabeth prohibited any new buildings within three miles of London, in this preamble: "That seeing the great and manifold inconveniences and mischiefs which daily grow, and are likely to increase, in the city of London, and that such multitudes can hardly be governed, and provided with food and other necessaries at a reasonable price, without adding new officers and enlarging their authority. Many of those who are poor must live by begging or worse means, and are heaped up together—many children and servants in one house or small tenement."

Lord Kames, in his "Sketches of Man," says: "Mexico and Peru afforded to their numerous inhabitants the necessaries of life in profusion. Cotton was plentiful, more than sufficient for the clothing. Indian wheat was universal, and was cultivated without much labor. The natural wants of the inhabitants were thus easily supplied, and artificial wants had made no progress. The Indians have learned from their conquerors a multitude of artificial wants, variety of food, and rich clothing.

"The Peruvian constitution seems to have been an agrarian law of the strictest kind. To the sovereign was given a large portion of the land for the expenses of the government; and the remainder was divided among his subjects. Every man plowed his own field, and then assisted his neighbor. Individuals were taught to do every thing for themselves. Every one knew how to plow and manure his land. Every one was a carpenter, mason, shoemaker, and weaver; and they were obliged to assist each other in sowing, reaping, and building without any reward."

* "None were idle or fatigued with labor; the food was wholesome, plentiful, and equal to all; every one was conveniently lodged and well clothed; the aged, sick, widows, and orphans, were assisted in a manner unknown in any other part of the world; every one married from choice

* Description of the Paraguay Indians, by Abbe Raynal, in his History.

and not from interest, and children were considered a blessing, and could never be burdensome. Debauchery, the
necessary consequence of idleness, which equally corrupts
the opulent and the poor, never tended to abridge the term
of human life; nothing served to excite artificial passions,
or contradicted those that were regulated by nature and reason; the people enjoyed the advantages of trade, and were
not exposed to the contagion of vice and luxury; plentiful
magazines, and a friendly intercourse between nations united
in the bonds of the same religion, were a security against
any scarcity that might happen from the inclemency of the
seasons; public justice had never been reduced to the necessity of *condemning* a single malefactor to death, to igno-
my, or to any punishment of long duration; the very names
of a tax or lawsuit, those two terrible scourges which every
where else afflict mankind, were unknown."

Civilization can give us no such a picture as this. Bolts
and locks, constables and watchmen, jails and prisons are
to be seen every-where. The causes of which are, men
are taken from useful pursuits to manage the money affairs,
to engage in commercial pursuits, and to govern the nation.
These are so numerous, men are poor. They cause crime
and celibacy. There are two classes in large cities that deserve our pity, servant women and milliners. They work
from morn to night on gay dresses covered with beads, ribbons, and spangles, which makes the wearer look like a
harlequin, and who is often an idle woman. This gay robe
often sweeps the streets, as trains are in fashion in 1868.
The poor girls at night can work on their own scanty dresses
to the injury of their eye-sight. Strangers who come to a
very large city observe some streets are occupied by inferior merchants, whose families live up stairs. From the
front part runs a long narrow building, which contains the

cooking, dining, and washing-room; all this is sacred to the maid of all work; over this is her sleeping cell. In this place she cooks, scrubs and washes thirteen hours in the day. She has brick walls around her and can see nothing. The alley emits vile smells which can not be cured. She is a stranger to the pleasures of home or friends.

This woman is not as happy as a monk. Abbe Raynal tells us a beaver is happier than a monk. This writer tells how these animals saw down a tree with their teeth, and it falls across the stream, the branches are gnawed off, and pieces of trees are floated down. A solid dam is made. It has openings to let off the surplus water. The beaver has his house on the top of the dam; it is made of mud and sticks; it is plastered inside very smooth, the floor is kept very clean, and covered with hay. A man can repose very comfortably in their huts. They build store houses for food, and it is divided without contest.

"A male and female get acquainted when laboring on the public works, and agree to pass the winter together; for this they lay up food. The happy couple retire to their hut in September. The winter gives leisure for amorous pursuits. The couple never leave each other. Their time is consecrated to love. On sunshiny days the loving pair walk on the banks of the river, eat some fresh bark, and breathe earth's exhalations. Toward the end of winter the female has those endearing pledges of this universal passion of nature. The father leaves his cell to his family, as it is spring. The mother goes out and feeds her charge on fish and bark."

CHAPTER VIII.

GOLD, SILVER, AND PAPER MONEY.

MONEY HAS ITS ORIGIN IN THE LOVE OF ORNAMENT—A MEANS OF KEEPING
THE PEOPLE POOR—WHAT MONEY COSTS SOCIETY—THE CAUSES OF METAL
MONEY—THE HISTORY OF PAPER MONEY—OPINIONS OF ANDREW JACKSON.

"Gold 'tis trash, it is the worldling's god."—POLLOK.

SOME village mechanics living in Europe were
watching some street occurrence, which caused the
magistrate to come to them and tell them to go
to work. This was very thoughtful in the magistrate. He
no doubt thought much was depending on their labors, and
he was right. It probably never occurred to the mind of
the magistrate, that if he and many others would go to work
at something of utility there would be such an abundance in
the world that disputes would never occur at all. Suppose
these laborers should go along the banks of a stream and
seek for shells and convert them into rings and ornaments,
men would not be any richer. If the magistrate should say
to these men, poverty will overtake you, it would be the
truth. If these persons should go and seek for gold, bitter
poverty would be felt somewhere.

Adam Smith, in his "Wealth of Nations," says:
"Among civilized nations many do not labor at all, many
of whom consume the produce of ten times, frequently a
hundred times, more than those who work." Nature
never designed this. As labor gives aching bones and limbs,

(169)

men are continually trying to throw the burden of their keeping on those who labor. A more prolific source of living without laboring, consuming without producing, can not be found than in money, which is truly an invention to get others' wealth and labor; which takes from him who labors the fruits of that labor, and gives it to him who will not labor.

Money had its origin in a period of the world when the condition of mankind was equal, when they had nothing to exchange. It is probable that we are indebted to the love of ornament for money. It is said that John Lander, the African traveler, had with him the same medals of brass that were used by the British Government to get the American Indians to fight against the American people. To get these medals the Indians will sell the lands of his ancestors; the African will set fire to the villages of neighboring tribes, for the purpose of selling the fleeing inhabitants into slavery, so as to get these ornaments. What a fearful price do the savages pay for these mean ornaments! With what pride do they wear them! Ships go to Africa with beads and copper coins, which are exchanged for gold dust, and ivory. No doubt these beads and coins could be exchanged for wheat if the natives had it. Some of the Chinese hang their money around their necks as an ornament.

When the poor inhabitants of Cuba and St. Domingo, were first visited by the Spaniards, they had little pieces of gold in their hair and other parts of their dress as ornaments. They were astonished at the rage of the Spaniards to obtain these, and to give their food and clothing for that which was of no value to them, nor of any great value to the Spaniards.

The name money comes from the Latin word *moneta*,

a piece of stamped metal. A slave, to whom a sheep was due, could he be persuaded to receive a coin instead of it, would have no motive to receive it except for ornament.

Those who rule a country always contrive to own the copper, silver, and gold mines. William the Norman gave these to his favorites, and forbid all others to seek for silver or gold. The Duke of Cornwall owned the copper mines. He could make copper money and give it for what he liked. Wages were once a penny a day. If a penny was coined in five minutes, it got a day's labor out of the slave. Money at first was rude bars, till human ingenuity found out how to stamp on them the monarch's image.

William I ordered that twelve ounces of silver should be coined into twenty parts, each part to be called a shilling. Each succeeding monarch made it to weigh less at every coinage, a grain or more at a time. In the time of Philip and Mary, the twenty shillings only weighed five ounces. If wheat was a shilling a bushel in the time of William, his pound of silver got twenty bushels of wheat. If the pound of silver was made into twenty-one shillings, the king had twenty-one bushels of wheat.

Charles I wanted money. He said: "Let the servants of the mint mix three penniesworth of silver, with as much alloy as will make a coin of the size of a shilling." He was told the servants of the mint would not do it. "Let them be sent to prison," said the angry monarch. The order was not obeyed. It would have been in the time of Henry VIII. European coins are shamefully alloyed.

If the State treasurer were to get in all his taxes, and get a decree passed that half a dollar should be of the value of a dollar, he would pay twice as many debts, so would all others. When the debts were paid, if another decree were to bring back again the money to its first value it would be a fraud. The king of France changed the *livre*, a coin that was divided into twenty-eight parts, to the value of forty parts. When the king had paid his debts, he changed the money back again to the first value.

The gold and silver in the English mines was exhausted about the time of Henry VIII. England has now obtained enormous supplies of gold from the mines of South America. Many a bagful of gold-dust has gone into the Mint, to be stamped into money, and then exchanged for the products of labor. This exchanging has been going on for generations, and it makes the people poorer. Such have been the accumulations of gold and silver in England, that twenty times as much is given for wages, as was five centuries ago. This does not improve the condition of the poor toiler. A bushel of wheat for ages has been the standard for a day's labor of a skilled laborer. If wages are a penny a day, the bushel of wheat is worth one penny. If a day's labor is five shillings, then is the bushel of wheat worth five shillings. Mechanics fall into a fatal error to think the higher their pay, the better is their condition.

Suppose the merchants of this country obtained gold amounting to $100,000,000, and spent it, the inhabitants would be that much poorer, with much less of the comforts of life. It is something we can not eat or wear. Simpletons will give their necessaries for superfluities. Stewart, of New York, one of the richest men there, has no gold on his person, proving that it is of no utility, except to surgeons and dentists. The papers tell us that during twenty years the California mines have yielded $1,200,000,000. This sum would have given 1,200,000 families a happy home, worth $1,000. A cottage worth $500 with barns and fences to that amount on land, would make many supremely happy. The Secretary of the Interior, tells us

FECTER

This boy, because he paid for the broom, is made a clerk, which has improved his looks, at the expense of some one else's comfort; to prove this his patron obtains a sum of money on a town-lot, or piece of wild land, the buyer of which has to practice unjust, pain and self-denial to obtain it. The Being who rules on high never designed that a part of his children should keep others in unproductive toil. In Cincinnati, there are 4,000 clerks and book-keepers; these working on level, fertile land, aided by machinery, can produce a sufficiency of food to maintain its 300,000 inhabitants. Of its 1,000 persons as police, sweepers of the streets, rulers of the city, etc., were to work on M. Greenwood's loom, they could clothe the city.

4

that when the Pacific Railroad is complete, the product of
the gold mines will be annually $150,000,000. Were
those who seek for gold to work at something else, it would
shorten the hours of labor more than a thirteenth. This
calculation supposes the diggers are laborers earning $500 in
a year, which will give us 300,000 laborers, who can spin
and weave, yearly, 1,350,000,000 yards of cloth, or find
one-third of the nation in food. Those who clothe and
feed the gold seekers—do not have much of the gold.

Gold has become so abundant in England that it is put
to strange uses. The Duke of Buckingham has two tons
of silver-ware. The Queen of England has changes of
gold-ware, sufficient to dine two hundred and forty persons.
The Earl of Carlisle has the dome of his mansion covered
with gold. The Duke of Devonshire has one of his gate-
ways covered with gold. Another nobleman has a gold
staircase. It is a frequent occurrence for an idle American
woman to wear jewelry worth $100,000. Ye statesmen
and philosophers, tell us, who are the humble ones, how
much of human happiness is sacrificed to promote all this
senseless vanity?

Gold and silver money became so abundant, men buried
it in the earth. The wealth of the Jews was in such things
as they could carry away; they were money-lenders and
exchangers. They were often plundered, persecuted, and
had to find a refuge in other countries, and then purchase
the privilege to return. They have paid at times one-third
of the king's revenue for protection. The Jews are the
same now as in the time of Moses—they had tables at the
door of the temple, and sold or exchanged half-shekels as
an offering to the Lord. Six centuries ago they might be
seen in the commercial marts of Europe, sitting on benches,
exchanging money for the Catholic pilgrims. The benches

16

on which they sat were called *banco*, the Italian name for a bench, from which comes the name of bank.

The increase of population made the hiding of money insecure. This led to the formation of banks of deposit by the Lombards and Jews. The crusades and religious pilgrimages led to the custom of loaning money to these bankers. These Jewish bankers often loaned money at twelve and twenty per cent; for this they may have thought they had divine permission. In the book of Deuteronomy it is written, "Of thy brother thou shalt not take usury, of the stranger thou shalt take usury."

The Bank of Venice was the first in Europe, and was established in 1171. The republic was pressed for money and it levied a forced contribution from the richest citizens, giving them in return a perpetual annuity of four per cent. An office was established for the payment of the interest. It was punctually paid, and became the Bank of Venice. At the office claims were registered, and the right to receive interest, which was transferable by purchase or death. It was a bank of deposit, begun without capital. The invasion of the French in 1797 ruined the bank. The republic was its security. In 1401, the Bank of Barcelona was established. In 1407, the Bank of Genoa was started.

The Bank of Amsterdam was started in 1609; the magistrates, by authority of the states, were declared perpetual cashiers to the inhabitants. All merchants were by law obliged to open an account with the bank, for which they paid a fee to the city. This bank was to assist the merchants in their commercial dealings. Creditors of merchants were to receive their dues at the bank, and the bills and receipts were recorded there. For deposits of silver or gold a certificate was given and recorded. In 1672, the French invaded the country, and the merchants went for their money, and it was there. The French invaded Holland in 1794; the merchants went to the bank for their money, and it was not there. This compelled the authorities to confess they had loaned the deposits to Holland, West Friesland, and the East India Company; the claims on these were given to those who had the certificates of the bank in their possession.

In 1640, the merchants of London carried their money to the Mint in the Tower. Charles I, wanting money, took £200,000. This destroyed its character as a place of security and deposit. The merchants then kept their money at home, and were robbed by their apprentices and clerks. This caused the merchants to take their money to the goldsmiths, who had vaults. The goldsmiths received money on trust, and allowed interest on it. The receipt passed from hand to hand as bank notes do now. The goldsmiths reloaned this money to the king, on the security of the taxes. This suggested the Bank of England, in 1694.

The mayor and council of London, with some of the nobility, invited William III and Mary, his queen, to come from Holland and rule them. Mary was the next heir to the throne. William wanted to have a war with France. He did not like to tax the people, for fear he might be exiled like James II, or lose his head, as did Charles I. He got a charter for the Bank of England on condition it loaned money to the government. The first loan was the sum of $6,000,000. The bank was to receive as interest $500,000. The next sum borrowed was $10,000,000, to pay a debt to the East India Company. The interest on this was $800,000. Charles II took out of the treasury $3,500,000. This belonged to some merchants who had it in the treasury. Charles's unjust appropriation was made a small part of the national debt. The people have paid this amount fifteen times over, in the shape of interest. A king dare not ask his subjects for money to carry on a war, and yet, for pieces of paper money, they will give salaries to his officers , food and clothing to his soldiers. Strange infatuation! These sums, when put together, were called "The Consolidated Debt." This term is now abbreviated to "Consols."

In seven years the bank had loaned $80,000,000, a small trifle. It was the beginning of a source of misery; and the germ of a plague that has ravaged England from that day to this. The Bank of England has contributed from 1694 to 1815, for carrying on useless and desolating wars, the enormous sum of $6,050,000,000. This borrowing has made the people of England pay three times this amount in interest, which amounts with the interest and principal to $26,050,000,000. Had money never been invented this enormous sum would never have been got out of the people. There are 50,000,000 of acres of land in Great Britain, were they to be sold for $100 an acre, and this added to the value of the peoples' dwellings, it would equal only half of this amount. The funding or banking system has enabled a few to get from those who labor, the value of all of England's accumulated labor, excepting the silver and gold. This calculation supposes the familes number 6,000,000, and that the habitation of each family is worth $1,000.

The reign of William III may be styled the most unfortunate that England ever saw; during its pernicious progress were sown the seeds of a system which has poisoned the happiness of Englishmen, and reduced them from a state of wealth and universal comfort and ease to a land of toiling slaves and spirit-broken paupers; who are lorded over by a moneyed and landed aristocracy,who have divided the government between them, and by a mixture of crime and error, in a century and a half, have induced a state of suffering and insecurity that bids fair to destroy the safety of the people. The Bank of England was a means of introducing the folly and wickedness of mortgaging the future happiness and labor of posterity, and also the means of introducing among the industrious classes pauperism, crime, and destitution; while the wealth of the country is drawn into huge masses and placed in the grasp of Jews, loan-mongers, gamblers in stocks, and every conceivable kind of swindling. It was the means of changing a country of wealth and happiness into a land of discontented, rebellious paupers, kept quiet by a standing army. The people are crushed in to the earth by a paper money aristocracy.

The sum borrowed to carry on the American Revolution was $695,000,000; this has been paid four times over in interest. The whole sum is $3,500,000,000. The English wars in France cost $4,250,000,000, from 1793 to 1815. This sum has been paid twice as interest, which makes the amount to be $12,750,000,000. All this was used to destroy the happiness of mankind and the principles of liberty. They were gigantic efforts of the privileged classes to prevent the amelioration of society, and to render mankind the *eternal* victims of oppression. Those who have contributed this amount went hungry and naked. The banking system was the reconquest of England to a worse condition of slavery than that of the feudal ages.

It is a truth, the issues of paper, gold, and silver money raise the necessaries of life, without giving the worker any more abilities to produce. The first loan increases the price of provisions, and the second loan has to be larger to to purchase them. The paying out of this loan makes the necessaries of life still higher. Loans and necessaries go up at a fearful ratio, increasing the wages of the soldier and producer. This expanding of the currency has been compared to blowing up a bubble till it bursts, then comes the misery. Mankind have invented the funding system, or the putting away paper money at interest. This may be an evil, it is probably the least of many evils. It would be a serious evil to get ten dollars for a day's labor and then pay it out for a bushel of wheat. It would require large bags to contain the money. It is a serious evil to create a large public debt with an expanded currency, and pay it with a contracted one.

In 1716, John Law started the Bank of France, " To put a stop to usury, to facilitate exchanges, to increase manufactures, and to enable people to pay more easily their taxes." These were the motives this man put forth to get the labor of others. In 1718, the king bought the bank. To save this bank from demand for specie, the king forbid the making of silver plate, the payment of debts in specie, all rents, taxes, and customs were to be paid in paper money. Fines, imprisonment, and confiscation, was enforced against those who had in their possession more than 500 silver livres.

The paper fabric fell. Its fall ruined thousands and reduced them to beggary and want; and well it might, by means of this paper money. The king got $420,000,000 out of their property in the space of four years. To absorb this paper money, pensions were granted to run twenty and forty years. Those who had these annuities became public paupers, and lived on the labor of others. It is said plenty of money makes good times. Then these French men ought to have had good times. They gave their labor for paper and got state paupers to keep. This money was used to find gold in Louisiana, and found cities there.

During the French revolution there was issued paper money, secured by the property of the church and exiled nobles. When the English and French engaged in war, the English counterfeited a great many bales of this money, and caused it to be circulated in France; the government would not redeem it.

The Bank of the United States was started in 1781, with a capital of gold and silver to the amount of $400,000. It was owing to this bank that the war of the revolution was carried to a successful issue. The government got loans from it to the amount of $200,000,000. This bank was re-chartered in 1790 and 1816. In 1836 it was vetoed by Andrew Jackson. Its capital, by its last charter, was the sum of $35,000,000, of which the United States contributed $7,000,000.

It becomes the laborer to get a clear idea of what capital is. It is not the duty of the laborer to take the definition of this word from the princely merchant or banker, who finds it to his interest to mislead the laborer, and get his surplus labor away from him. Capital, was in olden times, an accumulation of food and clothes to consume while men built their houses or engaged in any useful pursuit. This is still capital, and the creator of it can share it with others, on condition they help him. If there was no paper money to get a railroad, men would have to go and hunt for silver and gold, and pay the builders of the railroad with this when coined. If these miners concluded that if they built the road with their own hands, it would be the same as to seek gold. The labor spent on the road is equivalent to labor spent on the silver and gold. In the period of a gold and silver currency the State built all great works by taxes, and applied the profits to the expenses of the State. Since the art of printing has been discovered, and causes have led to paper money, men can get railroads, canals, bridges, and turnpikes for nearly nothing.   Men, when they want to own these things, pledge State debts and mortgages, to the State authorities, who give the beautiful money to them in bales.   This money costs two dollars a thousand, and it is exchanged for the mechanic's skill, and the farmer's toil, at the ratio of two to a thousand.   It probably takes half a day to print this $1,000, and it buys 500 days' labor from the railroad workers, who will get 250 days' labor from the farmer and mechanic for it.

Canals were not used in England before the year 1760. The Duke of Bridgewater conceived the idea of digging a canal to carry coals into the city of Manchester.   He got a bank note plate; and the money, when printed, read, "The Duke of Bridgewater will pay this on demand." Those who dug the canal got the notes, these were taken by the farmer and merchant, who believed the duke's promises, so they let the laborer have real capital food and raiment.   When the canal came into use the profits redeemed the notes, and the duke and his family had a means of support forever.   He did not furnish the capital; he only used cunning to get others to build this canal.   The opinion that he was rich built the canal.

Before this time coal was carried in wagons, and on the backs of asses.   It was a strange sight to see a long train of these little creatures, having on their backs a bushel of coal.   The duke, by his enterprise, sent hundreds of men and boys to other pursuits, perhaps to create luxuries.   It would have been far more rational had the authorities of Manchester issued the money and made the canal, the persons who fed and clothed the laborers would have got some of the profits.   This would consign to the workshop and plow, the duke and his family, and many tax-gatherers.

In this manner railroads, bridges, and turnpikes can be obtained by the State becoming like a pawnbroker, to receive property as pledges, and to issue money on it. In this way a person can become twice as rich as he was before. This makes the condition of men very unequal—one part toil hard to minister to the idleness and luxury of the other. Suppose five persons each pledge $20,000 worth of interest-bearing property, with the comptroller; they receive the sum of $100,000, which was the plan in 1860, now it is to pledge government securities, which bear interest while in pledge. If one of the persons who has received the $20,000 were to build a bridge with the money, his family would have a means of support forever. The same with a turnpike or a railroad.

It is the duty of society to own these, and get their revenues. If society can get a revenue from these sources, it will send the tax-gatherer to more useful work, and it will do the same to those who live on these profits. The United States banks have carried thousands from affluence to poverty. Many a person has got his father's patrimony, and then pledged it to some bank; the speculation not proving successful, the estate was lost. The natural employment of man is to cultivate the earth—banks allure him from it.

Hon. S. P. Chase, when governor of Ohio, in his message, said: "No system of currency can insure complete protection against speculation, debt, and revulsion. Credit currency in the United States is supplied by banks in the form of notes circulating as money. The number of banks, in 1858, exceeded 1,400; their circulation is $214,778,822; deposits, $230,358,352; capital, $370,686; discounts, $684,456,887; and specie, $60,000,000. It needs but a glance at this statement to perceive that a currency so expanded

17

must greatly stimulate hazardous speculation, and tend to financial disorder. The credit currency must become, in part or all together, incontrovertible into coin."

The capital of these banks is in the hands of the comptroller, and is earning six per cent. interest; add this interest to the interest the discounts earn, and add $5,000,000 to the two interests, and you have $40,000,000, the probable annual cost of the paper money of this land. The first sum is what the banks gain by their money getting destroyed, burnt, and wrecked. It is said a Lowell factory girl can make 1,000 yards of cotton cloth in a week; hence, if the bankers, their families, and dependents were to become workers, they could make for this people 4,000,000,000 yards of cotton cloth.

Said Helvetius to Frederick the Great, in alluding to some petitions for monopolies: "Sire, you need not trouble yourself to read them through; they all speak the same language. We beseech your Majesty to grant us leave to rob your people of such a sum; in consideration of which, we engage to pay you a share of the pillage."

Professor Vethake in his book on Political Economy, when speaking of bank expansions and contractions, says: "Profits, too, made in this manner can not be classed with those which result from ordinary gaming. They are precisely of the same nature with the winnings of the gambler, who uses false *dice*, or marked cards, unknown to his victim; and the act of obtaining them is deserving of no milder epithet than that of swindling or *robbery*."

In 1831, Mr Stephen Simpson, Cashier of the United States Bank, published the "Working-Man's Manual," in which the evils of banking are well portrayed. Page 48 says: "It is a singular infatuation, prevailing among Political Economists, that the scarcity of food that exists among the laboring people is attributable to the excess of population, while the palpable fact was staring them in the face, that the excess of the rich demonstrated the falsity of the hypothesis.

"The stinted measure of the wages of labor may be justly termed the evil principle of the age. If we substitute capital, banks, and monopolies, for the barons, lords, and bishops of the feudal time, we shall realize a juncture so precisely similar, as to carry out in full an illustration of the abuses under which the sons of labor now suffer oppression and injustice. But the laws have made it a just and meritorious act, that capitalists shall combine to strip the man of labor of his earnings, and reduce him to a dry crust and a gourd of water. Thus does power invert justice, and derange the order of nature. He who sows, shall reap; he who builds, shall inhabit; he who produces, shall possess! This is the dictate of nature, justice, reason, instinct and common sense. This instinct is crushed by the power of law and capital. Why should the working classes be stripped of the fruits of their labor? Simply because they are defenceless, and custom has, from time immemorial, classed them with slaves and servants."

In Spark's "Life of Washington," is a letter to Thos. Stone, in which the General says: "I do not scruple to declare that, if I had a voice in your legislature, it would have been given decidedly against a paper emission. The wisdom of man, in my humble opinion, can not devise a plan by which the credit of paper money would be long supported; consequently depreciation keeps pace with the quantity of the emission, and articles for which it is exchanged rise in a greater ratio than the sinking value of the money. An evil equally great is the door it immediately opens for speculation, by which the least designing, and, perhaps, most valuable part of community are preyed upon by the more knowing and crafty speculators."

John Q. Adams says: "As to bankers, there is but little difference between them and the counterfeiter. If I should give any preference, the counterfeiter is the best, for neither of them ever expected nor intended to pay their notes. The banker, more bold and daring, robs the people under cover and pretense of the law; the counterfeiter, more diffident and unassuming, robs the people without law."

Daniel Webster, in 1812, in the U. S. Senate, said: "Of all the contrivances for cheating the laboring classes of mankind, none is so effectual as that which deludes with paper money! It is the most perfect expedient ever invented for fertilizing the rich man's field by the sweat of the poor man's brow."

Thomas Jefferson, in a letter to J. Taylor, said: "The system of banking we have both equally and ever reprobated. I contemplate it as a blot left in our institutions, which, if not corrected, will end in their *destruction*, which is already hit by gamblers in corruption, and is sweeping away in its progress the fortunes and morals of our citizens. And I sincerely believe with you, that bank establishments are more dangerous than standing armies."

Andrew Jackson, in a letter to M. Dawson, in 1840, said: "A national paper currency is a great curse to any people, and a curse to the laborer of any country, for its depreciation falls on the working classes."

Wm. H. Harrison, in a speech made at Dayton, said: "I am not a bank man; I was once, and they cheated me out of every dollar I had placed in their hands."

Wm. Pitt said: "Let the Americans adopt their funding system, and go on with their banking institutions, and their boasted independence will be a mere phantom."

It may seem strange to many why American liberty is imaginary; it is so, unless it means every man to get all he can of his neighbor's labor, and keep it. It is self-evident that the man who is possessed of abundant riches has not earned them, and the causes that made him rich will make riches universal, if men will turn the money into other channels. We say of a slave he is not a freeman, because others get his toil, and leave him a very small share.

What shall we say of a community that gives a few the privilege of issuing millions of money, which gets the labor of others when issued, and the people pay every year for its use $40,000,000? This is a large sum and would find 80,000 homes at a cost of $500 each. This was brought about in this manner. Soon after the Revolution, the State Legislatures gave bank charters to a favored few at the expense of the many. The banks were required by law to have a third of their issues in gold. Every ten years there have been "runs" on the bank. When the gold was gone then came suspension, which means merchants and others who owe the banks must come and pay. The merchant sells his soap, sugar, hats, shoes, and clothes for the suspended money, which he is glad to get. The people are glad to get these things. They are what they work for. Society has now no money, which brings misery to the daily laborer, to those who are in debt, or have taxes to pay.

The Guernsey Times says: "In Muskingum the sheriff, in 1842, sold at auction a wagon for $5.50; ten hogs at six and a quarter cents each; two horses (said to be worth sixty dollars each) for four dollars; two cows for one dollar each; and a barrel of sugar for $1.50. In Pike County, Missouri, the sheriff sold three horses for $1.50 each; five cows, two steers, and a calf for $3.25; twenty sheep for $2.70; twenty-four hogs for twenty-five cents; eight hogsheads of tobacco for $5.00; three stacks of hay for seventy-five cents." Henry Clay tells us, in 1837 the people lost in four years by bank failures and depreciation of property $782,000,000, or one-sixth of the property of the Union. The losses of the country, in 1858, by bank failures was nearly the same. By the periodical revulsions we have had for ninety years, or the losses or changes that have occurred, one part of the community has lost $2,000,000,000. To make this subject plainer, we will suppose a person has property to the amount of $1,000, and he owes $100; when his property is sold at auction, and the property sells for $100, it involves a great loss. The person who purchased the property, may have earned his money by 100 days' labor; the other has lost what may have cost him a 1,000 days' labor. The human mind can not tell or describe how this land has been blighted by banks of discount, which tempt men to run in debt. To the bankers, for encouraging these treacherous institutions, the people will have paid in ninety years $1,000,000,000.

Suppose a laborer earns in one year $500, and he saves half of it for sickness and age, in two years he has saved $500; this will keep him two years. If by an inundation of paper money the commodities of life become twice as high, he has only what will keep him one year. This man has labored a day, and he ought to exchange it so as to get a day's labor from another laborer. To prevent this is an injury. The issues of the late war have affected those who live by incomes. The money received from interest has not purchased half as much as before. The plan of many of the Democrats is to issue more paper money, to pay the national debt. This will enable a person to pay his debts with half the labor. A person sells two barrels of flour for ten dollars, and lends the money, when he gets his money,

back again it will only purchase one barrel of flour. We
can judge a person if he is rich by the position he assumes.
If a man has plenty of money at interest, he will want paper
and gold money alike in value, so that he can purchase
much with the interest. If a person is in debt he will favor
a flood of paper money so that he can pay his debts easily
At the present time (1868), the currency is all paper, and it
is to be hoped paper money will never again be founded on
gold. The past shows how dangerous is a currency based
on gold, it rises and falls, causing the fortunes and happiness of men be very uncertain.

What better money can we make than by pledging houses
and lands to the authorities. It can be well secured and save
runs on the banks, and then we will have a uniform currency. In Franklin's boyhood books and papers were not
plentiful. A favorite way to obtain knowlege was by debate. Franklin started this question: "Is the emission of
paper money safe?" In 1729, he wrote an essay on paper
money. The State of Pennsylvania acted on his thoughts;
and issued £15,000, then £30,000. In 1736, the assembly issued £800,000, or $4,000,000. The money was
loaned to the borrowers from a loan office.

Five persons were made trustees of the loan office, under
whose care and direction the bills or notes were printed;
they were of various denominations, from twenty shillings
to one shilling; this created no necessity for much silver
money. The trustees took an oath, and gave security for
the due and faithful execution of their office; they were to
lend out the bills on real security for double that amount.
The borrowers were to pay the sum in sixteen years, one
sixteenth was to be paid every year with interest; the principal was loaned out again to others, and the interest was
applied to the expenses of the State. The trustees were

taken from different parts of the State, and were to continue in office four years, and to account to the committee of the assembly. At the expiration of the term they were to give up all moneys and securities into the hands of their successors before their bonds and securities could be discharged. This money was in use up to 1774.

A writer of this period says: "Paper money thus lent upon interest will create gold and silver in principal, while the interest becomes a resource that pays the *charges of the government*. This currency is the stream which converts all into gold that is washed by it. It is upon this principle that the wisdom and virtue of the assembly of Pennsylvania established an office for the emission of paper money by loans."

Adam Smith says: "The government of Pennsylvania without amassing any treasure, invented a method of lending, not money indeed, but what is equivalent to money to its subjects, by advancing to private people, at interest, and upon land security, paper bills of credit, and transferable from hand to hand like bank notes, and declared by an act of assembly to be a legal tender in all payments. It raised a moderate revenue toward defraying an annual expense of $22,000. Pennsylvania was always moderate in her emissions of paper money, which never sunk below the value of coin."

Franklin states that, "The colony of Massachusetts gave bills of credit, bearing interest, for which the people loaned coin, and afterward passed the bills. He calls it convenient money, bearing interest while in the pocket, and when passed the interest was calculated."

The citizens of Pittsburg, in 1847, or near that time, built water-works; the corporation got a note-plate and printed money, which paid the workmen for their labor and circulated as money. These notes were the same in appearance as other bank notes; there was written on them, "The city will receive this one dollar in payment for taxes." If the water-works cost $100,000, and capitalists had built them, they would have done it with credit paper money. For the use of this capital the citizens would pay $7,000 annually, and pay it for generations till the principal was paid. This $100,000 cost to print it $200, and why should the citizens of this city pay annually $7,000? Are not 100,000 citizens as rich as 100 bankers, and can they not give security to their own money? Why should these industrious iron-workers be guilty of the absurd folly of keeping a parcel of fellows in idleness for supplying some paper money? These notes could be carried in to pay water-rents, and be destroyed, or they can be re-issued to pay teachers or city officers. In this way the city can have money.

In olden times cities and governments did more for the people than is done now. Men are degenerating. The city of Hamburg, to maintain its poor, opened a pawn-broker's shop and took goods as pledges. The city, in one year made $160,000. The sale of unredeemed goods increased this fund.

If we had such patriots as Franklin, men who loved the country, who had some regard for the humble poor, and who did not look on them as things to live on, such men would give us a currency that would not fatten idlers to riot on the labor of others. Why should not the currency pay the expenses as it has done? Good men yet are to be found; they are modest, unassuming, and never seek for office. There are many who would serve the State with pride and fidelity as loan commissioners.

What a happiness it would be if the hard-working, wood-chopping, land-clearing farmer could borrow money, on easy terms. How he could furnish his farm! There is an other source of secure and profitable lending—it is the towns that want to make improvements, and can give the taxes as security. These two—land and taxes—a great State can loan on with great safety.

The county of Miami, State of Ohio, had, in 1854, made improvements to the amount of $94,000. First, a union school, at a cost of $13,000; then a poor-house, at the cost of $20,000; then a jail, at the cost of $30,000; and then another union school-house, at a cost of $33,000. These improvements were made in the space of ten years, for which the officers agreed to give as interest $9,400. This interest would keep twenty men in idleness. If the State had loaned its notes to this county it would have the interest to pay its expenses. In 1857, the authorities of the town of Cohoes built water works at a cost of $60,000, for the use of which they agreed to give annually $4,200, and give it for twenty years, the length of time agreed on. In this time the citizens of Cohoes will have paid $84,000, in interest, which will make the water-works cost $144,000. It would have been wise to let the State have this interest on notes it could issue. It would be wiser still to have built them a little every year.

In one year the United States had a surplus revenue. It was divided among the States. The State of New York received as its share $3,580,494, which loan commissioners lent out for the benefit of the school fund. The State of Connecticut sold the lands of the Western Reserve, and for three-fourths of a century has loaned the money for the benefit of schools. This proves a great State can become lenders of money.

The governor of Ohio, in his message for 1857, says the amount of the state and county taxes were $9,000,000, and the people of the State of Ohio on $221,000,000 pay interest.   The debts of the State are $16,402,095; cities, counties, towns are $15,000,000; recorded mortgages are $50,000,000; and railroad debts are $50,000,000." The interest is $15,000,000. This will make the whole nation to pay $150,000,000, interest for their debts. This will keep many from productive labor, who could if they were farmers find one-third of the nation in food. There are some debts on which the State might loan.

Jay Cooke, a famous banker, has made enormous wealth; he has a summer house among the lakes worth $10,000. His home cost more than $1,000,000, and is filled with the treasures of art, and all the creations of modern luxury. This man has the arrogance and the insolence to tell us in his pamplet that "a national debt is a national blessing." This book will rank with "Taxation is not Tyranny."

Andrew Jackson, says: "The paper system being founded on public confidence, and having of itself no intrinsic value, it is liable to great and sudden fluctuations, thereby rendering property insecure, and the wages of labor unsteady and uncertain. The corporations which create the paper money can not be relied on to keep the circulating medium uniform in amount. In times of prosperity, when confidence is high, they are tempted by prospects of gain, or by the influence of those who hope to profit by it, to extend the issues of paper beyond the bounds of discretion and the reasonable demands of business. And when these issues have been pushed from day to day, until public confidence is at length shaken, then a reaction takes place, and they immediately withdraw the credits they have given, and suddenly curtail their issues, and produce an unexpected and ruinous contraction of the circulating medium, which is felt by the whole community. The banks, by this means, save themselves, and the mischievous consequences of their imprudence or cupidity are visited on the public. Nor does the evil stop here. These ebbs and flows in the currency, and these indiscreet extensions of credit, naturally engender a spirit of speculation injurious to the habits and character of the people. We have already seen its effects in the wild spirit of speculation in the public lands, and various kinds of stock, which, within the last year or two, seized upon such multitudes of our citizens, and threatened to pervade all classes of society, and to withdraw their attention from the sober pursuits of honest industry.

"It is not by encouraging this spirit that we shall best preserve public virtue, and promote the true interest of our country. If the currency continues as exclusively paper as it is now, it will foster the desire to obtain wealth without labor; it will multiply the number of dependents on bank favors; the temptations to obtain money at any sacrifice will become strong, and lead to corruption, which will find its way into your public councils, and *destroy*, at no distant day, the purity of your government. Some of the evils of this system, press with hardship upon a class least able to bear them. A part of this currency often becomes worthless." This list of the evils of paper money, should warn us never to found paper money on gold, but on houses and lands.

Harper's Magazine, April, 1858, says: "The result of our commercial revulsion has been a wholesale confiscation of property, and had it been done by government would have led to civil war." Robberies are among the risks of bank capital.

CHAPTER IX.

A CENTURY OF INVENTIONS.

WANT A MOTIVE FOR INVENTION—UNIVERSAL RICHES WILL PREVENT INVENTION—ARKWRIGHT'S POVERTY AND INVENTION—WATT'S IMPROVEMENT ON THE STEAM ENGINE.

"Invent or perish."—MICHELET.

VISITING a State fair and seeing there the contrivances to shorten human labor should convince the most unbelieving that the hours of toil can be shortened. What an arena of industry is there! Who can contemplate such a scene without emotion? Here are monuments to plenty, and the evidence that famine shall no more afflict the land. Such a scene would lead us to suppose that this plenty is universal. It is not so. Cowper, when speaking of the plenty in England, makes one exception. This painful contrast is to be seen here. He says:

> " From east to west, no sorrow can be found ;
> Or only what in cottages confined
> Sighs unregarded to the winds."

There is evidence in this fair that the inequalities of life will some day or other cease. The changes in the people's amusements indicate this. The Romans could find pleasure in their gladiatorial shows, which were scenes of cruelty. The Middle Ages had their mock battles and single combats, called jousts and tournaments. Henry the VIII

(193)

paid a visit to the French king. Beneath a canopy of gold cloth the two sovereigns met. The gay pageantry displayed on that occasion has obtained for the place of meeting the name of "The Field of the Cloth of Gold." The time of Elizabeth had its field sports, bull and bear baiting, which consisted in setting dogs on these poor animals. We have cause for congratulation that these scenes have passed away, and are superseded by something more ennobling, the sight of which is calculated to provoke a spirit that will do some good to ourselves and others.

The youth of this land have the story of "Aladdin and his Wonderful Lamp." The story says that Aladdin had only to rub his lamp, when, whatever he wished for would appear, be it a beautiful mansion, a mine of gold or jewels, or a garden full of enchanting scenery. The scenes in the State fair are a reality—no conjuration is there. The creations of the brains of men are wonderful.

Franklin said he would like to see the time come when a person could twist more than one thread at a time. He lived to see one hundred spun by a single person. At the present time a man and two boys can tend 300 spindles, going with three times the speed of a hand-spindle. Since 1760, a community of workers each have received machinery to assist them to be equivalent to forty persons.

A State fair is a wonderful display of man's skill. In one part of this arena of industry may be seen the stationary engine, doing the labor of ten, perhaps a hundred horses. How quietly it performs its work ; it never murmurs or tires. It is the inanimate slave of man. A few years ago wheat was beaten out of the straw by tying two sticks together, and then throwing up the wheat in the air and letting the wind blow away the chaff. In this manner a person could thrash and clean twelve bushels in a day. A thrashing ma-

machine attended by seven persons will thrash and clean 700 bushels of wheat in a day. In a State fair it is not uncommon to see attached to the pulleys, which are moved by the engine, three thrashing machines, mills to grind sugar-canes, wheat into flour, clay for bricks, and draining tiles. In addition to all this, the engine makes shingles, saws logs, and splits wood.

In another part of this arena of industry may be seen machines, whose moving power is horses. A machine is to be seen that rakes hay, and lifts it into the wagon. A load is gathered in five minutes. Another contrivance lifts with a horse, rope, and tackle the load into the barn. The machinery that has been invented during the last twenty years for saving hay, cuts off two-thirds of the labor in the hot part of the year. In the fair is exhibited a huge saw six feet in diameter; the teeth are six inches wide. With this a strong man and horse can saw or trench in the soil 100 rods in a day. This saves the labor of ten persons. The arches or tiles to put in this drain, are made by machinery in a rapid manner.

Seed drilling machines are very numerous and get in the seed at the proper period. A person having these has eight laborers to work for him. Numerous mowing machines are to be seen beautifully polished. One of these can cut down more wheat or grass than ten men. Gang plows have been invented on which men can ride, and do twice or three times as much as with a common plow. Steam plows have been invented, one of which has plowed 400 acres of land in a season. Corn cultivators have been invented. With the aid of these a single man can cultivate sixty acres of corn. These implements were unknown a century ago. Time would fail to tell the wonders seen in a State fair. It is a scene which the nations of antiquity, the Saxons and Normans never saw.   This scene is an invention of modern times.   The fruits and vegetables displayed there were unknown four centuries ago, and have been collected by enterprising navigators, who have given us a more pleasing variety of food.

If Franklin could say in his time "Want and misery would be unknown if all would work at something useful," what would he say now?   The time has now come, when the laborer should work for himself only and it will result in the non-workers going to work, who will make such an abundance, that men will not torture their brains making labor-saving machines.

That want leads to invention may be proved by Richard Arkwright, who was the youngest of thirteen children of ignorance and poverty.   He never was at school.   He was a barber and rented a basement, and put out this as a sign,

A barber on the opposite side of the street put out this sign,

COME TO THE SUBTERRANEAN BARBER
AND BE SHAVED FOR A HALFPENNY.

Men are selfish and avaricious.   They try to get each other's work away, which is not right when we consider how much land there is unoccupied.   Arkwright was forced to quit the business and go to the country and collect hair for the wig-maker.   His mind seems to have been drawn out to schemes for the abridgment of labor by machinery, from which no change of time or place could divert him from making plans or models of what his brain conceived. This sometimes interfered with his business, and his wife, convinced that he would starve his family by scheming, when he ought to be shaving, in a fit of anger destroyed his models, and annihilated his prospects for *wealth* and *fame*. It is said he never forgave the ruthless deed, but separated from her at once, and nothing would induce him to live with her again.

His thoughts had often been drawn to mechanical inventions. This led him to abandon his hair speculations, and give his mind to the construction of a machine for spinning cotton by rollers. His model was patented in 1796. At fifty, he applied himself to the study of grammar, and to improvement in writing and spelling. He amassed a large fortune, and the order of knighthood was conferred on him by George III.

Arkwright substituted rollers in place of human fingers. Before he made his machinery 50,000 people obtained their bread by working by hand ; after his invention, 2,000,000 of persons got their bread from cotton. This must include the families of the cotton-workers. The importation of cotton before the invention was annually 2,000,000 lbs. now it is 500,000,000 lbs. There was 50,000 hand-spindles, now 12,000,000 machine spindles. The annual value of cotton goods ninety years ago was £200,000. The value now is £34,000,000. This invention has made cotton cloth five-pence a yard. It was ten times this sum. The people use now twenty-six yards where one was used. The annual consumption is 700,000,000 yards. The quantity sent abroad is 560,000,000 yards. In 1825, the spinning machinery of Lancashire was computed to be equal to 21,320,000 of

18

hand-spinners.   India is the home of cotton and cotton cloth, and was obtained from there before its introduction into England and America.   It has been among us one hundred years.

In 1540, Bernhard Palissey, of France, spent sixteen years trying to make enameled pottery. His motive was "to provide a handsome *support* for his wife and children." He was ambitious to be the prince of potters. He succeeded, after years of sorrow, difficulty, and trial.   To procure chemicals his family suffered for the comforts of life.   To feed his furnaces, he burnt the palings surrounding his house, and even its doors.   He endured the ridicule of his friends, the reproaches of his wife, and the persecutions of his king, whose minister put him to death for his Protestant religion. The king, to save him, wanted him to change his religion. Said Palissey, "I can die."

Charles Goodyear the inventor of India-rubber cloth, or enameled cloth, and many other things of this material, for many years suffered the bitterness of poverty while inventing. His wife used to often say: "Charles, you must provide better for me or I will go home." His answer was, "A little while longer and we shall have splendid wealth."   It came; he triumphed.

James Watt is another example of the impelling power of poverty, and the desire to attain those pleasures that the rich gather around them.   He was a mathematical instrument-maker.   He removed to Edinburgh.   He was not allowed to start a shop there, for the reason that he had not learned his trade in that city.   He was allowed a room in the college, where he was called to repair a Savery steam-engine.   While doing this work he thought he could make an improvement which he did, and it brought the engine into varied and extensive uses.   Previous to this time the

engine was used for pumping out mines. Had Watt been
rich he would have had no motive to make the improvements he did.   There is such an abundance in the world,
and the productive powers of man is so great, that riches,
some time or other will be universal.   Riches will be universal when universal labor prevails.

Says a writer, in Harper's "History of Inventions:"
"The power of steam far surpasses all the fabulous wonders
which imaginative genius have attributed to the genii of the
East, or the invisible fairies who are made to perform such
marvels in old English legends.   The very elements are
conquered by this mighty agency; both wind and tide may
oppose, but still the vessel plunges onward in spite of all
opposition, paddling against breeze and billow, like some
extinct monster of the early world, armed with those sweeping fins that fill the mind of the geologist with wonder.
This new-born giant thrusteth his iron arm into the bowels of the earth, and throws up its treasures by thousands
of tons, emptying the dark mine of its wealth, then leaping
on the surface, melting with its hot breath the weighty
metal, and rolling and beating it into massive bars.   As if
struck by the wand of a magician, the iron vessel springs
out of the shapeless mass of ore, by the power of steam is
launched upon the deep, and stands, as if in mockery, beside its oak-built rival, every rib of which was the growth
of a long century.   The very leaves that rustle in our hands
while we read were formed by it, and every letter in the
large sheet of daily news bears the imprint of its majestic
footstep.

"Even printing, the grandest of all human inventions, was
but in comparison the slow copying of the clerk, beside this
ready-writer, which now throws off its thousands of perfect
impressions within the brief space of a single hour.   It

grinds the bread we eat, and gives all the variety and beauty to the garments we wear. It stamps the wreath of flowers upon the flimsy foundation of cotton. And yet the whole of this moving power can be stopped by a child."

Dr. Lardner says: "A pint of water may be evaporated by two ounces of coal, into two hundred and sixteen gallons of steam, which will lift thirty-seven tons a foot high. A pound of coke (charred coal), burned in a locomotive, will evaporate five pints of water, and draw two tons on a railroad one mile in two minutes.

"A train of cars, weighing eighty tons, and containing 240 passengers, drawn by an engine, have gone from Liverpool to Birmingham, a distance of ninety-five miles, in four hours and a quarter, consuming two tons of coke, the cost of which is two and a half pounds ($12\frac{1}{2}$). To carry these, twenty stage coaches would be required. It would take 600 horses to accomplish this journey in twelve hours.

"In the draining of the Cornish mines the economy of fuel is attended too, and coal is there made to do more work than elsewhere. A bushel of coal raises usually 40,000 tons of water a foot high."

Nations that have no machinery have no coal fires. The mines require constant pumping to prevent them from filling with water. The same engine that pumps out the mines lifts up the coal to the pit's mouth. The railroads take coal to every part of England. A single blast of powder will detach more coal than a laborer can loosen in a week. Captain Thomas Savery devised, in 1698, a machine for drawing water from the mines.

The French assert that the Marquis of Worcester took the idea of the steam engine from Solomon De Caus, who published a book at Frankfort, in 1615, on steam as a power. A letter teaches us he went to Cardinal Richelieu who dismissed him as a madman without hearing him. He still importuned the Cardinal, who ordered him to prison. He had been there three years and a half, when the Marquis saw him. De Caus said, "I am not mad! I have made a discovery that will enrich any country that puts it in operation." His lordship returned, sad and thoughtful, and said: "He is indeed mad; misfortune and captivity have destroyed forever his reason. You have made him mad; when you cast him into this dungeon you cast there the greatest genius of his time, and, in my country, instead of being imprisoned. he would have been loaded with riches."

The Marquis of Worcester, living during the civil wars of Charles I and his parliament, took sides with the king, and lost his fortune, and was imprisoned in Ireland. He managed to escape to France. He became a secret agent afterward in England for the king; he was detected and put in the Tower. When cooking his dinner there, he observed that the steam forced upward the lid of his pot. It occurred to him that this power might be applied to useful purposes. When he got his liberty he went to work and made a machine, which he described in his book.

The steam-engine is a succession of improvements from the time of De Caus to the time of Watt. Those who have made changes on the engine are the Marquis of Worcester, Savery, Papin, Newcomen, Brindley, and Smeaton. Their contrivances seem to have been how to get the piston-rod back again after the steam had lifted it up. This was done by a boy who opened valves or cocks. To give the reader an idea how the engine of these men worked, take an iron barrel and partially fill it with water, under the bottom of the barrel kindle a fire, and you make steam; on the top open a valve and the steam escapes. To get service from this escaping steam construct another iron barrel,

closed at one end and a rim on the other, smooth and turned straight within.   In this barrel you want a movable,
flat, edge-turned piece of metal.   If you let in steam at one
end its expansibility lifts up the sliding plate, till it is stopped by the rim.   A contrivance is used to cut off the supply
of steam.   If water is thrown on the outside of the barrel
containing steam, the steam will become condensed, or become water again; this leaves a vacuum and causes the flat
piece of metal to fall down; by the pressure of the atmosphere.   That the atmosphere has power is evident, when
set in motion it throws down trees and houses, and moves
great ships.   When in a state of rest the atmospheric weight
is fifteen pounds to the square inch.   To reduce this principle to utility, you must put a rod in this moving piece of
iron and fasten it to a pump-handle; steam will force up
the handle, atmospheric pressure bring it down.   This engine required a boy to open cocks, and force water into
the cylinder to condense the steam.

" Humphrey Potter, a mere lad, who was occupied in attending to the cocks of an atmospheric engine, becoming
anxious to escape from the monotonous drudgery imposed
upon him, ingeniously contrived the adjustment of a number
of strings, which, being attached to the beam of the engine,
opened and closed the cocks with the most perfect regularity and certainty, thus rendering the machine totally independent of manual superintendence.   The contrivance
of Potter was soon improved upon.   The whole apparatus
was subsequently, about the year 1718, brought into complete working order by an engineer named Beighton.

" Watt's first improvement was an alteration of the mode
of condensing the steam.   Instead of using the method described, he had a condenser attached to the cylinder, and
he still further improved upon it by surrounding it with a

tank of cold water, which was drawn from an adjoining re-
servoir by the pump of the engine. An improvement effected in the steam-engine, was the custom adopted by
Watt, of closing the top of the cylinder, the piston being
made to work through a neck called a stuffing-box, which
was rendered steam-tight by being lined with tow saturated
with grease, which rubbed and greased the rod and made it
move easily.

"By this alteration the elastic force of steam was used,
as it is now, to impel the piston downward as well as upward. The machine hence became a steam-engine instead
of an atmospheric one, with that continuous action from
which so much benefit has been enjoyed by this simple
device.

"Notwithstanding these important advantages, Watt and
Boulton were compelled to make large sacrifices to bring
their engines into use, as will be seen by the proposition
of Mr. Boulton to the Carron Company:—'We contract to
direct the making of an engine. * * * * * We do not
aim at profits in engine-building, but shall take out our profits in the saving of fuel; so that if we save nothing, we
shall take nothing. We will guarantee that the engine so
constructed shall raise at least 20,000 cubic feet of water
twenty-four feet high, with each hundred weight of coal
burned.'"

Those who obtained these engines commuted the saving
of the coal, which Watt's engine saved over the others, to
an annual rent. The lessees of the Chacewater mine paid
an annual rent-charge for three engines $12,000. This
inventor had a splendid rural home, and spent the last years
of his life in literary pursuits. In Handsworth Church he
is represented sitting in a chair, with compass and paper, in
the act of drawing. His fame will be as enduring as the

the marble in which his effigy is chiseled. He has given his name to the steam-engine that may never be laid aside. We can form some conception of the magnitude of his gift to man, if we will try and raise coal by hand. An opening is made in the earth, it soon fills up with water; a windlass when turned with human strength, will some time or other draw out all the water; then the digging is resumed, after much lifting of mud and water the coal-vein is reached. The future labor is now to lift up the coal and water, it may be done with horse-power, it takes much human labor to procure food for the horses. Without steam-power the bushel of coal will be equal or worth a day's labor. Now a day's work of a common laborer will get twenty bushels of coal.

The fame of the inventions and experiments that had been made in France and Scotland, in navigating with steam, induced Fulton to cross the ocean to get these inventions on our long rivers. In 1775, John Fitch made a steam-boat, with which he made eleven voyages from Philadelphia to a town distant eleven miles. Washington and his companions were invited to ride in the boat. The maker of this boat was poor, his machinery was badly made, and he was unable to repair his boat.

Fulton got Watt and Boulton to make his machinery, with money obtained from Livingston, who was an embassador to France. Both saw on the Seine a discarded steam-boat. Unitedly they perfected a steam-boat on the Hudson in 1807. That Fulton was poor may be inferred from this narrative. A gentleman from New York was in Albany when the *Clermont* first arrived there. He found that the boat was a general object of wonder, but few were willing to trust themselves on it as a means of conveyance. He, however, determined to go in this boat to New York.

In the cabin he found a plain gentleman, quite alone, and engaged in writing. This was Fulton, and this conversation took place:—

Stranger. Do you intend to return to New York with this boat?

Fulton. We mean to try and get back with her, sir.

Stranger. Can I have a passage?

Fulton. Yes, if you choose to take your *chance* with us.

Six dollars was paid as the passage money. With his eye fixed on this money, which he retained in his open hand, Fulton remained so long motionless, that the stranger supposed he had miscounted the sum, and asked, "Is that right, sir?" This roused the projector from his reverie, and, as he looked up, the big tear was brimming in his eye, and his voice faltered as he said—"Excuse me, sir, but memory was busy as I contemplated that this is the first pecuniary reward that I have ever received for all my exertions for adapting steam to navigation. I would gladly commemorate the event over a bottle of wine with you. I am too poor for that now, yet I trust we shall meet again when this will not be so." They did meet again after four years, and the wine was not spared.

Fulton observes: "When I was building my first steamboat at New York the project was viewed with indifference and contempt or as a visionary scheme. My friends, indeed, were civil, but they were shy. They listened with patience to my explanations, but with a settled cast of incredulity on their countenances. As I had occasion to pass daily to and from the building-yard while my boat was in progress, I have often loitered unknown near the idle groups of strangers, gathered in little circles, and heard various inquiries as to the object of this new vehicle. The language was uniformly that of scorn, or sneer, or ridicule. The

19

loud laugh often rose at my expense; the dry jest; the wise calculation of losses and expenditures, the dull but endless repetition of the Fulton folly.   Never did a single encouraging remark, a bright hope, or a warm wish cross my path. Silence itself was but politeness veiling its doubts, or hiding its reproaches."

Fulton's biographer says: "Before the boat had made the progress of a quarter of a mile the greatest unbeliever was converted!   The man, who while he had looked on the expensive machine, thanked his stars that he had more sense than to waste his money on such idle schemes, changed the expression of his features as the boat moved from the wharf and gained her speed; the jeers of the ignorant, who had neither sense nor feeling enough to repress their contemptuous ridicule, were silenced for the moment by a vulgar astonishment which deprived them of the power of utterance, till the triumph extorted from the incredulous multitude which crowded the shores, was shouts and acclamations of congratulation and applause!

"The whole of the progress up the Hudson was a continued triumph.   Those on board of the several vessels which she met looked with astonishment at the progress of a ship, which appeared to be a thing instinct with life rather than a fabric moved by mechanical means.   It was said that to them she had a most terrific appearance.   The first steamers used pine wood for fuel, which sent forth a column of ignited vapor many feet above the flue, and whenever the fire was stirred, a galaxy of sparks flew off, and in the night had a very beautiful appearance.   Notwithstanding the wind and tide were adverse to its approach, they saw with astonishment the vessel was rapidly coming toward them; and when it came so near that the noise of the machinery and paddles was heard, the crews in some instances, shrunk beneath their decks from the terrific sight, and left their vessels to go on shore, while others besought Providence to protect them from the approach of the monster, which was marching on the tide, and lighting its path by the fire which it vomited."

Mr. Stephens, of Hoboken, soon after this launched a steam-vessel which was taken to the Delaware by the way of the ocean.   His son improved on Fulton's models, and gave to vessels which he built that beauty of form they now possess, and a capability of cutting through the water at the speed of thirteen miles an hour.   From that time steam-boats have multiplied, till all large rivers are studded with them.   The Marquis of Worcester tells us, in 1655, in an obscure statement of a vessel moved by steam, "which should, if need be, pass London Bridge against the current at low water."   Twenty years after Captain Savery tried to urge a vessel by means of an atmospheric engine.   He had no success.   At the same time, Denis Papin, a French philosopher, tried to prove in theory that steam would move a boat.   Half a century, later, Jonathan Hulls took out a patent for moving vessels by steam.   His plans failed.

At length, in 1774, the Comte D'Auxiron, a French nobleman, succeeded in the construction of a boat, which, when tried on the Seine, near Paris, moved against the stream, though slowly, the engine being of insufficient power. In his efforts he was assisted by a countryman of his, named Perier, who, in the year following placed a steam boat on the river, with an engine of one-horse power. His means were also insufficient. The Marquis de Jouffroy, on the Saone, at Lyons, tried a boat which excited much attention. The dreadful disturbances in France compelled him to leave his native land. On his return, in 1796, he learned that M. Des Blancs had obtained his plans and got them patented.	The government would give no redress to the marquis.	Robert Fulton was at that time experimenting in France, and had adopted a series of float-boards, that were fastened perpendicular on an endless chain, which was stretched over two wheels; these were fastened on each end of the boat; the working of this chain was the same as a belt over two pulleys; a part of these float-boards were always out of the water.	Fulton afterward used paddles. Des Blancs complained of the infringement on his patent; Fulton showed him the difference between the two machines, and offered him a share of the gains, if he would bear part of the expense.	No agreement was made.

In 1784, Rumsey was the rival of Fitch.	He made a steam-boat on the Potomac.	The coal used was half a bushel in an hour.	When the boat was loaded, with three tons' weight, its speed was four miles an hour.	In 1793, Rumsey went to England; assisted by others he had a vessel on the Thames that went against the wind and tide at the rate of four miles an hour.

In 1787, Wm. Symington made, in Edinburgh, a boat that attained five miles in an hour.	In 1788, Mr. Miller had an engine of twelve-horse power made and put in a boat, which caused it to go with a speed of eight miles an hour. Mr. Miller spent a handsome fortune in obtaining this public benefit.	Symington still continued to persevere, and in 1802, he made for Lord Dundas a steam-tug that pulled two vessels containing seventy tons of goods.	Fulton saw the vessels of Symington, and had been on a successful voyage with him in Scotland.	Fulton made notes of every thing that was shown him, and it appears he was let into all of Symington's secrets.	Every-thing connected with steam was explained to Fulton.	Mr. Henry Bell, of Glasgow, was the medium of communication between Fulton and the con-

trivers and improvers of the steamboat. Fulton received
from Mr. Bell drawings of the boat and engines which they
had used. Sometime after Fulton had received these drawings, he wrote to Mr. Bell, to say he had constructed a boat
from them, which prompted his correspondent to turn his
attention to the introduction of steam-navigation in his own
country. He set to work and made a model, which he put
into the hands of John Wood & Co., who built for him a
boat of forty tons burthen, with an engine of three-horse
power. In 1812, Mr. Hutchinson had a boat made with an
engine of ten-horse power, that carried one hundred passengers to Greenock, twenty-seven miles, in three hours.

The history of steam-navigation is a long series of experiments on which labor, ingenuity, money, and time,
have been spent, impoverishing and making the heart sick
by the failure of the plans of those who engaged in the enterprise of giving the world steamboats.

If we could visit an English monastery in the olden time,
we should see the patient monks sitting at their desks, with
ink, pens, brushes, gold, and colors, adding letter to letter,
and word to word, in thick, angular, black-letter characters,
from month to month, never ceasing except to eat, sleep, and
attend prayers. Their work is beautiful, and will, when
seen, call for our admiration. These written books were to
survive when the hand that wrote them was paralyzed in
death. It was not running writing as is used now. Every
letter had many strokes, or it may have been done with a
brush, and it may have taken six or ten times the labor that
writing now requires. The initial letters were highly orna-
mented with flourishes. This was, no doubt, done by those
who had the taste for it. Where *Italic letters* are used now,
the manuscript letters were done in red ink, which are as
bright as they were five hundred years ago. The parch-

ment was as fine and as thin as paper. It was very smooth, uniform, and white. It was made from skins.

This method of communicating knowledge was confined to a few. The cheap and rapid multiplication of books has been accomplished by applying steam-power to printing. In ancient times the thinking men got a glimpse at printing. The Romans could take movable type and stamp clay. For centuries before the Christian era, the Chinese used, no doubt, blocks or pages of characters. The printing of playing-cards was done before printing words or thoughts ; this may have done much toward suggesting the idea of letter-making, or movable type.

However much printing may do to record the deeds of nations, or keep from forgetfulness the virtues and achievments of men, it has not recorded its own origin, but left it in much obscurity. In 1499, the "Cologne Chronicle," forty-four years from the advent of printing to the world, gathered all it could relating to this wondrous art. The only source from which it could draw its materials was the traditions of men, and from two recorded lawsuits which the inventors of printing had.

John Gansfleisch was born in 1397. When a youth he lived in Mentz, with a family of the name of Guttenberg, whose name he adopted, as it was a custom. He became implicated in one of the insurrections against the nobility, so frequent at that time, and which resulted in the freedom of the commercial classes of Germany. This revolt was not successful, and he went to Strasburg. It is supposed he engaged in the occupation of taking off other's writings from carved blocks. His enterprising intellect was directed to some means of hastening the process. A thought broke upon him, the full development of which was to produce such glorious results. The supposition came on him that if the letters he saw upon the block could be separated from each other, they might be put together again in different positions, and form other words; and thus there would be a power of endless combination with a small stock of materials. How he did this we have no certain means of knowing, as he would keep this discovery to himself.

He returned to Mentz or Mayence, where he met a wealthy goldsmith of the name of Faust; and, together, they entered upon an undertaking to supersede the laborious occupation of the manuscript writer. Between them they hit on the expedient of casting types in metal, it being a more durable substance, and likely to increase their profits. Faust had in his employ a young man of the name of Peter Schoeffer, who suggested the stamping of letters in lead, so that they could be changed or renewed. This was accomplished, and the process of printing obtained. The partnership of these three men was begun in 1440; and was not productive till ten years after.

Letters at first were made of wood, which were not very enduring. Schoeffer discovered a method of molding letters in metal, which so pleased Faust that he gave him his only daughter in marriage. In 1458, Guttenberg retired from the concern from a want of harmony. They completed several works of importance, among them a Bible. Bibles were made so rapidly that these men were said to be in league with the devil. The storming of Mentz, in 1462, by an enemy, scattered the workmen. Printing was commenced in Italy, in 1466; in Paris, in 1469; in London, in 1474; in Massachusetts, in 1639; in Virginia, in 1739, and in Cincinnati, in 1793.

The press was a screw, and made of wood, till the Earl of Stanhope, a nobleman of great ingenuity, and an amateur printer, had an iron lever and press made, in 1790. In this year, W. Nicholson took out a patent for printing books, paper-hangings, calico, etc., on a cylinder, and the motive power was to be steam or water. Lord Camelford, his patron, died, which prevented the machine from being made. Konig, a German, came to England and tried to apply steam-power to a common press, without any success. He then applied himself to cylindrical printing, and succeeded in printing in an hour 1,000 copies. He was attended by two boys. In 1811, the "New Annual Register" was printed by steam. Mr. Nicholson may have helped Konig. He gave his drawings to the public. An agreement was made with Konig to make for the "Times" paper two presses. On the 28th of November, 1814, this paper told its readers, that they were for the first time reading a paper printed by the power of steam.

In order to show how steam-power saves labor, look at "The Cincinnati Commercial." Its owners have to supply to their customers 35,000 daily papers, or near that number. This paper is "set up" by thirty "compositors." On a hand-press two men will throw off 1,000 papers in ten hours. To supply the demand would require thirty-five presses, and 1,000 compositors or type-setters. One set of hands set up the copy. Then it is multiplied thirty-five times for the rest, who set up matter for the presses to work next day. At night the number of papers required are done. The first set of compositors, by having a small "take," need only be half an hour in advance of all the rest.

What mighty results come from steam working for us. After the thirty printers have done their work, four stereotypers take and double it, which is done in this manner: Three sheets of a peculiar kind of paper are pasted together; it is laid on a page of the type, and then beaten gently with a brush till the paper fills up the crevices of the type, the form is laid on a steam-heated stone, a powerful screw presses the soft paper on the face of the type, and in ten minutes it is hardened; this paper sheet is put in a mold, and the melted metal is poured in. The casting is formed so as to fit the cylinder. The Commercial uses two presses, which makes the stereotypers do the labor of thirty compositors. In six hours these four men have cast sixteen pages of the Commercial. If stereotyping were unknown, this paper would require sixty compositors.

The metal pages go to the basement press-room. One of these cylinder presses gives 12,000 impressions in an hour, the other 8,000. If one of the monk scribes could see this revolving printing machine, he would be speechless with wonder for some time. The large machine is thirty-two feet high and forty feet long. It is fed by eight persons. The papers are folded by machinery. A machine will fold 10,000 papers in an hour. The compositors, proof-readers, stereotypers, folders, and pressmen of the Commercial office number, perhaps, sixty persons. These working ten hours a day will produce as much writing as 6,000,000 of the monkish writers. A compositor will set up six of these pages in a day. A writer can do the same amount of writing. A printer can bring to help him machinery to multiply his work to an enormous extent.

The invention of stereotyping is an important one. It is to cast a page of type, so that it will be solid, an eighth of an inch thick. In 1725, Wm. Ged, of Edinburgh, made an arrangement with the University of Cambridge to cast Bibles and Prayer-Books. It received so much opposition from the workmen, that it was discontinued. In 1804, this art was brought into use again. This plan is used for books: The face of the type is oiled, plaster of Paris is mixed with water till it is as thick as cream, then it is poured on the type. To keep it from running off a frame is put around the edge of the page, which makes the plaster to be half of an inch thick. A screw is at each corner of the frame to lift it up. The cast is put in a flat pan, the lid is fastened on; it is put in a cauldron of melted metal. When filled up it is allowed to stand in water till cooled. The plate is shaved on the back, then it is *picked*, which means the bad letters are to be repaired, or others inserted. One molder, one caster, and two others will finish 100 plates in a day.

A cast plate taken from a type page of this book will weigh one pound, and cost fifty-five cents, as wages are high on account of the abundance of paper money. A page of this book in type will weigh seven pounds and will cost $3.85. The type-setting adds fifty cents more to the page. When the pressman makes up the "form," it saves his time to handle only 400 lbs in place of 2,800 lbs. The page of type is liable to be broken, or, lose a part of its letters, the type page requires very careful handling.

Twenty years ago electrotyping was applied to printing. This art takes beeswax and melts it with other substances. By means of heat this wax flows level on a plate, and it is placed on pages of type and wood-engravings; then it is put when cold, under a very powerful press. The impression is put in a trough containing sulphuric acid, in which has been dissolved pieces of copper. A galvanic battery causes the copper to deposit on the wax. The result is an indestructible copper page, or an engraving that is hard and will not wear out like a wood-engraving. This invention has set aside the costly copper engraving. Messrs. O'Ferral and Daniel, of Piqua O., wish to advertise a new agricultural machine; they will send a drawing to a wood-engraver, for an engraving he will charge near $20. The electrotyper will reproduce it for fifty cents a copy, which, when multiplied, can be sent to every paper in the State. The initial letter, head, and ending of these chapters are electrotype engraved.

Machinery, when used on women's shoes, enables a man to sew a pair of soles on in three minutes; and a pair of good "lasting shoes" can be made, by a division of labor, by each workman, in twelve minutes.

Furniture making is not the laborious business it was. A table-frame can be made in twelve minutes, that used to take five hours by hand labor. It is painful work to plane hard and knotted wood. The planing machine takes the cross-grained oak, gnarled ash, curled maple, and tough walnut, and planes them so accurately that it can not be attained by hand. The face of a board, twelve feet in length, can be planed in a minute. It used to take a day to plane, tongue, and groove fifty floor boards; now machinery will do this to 1,000 boards in a day. A century ago a saw-mill was unknown. Timber was sawn by hand over a pit by two persons; one above, the other under the log.

Machinery has been introduced into the tinner's trade. It does many things that once were done by hand. To make a plate, a dipper, a basin, will require much marking, clipping, and soldering; by steam machinery each of these, and other things, too, can be made at a single stroke.

Aided by steam a workman can make in, a day, ten carriage wheels. It will take a day to make a carriage wheel by hand. Plow handles can be made so fast with steam that a man can make 100 smooth, bent handles in a day.

Steam helps the blacksmith in a wonderful manner. He does not have to heat and pound his scraps together, to make a fire-shovel. By railroad his scraps are taken to the rolling-mill, where they are made into iron sheets of various thicknesses, or into bars, round, oval, and flat. These

make the forming of the shovel an easy task.   Steam-power
rolls out the railroad-tie, clips the massive bar, hammers
out the ponderous anchor, and shapes the little nail.

When your ancestors were fighting to be free from England, a noble Englishman invented the moving rest, that
holds the cutting point to the revolving surface of a steam-
boat shaft, that is held in a lathe.   This contrivance saves
the workman from standing and holding his tool to what is
turning.   This gives leisure for reading.   So does the iron
planer, it saves men from "chipping" and "filing."

Steam cuts the edges of books with great rapidity.   Book-
binder's tools twenty years ago were simple.   The hand-
knife would scarcely cut a dozen pages.   Six of these books
are put under the steam-moved knife, and their edges are cut
in an instant.   Steam now makes paper very rapidly.

The New England Indian had no iron.   He peeled birch-
bark off the trees with his hands to make a house.   He burned
down the trees to have fire.   His food and clothes had to be
sufficient, or he would perish from the earth with want.

The living of some of our people is as precarious as the
Indian's.   Steam is making its encroachments, it mixes and
bakes bread, does washing, wood-sawing, and needle-work.
These things make the living laborer feel sad ; he feels he is
not wanted here.   The difficulties of obtaining employment
are increased by doing every thing by steam.   We ought to
live easy and free from care with such a power to work for
us.   Suffering is going to teach the American people how
base rulers have acted to let speculators have public lands.

CHAPTER X.

MERCHANTS AND LAWYERS.

MERCHANTS ARE THE FOUNDERS OF CITIES—A CAUSE OF THE OVERTHROW OF SLAVERY—MERCHANTS ARE TOO NUMEROUS—THE CAUSES WHY LAWYERS EXIST—THE LAWYERS ARE TOO NUMEROUS—An INJURY TO SOCIETY.

"Do you want any needles, any thread, any lace for your cape."-SHAKSPEARE;
"A Lawyer takes your estate from your enemy and keeps it himself."-ERSKINE.

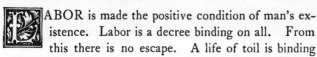ABOR is made the positive condition of man's existence. Labor is a decree binding on all. From this there is no escape. A life of toil is binding on all animated nature, from the stupendous whale that dives in the ocean, to the ephemeral insect whose existence is but for a single day. All men have the same form and appearance: it follows all men ought to labor. As all men are the same in their wants and conditions, all ought to have the same rewards for their labor, and an equal right to the earth, in which are the means of happiness. If a man has to labor for himself and another, he has to labor twice as hard, or twice as long. In civilized society as it progresses, few have to maintain many.

Those who seek for easy work do an injustice to those who do the hard work. It should be borne equally alike by all. There seems to be a disposition among the humble classes to dispense with retail merchants, and to divert the wealth that flows into the coffers of the merchant into their own slender purses. Merchants have exercised a tremen-

(217)

dous influence on this earth. The time may come when the humble workers will break up their power. It can not be that hundreds of thousands of bales of paper are converted into newspapers, and then scattered over the land, each of which contains the wholesale price of the necessaries of life, and not teach the working people to combine to get them at cost price.

Eight centuries ago the merchant in England was despised by the lords of the manors; he went from place to place with his goods, and was often robbed, or paid a large tribute or toll to be exempt from pillage. He settled the towns, and gathered around him the men of toil and sorrow. These became opulent by engaging in manufactures and commerce. The favor of these merchants was courted by kings and lords, to gain the ascendency over each other. These sent deputies to London, who at first sat at the foot of the House of Lords. These deputies were put in a room by themselves. Merchants and manufacturers have become titled lords, and have purchased manors and manor houses. William Pitt came from a family of merchants. The Peel family came from a calico printer, and own the Drayton manor.

Ricardo, a Jewish banker, had a way of "watching the turn and variations of the [money] market." This watching yielded him millions of dollars, with which he bought the estate of two Norman families, Honeywood Yates and a Scudamore. These estates give a rent of $50,000 a year. Holland, one of Baring's partners, has bought an estate of Lord Somers, for $4,000,000. The same lord has sold an estate to a Birmingham banker, of the name of Taylor, for $3,500,000. Mr. Drummond, a banker, bought an estate, pulled down the manor house, and blotted out the memory of the Goodshalls. Mr. Tinkler, a powder-maker, got the old mansion and estate of the Duchess of Marlborough. Mr. Laing, a West Indian merchant, has a place once owned by Sir Wm. Temple. Alexander Baring has the mansion and estate of the Duke of Bolton, and also the noble mansion, park, and estate of Lord Northington. Sir Thomas Baring has succeeded the Russells to the estates of Stratton and Micheldover, which were once owned by King Alfred. It has been computed that the Barings have swallowed up more than thirty of the estates of the small nobility. These sharks that have devoured so many fish, can yet be destroyed by the working people, if they will only act soberly and prudently.

There seems to be a mighty change coming over the English working people: they are forming partnerships to carry on their trades; others are taken into partnerships by their employers, who give them a share of the profits. The greatest change of all is to buy the goods of the wholesale merchant, and then divide them without using merchants. This plan uses no bankers.

The most remarkable case of co-operation is that of the ☞ "Equitable Pioneers' Society of Rochdale." ☜ This is in England, and was commenced in 1844, by some forty poor and humble working-men, with less than ten dollars in their treasury, and an income of two pence in a week from each shareholder—its object being that of pecuniary benefit and improvement of the social and domestic condition of its members. From this simple beginning it has grown to have seven departments, and the capital is now $75,000, and its shares are five dollars, of which $18,000 are in the mill.

The pioneers have incurred no debts and made no losses. Their aggregate dealings have amounted to $1,500,000. They have never had a lawsuit, and nearly a hundred per-

sons are employed by the society. Twelve are employed
in the store. Over the store is a reading-room of papers,
and a library, containing 2,200 books, for the families of the
members. Toad Lane is crowded with cheerful co-oper-
atives; as much as $2,000 are taken in a single day and
night. Says a writer: " It is not the brilliancy of commercial activity, in which the reader will take any interest; it
is the new and improved spirit animating this intercourse of
trade. Buyer and seller meet as friends. Toad Lane, on
Saturday night, is as gay as the Lowth Arcade in London,
and ten times more moral.

"These crowds of hard-working men once never knew
when they had good food; their dinners were adulterated;
their shoes let in water too soon; their coats shone with
devil's dust, and their wives wore calicoes that would not
wash. These now buy like millionaires, and get as pure
food as the lords. They are weaving their own stuffs, making their own shoes, sewing their own garments, grinding
their own wheat, slaughtering their own cattle, buying the
purest sugar, and the best tea and coffee. The finest beasts
of the land waddle down the streets of Rochdale, for the
consumption of flannel weavers and cobblers.

" When did competition give poor men these advantages?
And will any man say the moral character of this people is
not improved under these influences? The teetotalers of
Rochdale acknowledge that the *store* has made more men
sober than all their efforts have done. Husbands, who never
knew what it was to be out of debt, and poor wives, who,
during forty years, never had a six-pence unmortgaged in
their pockets, have now little stores of money sufficient
to build a cottage. In their own market there is no dis-
trust, no deception, no adulteration, and no second price.
Those who serve neither hurry, nor flatter. They have but

one duty to perform—that of giving full weight, fair measure, and a pure article.   In other parts of the town where competition is the principle of trade, all the preaching of Rochdale can not produce effects like these."

The "London Morning Star" gives the following interesting account of a co-operative experiment in England, which has been productive of excellent results, and saves twenty per cent. of family supplies: "Of all the branches of the civil service the Post-office is the most enterprising, and it was in this department a co-operative movement began.   In 1865, the increased dearness of living was pressing severely on those with fixed incomes.   Half a dozen members of the Post-office determined to try whether, by buying in large quantities, and dividing the articles so bought among themselves, they could not get supplied more cheaply than in the ordinary manner.   In order that the purchases be made on the lowest terms, it was settled that all payments should be in ready money.

"The experiment was commenced on a small scale, with fifty pounds of tea.   Each individual received a share of tea, which he paid for.   It was found that a shilling was saved on a pound.   Whole chests were obtained, and the consumers increased rapidly.   Other articles were also obtained.   In the course of a month a little society was at first formed, and, after much anxious deliberation as to whether the expense could be met, a small store-room near the office was obtained, so as to be easy of access.   Wholesale houses agreed to let the members have, for ready money, goods at reduced prices, on condition that they call on certain days, and at stated hours.

"From a small beginning this supply association went on, till it had several rooms, in which were hosiery and stationery.   The amount of the sales in one year was $100,000.
20

There was divided 50,000 lbs of tea, 20,000 lbs of coffee, 180,000 lbs of sugar, 20,000 lbs of candles, 23,000 lbs of rice, 12,000 lbs of soap. This association numbers 4,000 members, and they have physicians, lawyers, brokers, and architects, who charge lower rates to each other. These statements show that, by the co-operation of consumers, the cost of family supplies may be reduced one-fifth. Similar experiments have recently been made in France with the same good results."

There are many American mechanics who earn $1,000 in a year; by adopting this plan $200 a year can be saved. This, in ten years, will give $2,000, which will obtain a fine house and furniture. Americans can see the injustice of slaves supporting masters, they can not see the injustice they do themselves by keeping merchants. In the streets of Cincinnati, in the fall of 1867, men offered the forequarters of beef for five cents a pound, and the hind-quarters for six. In the market beef sold from ten to twenty cents a pound. It seems the Englishman buys the fat ox, hires the butcher to kill him, and distributes the meat. Is not this evidence that the laborer will prevent the merchant from buying any more baronial halls or manor lands.

In 1867, dressed hogs sold for seven and a half cents a pound in Cincinnati. The pork merchants buy these and cure them; the retail dealers charge for this meat in the form of hams, lard, and bacon, from eighteen to twenty-five cents a pound. As the present generation do not know how the people lived thirty years ago, it may not be amiss to tell them. In those days men did not live in cellars and garrets. The cellar was a store-room for meat, apples, and potatoes. The meat, when cured, had a piece of wood attached to it, on which was carved the owner's name, who sent it to the public smoke-house, the owner of which charged two cents for smoking a ham. The wife and children went and gathered a load of apples, or twenty bushels at a cost of twenty cents a bushel. The farmer brought to the town family a winter's supply of potatoes, without the merchant's profits. A barrel of cider cost a dollar, which made vinegar for a year. At the present time the merchant fills his cellar with potatoes, at a cost of a dollar a bushel; they are sold, too often, to the improvident laborer for $1.25 to $2.00 a bushel. This was the price at the gathering time in 1867. In the spring the price was $2.00. Apples sold at the same rates.

The "North British Review," November, 1852, said: "The number of retail trades and shop-keepers is out of proportion to the requirements of society, or the number of the producing classes. There are in many places ten shop-keepers to do the work of one, such at least is Mr. Mill's estimate. Now these men, industrious and energetic as they are, do not add to the wealth of the community; they merely distribute what others produce. Nay more, in proportion as they are too numerous do they diminish the wealth of the community. They live, it is true, many of them, by snatching the bread out of each other's mouths; but still they do live, and often make great profits.

"These profits are made, by charging a per centage on all articles they sell. If, therefore, there are two of these retail dealers to be supported by a community when one would suffice to do the work, the articles they sell must cost that community more than needs be the case, and so far the country is impoverished by supporting one unproductive laborer too many. Any one who has examined into the subject is surprised to find how small a portion goes to the producer or importer, and how large a portion is absorbed by the distributer."

There is another movement in England worthy the attention of the American who sells his labor, on which the employer frequently makes one-half of the amount of his wages. Thomas Hughes says: "That by far the most important question arising, on the occasion of the recent gathering of the Social Science Congress at Manchester, is co-operation, a term which expresses a fair compromise between capitalists and laborers, whose contests for so many years in England have been severe and expensive to both. Co-operation, within the last twelve months, has taken a new start in England.

"The antiquated trammels in which the law bound all industrial enterprises in favor of great capitalists, were only finally broken through in 1865. In that year a short act was passed, for further amending the law of partnerships, in to which was slipped a clause, enacting that paying work people or agents by, a share of the business, instead of fixed wages, should not constitute such work people or agents partners or enable them in any way to interfere with the management of the business.

"Immediately after the passage of this act, the firm of Briggs & Son, very large coal owners in the West Riding of Yorkshire, converted their business into a joint stock association, and declared that their work-people should be henceforth entitled to a share of all the profits made beyond ten per cent., which sum has been estimated to be a fair interest on capital in coal mines. This step was taken at the suggestion of Mr. Currer Briggs, the eldest son of Mr. Henry Briggs. The latter gentleman had incurred a great amount of odium with his men. He received letters threatening his life. He was denounced in the men's union, where it passed into a proverb that 'coal owners were devils, and Briggs is the chief of devils.' In 1863, things had come to

such a pass that he had to work under the protection of the
county police. His capital yielded him and sons only four
per cent. He proposed to sell the pits, and take their capital where they could get better interest for it, without constant quarreling. The son said: 'Let us try the plan of
giving the workmen a share in the profits before giving up.'
The father and the other partners consented. The capital
of the concern was divided into shares, small enough for the
work people to buy with ease. They were invited to buy,
and at the same time, whether as shareholders or not, every
man who had worked for a certain time was entitled to a
bonus out of the surplus profits, after the ten per cent. on
the capital was paid, in proportion to his wages earned in
the mines.

"The result of the first year's working has been such a
complete success as to almost stagger those, who for many
years, advocated such plans as the only method of securing
peace between employers and employed. The company
has actually earned nineteen per cent. clear profit. These
results were celebrated at the town hall, in Leeds, on the
evening before the meeting of the Social Science Congress.
The colliery hands, nearly 1,400 strong, came in two special
trains, and met the Briggs family in the hall.

"The workmen gave some silverware to Mr. Currer
Briggs, which was paid for by subscription. Several of the
leaders of the miners, who had been the most bitter opponents of Mr. Briggs in the old days, stood upon the plat-
form, and spoke from their hearts as to the blessings which
the change had wrought and would bring. Every man
was full of loyalty to the concern, which he now felt to be
his own, and there was a resolution to double the bonus during the coming winter. It is believed that the immense
industries of England will be peacefully united."

These plans show that the Englishman will some time or other arrive at liberty and independence, though he has no fourth of July orators or writers on liberty. His savings will enable him to go to some foreign country where land is free. It is possible, by virtue and intelligence, for the toiling men of England to emancipate themselves and leave the merchants and bankers to wait on themselves, and cultivate their newly-acquired manor lands.

The Americans have need of co-operative stores. Are not many of them the subjects of severe toil. Why should they give ten dollars for a clock, when it costs at the factory two dollars and twenty-five cents, and the carriage to Ohio is fifty cents. This was ten years ago. There are women's stuffs, having French fancy names, made in Lowell for twenty-two cents a yard, for which the retail buyer pays sixty cents. It becomes Americans to use the learning, they have acquired at such an immense public cost to learn the cost of the many articles they use, and not be the victims of the thinking merchants. Printers, with their ink and paper, will enlighten men on the cost of production of commodities, if men will find the light.

All merchants do not gain splendid wealth; some gain very bitter poverty in old age, and wear thread-bare coats, and feed their children on bread and molasses. This is often contrasted with the house, garden, lawns, and fruit trees of a less gifted person, the labor of a carpenter and farmer, who did not understand the mysteries of trade, or the art of keeping books by single entry. The two Preston barbers began to compete with each other. The one who offered to shave for a halfpenny to do his best could only earn thirty pence a day, which did not obtain good and sufficient food. It often happens that the merchants compete with each other. One richer than all the rest destroys the

others.   At one time a merchant in Cincinnati, supposed
to be worth a great deal more than a million, had a neighbor merchant, who was supposed to be worth less than a
million.   Each commenced to put forth arts to get each
other's custom, which resulted in selling at cost and below
cost.   It was a strange sight to see thousands of people at
a palace of trade, waited on by hundreds of clerks.   The
conclusion of this was the little merchant retired broken and
discomfited.   The mischief did not end here; all the other
stores in the city who sold dry goods, had to sell at prices
that yielded no profits.   A winter at this gave no rent, no
salary, no money to pay debts, and caused many to go under
the stream of competition, who, if brought to the surface,
will appear in new characters as clerks; when beauty and
activity is gone, they become street merchants, venders of
stockings, shoe laces, papers, apples, and figs.

Many a one in early life has become a merchant, and
had visions of the pleasures of wealth, such as riding in a
carriage and receiving the homage of men; it has ended in
becoming the sweeper of a crossing, or the owner of a pea-
nut stand.   Happy are those who fail early; they avoid calamities like these; it gives them time to plant a vine, and
enjoy the fruit thereof.   It has been computed that all the
merchants fail except six in the hundred, which must be a
cause of sorrow.   Merchants have erected walled towns,
which have become to panting, fleeing slaves a city of refuge
from a master's fury.   Merchants have done all the good
they can; it is time their costly power was broken

Merchants brought tulips from Constantinople, in 1611.
In Holland these became a source of speculation.   Chim-
ney-sweeps, servants, and noblemen went into a mania on
buying and selling tulips.   The demand for them became
great, they kept rising in value.   The first buyers made large

fortunes. The prices went up as high as they could, and then went down. The last buyers lost their money. For a tulip root twelve acres of land was given. Another gave a carriage, two gray horses, and the harness for a root. A species of gambling came from this. A nobleman says to a merchant, "I will give for a tulip three months from now 1,000 florins." At that time it was worth 800 florins, at the time of delivery tulips were worth 1,200 florins [$300]. The merchant gave the nobleman 200 florins; if the price was 800 florins the merchant received 200 florins. There are now men who gamble in stocks, it shows how corrupt is human society or these men would be at productive labor, at something that will make men happier.

Mr. Holland, in his book called Plain Talks, says: "A stock exchange is a paradise of shirks [men who don't work], a place where not the first particle of wealth was ever produced or ever will be produced; where great games of chance are played in a strictly legal and moral way; where men combine to break down the credit of worthy associations; conspire to give a fictitious value to things that are of no value, and make a business of cheating each other and swindling the world.

"I can perceive no difference between the professional gamblers in stocks, and any other professional gamblers. Both are men who produce nothing; who play at games of skill and hazard for money; who never win a dollar that does not leave some other man poorer. The commercial exchanges are points of attraction for the shirks of the world. They stand ready to grasp at some portion of the profits of trade—men who minister to the vices of the rich, who speculate in the necessaries of life, who invent fancy schemes of plunder, who eat the subsistence of needle-women, who stand at the counter instead of plowing."

This boy has now become an adopted son, and has abundant leisure to destroy labor he never created. He visits a hospital, it may be to stifle his conscience, which upbraids him for not assisting those who sustain him, for not enduring the summer's heat and winter's cold. "Bear ye one another's burdens," is a command which we truly observe when we share with those who do them—the severe duties of life. Lord Oliphant convinced of the injustice of being supported by others' labor, left the pleasurers of his English home, his country's honors, and united with a body of co-religionists on the banks of Lake Erie, where he plows and wears home-spun. If all will practice this, hospitals for sick will be unknown.

5

The law has been regarded as the standard by which to measure all offenses and irregularities, as affording information to the different members of community, respecting the principles which shall be adopted in deciding their actions. One result of the institution of the law is, that the institution, when once it is begun, can never be brought to a close. Edict upon edict is heaped up, volume to volume is added. It is said the published laws of England are contained in forty folio volumes, to read which will take a lifetime. Every body in England is supposed to know the law; many suffer from not knowing it. To many its stern code of laws is darker than the Egyptian hieroglyphics.

"There is no maxim more clear than this, 'Every case is a rule in itself.' It seems to be the business of justice to distinguish the qualities of men, and not confound them. As new cases occur, the law is perpetually found deficient. Lawyers have not the faculty to look into the future, and can not define that which is boundless. Hence lawyers are continually wresting the law to include a case which was never in contemplation by its authors, or else get laws made to suit the case. The quibbles of lawyers, and the arts by which they refine and distort the sense of the law are proverbial.

"The education of a lawyer enables him, when employed by a prosecutor, to find out offenses the lawmaker never meant; to discover subterfuges that reduce the law to a nullity. The laws, in order to escape evasion, are frequently tedious, minute, and circumlocutory. The volume in which justice records her prescriptions, is forever increasing, and the world will not contain all that might be written.

"The consequence of the infinitude of law is its uncertainty. Laws were made to put an end to ambiguity, and that each man might know what he had to expect. Two

21

men would not go to law unless they were both promised success by their lawyers. Law was made for a plain man to understand. Yet lawyers differ about the results. Does it make the case any the less uncertain, if it had been trusted to a jury of neighbors with the ideas they entertained of natural justice? Lawyers absurdly maintain that the expensiveness of law prevents the multiplication of suits; when the true source is the uncertainty of the law, which is a code none can master; a labyrinth without an end; it is a mass of contradictions that can not be disentangled. Study will enable a lawyer to find plausible, perhaps, unanswerable arguments for almost any side of any question. It will be the utmost folly to suppose that the study of the law can lead to knowledge and certainty.

"The task of the law is to describe what shall be the actions of men, and to dictate discussions respecting them. Law says it is so wise, that it can not draw additional knowledge from future circumstances, and that future knowledge which may be acquired shall have no effect. Law tends to fix the human mind in a stagnant condition, and substitute duration in the room of unceasing progress.

"If a code of laws is wrong, a lawyer is a dishonest man, a subject for censure and regret. Men are the creatures of circumstances under which they are placed. To be surrounded by vice is to be vicious. To be dealing in quibbles, false colors, and sophistry can not fail to make lawyers lose the generous emotions of the soul, and the discernment of rectitude. The more successful he is in quibbling the worse he is tainted with evil. A lawyer may be full of sublime virtues, in time he becomes inconsistent and accessible to a bribe.

"A lawyer designs to plead no cause that is unjust, and use no arguments that are not truth, but strip law of its ambiguities, and talk rationally. Still he is a pernicious member of society. He retards the progress of mankind, defers the advent of a sounder policy, and renders mankind satisfied with imperfection and ignorance. In a word, if there were no lawyers men would plead their own causes, and justice would be easily attained.

"The law is wrong in exercising a jurisdiction upon the circumstances of the case. Men are not wanting whose ideas of right and wrong are as correct as the law, and who can come to the same conclusion as the learned judge. The law is called the wisdom of ages. What arrogance! Law is a compound of passion, timidity, jealousy, monopoly, and a lust of power. The wisdom of ages has to be corrected every year, its ignorance pointed out, its intolerance made easy.

"Men having reason given them, why should they not obey that? The Creator has engraven on the mind a code of right and wrong. The mountains of parchment to which he refers only impose on him. They are the remains of superstition and ignorance. Frequently it happens a piece of property has been willed to a person; another claims it. It is put to the decision of a court, and it is appealed to another court. On the one side is cheating; on the other anguish and misery, baffled hopes, fruitless years of expectation, which consume the strength of men in lawsuits. Trifles make endless controversies." *

"I propose only to consult the volume of nature; I knew, to a certain degree, what was the task I undertook. All the evidence I collected bore immediately upon the point under consideration. But now the principal point becomes involved with innumerable subordinate ones. I have no longer merely to be satisfied, by a long compendious course,

* This language is taken from Wm Godwin's "Political Justice."

to arrive at that which is right. With laws I am concerned with the construction of phrases, the removing of what is doubtful, the reconciling of contradictions, the ascertaining of the mind of the composer; and for this purpose the consulting of history, the ascertaining of the occasions of the institutions, and even the collecting, as far as possible, every anecdote that relates to their origin. I am concerned with commentators as much as I am with the text, not merely to assist my own deductions, but because they have a certain authority fettering and enchaining my deductions. I sought it may be repose for my indolence; but I have found an eternal labor. I have exchanged a task comparatively easy for difficulties unconquerable and endless.

"Such is the mode in which a lawyer forms his creed. It is necessarily captious and technically pregnant with petty subtilties and unmeaning distinctions. But the evil does not stop here. It would be a mistake, peculiarly glaring and gross, to suppose that a lawyer studies the law principally that he may understand it. No, his great object is to puzzle and perplex. His attention is given to the inquiry how he may distort the law to suit the cause in which he is engaged. This is a necessary consequence of one man being hired to tell another man's story. The principal, however, erroneous he may be, is expected to express himself in good faith. The agent is careless himself about the merits of the cause. He is indifferent whether his client is right or wrong. He will plead for the plaintiff to day, and the opposite side to morrow. He stands up before a judge and jury, on the most important questions, upon which are the peace, the lives, and the liberties of familes. If he has an honest tale to tell, it is well. But if he has the weaker side, he undertakes by a solemm argument to mislead, if he is able the court and the jury. He justifies himself thus; if men are to have their causes plead by others, the greatest delinquent is entitled to the same privilege. To reject his application would be to prejudice his cause.

"Law, we are told, is that by which one man is secured against the passion and injustice of the other. It is an inflexible and impartial principle, holding out one standard of right and wrong to all mankind. It has been devised by the wisdom of sages, in the tranquillity of the closet, not to accommodate particular interests, but to provide for the welfare of the whole. Its view is sublime and universal. It can not be warped to suit temporary and personal objects of men.

"It teaches every man what he has to depend on, not suffering himself to be condemned at the caprices of his judges, but by maxims already promulgated and made known to all. It gives a fair warning to one party of the punishment which a certain conduct will incur. It affords also the other party a remedy against the usurpation of his neighbor.

"If law be, to this eminent extent, the benefactor and preserver of mankind, must it not reflect some of its own luster upon its professors? What character can be more venerable than an expounder of the law, whether we apply this to the judge, who authoritatively declares its meaning from the bench; to the pleader, who takes care to do justice to himself, or to the less brilliant, but not less useful functions of him who, from his chamber, communicates the results of the researches of years to the client, who would otherwise be unable to find his way amidst the complexities of statutes, glosses, and precedents?

"We will not inquire into the soundness of this panegyric, which has been so often produced on the institutions of the law. All that our present subject requires of us is to as-

certain what sort of character is the study of the law likely
to entail on its professors. The business of a man is to inquire into the dictates of reason and the principles of justice.
The business of a lawyer is of a very different character;
he has nothing to do with generous and impartial reason;
his concern is with edicts and acts of parliaments. He is
to consider these as the standards of right and wrong. He
must expel from his mind all notions of independent investigation, or he must submit to the necessity of maintaining
that to be right, because it is conformable to law, which he
knows to be wrong and irreconcilable to justice.

"This is too plain to need any profound elucidation, that
laws, in their great outline, are the *prejudices of a barbarous
age*, artificially kept alive and entailed upon a civilized one.
Laws that are of long standing derive their character from
principles and systems that are exploded and out of use.
Such of them as are of recent date have often originated in
temporary objects, in anti-social passions, in the intemper-
ate desires of giving strength to monopolies, and firmness to
the usurpations of the few over the many. From this het-
erogeneous mass the lawyer extracts his rules, which he
thinks is for the good of men. Nothing is more usual
among persons of this profession, than to see them express
their sensation by a look of contempt and astonishment if
men doubt the infallibility of the law, or question the truth
of its decisions.

"The human mind is to bring every principle of ethics
within the scope of its own examination; to derive assistance
from every means of information, oral or sciptory; but to
admit nothing on authority that supersedes reason. If I
would estimate the means of human happiness; if I would
judge truly of the conduct of my neighbor, or know rightly
how to fashion my own, I must inquire deeply, not super-

ficially, I must enter into the principles of things, and not suffer conclusions to steal on me unawares, I must proceed step by step; and then there will be some chance that the notions I form will be found harmonious with each other. But when, instead of adopting my opinions with this degree of caution and deliberation, I am induced to admit, at a single stroke, whole volumes of propositions as unapproachable and decisive, I resign the most beneficient prerogative of the human understanding." *

Mr. Maxwell says: "In every school district, in Norway, is a Court of Reconciliation. Every law-suit is brought before the justice in person; no lawyer is allowed in this court. The parties state their complaints, and the justice notes the facts of both sides, considers and arranges the matter, and proposes what is fair in the case. If accepted, it is entered in a Court of Record. If appealed, it goes to the district court. The writings of the justice are taken as evidence, and none other. If the justice was right, the party appealing pays the cost of appeal. This system of minor courts prevents unnecessary litigation. The case can go to another court, on the same evidence, without any trick or circumlocution from either party. There is no chance for pettifoggers, the banditti of the bar. No deluding of the clients, or mystifying the judge or jury by sharp practice. Two-thirds of the suits are settled in this court. Of the remainder, not more than one-tenth are ever carried up. The judges are responsible for errors of judgment, delay, ignorance, carelessness, or prejudice. They may be summoned and tried in a superior court, and, if convicted, are liable for damage to the injured party. The lawyers of Norway have integrity and learning."

* The reader is kindly referred to Wm. Godwin's "Enquirer" and "Political Justice" for a continuation of this subiect, from which this is abbreviated.

There exists in large cities in England courts of reconciliation, where three magistrates persuade men to be reconciled with as little cost as possible. This is a consequence of being ruled by a king, who promotes economy, so as to have a greater share of the plunder. Where the people are all sovereigns, they plunder each other.

Blackstone says: "Laws are to prevent what is wrong, and promote what is right." This language is sublime if it be the truth; it seems not to be so. To prove this, take two examples; the year 1857 was one of universal bankruptcy made so by paper-money makers. This caused the writer unwillingly to have some leisure to observe the administration of justice. In the court at Schenectady was tried a man for going into the woods of his neighbor, on Saturday afternoon, at five o'clock, and taking a quarter of a cord of wood. On Sunday, the man who took the wood paid a friendly visit to the owner of it; the owner of which, the next day, found out his loss, and told his neighbor to bring the wood back again, who then offered a dollar and a quarter for it, which the owner refused to take, and in a spirit of revenge had his neighbor charged with stealing. The witnesses testified that these two men were friendly, they exchanged labor with each other, and borrowed each other's tools. To try this cause required twelve jurymen, two advocates, three judges, two constables, a sheriff, and a fire-maker. The jury could not agree, and call the fault stealing.

The court, the next day, tried a man for getting into a sleigh, and driving the horse seventeen miles. This man was drunk; and when his reason returned, he told his brother what he had done, who returned with the sleigh and offered the owner six dollars to be reconciled, which he would not take; he must have the man prosecuted for stealing. The same number of men were employed in trying this cause. The jury could not agree, and call this horse stealing. The two trials took each a day, and cost the county $150. Is not this a robbery on the people? It is time it were ended!

The writer, with four others, made for two employers a set of wood patterns for a hot air-furnace. These were to be made in a month. The person who had the work done was taken with the cholera, which prevented him from overseeing us. When he saw the work, some part of it had to be changed. The man for whom the work was done examined it well, and took it away. The makers asked for $150, their due, a part of which was for making the changes. The man refused to pay, and the debt was taken to a magistrate. The defendant had for a witness his foreman, who said the work was bad. A rival pattern-maker, having feelings of animosity, said, " I have made changes on the work, and it is not workman-like." The judge could not decide. Had a pattern-maker been chosen a judge, each plead his own cause, each witness told his tale, the result would have been, the two contractors would have got some pay. No cheating with such a judge. The work could not have been done any better. The Anglo-Saxons had their disputes decided by the witnesses. Have we improved?

Dean Swift, in his " Gulliver's Travels," which he wrote to satirize the follies of mankind, in a conversation with the people he visited, speaks of lawyers thus: " There was a society among us, bred up from their youth in the art of proving, by words multiplied for that purpose, that white is black, and black is white, according as they are paid. To this society all the rest of the people are slaves. For example, if my neighbor has a mind to my cow, he has a lawyer to prove that he ought to have it from me; I must then hire another to defend my rights, it being against the rules of the law that any man shall speak for himself. Now, in this case, I who am the rightful owner, lie under two great disadvantages: first, my lawyer, being practiced almost from his cradle in defending falsehood, is quite out of his element when he would be an advocate for justice, which is an unnatural office he attempts with awkwardness, if not with ill will. A second disadvantage is, that my lawyer must proceed with great caution, or else he will be reprimanded by the judges, and abhorred by his brethren as one that would lessen the practice of the law. I have but two methods to preserve my cow. The first is to gain over my adversary's lawyer by a double fee, who will betray his client by insinuating that he has justice on his side. The second way is for my lawyer to make my cause appear as unjust as he can, by allowing the cow to belong to my adversary; and this if skillfully done, will certainly bespeak the favor of the bench.

"These judges are persons appointed to decide all controversies of property, as well as the trials of criminals, and are picked out from the most dextrous of lawyers, who have grown old or lazy, and have been biased against truth and equity, and lie under such a fatal necessity of favoring oppression, fraud, and perjury, that I have known some of them refuse a large bribe from the side where justice lay, rather than injure the faculty by doing any thing unbecoming their office. It is a maxim among lawyers, whatever has been done before may be done legally again; and therefore they take special care to record all the decisions formerly made against common justice, and the general reason of mankind. These, under the name of precedents, they produce as authorities to justify the most iniquitous opinions, and the judges never fail of directing accordingly. In pleading, they studiously avoid entering into the merits of the cause; but are loud, violent, and tedious in dwelling on all circumstances which are not to the purpose. For instance, in the case already mentioned, they never desire to know what title or claim my adversary has to my cow; but whether the said cow was red or black; her horns long or short; whether the field I graze her in be round or square; whether she is milked at home or abroad; what diseases she is subjected to, after which they consult precedents, adjourn the cause from time to time, and in ten, twenty, or thirty years, come to an issue.

"It is likewise to be observed that this society has a peculiar cant or jargon of its own that no other mortal can understand, and wherein all their laws are written, which they take care to multiply—whereby they have wholly confounded the very essence of truth and falsehood, of right and wrong—so that it will take thirty years to decide if the field, left me by my ancestors for six generations, belong to me or to a stranger three hundred miles off.

"In the trial of persons accused of crime against the State, the method is much more short and commendable; the first judge sends to sound the disposition of those in power, after which he can easily save or hang a criminal, strictly preserving all due forms of law.

"Here the listener interposed and said: 'It is a pity that creatures, endowed with such prodigious abilities of mind, as these lawyers must certainly be, and were they not rather encouraged to be the instructors of others in wisdom and knowledge.' In answer to which I assured him, that in all points out of their own trade, they were usually the most stupid, ignorant generation among us, the most despicable in common conversation, avowed enemies to all knowledge and learning, and equally disposed to pervert the general reason of mankind in every other discourse as in that of their own profession."

This description may be distorted and extreme. It can not be denied that the lawyer does mischief. With what eagerness did one try to prove my employers were not entitled to the balance due on the patterns. Each of us had sixty dollars for our month's work, which was obtained from the defendant in advance. The employers had nothing for their rent, lumber, skill, and time. We had in the shop the patterns of a furnace to guide us, made by the rival witness. I saw his work was nailed together and broken. I dovetailed together what I did, so that it could not break. Dovetailing was done where it could be. It was afterward ascertained the rival witness made changes on the patterns to the amount of *twelve* dollars.

Jefferson said: "A court of justice was an old English aristocratic institution, and a natural enemy to the common people." The census book says we have " 33,980 lawyers, 123,378 merchants, 184,485 clerks." It would be a good plan to set the lawyers and nine-tenths of the merchants at something else. These have abilities to clothe and feed as many as 10,000,000 of people.

Dean Swift said : " He who made two grains of corn, two blades of grass grow where one grew before, would deserve well of mankind, and do more service than the whole race of politicians. In England is produced three times more food than the people consume. The greater part goes to foreign countries. In return we obtain diseases, vices, and follies. The rich men enjoy the poor man's labor, who lives miserably on small wages that they may live plentifully."

CHAPTER XI.

PHYSICIANS AND MINISTERS.

John Wesley's Remedies for Sickness—The Opinions of the Democratic Review—Jefferson—Priessnitz—Bulwer—Havelock—Volney—The Early Christians—St. Chrysostom—Tertullian—The Moravians.

"Medicine is the destructive art of healing diseases."—Lord Byron.
"Early piety, if persisted in, prepares for a good old age."—J. A. James.

JOHN WESLEY believed that every disease under the sun could be cured with cold water, herbs, and the juices of fruits. He cared for the bodies of men as well as their souls. He gave to his humble followers and to the world a book, containing 450 pages [12mo Pica], called "Primitive Physic, or a Natural Method of Curing Diseases." This book enumerates 290 diseases, and gives 925 remedies. Dr. Abernethy tells us the older a medical practitioner gets the fewer medicines he uses. He tells us of an apothecary who took a room in London, and from six black bottles he compounded and dispensed medicines for the poor, from whom he made an enormous fortune. A prescription in the time of James I was a very long list of strange incongruous substances, under the name of boluses and doses, which, when compared with the few and simple drugs the physician uses now, gives hope that future generations in a century or two, will use no medicines at all.

It is some consolation to know that the formidable array of cures and receipts given us by Mr. Wesley, have been, by modern innovators reduced to six, the juices of fruits, one internal and four different outside applications of water. In his book he says: "It is probable physic, as well as religion, was, in the first ages of the world chiefly traditional—every father delivering to his sons what he had received concerning the manner of healing hurts, the diseases of climate and season, and the medicines of the greatest efficacy. This is the method of preserving the healing art among the Americans [written in 1747] to this day. Their diseases are few and do not often occur, by reason of continual exertion and temperance. If any are sick or torn by a wild beast, the fathers tell what remedies to apply. It is seldom the patient suffers long—these medicines being quick as well as generally infallible.

"Has not the Author of Nature taught us many medicines by accident? Thus, one was walking in a pine grove, at a time when many were afflicted with sores in the mouth. A drop of gum fell from one of the trees on the book he was reading; this he applied to one of the sore places. Finding the pain ceased, he applied it to another place, which it healed. Numberless remedies have thus been casually discovered in every age and nation.

"Physic was wholly founded on experiment. The European, as well as the American, said to his neighbor, "Are you sick? Drink the juice of this herb, and your sickness will be at an end. Are you in a burning heat? Leap into that river and sweat till you are well. Thus ancient men, having a little experience, joined with common sense, and common humanity, cured both themselves and their neighbors of most of their distempers.

"In process of time, men of a philosophical turn were not satisfied with this. They began to inquire how they might account for these things. How such medicines wrought such effects? They examined the human body in all its parts; the nature of the flesh, veins, arteries, nerves; the structure of the brain, heart, lungs, stomach, and bowels They explored the several kinds of mineral and vegetable substances. Hence the whole order of physic. Men of learning began to set experience aside; to build physic from hypothesis; to form theories of diseases and their cure, and to substitute these in place of experiments.

"As theories increased, simple medicines were disused; in the course of years, the greater part were forgotten. In room of these, abundance of new ones were introduced by speculative men, and these more difficult to be applied, as being more remote from common observation. Hence rules for the application of these. Medical books were multiplied, till at length physic became an obtuse science, quite out of the reach of ordinary men.

"Physicians now began to be held in admiration, as persons who were something more than human, and profit attended their employment as well as honor; so that they had now two weighty reasons for keeping the bulk of mankind at a distance, that they might not pry into the mysteries of the profession. To this end they increased their difficulties by design. They have filled their writings with terms unintelligible to plain men. They affected to deliver their rules, and to reason on them in an obtuse and affected manner. These introduced into practice compound medicines, containing so many ingredients that it was scarce possible for a common person to know which wrought the cure. They used exotics not understood, chemicals that can only be used with the advice of the physician. Thus honor and gain were secured—a vast majority of mankind being cut off from helping themselves or their neighbors, or once daring to attempt it.

"There have not been wanting lovers of mankind who have endeavored to reduce physic to its ancient standard, to explode all hypotheses and fine-spun theories, to make it intelligible as it was, having no mystery in it, so that every man of common sense may prescribe to himself and neighbor.   A mean hand has here made some little attempt toward a plain and easy way of curing diseases.   I have consulted common sense, experience, and the interests of mankind.   Is it not needful, in the highest degree, to rescue men from destruction, from wasting their fortunes, from sickness and pain, from throwing away their lives, health, time, and substance.

"The method of compounding medicines can never be reconciled with common sense.   Experience shows that one thing will cure most disorders as well as twenty.   Then why add the other nineteen to swell the apothecary's bill.   Nay, possibly, on purpose to prolong the distemper, that the doctor and he may divide the spoil." *

These are a few of Mr. Wesley's remedies, some of which he tried on himself successfully :

For an ague.—Go into the cold water bath before the cold fit.   Never bathe on a full stomach.   Go to bed and sweat after the bath.

Asthma.—Take a pint of cold water every night when you lie down.   Vomit by taking a quart of warm water. The more you drink the better.

Hooping-Cough.—Use the cold water bath daily.

Cholera Morbus, or flux and vomiting—Drink two or three quarts of cold water, or a drink of vinegar and water.

A Cold.—Drink a pint of cold water, or add a spoonful of molasses.   Tried.

A Colic.—Drink a pint of cold water.   Tried.

* Sentences here and there are taken from Mr. W's book ; the words are his.

An Inveterate Cough.—Wash the head in cold water every morning, or use the cold bath.

The Dropsy.—Use the cold bath daily after purging.

A Fever.—Drink a quart of cold water in the beginning of any fever. It is safe and sure. Lie down when taken.

Weak Eyes.—Wash the head daily with cold water.

The Measles.—Drink only thin water gruel, or milk and water, or toast and water.

The Rheumatism.—Use the cold water bath with rubbing and sweating.

A Sprain.—Hold the part two hours in very cold water.

The Scurvy.—Live on turnips for a month, or an entire milk diet for six months, or lemon juice and sugar.

A Sore Throat.—Take a pint of cold water and lie down.

For Worms.—Use the juice of lemons.

A Flux.—Use the cold bath daily, and drink water from the spring largely, taking nothing else till it stops.

Consumption has been cured by cold bath. A consumptive man was advised to drink water gruel without sugar or salt. In three weeks he was well. Use as a drink cold water and new milk. To each quart add two ounces of sugar.

A middle-aged man drank five quarts of cider every day, and was cured of a dropsy, supposed to be incurable, in a few weeks. A farmer, aged seventy, was given over to die. Being desperate, he drank three quarts of cold water every twenty-four hours. His whole food was sea biscuit. For sixteen days he seemed worse; then he had watery discharges for a week, and was soon well.

The Gravel.—Eat abundantly of spinage, or drink largely of warm water sweetened with honey, or peach-leaf tea, or infuse an ounce of wild parsley seeds in a pint of white wine, for twelve days. Drink a glass of it, fasting daily, for three months. To prevent its return, breakfast on agrimony tea.

22

It cured me [Mr. Wesley] twenty years ago, nor have I had the least symptom of it since.

Mr. Wesley says: "A prejudice prevails, that fruits are noxious in a dysentery. Whereas, ripe fruits, of whatever species, especially summer fruits, are the real preservatives from it. They thin down the thick bile. Ripe fruits are the true solvents of it. They may bring on purging, but such as guard against dysentery.

"We had an extraordinary abundance of fruit, in 1759, and in 1760, and scarcely any dysenteries. Whenever dysenteries prevail, I eat less meat and more fruit; and several physicians adopted this caution with the same success. I have seen eleven patients in one house with the dysentery, of whom nine ate fruit and recovered. The grandmother managed a child her own way, with burnt wine and spices, but no fruit. She conducted herself in the very same manner, and both died.

"In a country seat near Berne, in 1751, the flux made great havoc, and the people were warned against the use of fruits. Ten out of eleven persons ate plentifully of plums, and not one of them was seized with it. The poor coachman alone rigidly observed that abstinence, and took a terrible dysentery.

"This distemper had nearly destroyed a Swiss regiment, in a garrison, in the south of France; the captains then purchased a vineyard, where they carried the sick soldiers, and gathered grapes for them. After this not one died, nor were any more attacked with the dysentery.*

---

* In 1866, the cholera prevailed in Cincinnati. Said a shop-mate to the writer, "I am sick, I will go home." He had the cholera; his mistaken friends gave him brandy and pepper. I prepared him, aided by another, for his coffin. Around my home three died with this disease. I had the diarrhea come on me, I took two lemons and a bunch of grapes. I have not much faith in the physician's skill. I had once a diarrhea when many were dying

"A clergyman was seized with a dysentery, which was not mitigated in the least by any medicines he had taken. By mere chance he saw some red currants. He took a fancy to them, and eat three pounds in two hours in the morning. He became better that very day, and the next day was entirely well."

"In modern times it is the fortune of an unlettered peasant to work marvels in the healing art, and to deprive it of its air of mystery. The name of Priessnitz belongs to history. He is remembered by those whom he has restored to health, and taught to avoid suffering by his water-cure. He has been the means of working out a great change in the preventing and the curing of diseases. Future generations will bless the peasant philosopher for his untiring labors. His birthplace was on the mountains of Grafenberg, in Silesia, in Austria. At twenty he managed a small farm, and was capable of great exertion. During the latter part of his life his drink was water. Most of his reflections and observations are directed by common sense.

"The first idea he had of the healing power of water was from a man in some iron-works, who used it for burns and injuries. He began to reflect on health and disease. He noticed that the ruddy-faced and bare-footed plowman did not complain of head or stomach aches, and he was unac-

with this disease. I invited a physician to heal me. He gave me "blue-mass," which, he said, made me worse. He paid me eight visits, and gave me many medicines. Then he left me, saying, "I must take laudanum." Another doctor gave me twenty doses of rhubarb and morphine. I was as weak as a child. The thought came into my mind, if I would live like a child I should get up again. I made a vow I would throw the medicines away, and live a week on milk. I was, at the end of the week, able to work. Another time I was a great sufferer from this very painful complaint, and I cured it by drinking daily a quart of cider. I was well in a week. The idea was obtained by reading a newspaper. The theory of this disease is—the digestive organs need repairs. The juices of fruits help wonderfully.

quainted with anxiety or the blues; and that after being
wet for hours, he did not take cold or shiver. He also
observed those who had gone through the dissipations of
Vienna, or who had passed a studious life in warm rooms.
He also observed the dairy-maid, the seamstress, and the
fine lady, who seldom walked. From these contrasts he
formed his notions of health, life, and disease. He began
practicing on the injuries and slight ailments of his neighbors, applying his compresses, warm or cold, according to
the state of the inflammation. To this he added sponging
different parts, and sometimes the whole body, with water,
with plain diet, and water drinking at the same time.

"In the midst of these trials a wagon went over him,
and broke some of his ribs. Two practitioners of the village gave him no hope of recovery. He took the resolution
of trying his own plan. He recovered very rapidly. His
cure made a sensation, after such an unfavorable opinion.
Many now applied for advice, and he made many cures. It
gave him an opportunity of studying the phenomena of disease, and the different effects produced by water. From this
he formed a theory, and contrived new modes of applying
his remedies to gain certain results.

"The powerful aid of sweating dwelt on his mind, and
he contrived the plan of enveloping his patients in blankets.
This answered his views, when properly used and followed
by a bath. This was not attended with any debility and it
relieved the internal organs, and the constitutional powers.
He was puzzled how to treat the critical phenomena,
which took place during the water treatment, and here the
water-cure has gained by being thrown on its own resources.
Had he been licensed to use medicines, in many of his di-
lemmas he probably would have resorted to them, instead
of finding out a surer and safer plan of treatment—the di-

versified modes of using water. He was also dissatisfied
with his imperfect plan of treating fevers and inflammations.
By continual reflection, he arrived at the process of enveloping in the wet sheet, the crowning discovery of the water
cure. With the aid of this valuable remedy, he was able
to modify his treatment as he pleased. He soon discovered
its powerful effects, when used in the treatment of chronic
diseases.

" All this however did not go on smoothly, or without
obstacles. He was denounced as an unlicensed and dangerous impostor. He was fined, and his treatment was suspended. Confident in the goodness of his cause, and backed
by numerous patients, he appealed against the sentence, and
it was set aside. Priessnitz and his system became important. It attracted the attention of the government at Vienna.
A commission of medical men went to inquire into the new
water-cure. Old Baron Turkheim, at the head of the medical department was at the head of this, a man of spirit, and
learning. On his return to Vienna, at the medical society,
he was asked 'what he thought of the new charlatanism.'
He replied, 'Priessnitz is an honest man, and no impostor,
and his mode of treatment is *superior* to ours. Believe me,
gentlemen, we have much to learn from this countryman.'
This made the sages of Vienna angry at the founder of the
water-cure. Those who left their care and went to this
water-cure returned with perfect health.

" The commission analyzed the water to discover its
mystic virtue! They found it was spring water! They examined the sponges with great care, to see if they contained
any secret remedies. He was now taken under the protection of the government, and a policeman was stationed at
his hospital, to note the number of the patients, and report
the deaths, and other results of the treatment. Up to 1841,

he had treated 7,219 strangers, and there had been thirty-nine deaths.* Some of these died before commencing the treatment, and were in a dangerous condition. This peasant doctor made $750,000. Nobles and the sons of kings were among his patients." †

There was a ship from Africa, laden with blacks, destined for Cuba. They overpowered the crew, and compelled them to steer for home. This ship was picked up on the coast of Connecticut. It was resolved by some good people to send these Mendians back to Africa. Mr. George Thompson of Ohio became their missionary. In his "Observations on Africa," he says: "To take medicine is unnecessary. In the most violent attacks of fever, pure water, well administered, is more salutary than the whole list of medicines. Rightly applied, it relieves pain in the head, bowels, and limbs; it purges or vomits; it strengthens, enlivens, and invigorates; it carries safely through the fever. All persons going to live in Africa, should acquire the true principles of hydropathy.'

General Havelock, in India, could get no relief from his chronic sickness. The English physicians in that country could do him no good. When he went to England, none could help him there. He then made a pilgrimage to the Silesian peasant's hospital to be cured. In a letter to a friend he says: "I can hardly describe to you how much I have already gained by these potations and immersions. * * * * I am to devour eight pounds of grapes per diem." His biographer adds: "What with the grapes and hydropathy together he rallied yet more sensibly, and became comparatively a vigorous, healthy man." ‡

* Among 100 well persons three die in a year. A good test of Mr. P's skill.
† The practice of Water-cure, by Dr. J. Wilson. Fowler & Wells, 1855.
‡ Life of Wm. Havelock, by Rev. Wm. Brock. Carter & Brother, 1858

Volney, in his travels in the United States, says: "I have been attacked with an habitual flux in Georgia, in consequence of fatigue. In whatever climate it originates, it yields to no remedy. No astringent was of any use to me, not even rhubarb and ipecacuanha was of any service to me. I took doses of opium. The relief was momentary. Where plums grew, by eating this excellent fruit I was relieved for that season; and no sooner was I obliged to abandon this fruit, the disease prevailed again. The cold bath I found of some benefit to me." *

Thomas Jefferson said: "A physician was one who put medicines, that he knew but little about, into a human stomach that he knows nothing about." Such were his prejudices against this class, that he was unwilling for his young relatives to enter the profession.

Says the "Democratic Review:" "Among the allopathic medicines in common use, we have the *paralyzers*, aconitic and hemlock; the *convulsives*, strychnia and prussic acid; and the *delirafacients* are henbane, stramonium, and the deadly night-shade—seven poisons of the most virulent and sudden in the whole kingdom of nature. Using these, we can only wonder that the virus of the rattlesnake, or the saliva of hydrophobia was not added to the list, and dealt out to suffering invalids on the authority of formal receipts. Next to these we have the less active, but still powerful poisons, opium, cinchona, digitalis, scammony, gamboge, hellebore, croton oil, colocynth, and a long list of vegetable poisons, as if the whole vegetable kingdom had been ransacked; and when any substance was found, fetid to the smell, nauseous to the taste, and deadly in its action, it follows that men must take it for medicine—for health."

* A view of the climate and soil of the United States, by C. F. Volney. Page 309. Conrad, publisher. Philadelphia, 1804.

The "Scientific American" tells us that a blister made in the hand by a hoe, or some other implement of industry, will cure sickness.   This seems to have been a remedy of Mr. Lyman Beecher, to work away the symptoms of sickness, by working on some land.   This seems to be true.   If we become indolent, and keep on the sofa, we shall be sick. Oliver Goldsmith was a literary physician, a class, people think, are not good at healing.   At one time he sent a sick person a round box, labeled to be taken as often as necessities require it.   It contained ten pieces of gold.

It can not be denied that mankind need a class to be so skilled that they can amputate a limb, sew up an artery, or trepan a dented skull.   This is no evidence that physicians should be so numerous.   Select one or two in a town, and give them all the custom, who will make you well quicker, and, perhaps, charge you less.   Dr. Abernethy had a large practice to make $100,000 a year.   People had to be brief when they came to him.   A lady showed him her finger He said "a poultice."   She came again and showed it and said, "Better; how much do you charge?"   The reply was, "Nothing; you have the art of holding your tongue." He used to tell some to earn sixpence a day, and live on it.

Bulwer said a physician "was one who relieved you of your money, not of your malady."   In his "Confessions on the Water-Cure," which contains a description how he was cured by water when the physician failed, he says: "A little reflection taught me the learned professions are not disposed to favor innovation on that which is sacred in their eyes.   A physician can not be expected to own that a Silesian peasant can cure with water the diseases that resist an armament of phials.   I threw physic to the dogs." *

* The reader is referred to the books of Fowlers & Wells, hydropathic publishers, city of New York, for that knowledge to enable him to cure himself.

The advent of Jesus Christ into the world is the most remarkable event in its history. At the present time, fully a
fifth of the human race believe in his name. He was full
of kindness, benignity, and devotion to men. His object was
to benefit them on earth and in heaven. His career was an
extraordinary one. His death was very painful. He was the
victim of prejudice and superstition. He came to level the
galling distinctions of human society; to make the painful
inequalities of life to cease; to add what was lacking in the
Jewish law; to make the moral laws of man complete. He
showed how absurd was the Jewish law of retaliation. In its
place he gave the law of kindness and forbearance. He
came to give men light for their darkness, happiness for
their fears. Men desired immortality. He showed them it
could be obtained, and there was an inheritance beyond the
grave. He upbraided mankind for their wickedness, luxury, and superstition. In him there was no hypocrisy or
dissimulation, no sin or vice, no desire to be rich.

That he was a reformer, may be inferred from the language of his commission: "The Spirit of the Lord is upon
me; because he hath chosen me to preach the Gospel to the
poor, he hath sent me to heal the broken-hearted, to preach
deliverance to the captives, and recovering of sight to the
blind, and to set at liberty them that are bruised." [Luke,
ch. iv., v. 18.] For this kindness to the human race, men
should adore and love him. There have appeared many reformers who loved the human race, and gave them noble
precepts for their moral conduct. The precepts of Jesus
are nobler than them all.

Plato wrote the scheme of a republic, in which the law
should watch over the equal distribution of the external instruments of unequal power, honors, property, etc.

Confucius said: "If a state is governed by the principles
23

of reason, poverty and misery are the subjects of shame; if a state is not governed by the principles of reason, riches and honors are the subjects of shame."

Diogenes devised a noble and worthy plan of opposition to the system of master and slave. He said: "It is in the power of each individual to level the inequality which is the topic of the complaint of mankind. Let him be aware of his own worth, and the station he occupies in the scale of moral beings. Diamonds and gold, palaces and scepters, derive their value from the opinion of mankind. The only sumptuary law which can be imposed on the use and fabrication of these instruments of mischief and deceit, these symbols of successful injustice, is the *law* of *opinion*. Every man possesses the power, in this respect, to legislate for himself. Let him be well aware of his own worth and moral dignity. Let him yield in meek reverence to any worthier or wiser than he, so long as he accords no veneration to the splendor of his apparel, the luxury of his food, the multitude of his flatterers and slaves. It is because ye value and seek the empty pageantry of wealth and social power that ye are enslaved to its possessions. Decrease your physical wants; learn to live, like the beasts of the forest and the birds of the air, so far as nourishment and shelter is concerned; ye will not need to complain that other individuals of your species are surrounded by the diseases of subserviency and oppression."

Jesus of Nazareth saw that the majority of men were in poverty and ignorance, gratifying the luxury of many at the expense of their comfort. These few did not try to govern their own evil passions. They sought to gain majesty, rank, wealth, and power over the weaker part of men. It was for these proud ones that these precepts were given, to bring them to a better feeling, to teach love and kindness to men.

He opened his mouth and taught them, saying: Blessed are the poor in spirit: for theirs is the kingdom of heaven.

Blessed are they that mourn: for they shall be comforted.

Blessed are the meek: for they shall inherit the earth.

Blessed are they which do hunger and thirst after righteousness: for they shall be filled.

Blessed are the merciful: for they shall obtain mercy.

Blessed are the pure in heart: for they shall see God.

Blessed are the peace-makers: for they shall be called the children of God.

Blessed are they which are persecuted for righteousness' sake: for theirs is the kingdom of heaven.

Blessed are ye, when men shall revile you, and persecute you, and shall say all manner of evil against you falsely, for my sake.

How grand! How noble! How sublime are these precepts! A belief in them makes men love and pity their race, and not trample upon them, nor regard them as beasts of burden to ride into power, or stepping stones to ease and leisure. The eloquence of Jesus was directed to the enslaving vices of mankind that have made them miserable for ages. Nations had warred against nations, they had employed the ingenuity of men for destroying property, and lives. Instead of one grand community, mankind were divided into many, each so organized that they could ruin one another. To carry out these plans required that millions of sensitive beings should suffer agony and want.

How much superior are these precepts to the meaningless, inexplicable code that councils make for us to square our lives by, and which needs an interpreter. Men are destitute; and were law-makers, interpreters, and judges to do something else, some misery would disappear. It is only during the past four hundred years that men have had a

printed code to refer to. The time was when the decision of the magistrate was common law. He was supposed
to be full of piety, justice, and wisdom. An analysis of law
cases show that they are the disputes of men worth millions
with those worth nothing; those worth four thousand with
those worth forty dollars, or some other· extreme. If the
usages of society were different, or the laboring man was
more enlightened, the future creations of labor would be retained more by those who make them. The inequalities of
life cause endless lawsuits, which will cease when the poor
possess more.

Crimes and wrongs are on the increase in this Republic.
Legislation is an attempt to provide against the mistakes of
men, and to assign penalties for injuries; it destroys as
much as it preserves. The command of Jesus Christ is,
"Love your enemies; bless them that curse you, that you
may be the sons of your Heavenly Father." If men would
obey this command, be forgiving and forbearing they would
be happier and better.

An Athenian soldier accidently set fire to the city of Sar-
dis. It was burned to the ground. The Persians retaliated on Athens. They assembled successive expeditions
on the most extensive scale. Athens was burned to the
ground, the territory was laid waste, and every living thing
destroyed. The Persians desisted when not able to do any
more mischief. Alexander retaliated by destroying Persia.
If men would be forgiving, how much happier the world
would be. If the sums or the time that is spent in war,
were employed in promoting the welfare of man, how different would be human society !

"Be ye perfect, as your Father in heaven is perfect." If
men will obey this sentence, it is better than volumes of
laws. To understand the whole moral duty of man, the

Decalogue must be studied, of which one single precept, strikes at the root of all wrongs: "Thou shalt not covet."

The followers of Christ after his death, or "They that believed, were together, and had all things common; and sold their possessions and goods, and parted them to all men, as every man had need. And they continuing daily with one accord in the temple, and breaking bread from house to house, did eat their meat with gladness and singleness of heart, praising God." [Acts, ch. 2., v. 45].

This was a severe blow to pride, to ample possessions, to costly food and raiment, and to magnificent rooms. No great moral improvement of mankind can take place till a system of equality like this prevails.

These Christians increased rapidly in spite of persecution and torture. Pliny, a governor of a Roman province, in the year 104, tells Trajan, the Roman Emperor, "That the Christians are not guilty of theft or adultery ; they observed their word and were true to their trust." Tertullian says: "Were the Christians to retire to another country, the Romans would have a frightful solitude." In the third century there were Christians in the camp, the senate, and every-where but in the temple and theater. St. Chrysostom examining from what source the eminent virtues of the first Christians flowed, ascribes it principally to their divesting themselves of their possessions. He says: "Whosoever hath a large possession, hath a tempter to draw him into hell."

It is a source of regret that there are so many divisions in the Christian Church. It would be better for mankind if they would unite and form one church. How many ministers it would send to the plow! The town of T——, on the Miami Canal, contains three thousand five hundred inhabitants, and has eleven churches. Two churches would be sufficient to contain all the church-goers. There are two kinds of Methodists and Presbyterians. The Baptist Church had forty members, most of whom were poor, and homeless. Their church cost $4,000, which is on each member $100. These forty members pay an annual salary of $800 to their minister, which is twenty dollars on each member. If one of these homeless members, at the close of life, should say, Why am I homeless? the answer might be, You have given sufficient to have made you a good home. Religion does not demand these sacrifices. The truth can be found at a cheaper rate.

The Primitive Methodists were also poor. The basement of their church was divided into cells, the abodes of women in years. While looking at these poor, cheerless homes, the thought occurred, if the labor that is in superfluous monuments were in cottage homes for widows, it would promote their happiness. The time is coming when the most costly monuments will tell that those beneath have been successful plunderers of others' labor.

The Methodists have local preachers who are as good as the itinerants. The world is very wicked, and something must be done to make it better. To induce the people to come to church, it should be made attractive by organs and beautiful architecture. To such a church there might be half a dozen preachers who could preach gratuitously and by turns. Among the Dunkers and Friends you will find no paid preachers. Among them the strictest honesty prevails. These have volunteer preachers. There are many of the sermons of Wesley, Watts, Whitefield and others, that can be read with profit. To make a sermon, requires three days' time. There will not be wanting men full of benevolence and the spirit of Jesus, who will teach his precepts, without any reward. A paid ministry has its evils. It can

not strike as heavy blows at folly and weakness, which many
in the congregation practice.   The minister must treat in a
dainty manner the faults of some, or he will lose a part of
his salary.   The early Christians received no pay for preaching.   Paul could work and preach.   Franklin told Paine not
to publish his "Age of Reason."   He said: "Don't un-
chain the tiger; men are wicked with religion, they will be
worse without it."   The Bible pronounces woes on those
who "add house to house," on the lawyers, on those who
are rich, and oppress the poor.   See James, ch. v.

These examples prove that men can be reclaimed from
sin.   Mrs. E. Fry went to Newgate Prison, where three
hundred ferocious and riotous females were confined.   She
proposed to find them employment and instruction.   She
told them of the comfort to be derived from industry and
sobriety, the pleasure and profit of doing right and acquiring knowledge, the happiness and joy of a religious life.   So
great was the change, at the end of two weeks the Governor hardly knew the prison again.   The Lord Mayor, Al-
dermen, and Sheriffs were astonished at the orderly deportment of the prisoners—their attention to the Scriptures—the
obedience and respect shown to visitors—their cheerful manners and the absence of noise, tumult, and contention.   Licentiousness and rioting were exchanged for sobriety and
cleanliness.   Hundreds were made better.   One said to
Mrs Fry: "From you I learned to flee the road that leads
to hell, and to look to my Savior for pardon.   This doctrine teaches me to deny all ungodliness and wordly pleas-
sures.   Dear Madam, permit me to give you two pounds for
benevolent purposes, which I have earned."

Isaac T. Hopper, a Friend, spent fifty years helping poor
people to work, and slaves to freedom.   He used to preach
to the inmates of Sing Sing Prison.   He often moved a

large part of his unhappy audience to tears. His friendly counsel produced permanent effects on their characters. In a letter to his daughter, he says "One of these poor fellows attacked the life of his keeper. I had an interview with him. He received what I said kindly, and said he could not control his passion. I tried to convince him he had power to govern his temper. Since I have talked to him, he has become better. I hardly ever saw a more changed man."

Burke, in his "Reflections on the French Revolution," says: "When the Anabaptists of Munster, in the sixteenth century, had filled Germany with confusion, by their system of *levelling*, and wild opinions concerning property, what country in Europe did not feel just cause of alarm at the progress of their fury?" The Anabaptists arose in 1521. They taught that to Christians who had the Gospel to guide them, magistrates were unnecessary; that the distinctions of birth, rank, or wealth should be abolished, and that all Christians should live together in a state of equality, throwing their possessions into one stock, and live as one family. In 1525, Munzer and his associates put themselves at the head of a large army, and declared against all laws, governments, and magistrates of every kind. They got possession of Munster city, deposed the magistrates, and confiscated their estates for public good. It is reported that 100,000 fell by the sword. It is supposed a part of these were Catholics, and others having no religion. The first insurgents groaned under oppression, and took up arms for civil defense. It was not a war about baptism. It was in opposition to the feudal system, and the oppression of the German princes.

The Dunkers arose in 1724, Corneal Reissel, a German, was their founder. Persecution compelled them to settle fifty miles from Philadelphia. They do not shave; their best speakers are ordained to be ministers. They still are of the same faith as their fathers. They work at agriculture, and are very plain in their apparel and furniture. The Moravians derive their origin from the Greek Church. In the ninth century, the kings of Bulgaria and Moravia were converted to this faith. The Romish Church compelled some to submit to its dictates. Some united with the Waldenses.* In 1547, they were called "The Brethren of the Law of Christ." A civil war broke out in Bohemia, which compelled them to scatter to other places. A colony, under Christian David, in 1722, went for protection to Count Zinzendorf, who helped them to lands, and to a town which was called Hernhutt. From this place has gone forth many a noble colony of plain, pious people to every quarter of the earth. The Count became a convert to their faith. They have economies, or choir-houses, where they live in *communities*. The single men and women, and the widows and widowers, there support themselves. They have established fifty missions, which have been a great blessing to men. Their Greenland mission was begun in 1733; in North America in 1734; in Crimea, in 1765. This last mission was among the Tartars, to whom industry was taught by example. The Moravians had a moat for protection around their town.

An ancient Inquisitor says of the Waldenses: "These heretics are known by their manners and conversation; they are orderly and modest in their deportment; they avoid all pride in their dress, they neither indulge in finery, nor are they ragged and mean. They avoid *commerce*, that they may be free from deceit and falsehood. They get their living by manual industry. They are not anxious about

* Christians who never submitted to the Roman Catholic Church. They reside in the valley of Piedmont, in Italy.

amassing *riches*, but content themselves with the necessaries of life. They are chaste, temperate, and sober. They abstain from anger." The Archbishop of Turin says: "Their heresy, excepted, they generally live a purer life than other Christians."

The Friends [Quakers] came from the teachings of a weaver, in the fifteenth century. He taught men to despise gold and silver lace, embroidery, laces and ruffles; not to use the word master or servant, or address others with titles. He taught that, to attack others, violated the laws of humanity; to defend one's self broke those of Christianity. If any asked for his coat, he got his waistcoat too. They who struck one cheek were invited to strike the other also. The Friends would take no oaths, pay no tithes, for which they were whipped, imprisoned, and put in pillories and in madhouses. Wm. Penn, in 1681, obtained for them Pennsylvania, to which these people went in large numbers. Said Cromwell: "This is the only religion I can not bribe."

The monks were of various kinds. The meaning of the word is "solitary," and is from *monachus*. Persecution was the cause of men living in deserts. Some lived in communities under a superior, and their houses were called monasteries. Those who lived in cells apart were called *lauræ*. Those having a fixed place were called Chartreux, Benedictines, and Bernardines. Strolling, begging monks were the Capuchins and Franciscans. St. Anthony, at the close of the fourth century, engaged them to live in societies, and have fixed rules for their conduct. They were first in Egypt, then in Palestine and Syria. They went to Italy, France, and Britain. Monks were distinguished by the color of their habit—black, white, and gray. There were monks of the choir and the cloister, professed monks, and lay monks. The latter had priesthood conferred on them.

From these examples we learn what undefiled religion does for a guilty world. It is a remedy for its wrongs. Jesus commands us to put away all avarice and selfishness. Do all Christians do this? No. Many of the children of light and grace are full of selfishness. Religion makes some industrious, frugal, and saving, who will buy wild lands, town lots, stocks, and merchandise, with which to get the earnings of others, forgetting that the Scriptures say "having food and raiment let us therewith be content." Many think that giving to the heathen will cure faults. It is not to be denied that this is a noble charity. Many triumphs have been won where the heathen have been taught productive industry. Where a people have the arts, the converts are costly. In Turkey, a worldly paper has made a calculation, the converts cost each $20,000, and a less sum converts here. The Christians deserve our admiration.

New York City has one church member to fifteen who are not. These few build the churches, support societies that benefit men. The extreme poor do not go to church. Their dingy hats, faded clothes, ill contrasts with the gayety there. The poor can enjoy the pleasing strains of the organ, and the choir singing the songs of the ecstatic Wesley, the pious Watts, or the gifted Montgomery. In a gothic church, having an organ, and a quartette choir, the writer counted fifty persons on a summer's Sunday eve. Another church, having seats for 2,000, had 120 persons in attendance. A gothic church hangs out a sign "Seats are Free." Add to this, the brothers wear home-spuns, and the sisters calicoes. This will induce the poor to attend.

In this city [Cincinnati] is a Female Methodist College, which looks like an abbey of the olden time. It has rooms for 100 ladies, in which to learn the Latin name of a dog, and the Greek name of a sheep. To learn these languages requires four years, and will be forgotten in five unless used. That these ladies may be refined and polished, others must be rude and ignorant. To sweep halls, and cook their food in the basement requires ten servants. At night they will retire to the attics. These polished ladies will require at least twenty persons to create their food and clothing. The wages of these give no books, no leisure, no learning. If all would labor eight hours in a day, learning would be equal. Eight hours daily could be spent conjugating Latin verbs, or declining Greek nouns. The strangest feature is that a hall of learning must be endowed, the Latin and Greek paid for by human society. Says a manager of one of these colleges to the Cincinnati Suspension Bridge Co., we will take $500,000 worth of shares, to give us yearly $50,000 to pay the teachers. Suppose the people of Cincinnati borrow the money of the State, and give to it every year the tolls; in ten years the bridge would be free, and persons can keep their money for their own accomplishments.

To take interest on money is condemned by the Bible. Our Lord says: "*Do good and lend, hoping for nothing again.*" [Luke ch., vi, 35]. Webster says "Usury comes from the Latin word *usura*, to use—a premium stipulated to be paid for the use of money. *Usury* formerly denoted any legal interest. In this sense the word is no longer in use." Nothing can be plainer that interest is forbidden. It was so understood by the "Fathers." Ezekiel [ch. 18, v. 13] says: "Hath given forth upon usury, and hath taken *increase* [interest]: shall he then live? He shall not live." These texts refer to usury. Matt. 5, 42; Exod. 22, 25; Levit. 25, 35; Deut. 23, 19; Psalm 15, 5; Ezek. 18. 17; Gal. 6, 2.

CHAPTER XII.

FARMERS AND MECHANICS.

THE FARMER'S BURDENS ARE TOO HEAVY—IT IS HIS DUTY TO MAKE THEM LIGHT—HOW TO EDUCATE HIS CHILDREN—TO FERTILIZE THE SOIL—HOW THE MECHANIC MAY SHORTEN HIS LABOR—HOW TO OBTAIN A HOME.

"Agriculture is the only honest way of living."—BENJAMIN FRANKLIN.
"Have but few wants, and the means to supply them."—DE WARVILLE.

YOU who are farmers are almost crushed to the earth, with unrequited toil. Like beasts of burden you bear with patience heavy loads. The injustice of society, the remains of barbarism, bind burdens on the farmer that should not be endured. For instance, a number of idle ruffians meet to see a "mill," or two persons maim each other. A number of pale, smooth-faced gentlemen in women's toggery, met to try a MAN, not for *crime* or outrage on men's moral feelings, but for preaching in a Methodist meeting house, for persuading men "to cease to do evil, to learn to do well." For this he was arraigned before a tribunal of Episcopal clergymen, who should have been better employed. There were many outcasts around them, suffering for the necessaries of life. Had these men first created their food and clothes, their faults would not have been so great. Like worms in the peach, they only destroy, they do not create. This was in 1868.

If the farmer would spend a portion of his time making cloth, beet or maple sugar for his own consumption, there

(265)

would be a mighty change—many in society would have to toil.   The corruptions of society enable thousands to live without doing any work.

Farmers are at the bottom of the social column.   When a farmer visits a large city, he should have these reflections: This large multitude I help to feed and find in clothing materials.   What do I gain?   Am I a freeman or a slave?   Why do I toil so incessantly?   The unproductive classes become more numerous every day.   The farmers do not increase in proportion.   The farmer, by selling his grain and grass, impoverishes his land.   Many farms in New England which once gave thirty bushels of wheat to an acre, now only give twelve.   The wheat was eaten in cities, and wasted so that the soil was not fertilized.   In the same manner are the Western States becoming barren.   In half a century sterility will prevail, unless prevented.

The ruins of cities show they have been once populous. Why is it a desert around them?   This land was once a woodland covered with trees, the leaves of which decay and mixed with sand form the soil.   What has taken ages to form may be destroyed in a generation—which is done in this manner.   The soil was planted, and the products consumed in cities, which are on river banks.   Water carries away what should be put on the soil.

A Southern journal says: "Cotton is an exhausting crop; it leaves so little to manure the soil.   Cotton has destroyed more than earthquakes or volcanoes.   South Carolina has produced cotton, to the last dying gasp, till the soil forbids cultivation, and is turned out to nature, reminding travelers of the dilapidated condition of Greece."

Thomas Jefferson said: "Cultivators of the earth are the most valuable citizens.   They are the most independent, the most virtuous, and they are tied to their country,

and wedded to its liberties and interests, by the most lasting
bonds. As long, therefore, as they can find employment
in this line, I would not convert them into artisans, mari-
ners, or any thing else. Our citizens will find employment
in this line till their numbers, and of course their productions, become too great for the demand, both internal and
foreign. This is not the case as yet, and probably will not
be for a considerable time. As soon as the surplus of hands
must be turned into something else, I should then, perhaps,
turn them into the sea, in preference to manufactures. I
consider this class of artificers as the panderers to vice, and
the instruments by which the liberties of a country are generally overturned. However, we are not at liberty to decide
this question on principle of theory only. Our people are
decided in the opinion that it is necessary for us to take a
share in the ocean. I think it is a duty in those intrusted with
the administration of affairs, to conform themselves to the
decided choice of their constituents; and that, therefore, we
should, in every instance, preserve an equality of right to
them, in the transportation of commodities, in the right of
fishing, and the other uses of the sea. But what will be
the consequence? Frequent wars, beyond a doubt!"

Mr. Jefferson never ceased to believe only in simple, rural
life—moderation in living—daily toil; and no greater aggre-
gation of human beings than is to be found in the family on
each farm. He was opposed to the building of a Federal
town for the seat of government.

It is the duty of the father who owns a farm, to leave it
for all future time to his descendants. Why should the father,
who has felled trees, dug up stumps, drained marshes, cultivated hedges, planted orchards, and erected the home with
its green lawns, graveled walks, flowering shrubbery, and
climbing grape vines—why should all this, at the father's

death, pass into the hands of strangers? It is better that the offspring should bless the parent or ancestor for his industry, than a stranger should rejoice in having obtained a possession for a small bale of paper money. When an estate is sold, many a tree and shrub, brick and nail, is not paid for. The purchaser hardly ever pays the full value.

Mr. Wilkinson P————, of Miami Co., Ohio, told the writer, when stopping with him, as a school-teacher, that he "bought his farm, containing 130 acres, for $3.00 an acre, and he paid for it by driving cattle, for thirty-three cents and a third of a cent for a day." He then got married and had seven children. Said he: "I calculate to give my boys, when twenty one, 100 acres each, and the youngest is to have the home farm." This he has done, and he gave his daughter for a marriage portion $2,000. Since he started them in life, he has saved for each $2,000. From this farm this father has saved, in forty years, $30,000; perhaps more. This family had every luxury. This farmer had a way of increasing or multiplying his money, by interest, which is a plan of getting from others. His conscience did not see it was wrong, and he may be forgiven. This case proves that the home should be in the family as a monument after death, and a fountain of supplies, for the members of the family to draw from while creating a new home. These boys were put to work at proper age and earned their farms. Some of them understand algebra and the sciences. These boys cleared their own land.

The writer, became acquainted, in Clinton Co., Ill., with seven brothers of the name of Sharp. Their father taught them to farm, and then gave each 100 acres of land. One brother now has 500 acres, and is a local preacher; the excess of food his sons, tenantry, and himself make will keep his congregation 150 persons all the year. One has the home.

In Sweden the youngest son takes the homestead and keeps the parents; the surplus goes to supply the others. A division takes place where the estate is large.

It is to be hoped the time will come when men will believe again it is sinful to take interest, and that the laboring men will be their own merchants. If justice had been done to society, it would be the owner of all the turnpikes and railroads. If such a period should ever come, men would have to build their own homes. It is from these sources that wealth is obtained that enables men to buy costly homes.

There are three sources that impoverish a farmer's lands: The first is to buy the land on credit, and pay for it by selling its crops; the second is to sell crops to pay the taxes; the third is to sell crops to buy shoddy cloth. If these drains on the land were to cease, a greater number of the farmer's children might find support from the soil. Two of these will be done away with when men know their political rights; the latter when men discipline their mechanical faculties.

To buy cloth abroad introduces the evils of cities. Says Bismark: "Large cities are in the highest degree obnoxious to the welfare of nations." This fact should make the farmer, joined with others, resolve to possess some simple and cheap twisting and weaving machinery. Porter, in his "Progress of the British Nation," says: "A *curious* trade has of late years sprung up, that of importing rags for the purpose of re-manufacture. These are assorted, torn up, and twisted with wool of a low quality, and inferior cloth is made from the mixture."

The farmers, in olden times, supported many scholars. Wm. Godwin, in his "Enquirer," says: "About the fifteenth century the human mind began to shake off its slum-

24

bers.   The principal causes of the revival of learning was
the study of the classics [writings of the ancients].   The
desire of rescuing the ancient manuscripts from oblivion
engaged the attention of kings and princes.   It was considered the most important task in which they could be engaged.   Hence they did not scruple to appropriate the resources of the nation for this purpose.   Scholars went from
country to country, with the hope of obtaining classical
manuscripts.   The recovery of one was the cause of as great
a triumph as if battles had been won, or nations plundered.
To illustrate these, authors and scholars arose, and considered it an honored task to translate and comment on them,
to remove their obscurities, so that the Greek and Roman
writers could be understood and their beauties admired."

At the present time it is the duty of all to become learned.
The ancient classics are translated, why should men go to
a large building to learn to read them.   The time spent at
this would open a new farm.   This course must make men
poor.   If they escape poverty it is a loss to others.   The colleges would make nice homes for aged women who are
homeless.   In a single year [1867], Harvard College had
gifts to the amount of $475,000.   George Peabody gave
$150,000 for archæological [the science of antiquities] and
ethnological [a science on the different races of men] purposes.

How much more it would add to the happiness of men
if this sum were spent in industrial schools for the poor.   It
is difficult for boys to get places, as wood and iron can be
made to do their work.   The boys in the "Ohio Reform
School" spend half of their time at learning, the other at
making their shoes and clothing.   They are taught to obtain their own food; what is left is sold.   The farmers are
in need of such a school, where their children can learn the

use of tools. How few farmers there are who can file saws or put an edge on steel tools. Every farmer should be able to keep his machines in repair, and for this purpose mechanical colleges should be built. There seems to be a disposition on the part of the authorities, to start such schools. If architecture and some of the ologies are taught, it will be of no benefit to those who labor.

C. B. Boynton, in his book, on Russia, says: "A farm of 700 acres had been laid out, under the direction of the government, and on the premises an agricultural school had been established, where both the theory and the practice of agriculture are taught to 200 peasants. An extensive museum is attached to this farm, containing whatever relates to the occupation of a farmer, including all descriptions of agricultural implements, even to the finest breeds of cattle. Model cottages are introduced. Each province is allowed to send annually a certain number to the school. In each year fifty graduates are distributed through the country after having obtained a four-years' course. The pupils are taught blacksmithing, carpenter work, cooperage, tailoring, shoemaking, cabinet-making, and agricultural implement making. Connected with this school is a brickyard, a pottery, a tanyard, and a windmill. Each graduate gets a farm and a 1,000 roubles [$750] to stock it. The pupil is encouraged to carry out these theories and teach others."

This is a model for the Americans. If they should teach the fine arts, only a few will enjoy them. The poor do not see a painting often. These mechanical colleges at present are supported by the sale of wild lands. The Government gives a State 100,000 acres, and it is sold for ten dollars an acre, the amount will be $1,000,000. A poor laborer has accumulated $800, by the most painful saving, such as abstinence from the best food and clothing, or doing without books and papers. This laborer, to obtain eighty acres, has to give his savings. It will take 1,250 laborers to purchase this land. Can any humane man say it is just and right that these laborers should suffer so much to found or endow a school like this. These laborers have to endure painful toil to clear and fence this land. They get the lowest pay, and it is a wrong to embarrass them, the most useful class, by such unequal burdens which are not imposed on the other classes. To save this sum will take a laborer eight to ten years. Statesmen and speculators do not build the school-houses and churches that surround this unimproved land; it is the settlers who make this land desirable, for which they ask nothing, and are glad to see one who will help them to build these. The mechanical colleges should be paid for by the State, and the tuition by the pupil.

It is the duty of every farmer to educate his children, so as to go through the world with ease and comfort, without care and anxiety. The parents of the child should hear it say its letters at three years of age, which will take ten minutes in the day. At four, it will be able to read an easy lesson. At this age the child can be taught to form letters on a small blackboard, resting on the lap. Chalk is used, and this should be the first lesson, *a a a a a a*; this is the second, *b b b b b b b*; this is the third, *c c c c c c c*. When the child has made eight letters, then give it this for a copy, *a b c d e f g h*. The remaining letters form two copies.

a b c d e f g h i j k l m n o p q r s t u v w x y z

This is the last copy. The child should practice on *a* till it can make it perfect, and make it without seeing the copy.

The writer learned this mode of teaching writing by accident. In 1858, the Government offered, in Missouri, a piece of land, one mile long and half a mile wide, for forty dollars. I went to Crawford Co. to see it. The land was hilly, and covered with small oaks. In the little valleys and creek bottom were opened farms. I was offered, by Wm. Keys, fifty dollars in gold to teach school ten weeks. The school-house had no windows. A log was left out to admit the light. In the loft were some boards; with them I made a row of desks, and a blackboard 6 by 3 feet. This I put on two poles, having on them a little fork, and placed it against the ugly fireplace, after filling it with green branches. There were some pieces of boards left; these I thought would, if planed and blackened, make a substitute for slates. I found out what books were wanting as near as I could. I was about to start to Steelville, fifteen miles distant, on foot to purchase them, when Mr. Keys offered me a horse to ride. This act gave me some surprise, as he had only known me five days. I can only account for this, that he did not know what crime was, as it is unknown in far-off rural districts. I purchased, among other books, some mental arithmetics. Said I to a druggist, "Let me have two pounds of chalk." Said he, "I have none." I said to him, with a feeling of disappointment, "What shall I do? I am going to hold a school, and I can not teach without chalk." Said the druggist, "Your scholars will find plenty of chalk in the hills."

I had the children of twelve families to teach. I had to "board around." Sometimes I had to go four miles to the farthest family, in a lonely path, with no houses on it, and liable to meet a wolf on the road. Seven of the fathers of these families could read, five write, and two cipher. I gathered the oldest scholars around my large blackboard, and showed them how addition was done, and what it was for, and then got them to do the same. In five weeks I got some of them through long division. I then showed them how numbers were to be used to find out the price of articles. I considered for what purposes they wanted arithmetic, and drilled them in those examples that they needed. I found out that nearly all could make the alphabet in chalk, from memory in a month. I then gave them an easy copy on their blackboards, which was afterward put on paper, in a neat manner. Writing was learned without pot-hooks or straight marks.

There was a man who persuaded two of the directors that I was not teaching arithmetic right, so I was discharged at the end of eight weeks. This man wanted his son to be the teacher. On the last day of school the circuit preacher was to preach at one o'clock. There was also to be a wedding. I showed how well my charge could read. I then caused them to write on the blackboard the alphabet. I showed their copy-books. I then asked the Presbyterian minister to examine some of them in interest, single rule of three, and in such problems as would occur in life. I had some boys who stepped up to the blackboard and showed to their parents, what they never saw before, how the value of their butter was obtained at so much a pound, the worth of a farm when the price per acre was given, and also the amount of a note. I kindly advise farmers to give this order to a pattern-maker or cabinet-maker.

Mr. ——— ———. Please plane for me, on both sides, a piece of board six inches wide, eighteen inches long, and half an inch thick. Let the wood be poplar. Black-walnut or pine will do. Varnish it with shellac varnish and lamp-black. Set your gauge one inch and a half, and gauge from each edge.

Parents, with this experiment of mine, can not fail to teach their children to write in a rapid manner. If shellac is not to be had, lamp-black, water and glue will answer to paint the board. The gauge lines are made after the board is painted. Parents do not know how easy it is to teach their children. If the teacher has thirty-six scholars, he gives to each scholar ten minutes of his time during the day. The parent spending this time every day in the year will make better scholars. If the mother will take her needle-work, and make her child sit on a low stool, with its back to her, she can hear and see the lesson, and lose no time. Only a few statesmen can spell well. Many scholars are deficient in orthography, in the " nature and power of letters, and the just method of spelling words." The country teacher does not stop to analyze words, to accent syllables, to give the varied sounds of letters, or to modulate the voice in reading. The school-books now are progressive, and adapted to all capacities of youth, which the mother can easily teach. It is the duty of the mother to teach her child that six added to six makes twelve, and three times five makes fifteen. It is her duty to teach the difference between nouns and pronouns, verbs and adverbs. If the mother will try she will be equal to the task, and quite an adept at teaching that which is difficult. It is her duty to begin at three years of age and teach to seven then if the child goes to school, it can sit on a bench without a back and its feet will touch the floor.

It will be difficult to tell what might have been the consequences if the Wesleys had not been taught by their mother. Watts, the poet, could read Latin at four years of age. Watt, the improver of the steam-engine, at six could work the problems of Euclid. Two of these lived to see eighty years, the others not quite that age.

NOTE.-Wilson, Hinkle & Co., Walnut St., Cin., publish school-books on every subject. These begin with the primary, and go up to that which is difficult.

Wm. Cobbett says: "I do not remember when I did not earn my living. My first occupation was driving away the birds from the turnip field. My next employment was harrowing barley with a single horse. This was followed by hoeing peas, reaping wheat, and plowing. My father said: 'He had four boys, the oldest fifteen, and they did as much work as any three men in the parish of Farnham.' In the winter evenings my father taught us all to read and write, and gave us a good knowledge of arithmetic and grammer." This man never was at any school. He earned $100,000 by his pen. He wrote 100 books to the working people, to get them to throw off their slavish chains.

The school-teachers of Cincinnati, in 1866 were paid $556,348. Each scholar costs annually $12.00. If parents would instruct their infant children, half of this might be saved for an industrial school. Parents should think the school-fund is often taken from those who do not need its benefits. They should save it as much as possible. Farmers are not sure their children will be scholars. I was in Illinois, a farmer and his boys were around a heap of corn shelling it. I said to the boys: "If a person can do a piece of work in two days, and another in three days, how long would it take both working together?" They could not tell. The mother and daughter were teachers, and could not tell. I said: "One can do half of the work in a day, the other can do one-third in a day: if you add one-third and one-half together, they will have done five-sixths in one day, and the remaining sixth will take one-fifth of the next day." Said the boys, "We see how it is done."

Parents must teach their children to think and reason. It is easy to do it. When I worked at clock-making I paid a boy $2.00 in advance to teach me arithmetic. I had my first lesson on a rock where he was fishing. I then taught myself.

The farmer must be a thoughtful, thinking being, or he will be imposed on. When the people were counted in 1859, it was ascertained that one in six had what was called an occupation. The remaining five-sixths were women and those under twenty-one. Half of the nation are under twenty-one. Half of the nation are females. Those employed were 5,700,000 and occupied as named:

Agriculturists	3,219,495
Mechanics and manufacturers	480,905
Day laborers	969,000
Servants	560,000
Merchants	123,378
Clerks	184,485
Physicians	54,000
Clergymen	37,000
Lawyers	33,193

Many of the last six classes could easily be more profitably employed at something else. The servants alone can produce food for 20,000,000 of persons. We often see them at the most frivolous pursuits, such as polishing a doorhandle, waiting on idle people, or driving a carriage, when those within can do it themselves. It is a great pity that men with minds, capable of great achievements, should be engaged in such ignoble employments. The poor slave once had a boundary line marked out for him, beyond which he could not go without permission; those lines were those that surrounded the farm on which he was doomed to work. Did he see the man who was free do his servile work? his language was "poor white trash." As much as if he had said, you can get an ax and a spade and create a home; selling your labor makes you but half a man; you are midway between a freeman and a slave. Is there "no independent wish implanted in your mind?" Is your sense of enjoyment so dull that you should be content with rudeness? Is your

25

faculty of invention so poor that you can not give beauty
and form to the materials that are so abundant? Is your reason so perverted that you can not see the wrong you do to
yourself, by taking so scanty a share of your toil for what
you endure? Is your moral sense so obtuse that you can not
see the injustice you do to yourself, by letting another filch
away the excess of labor you create, which is given to painters and sculptors, whose creations you are denied the poor
consolation of seeing? Our African had these conceptions.
Some men were trash, who could be removed and their loss
not felt. The time was when men had *coats-of-arms* to keep
themselves in remembrance, and this custom still exists.
Some might adopt this device—a chin surmounted by razors
sponges, and combs. Waiters can use an arm covered with
a towel, surrounded by blacking brushes, brooms, and dus-
ters. Others can use a curry-comb crossed with whips.
This table shows the proportion of men's pursuits.

A physician to every...	600 people.
A clergyman to every...	800. ,,
A lawyer to every...	1,000. ,,
A merchant to every...	250. ,,
A manufacturer to every...................................	65. ,,
A farmer to every...	10. ,,

In 1859, the value of the wheat crop was $223,000,000,
the corn was worth $180,000,000, the hay $200,000,000,
the butter and cheese $110,000,000, the wool $50,000,000,
the cotton $200,000,000, the tobacco $60,000,000, the
slaughtered animals $212,000,000, the sugar $30,000,000.
The cotton, woolen, and iron manufactures amounted to
$250,000,000 in 1859. The total amount of this labor is
$1,515,000,000. This quantity will keep 90,000,000 of
persons. This appeared in the daily papers: A *writer*, of
the name of Major Huntley, died in the streets of Albany,
of actual starvation. He left a wife and one child.

A mechanic or laborer, who resides in a large city, and is poor when he marries, the probabilities are that he will always remain homeless. Those who get homes in large cities are one in four. The only plan the laborer has to get a home is to remain single till he can get one. The Miami County farmer who earned $100 in a year, did not marry till he accumulated $400. Had he married without getting a home on the land, he could not have set his children to work. They would have been a burden to him, and made him unhappy. The children of a city poor man must do any thing they can find to be done. After waiting months, perhaps years, for something "respectable" to work at, the boy becomes a cigar-maker, or a barber.

When a poor father living in a large city dies, his daughters must go out to service, and work from five o'clock in the morning to eight in the evening, and then sleep in a room that has a window in the roof, or they must become sewing girls, to make fine clothes for others, while they are ragged. The only remedy is for men to go in companies to the wilderness and make homes. It can not be that man, with all his knowledge must be poor. It is what we do that makes us poor. In Cincinnati is a warehouse that has four large stone-brackets over the door, on the end of each is a huge face. The carver has dug the eyes out of two, which makes them look hideous. To dig out these eyes must have cost two dollars, which would give some poor child a pair of shoes. Some say this gives work to mechanics. It is very absurd reasoning. It is unnecessary labor, which, if not done, society would be just as well off. If the stone-carver had remained idle, he would not have destroyed his clothes or consumed as much food.

A man has money in his house. A bad man goes and takes it, for which he is arrested. The judge says to him,

"Why did you do this act?" The reply is, "I wanted to give work to mechanics. I know a stone-cutter who wants to make for me some stone ornaments, to obtain clothing for his family." Says the judge: "The family whom you deprived wanted the money for their own clothing. You must atone for your fault, by confinement, where you will be taught to make cloth. Let the stone-cutter get a loom, and make his own clothing, and society will be gainers."

There are in society men who get large quantities of others' labor by strange, queer ways which mankind, some time or other, will find out is wrong. They are guilty of the folly and wickedness of putting labor in the wrong place, thereby causing much sorrow and misery. There is no difference between building the Pyramids of Egypt and some of our modern stores. Both have caused men to go hungry and ill-clad.

One of the boys in Missouri to whom I taught arithmetic was seventeen. He could tan and dress a cow's hide, make the leather into a pair of boots. The hides were tanned in a hollow log. He could build log-houses and make furniture. I felt much admiration for Mrs. Keys when I saw her husband in a black suit of clothes, all wool, made, spun, cut, and dyed with her own hands. Many families make blankets, quilts, sheets, and linen for old age. It would fill a person with surprise to see the shelves laden with these goods. Their mechanical knowledge was very limited. If their boys could have learned better modes of working they would be richer. The men did not work more than four hours in the day on an average. They used wooden plows with a piece of iron on the point. The young people had never seen a sofa, brick or frame house. If you set this people to making stone faces and foolish things, families will freeze to death. This often occurs.

If a hundred mechanics will form a community, and subscribe $20,000, they can purchase looms, mill-stones, sawmills, wood-planing machines, wood and iron turning lathes, farming tools, and a steam engine. This amount will also build a shop. This community, occupying a tract of land, will escape many burdens, and their children will never do servile work for others.

The Plymouth pilgrims made a contract, that they should possess all things in common for seven years, after that they should be in separate families. In 1650, this instruction was given by the secretary of New Netherlands to the people how they should build houses: "Dig cellars six or seven feet deep, and as long as is necessary. To keep the earth from caving, fasten bark on the sides, and cover the floor with plank. Take spars for the roof, and cover with sods and bark." This was the mode of building in New England at first, so as not to waste time in procuring food. In the course of three or four years, the country became better adapted to agriculture, and then better houses were built.

"The 'Oneida Community' has been established twenty years, and consists of 200 persons, men, women, and children, who own 508 acres of good land. John Noyes organized the association. They believe the Bible is the Spirit of Truth. For tea and coffee substitutes are found. Tobacco and ardent spirits are not allowed. The sexes generally room apart. As far as their means allow, every man and woman has a private room, with furniture and library.

"There are twenty departments in business. Each person works at that for which he is fit. They make satchels, carpet and traveling bags, mouse and bear traps, and sewing silk. They are wholesale dealers in silk. They can immense quantities of fruit. Their orchard contains fifty acres, and it is full of strawberries, blackberries, grapes, apples, pears, and plums. Their barns and stables are large. The grounds are handsomely laid out in walks and drives. The house is three stories high, and 300 feet long, with two wings. They have a large hall, in which is held concerts, lectures, and occasional dancing. They have a band of music. The government is general *persuasion* and particular *criticism*. In sickness, "faith and nature" is preferred to medicine. Time has softened the virtuous indignation they endured. They now live on good terms with their neighbors. Their belief makes them quiet and industrious, and mind their own business. At the age of two, the children are given up to be taken care of *en masse*. At twelve they mingle with the others. The capital of two communities is $254,568. A large portion of the women are not very attractive. The men are thoughtful, with a tendency to reading. Their library contains 2,500 books.*

In 1817, some Wurtemburgers, for not fully believing the doctrines of Luther, had to leave that city. "A 'Friend' let them have, in Tuscarawas, Co., O., 5,500 acres or land at $3.00 an acre, and sixteen years to pay it. After they had tried other usual plans, in 1819 they became a social community in the strictest sense—a co-operation, where the strong should support the weak, and there be no wants that united effort can not relieve. They elected a secretary and treasurer. There are 300 persons; they elect three trustees to serve them three years, who subject all their business to a committee of five. They own thirty-three dwellings, a saw, flour, and woolen mill. The flower garden in the center of the village contains a hot-house. They milk 100 cows, and make 7,000 pounds of butter in a year. Fifty families get their milk and butter from the milk-house. The ma-

* Cincinnati Times, July 25, 1866.

terials for wearing apparel are kept in the "magazine," and given out by the housewife to each family on application. Each family draws bread from the bake-house, and sends their washing to the public wash-house. They are of the opinion that too much book-learning is not good for people of their habits. They have a school teacher among them, and also a flock of 1,500 sheep. The Justice of the Peace performs the marriage ceremony. They meet for worship twice on a Sunday, and sing, and hear a sermon read. No public prayers.

"They seem ignorant of social life. They work hard, and idleness is entirely unknown. The children begin working as soon as old enough, and their life, from the 'cradle to the grave,' seems an endless routine of labor. Few ever see any money. Their wants are supplied out of a common fund. There are no rich or poor; all are equal, and laboring for a common cause. Many of them are entirely ignorant of the world, or any thing pertaining to it; many never having been three miles from home. Having little care or anxiety, living a moral and industrious life, they are long-lived and healthy. No record is kept of the food and clothing consumed. Their wants are few, and supplied from the store-house. Beyond this they desire nothing. They use no tobacco. Sometimes they drink native wines. Their land and buildings are worth $1,500,000, which makes the share of each man, woman, and child to be $5,000. They wear blue fabrics of their own making. The women wear blue stuff gowns, short and scant. To them pomp and display is nothing but vanity. Devoid of ambition or fame, ignorant of the ways and wickedness of the world, they journey through life, without the many disappointed hopes and blasted expectations that the people of this world suffer."*

* Cincinnati Commercial, August 3, 1867.

"The Shakers owe their origin to the teachings of Ann Lee, who founded this sect a few years before our Revolution. A settlement of them, near Lexington, Ky., contains 400 persons, and they own 5,600 acres of land. No rich or poor are to be seen in their village. All their lands, cattle, horses, and sheep are held in common. "The house which we were shown was a model of neatness. The great wide hall was as cool as an iceberg, with its narrow strip of carpet, and painted floor, which was scoured till it glistened. All the furniture was home-made. The bottoms of the old-fashioned, high-backed chairs were woven out of narrow strips of white, black, brown, and green woolen cloth, and looked very beautiful indeed. The stove shone like a mirror, and the tongs, shovel, and wisp hung neatly by its side. Curtains of snowy muslin shaded the windows. Order and cleanliness prevailed every-where. They kept up their society by adopting children, of whom one in six stay to live a life of celibacy and holiness."*

The moulders of Louisville have an association for getting high wages. When they forbid others to work for the employers, and say that these shall have only one apprentice to ten workmen, they do what they have no power to do. Men are free. If one class of mechanics combine to raise their wages, the other should do the same to be equal. If the stove moulders combine, the stoves must sell high, and less will be sold. If the moulder has to pay the carpenter the increased rate of wages, he will see the absurdity of "strikes." The injury workmen do to themselves by strikes is to see their work done somewhere else. Strikes diminish the employer's capital, his machinery goes to ruin; and, after a strike, the employers use fewer workmen, and do not employ the leaders. A strike, many years ago, in

* Cincinnati Commercial, July, 1867.

England, among the cotton-cloth workers, made one employer gather up his machinery and start it in this country. A strike in England, among weavers, in 1830, led to the invention of the self-acting loom.   A strike among pit sawyers caused the universal introduction of steam-driven saws all over England. This was fortunate for the consumer, not so for the sawyer.   A moulder in Louisville struck a man down, and left him dying, for not working for the price he dictated.   The bricklayers of New York City, in 1868, made an unprofitable strike.   When they did go to work, it was, perhaps, on some gorgeous mansion, an unnecessary store, or an expensive stable.   When their work was done many of them went to eat and sleep in a place not fit for a habitation.   Striking mechanics seem to forget, they increase the difficulties of employers to get work for them.

A wood-chopper hauls wood to town for $3.00 a cord. Another wood-chopper says to him, let us have $5.00 for a cord, which we can bring about by combining, and not letting boys learn the work. This would lessen the amount of wood, and cause the bricklayers to shiver. The mechanic who would forbid a poor boy from learning a useful trade, has not much feeling, and would make a detestable tyrant. If mechanics will practice the industry and simplicity of the "Zoarites" and "Rappites," * they can not consume the food nor wear out the clothing they can create. Some can do more than others, and should have more pay. Hugh Miller, in his "School and School-masters," tells us of a man who asked for some stone-cutting. The foreman said, "Can you hew a column." He replied, "I think I can do it." On Monday he took a chip of his stone, and went a little

* Zoar is the name of the village in which the Ohio community live. Jacob Rapp, a German, with his followers, in Beaver Co., Penn., created millions of wealth, in the form of farms, mills, and stores. They are Communists.

distance and looked at it. Tuesday he trifled away. The strange Highlander on Wednesday began to work in earnest. The others ceased to laugh at him. On Thursday, at noon, he was even with them; the laugh was on the other side. He had done as much as they had. On Friday night his column was done. The others had a hard day's work to do. When paid, he said "I can hew a column." Mr. Miller said his uncle could build more stone wall than his two nephews, who worked as hard as they could. This proves that societies can not fix a uniform rate for other's wages. Some have more skill than others.

Two of the Harpers, in early life, worked sixteen hours a day, which has caused them to own the largest publishing house in this country. Their ambition is to supply us with good and cheap books. Some printers earn thirty-five cents an hour at their labor. There are others who endure the fierce heat, the bitter cold, and work for twenty cents an hour. There are boys who wish to be earning something. If the Harpers choose to employ these, if they can be taught to do the work, who has the right to interfere. The employing shoe-makers of Linn, and the shop-owning clock-makers of Winstead, work all the unskilled labor they can by a division of labor, which gives to printers and bricklayers cheap shoes and clocks. Why should the men who do the severe work have the least amount of comfort? All men are alike; all should have an equal share of the earth and its comforts.

This fact shows that strikes accomplish nothing. "The Scotch miners' strike was the most extensive and bitterly contested in Scotland. 40,000 men were engaged in it. The loss of wages was $2,500,000. The men have returned to their work under a very gloomy mood and a burning sense of injustice."—London paper, 1856.

English workmen have a way worthy of our imitation. In March, 1849, a few pianoforte makers commenced with a capital of $500. They went on increasing their business, till they were worth $10,000.

In August, 1848, fourteen workmen, with a capital of $550, formed the "Fraternal Association of Working File makers." Their numbers increased to forty-two, and they earned a fifth more than their wages.

In 1843, Mr. Laclere, of France, formed partnerships with his workmen, to save his tools and materials. Among fifty workmen he divided $3,500 in a year, in addition to their wages, which was a fifth.

A furniture factory in Indianapolis, containing an engine and abundant machinery, is owned by nineteen workmen. This shows that changes are made which will be beneficial to the working people. Many different trades are thus carried on in England. To see a number of journeymen shoe-makers or tailors in a town suffering a person to make gains from their labor is a reproach to them.

The poor mechanic and humble laborer often feel humbled, when they contrast their depressed condition with that of the wealthy. Some roll in a splendid carriage, driving helter skelter here and there, while they trudge on foot. Some have a pew in the church, in which to show their silks and satins, and to listen to the sweet tones of the organ, as they reverberate among groined arches, and along fretted aisles. Some are covered with costly laces, silks embroidered with silver and gold, or ermine-trimmed velvets resplendent with jewels. To see a person thus bedizened, putting on a defiant air and a haughty mien, must carry to the mind of that poor widow a sense of great injustice.

The laborer has but one method to rise above his condition, and that is, to leave such people to serve themselves.

By frugality and abstinence from marriage till a start is obtained, a home will be secured. The writer tried to sell his manuscript on labor to six publishers. Not one had the politeness to look at it. After much thought, I purchased $43.00 worth of type. I also purchased a hog at eight cents a pound, which I salted. I bought potatoes at $1.20 for a bushel. They rose in the spring to $2.00. I purchased beans at wholesale prices. Occasionally I had beef and mutton. My winter's daily food cost, with coffee and apples, eighteen cents. A pound of bread sells for ten cents.

A pound of good flour costs six cents, and will make twenty-one ounces of bread, at a cost of four and a half cents a pound. It is the duty of every housewife to use as much flour as possible. Make a batter of eggs, skimmed milk, and flour; ferment it, and bake into pancakes. Have a generous portion left, then put it in a cloth, boil it two or three hours, and serve it very hot for dinner. It is to be eaten with butter, sugar, and honey.

Roll out a portion of richly made paste to the diameter of a plate. Roll out six small pieces to the diameter of a saucer. On the large piece of paste spread a layer of apple sauce or blackberries; spread this on each layer of paste, and bring the outside layer over the whole mass. Put a plate on the joining place, and it will keep out the water. Boil in a cloth. Half a pound of chopped suet, mixed with a pound of flour in milk, and boiled in a cloth, makes good food, when eaten with honey and butter. Four cents' worth of wheat, pounded wet in a bag till hulled, and boiled in five quarts of milk, with six ounces of sugar, serves four men a meal.

Coarse beef, with one-third of salted pork, finely chopped with hatchets on the end of wood, makes excellent food.

CHAPTER XIII.

THE AMERICAN GOVERNMENT.

THE AMERICAN GOVERNMENT HAS NOT AMELIORATED THE CONDITION OF THE
WORKING PEOPLE—IT SHOULD BE CHANGED—IT BENEFITS THE RICH, NOT
THE POOR—OPINIONS OF BRISSOT DE WARVILLE—MARQUIS DE CHASTELLUX.

"Ill fares that State, to hastening ills a prey,
Where wealth accumulates and men decay."—GOLDSMITH.

GODWIN, in his "Inquirer," says: "In savage life
there is no invidious distinction. There is no one
unequal. None are insulted by the sight of insolent wealth and idleness. As soon as the distinction of
property exists, created by the labor of tenants and serfs,
then there must be a '*power*' vested in certain individuals,
to compel others to labor for their benefit."

To prove this, we need only to look at the varied disposi-
tions of men; some are good and kind, others are selfish,
cruel, and unjust. The benevolent Howard proposed to
his wife to visit London. She said, "The £100 it might
cost would build a laborer a cottage." The journey was
not made. He spent $50,000 in visiting European prisons,
trying to get their woes mitigated by their sovereigns. A
part of the Roman patricians could find pleasure in gladiatorial shows, where thousands of victims, monthly, must give
up their lives, to obtain which provinces were ruined. Some
can see others work for the necessaries of life, and not assist them. They would rather contrive schemes to plunder

them.   Franklin's satire on human society is true.   He says:

> "Some know no reason why they are born,
> Except it be to eat up the other's corn,
> To eat up all the fowl, flesh, and fish,
> And leave behind them an empty dish."

There are many who have acquired wealth by injustice and oppression, and who rely on the government to enable them to keep it.   Van Rensselaer, of N. Y. State, had given to him a piece of land, one hundred miles by fifty, containing 3,200,000 acres, which was rented to settlers, each to give a bushel of wheat for nine acres, a pair of chickens, and a day's labor every year.   The "Patroon" had the privilege of cutting all the wood he wanted; and when the settlers sold out, they had to give a fourth of the money to the Patroon.   His claim was given by Queen Anne.   In 1837, the settlers got it into their heads that Anne had no right to give away lands, to which they and their ancestors had acquired a title by cutting down the trees, fencing the fields, killing the wolves, conquering the Indians, constructing the roads, and fighting for it during the Revolution.   To put on a piece of land $10,000 worth of work, and when sold to give $2,500 of it to this Patroon was injustice.

This man had done nothing to the land to give it value. This person had rents from the cities of Albany, Troy, and many villages.   The "renters" had a revolt, and were subdued by policemen and soldiers.   An appeal to laws was in vain, as they were made by lawyers and men of wealth. This man had at least $200,000 as a yearly income.   It would bother him to eat $1,000 worth of fruits, vegetables, bread, and meat in a year.   This sum feeds idle servants, useless mechanics, sculptors, painters, and makers of curiosities.   These last make articles called *virtu*, which cause the Patroon to be a *virtuoso*, a *connoisseur* instead of a farmer.

After nearly a century of a national existence, it becomes us to inquire, Are we a happier and better people. Since the Revolution this country has been increasing in misery and crime, and nothing will save this land from wretchedness but to return to those habits that prevailed before our Revolution. Mrs. Grant came to America in 1760. In her book she says none were rich or poor. All had to work in their *gardens*, except Mr. Schuyler. This was in the city of Albany. The Marquis De Chastellux, a French officer, was in this country in 1783. In his book of travels, he says the only poor person he saw in America was a girl, who had escaped from the Wyoming massacre, and she was living in a tavern. This writer adds, food and lodging are abundant every-where.

The translator of Brissot De Warville's American Travels, says: "He was an indefatigable defender of the rights of mankind, an impartial reasoner and inquirer." In answer to an inquiry, "Can a people without any goverment be happy?" he says, "Yes, the numerous Quakers dispersed over Pennsylvania have passed half a century without municipal government or police. P. 16.

"We have often observed that civil legislation has corrupted the best political institutions; it is often a crime against society. * * * The timidity that wealth inspires, disposes the rich to regard the poor as capable of being restrained only by fetters. P. 35.

"In some houses you hear the piano. God grant that the Boston women may never attain the malady of perfection in this art! It is at the expense of domestic virtue. * * * The law has imprisonment for adultery. It is scarcely carried into execution—the families are pure and happy. * * * I see, with pain, they invoke the hair-dresser's art. This art, unhappily, has already crossed the seas. P. 73

" When riches are centered in a few hands, they have a
great superfluity to favor the agreeable and frivolous arts.
When riches are equally divided in society, there is very
little superfluity and means of encouraging the pleasing arts.
The ability to give encouragement to the agreeable arts is a
sympton of a national calamity.   P. 88

" The [Boston] work-house is not so much peopled as
you imagine.   Provisions are cheap, good morals predominate, and the number of thieves and vagabonds are small.
There is no *misery* here. * * * You travel without fear or
arms.   You sleep quietly in the woods, or in a house that
has no locks on the doors.   P. 99.

"Almost all these houses are inhabited by men who are
both cultivators and artisans.   One is a merchant, another a
tanner, etc.   All are farmers. * * Agriculture being the basis
of the riches of this state [Connecticut], they are here more
equally divided. * * You hear nothing of robberies, murders,
and mendicity.· The American poor do not abjure all ideas
of shame and equity.   P. 121.

"Agriculture abounds there [Albany], and the people do
not like to hazard themselves to the dangers of the sea for
a fortune they can draw from the bounty of the soil.   The
air is pure, the people are tolerably temperate, in good circumstances, and there are no poor, provisions being very
cheap.   P. 130.

"A man in that country [Ohio] works scarcely two *hours*
in a day. * * Philadelphia is already too large.   When
towns acquire this degree of population, you must have police, spies, soldiers, prisons, hospitals, and all the sweeping
train of luxury.   Wherever you find luxury, provisions are
dear. * * As to gold, it is degrading for a free country to
dig for it.   Gold has always served the cause of despotism.
Liberty will find less dangerous agents in its place." P. 416

This man was once a merchant, and failed. He now sells hot potatoes to poor
street boys. He might have been a happy farmer, if the speculators in wild lands
were unknown. Gen. Washington had 200,000 acres, Morris & Co., 6,000,000,
Albert Galatin and others, 225,000 acres of land for profit or rent. This made
them oppressors of the working-men, and gave them power to found banks, construct toll-roads, build bridges, and possess railroads. If the "Fathers" had given
to each mechanic a town-lot, to each farmer as much land as he could cultivate,
the inequalities that now exist would not be seen. The rulers of this nation, by
selling lands to those who will not cultivate them, make the work-people slaves.

This writer tells us of a visit paid to Gen. Washington, where Col. Humphrey assured him that the General planted 1,100 bushels of potatoes in a year, and his estate consisted of 200,000 acres of land. This language occurs in M. Brissot's second volume:

"When man has every convenience, he then thinks of ornament. The wants of luxury are in the imagination, and procure imaginary pleasures only. To wear lace clothing or drink coffee out of china is a want created by fancy. * * Men whose subsistence is precarious love their children less than the inhabitants of the country who have a small property. Paternity is a burden, and their children are ignorant of the soft caresses of paternal love. Manufacturers [workmen] are condemned to vegetate in dismal prisons, where they respire infection, and abridge their lives. This alone ought to decide the Americans to reject the painful state of manufactures.*

"If manufactures bring gold into the States they bring a poison that undermines them. They accustom men to servitude, and give to a republic a preponderance to aristocratical principles. Accumulating riches in a small number of hands inclines republics to aristocracy.

"Husbandmen are honest people. Workshops show interest struggling against interest, rich and indolent stupidity striving to cheat active indigence. If workshops do not make men rascals they dispose them to become so. * * In a republic none should be wretched—*want* obliges them to disturb civil order. They are paid by the rich, who may make use of them to destroy republicanism. * * * Plate is used in the South, where slavery reigns, and many are poor

---

* This writer had ample opportunities to observe how miserable were lacemakers, jewelers, silk weavers, and others. To his mind, to take the people from productive employment was to make them poor. He saw the people had good woolens and linens, which each made for himself.

there. There are none in the North—no plate is used there. * * America is not yet gnawed by the vermin which devour Europe, by indestructible mendicity. Thieves render not her forests dangerous. Her public roads are not stained with blood shed by assassins and robbers. There are no beggars, no indigent persons, no subjects forced to steal the subsistence of others to procure one for themselves. Every man finds land to produce him articles of subsistence, and it is not loaded with taxes, but renders him a recompense for his labor. A man who can live easily never consents to dishonor himself by useless crimes, the torments of remorse, and the vengeance of society." *

Mr. Winterbottom, in his "History of America," tells us : " The thirty-sixth article of the [Pennsylvania] constitution says : 'Every freeman, to preserve his independence, ought to have some profession, calling, trade, or farm, whereby he can honestly subsist. There can be no use in establishing offices of profit, the usual effects of which are dependence, servility, faction, contentions, corruptions, and disorders among the people. Wherefore, whenever an office, through increase of fees, becomes so profitable that many apply for it, the profit should be lessened.'

"The Americans pay few taxes, and no tithes. The rich have no power of oppressing there. Not many have great riches. Poverty is almost unknown. Mr. Cooper saw only one beggar, and he was an Englishman.

---

* This writer visited this land in 1787. His writings are full of instruction to the Americans. The troubles that he foresaw are upon us. He went back to France. On the 31st of Oct. 1793, he and nineteen others were guillotined for being in opposition to Robespierre, Barrere, and others. Their last words were "Vive la Republique." They all commenced to sing the Marseillese hymn at execution. As their voices became lessened, the sounds grew feeble. At last one stood up to sing, his voice was silenced. Their execution was concluded in thirty-seven minutes.

"The homestead is given to the youngest son. An unmarried man of thirty is scarcely to be found in the country towns. A grandmother at forty and her married daughter, each having an infant, are often seen together.

"The privileged aristocracy of Europe are often without a single virtue, rolling at ease in splendor, preying upon the fruits of honest industry, and devouring the earnings of the virtuous peasant. Their depraved manners extend poison through all the channels of human happiness.

"In America this class of persons is not known. The mass of inhabitants, exclusive of servants, consists of those who possess lands in fee simple. A mediocrity of situation is common in America. There are but few whose incomes will reach £2,000, and the numbers are nearly as small who are reduced to a dependent situation.

"There are in America but few people like the poor in England. There are few great proprietors of land, and few tenants. All follow some handicraft. Very few people are rich enough to live on rents or incomes, to pay the high price for paintings, statues, architecture, or any works of art more curious than useful. Wanton extravagance, useless parade, and quarrels are not common. Boxing matches are unknown. No military to keep the people in awe. A robbery is rare. There was none during the yellow fever in Philadelphia.

"In England, the young man flies to prostitution, for fear of the expense of a family. In America no man is anxious about the expense of his family. Every man feels the increase of his family to be an increase of riches, and no farmer doubts his ability to provide for them.

"In Great Britain, perpetual exertion, incessant industry, daily deprivation of the comforts of life, are incumbent on the man of middle life. In America it is otherwise. The

mass of the people are *untainted*, hence their freedom from
artificial poverty, and the diffusion of the common conveniences of life.

"In England, if a man is unfortunate, the crowd trample
on him. In America there is room to get up again. Part
of the tradesmen live in the country, and reside on from one
to one hundred and fifty acres, which they cultivate at their
leisure with their wives and children." *

Isaac Weld visited America in 1807. It seems from
reading his "Travels in North America," that he found
money did not command respect. If this Englishman had
seen any want or poverty he would have mentioned it. He
says: "The generality of servants, in Philadelphia, are emigrants. They remain in servitude till they can save some
money, then they quit their master for the independence so
natural to the mind of man. As to the Americans, none
but the most *indifferent* enter into service; it is considered
only suitable for negroes. *Civility* can not be purchased on
any terms. They consider it incompatible with freedom,
and that there is no other way of convincing a stranger he
is in a land of liberty, only by being surly and ill-mannered
in his presence.

"At the taverns the bread was sour, the fruit acrid, and it
was difficult to get a horse rubbed down." Mr. Weld describes how wretched slavery makes a people, and how the
common people fight, and how they gouge out the eye.
"In Virginia every fourth man appears with an eye out."

Duke De La Rochefoucalt Liancourt wandered up and
down this country from 1795 to 1797. His principles
were opposite to those of Brissot's. In his book of "Travels," he says: "The people of America live well. There

* This history was written in 1795, for circulation in England. It is
in four volumes, quarto size.

are few persons who do not possess more than they need
for their maintenance.   Hence the indolence of the inhabitants.   * * * There are seldom any poor in Roxborough
County [near Philadelphia].   Laborers are scarce in New-
ark.   The district contains no paupers, there exist no poor-
rates.   * * * Morristown is seven miles from Philadelphia.
Its jail is only inhabited by the keeper.   Poor-rates are seldom necessary.   At present no paupers are there.   * * *
The laws of the State of New York have established poor-
rates.   There are few to be found of this description in
that new country.   * * * Herkimer Co. contains 25,000,
persons.   Two of these received public relief.   * * * John
Schuyler has 1,500 acres of land ; 500 acres are cleared.
He owns three mills, and his yearly taxes were $35.00."

   " John Melish gives us two volumes of travels in this
country from, 1806 to 1809.   He says : " The people are
remarkably civil and industrious.   'The genius of architecture seems to have shed his maledictions over the land.'*
There are no large towns, there seems to be no *occasion* for
them.   Mankind are better accommodated in small towns
than in large cities.   The inhabitants are mostly farmers,
and produce on their farms every necessary of life.   One
day's labor was sufficient to keep the family a week."

   This writer, by this record, has given us the causes of the
poverty of this country.   "'The Ohio Company's purchase' is along the Ohio River seventy miles, from north
to south eighty, and contains 1,000,000 acres.   The retail
price of this land was from $2.00 to $20.00 an acre.

   "'The Symmes's purchase' is between the two Miamis,

---

* This writer paid a visit to Thos. Jefferson, and has saved us this one of his
noble sayings.   A beautiful store is built by profits the people have not yet
learned to save.   That imposing college is often built by speculations on
public lands.   The grand public edifice is often built by forced contributions.
Were the common people wise, this excessive labor would be on their homes.

it contained more than 1,000,000 of acres, and was sold for
$5.00 an acre.   Mr. Zane, of Wheeling, for surveying a
road, had given to him lands that are the sites of Zanesville,
New Lancaster, and a tract of bottom land opposite Chil-
licothe, one mile square. 'The Scioto Company's purchase' contained 2,000,000 of acres.

"'The Western Reserve lands' were 122 miles long,
and 45 wide, and contained 3,423,360 acres.   In 1795,
500,000 acres were given to those on the Connecticut sea-
shore, whose towns were burnt by the British during the
Revolution.   The remainder of the land, was sold by the
Connecticut Legislature, to Oliver Phelps and others for
$1,200,000.   This, land in, 1810 was re-sold for two and
four dollars an acre.

"'The Holland purchase' was 100 miles square, and contained 4,000,000 of acres, in the vicinity of Lake Ontario,
and the Genesee River.   The retail price was $3.50 for an
acre, five per cent. in cash, and the balance to be paid
in six annual payments."

This writer gives us a pleasing description of the "Rapp
Colony."   He says: "'The Harmonist Society' had its
origin in Wurtemberg.   The Lutheran religion had become predominate, to which every body had to contribute.
These men maintained that the religion taught by Luther
had been destroyed, and in place of it, to regulate the life,
and regenerate the mind, it was converted into an engine of
power, to the civil government, to keep the people in check.
They were subjected to fines and imprisonments.

"In 1805, they organized a constitution, and founded it
on Acts, ch. iv, v. 32. This society, in their new American
home, in 1809, had 4,500 bushels of wheat, 4,500 of rye,
4,500 of barley, 10,000 of potatoes, 4,000 lbs of flax,
and 1,000 sheep. In 1810, they numbered 800 persons.

"They owned 9,000 acres of land. Their mills, dwellings, and lands amount to $220,000. They live pure lives, and resign their offspring to the society at death. They have no fear of want, no care, no use for money. They help each other, and are free from the temptations that the rest of mankind are subject too. There is no crime or immorality among them."

Had these people lived in the city, and become chinshavers, head-washers, grotesque stone-carvers, toy-makers, wood-carvers, and frivolous workers, they would have been poor and miserable, their children drudges, sewing-girls in shops with the windows in dark, dirty alleys. Some of these societies are still prosperous and getting richer. The time may come when laborers will live in "baronial halls," surrounded with umbrageous walks, grassy lawns, beautiful conservatories, well filled graperies, abundant vineyards, bounteous orchards, flowery parterres, productive gardens, and pleasing apiaries.

The "Zoarites" do not increase, and their children wander off to enjoy gavety elsewhere. There can be no harm in making their home attractive to prevent this. When a man has a house, a granary, a fenced field, he may indulge in the fine arts; if he creates them with his own hands, then no one is injured. To take by force or fraud the food and clothes of another, and give them to scene painters and trifle makers is an injustice. Those who nourish these artists never see their wondrous productions.*

The writer resolved he would make a painting by getting up early in the morning at midsummer, and painting to seven o'clock, the hour for labor. With pencil I copied a book scene, and put on the varied colored paints. After sixty mornings I then showed the painting to a "tinner" and a "plumber," the two first to see it. One said: "Whoever saw such sharp rocks on a seashore." Said the other: "They are put there to find freight for the boat." The scene was a boat at sea, sailors on the shore, cottage and hills in the dis-

In 1818, a Philadelphia printer, of the name of H. Hall, printed a series of "Letters on Pennsylvania," written by C. B. Johns. He says: "There are no poor here. A laborer gets $1.25 for a day's labor. $1,00 will purchase 20 lbs of beef, or 20 lbs of pork, or 16 lbs of flour. The labor of four days will give him support for a month. I have been in four houses, and the men are sitting down instead of working. Sheep skins, heads, and breasts are thrown away."

The laborer of half a century ago did not accumulate a pile of money to generate stealers. He created a heap of food, and then ate it. A thief in these improved days stole some silver-plate. He sent a letter to his victim saying: "Allow me, sir respectfully to suggest to you in future you will content yourself with cheap spoons, and spend your surplus cash in the cause of humanity and Christ."

Abbe Raynal, when speaking of the criminals sent to this country, says: "If they had not quitted their country, disgrace and shame, which never fail to depress the mind, would have prevented them from recovering either regularity of manners or public esteem. But, in another country, where the experience they had of vice might prove a lesson of wisdom, and where they had no occasion to attempt to remove any unfavorable impressions, they found, after their misfortunes, a harbor in which they rested with safety. Industry made amends for their past follies. Men who had left Europe like vagabonds, and who had disgraced it, returned *honest* men and *useful* members of society.

"All these colonists had at their disposal, for clearing and tilling their lands, the most profligate set of men in

tance. I never painted a cloud, a tree, or a wave before. A determined will works wonders. My ambition is with my own hands to build a house and have some home-made paintings.

the three kingdoms, who had deserved death for capital
crimes, but who, from motives of humanity and policy,
were suffered to live and work for the benefit of the state.
These malefactors, who were transported for a term of
years, which they were to spend in slavery, became *industrious*, and acquired *manners*, which placed them once more in
the way to fortune. There were some of those who, when
restored to society by the freedom they had gained, became
planters, heads of families, and the owners of the best plantations—a proof of how much it is for the interest of a civilized society to admit this lenity in the penal laws, so conformable to human nature, which is frail, but capable of
sensibility, and of turning from evil to good."

Jeremy Bentham, in his "Theory of Legislation," says :
" The English, before the independence of America, were
in the habit of sending their convicts to that country. This
was slavery to some, to others pleasure. A rogue was a
fool if he did not commit some offense to get an outfit and
a free passage. Some of the convicts gained a *home* and
property."—Penal Code.

Lord Kames, in his "Sketches on Governments," says :
" Our American settlements are now so prosperous, banishment there is scarce a punishment. It may, however, be
now a sufficient punishment for theft."

Mrs. Kitty Trevelyan, in her diary of the "The Times
of Whitefield and Wesley," written in 1745, says : " There
are the convicts, our outcast countrymen, working out their
sentences beside the negroes on the plantations."

Voltaire, in a preface to another's book, speaks of transported criminals to America as becoming honest.* De
Toqueville, in his writings, alludes to this subject.

* The writer regrets that the note he made from Voltaire is mislaid. Men
are made bad by circumstances. If you change them, men become better.

27

James I "ordered dissolute persons to be sent to Virginia." Statutes were enacted that crimes punishable with death might be commuted by the courts to banishment. A reason for this act was "in many of the colonies there was a want of servants, who, by their labor and industry, might *improve* the said colonies and make them more *useful*."

The Legislature of Virginia passed an act, that persons who disposed of these convicts should give £100 security for their proper behavior. Those who purchased them gave £10 security that they should do no harm. In 1750, about 400 felons were yearly sent to Maryland.

In 1752, the New York "Independent Reflector" says: "Very surprising that a horde of the most flagitious banditti upon earth should be sent as agreeable companions to us! It is intended as a punishment. It is a mistake; they are highly rewarded. What can be more agreeable to a wretch, driven through necessity to seek a livelihood by housebreaking, and robbing on the highway, to be saved from the halter, the stench of a jail, and transported to a country where no man can reproach him for crimes; where labor is high, where a little will support him, and all his expenses will be moderate and low?"

The Revolution put an end to convict emigration. In 1801, Botany Bay had 5,000 convicts and 500 free people. This was the germ that will be a mighty nation. This infant people was divided into servants, soldiers, and masters. The poor convict had only a small burden to bear, he became virtuous. When the lawyer, clergyman, scholar, merchant, physician, philosopher and others are added to the burdens of the untaught convict, then the heavy, crushing machinery of government must be brought into requistion to compel submission. The result is jails, gibbets, gallows, engines of torture, well-dressed men with clubs, and soldiers

with bayonets. These convicts had in one year 10,000
acres of wheat, 7,000 sheep, 1,300 head of cattle, and 5,000
hogs. The convicts having to eat this themselves would
be virtuous. To fasten on them the various orders of society was to make them poor, and cause them to be criminal to their oppressors. In place of soldiers and masters if a
few mechanics had been given them to teach them how to
labor, a greater amount of justice would have been done to
them. Society makes men wicked. Put them in the way
of earning an easy living, and you do much toward making
men better.

O'Hara, in his "Hist. of New South Wales," says: "In
1819, the colony had 20,000 people. They had 170,920
sheep, 44,750 head of cattle, and the acres of land cultivated was 47,564. * * * Their "Gazette" tells us that "a
person is desirous of instructing children in polite diction."
In 1822, a commissioner was appointed to inquire into the
condition of the colony. He finds fault with setting convicts to work on public buildings with pilasters and pillars,
when many are wanting *covering*. The convict can buy his
time off the government for seven shillings a week. Samuel Terrey, a convict, has got 1,900 acres of land, 1,450
head of cattle, and 3,800 sheep."*

There are many people who have no governments, and
are virtuous. Lewis and Clark were sent to explore the
Rocky Mountains by President Jefferson. These men in
their journal tell us they saw tribes of Indians among whom
the crime of stealing was unknown. A traveler among the

* The avarice and selfishness of this man creates governments. The natives keep the colony together. This, with the sale of lands, makes the convict
a drudge to the more knowing. The discovery of gold in this land has made
bolts and locks necessary, and also governments. This gold caused crime,
which took men from productive labor to prevent and punish it. This land is
not as virtuous as it was. There are too few at useful work.

Esquimaux Indians says their oars, lances, and every thing of value was exposed, and none were guilty of stealing. Mr. Robert Percival says: "The Ceylonese are courteous and polite in their behavior. I have already exempted them from the censure of lying and stealing."

Lord Kames, in his "History of Man," says: "Riches, selfishness, and luxury are the diseases that weaken prosperous nations, that corrupt the heart, and dethrone the moral sense. Men hesitate at no expense to purchase pleasure, and at no vice to supply that expense. Looking back to the commencement of civil society, when no wants but those of nature were known, and when such wants were amply provided for, we find individuals of the same tribe living innocently and cordially together. They had no irregular appetites, nor any ground for strife. In that state moral principles joined their influence with that of national affection to secure individuals from harm. Savages, accordingly, who have plenty of food and are simple in habitation and clothing, seldom transgress the rules of morality within their own tribe.

"Didorus Siculus says the inhabitants of Britain dwelt in mean cottages, contented with plain and homely fare, and strangers to the excess and luxury of rich men. In Holland locks and keys were unknown, till the people became rich by commerce. The Laplanders have no notion of theft. This crime was unknown among the Caribbees. In the reign of Edwin, King of Northumberland, an historian reports that a child might have traveled with a purse of gold without hazard or robbery. In our days of luxury, so intolerable is want, that even the fear of *death* will not deter men. Paul Carpi, in 1246, said the Tartars were not addicted to thieving. Pagans in Siberia are a moral, good people. Among them thieving and fraud are rare."

Lord Kames goes through much reasoning to prove that governments introduce misery into society. It can not be denied that the people, before the Revolution, were virtuous and no crime prevailed. Thomas Jefferson, in his " Notes on Virginia," makes no allusion to crime or poverty, hence we may safely conclude there was none.* In these notes, he says: "I never saw a native begging. A subsistence is easily gained here. * * * Corruption of the mass of cultivators is a phenomenon, which no age or nation has ever produced an example."

The fathers of the Revolution, to judge by their acts, believed in a class "to do the mean duties of life, on which to build refinement and civilization." The first method is to let men have large quantities of land, not for the purpose of cultivation, but to sell for a high value, to get money without working for it. A laborer has not the time to read, or the money to purchase Smith's Theory of Moral Sentiments, Wayland's Moral Science, or Thomas Brown's Moral Philosophy. He must reason the question his own way. A thief wants money, so does a land speculator. The scheming of the one is legalized, the other is not. To the mind of a person not versed in moral ethics, as taught by college men, he must reason thus. The land was made by the Creator for his children, and he designs all to have an equal share. That one man should pay another for a piece of wild land is unjust, and a usurpation on the rights of men. The Creator designed land to be free.

For the fathers of the nation, to give whole districts to a few, was an outrage—it was giving the common people to be a prey to speculators. This later government has given to

---

* If the reader will examine this subject he will find this is truth. M. Brissot tells us that Boston took care off 150 old and diseased persons. These were mostly strangers. Boston then was a seaport town—a cause for poverty.

railroads 3,000,000 of acres, from which enormous fortunes will be made, and it will make the condition of many of the Americans but little better than serfs.   In an agricultural country the people labor four hours a day.   When railroads are built the farmers work ten hours a day.   They give their surplus for foreign luxuries.   A poor drudge, who handles this surplus in its transit, gets as pay for a week's work what will keep him two.   The farmer creates in one week what will keep him ten.   When the railroad laborer becomes as wise as the farmer, he will say to him, Risk your own life, do your own carrying.   It is the object of legislation to make a part of men drudges.   If the $30,000,000 that has been spent in Illinois on railroads had been used to introduce the manufacture of the various luxuries that come from abroad, the people would be happier and better. The people of Illinois should have built their own roads. To print $30,000,000 would have cost $15,000.   For these notes the merchants and farmers would support the roadmakers.   These two classes fed and clothed the workmen for the capitalists.   They should have done it for themselves, and owned the road.

The cost of the railroads in this land is $1,600,000,000. The cost of the railroads in Massachusetts is $18,000,000; the earnings yearly are $6,500,000.   The New York railroads cost $1,700,000, and earned yearly $50,000,000.   The Pennsylvania railroads cost $222,000,000, and earned one-fifth of this sum.   The Cleveland roads cost $4,868,427, and earned $2,659,346.   The Terre Haute railroad earned yearly $1,134,549, and cost $1,984,149.

In the island of Guernsey, near France, the authorities, to build a market-house, issued paper notes which circulated. The rent was paid in these notes.   This same plan would have gradually filled this land with railroads, the profits of

which would have raised a revenue sufficient fo the pur
poses for which taxes are assessed.　The canal built by the
Duke of Bridgewater, a century ago, pays enormous profits.
The £100 share sells for £1,500.　Had the city of Manchester issued notes, passed them as money, and built this
canal, the annual revenue derived from it would be equal
the first cost of it.

The "Prairie Farmer" notices some of the large farms
in the West: "Broadland's contains 23,000 acres.　Fowler & Earl's farm, in Benton County, Indiana, numbers
26,000 acres.　Sumner's farm contains 13,000 acres.　In
the same county is the Boswell farm, containing 8,000 acres.
Many farms in the Wabash Valley contain from 1,000 to
3,000 acres.　The owner of Broadland has in Ford County,
a farm of 40,000 acres.　Another has a farm of 17,000
acres.　Mr. Sullivant's farm, in Illinois, contains 40,000
acres.　This man has a large village, and all the inhabitants work for him under overseers."　This looks like feudalism—like scenes in Russia.　To see gangs of men working hard to enrich another, should arouse a feeling of indignation in the mind of every humane man.

It may be said with truth, that the owners of these large
farms give to their hands one-third of the crop.　A bar-
gain like this is often made.　For three centuries the African Moors had a habit of taking vessels, robbing them, and
carrying the sailors into slavery, who were allowed to have
one-third of what they earned.　General Eaton, at Tunis, in
1799, writes thus: "Truth and justice demand from me
this confession, that the Christian slaves among the barbarians of Africa are treated with more humanity than slaves
in civilized America."　These slaves could purchase their
time, and had Sunday and saint days to keep.　They were
out of the way of harm.　They could believe whatever they

pleased. At home, if they should change from Catholicism to Protestantism, the Inquisition behaved disagreeably to them. Even to be a Quaker was to suffer imprisonment. These slaves worked at trades, became merchants, accumulated fortunes, and purchased their freedom. In Christendom a poor man has been punished for stealing a pint of peas to satisfy hunger. The Algerine was indulgent. Stolen goods when found were taken away. The Koran said: "A slave was not a free agent; if he stole to satisfy hunger, he could not legally be punished for theft." Captain Pichellin had 800 slaves, and they had a good time at stealing. On one occasion a slave stole and sold the anchor of a galley. Said Pichellin: "You Christian dog, how dare you sell my anchor?" Said the slave: "I thought the galley would sail better without the additional weight." This reply caused a laugh.

All of these slaves could not rise above their condition. A successful expedition was gotten up to deliver them. A wrong exists among us. A class of men get possession of the public lands, and compel the most virtuous part of the community to work for them eight hours out of twelve. Sturgis, of Chicago, has 300,000 acres, which will take him two days to ride around it on horseback. This man has gone among the Kansas Indians and bought out their claim, which gives him 8,000,000 of acres more.

Since 1784, land speculators have made thousands of millions of dollars. Their plunderings are equal in value to the depredations of the thieves. If the farmers, merchants, and mechanics would unite with the laborers to get free homes, it would be done. "Harper's Magazine," for 1868, in an article called "Trip to Colorado," said: "In the stage was a person looking for lands to locate them." The stage was attacked by Indians, and found refuge at a fort

The speculators of the nation get the advance of the laborers when they locate lands before the Indians leave, and have the United States soldiers to protect them. The laborer, to get lands, must go over beyond those of the speculators, where the Indians will kill him.

Had the fathers of the nation not been so selfish, and given the lands to those only who would settle them in limited quantities, or 160 acres, the people of this nation would be more virtuous and happier. Men's inability to occupy lands makes them criminal. How noble it would have been had the fathers of the nation set apart, in every township two square miles of land for a town site! It would have given homes to 1,280 mechanics; to each two acres, on which to be happy, and not be the victims of base men.

There is another wrong government does: it encourages gold-seeking—to obtain which takes men from useful toil, and increases the toils of those who remain to do it. The amount of gold given us by California is $1,500,000,000. The labor to seek this gold would have made half of the American people good homes.

This extract shows how some people do not like to offer premiums to men to steal: "They say in Siberia—that a man *deserves* to be robbed who carries his money in such a small compass as silver coin in a purse." * This people find their safety in having their treasures in the form of goods. Paper money enables those who issue it to double their wealth. Wm. Penn sold 1,000 acres for $95, or he rented fifty acres for a yearly rent of a cent an acre. The farmer could borrow money off the State at six per cent., and have sixteen years to pay it. The interest paid the expenses of the State, and saved the people from taxation.

* "Travels in Siberia; or, Spectacles for Young Eyes." By Sarah W. Lander. Boston: Walker, Wise, & Company. 1864.

It has been computed that 2,300,000 white families in this land have no homes of their own. In New York city 750,000 persons live in tenant houses. These make 115,986 families; of these, 15,990 families have a separate house; 14,362 families live two in a house; 4,416 buildings each contains three families; 11,965 houses contain each seven families; 113 rear-houses each contains fifteen families or seventy persons; twenty-four houses each contains eighty persons; seventy-two houses each contains ninety-five persons; 193 houses each contains 111 persons; seventy-two houses each contains 140 persons; twenty-nine houses contain 5,449 persons, or 187 to each house.*

The reason of this destitution is, labor is put in a wrong place. A Presbyterian family resides in a house in this city [Cincinnati], that cost, with its furniture and surroundings, $300,000. The stone-carved front of the nice stable has a delicately stone-carved horse-head over the entrance, the labor on this would make plain homes for many widows. Jerome, a horse-racing banker, ornaments the inside of his stables with black walnut panels, grained and varnished woods, which cause many to be homeless.

One source of this nation's wrongs is to get the extreme rich to make the people's laws or rules that must govern

---

* The writer knew a man whose farm [160 acres] became part of a city. His plan was to divide each acre into lots of an eighth, and sell them for $175 or each acre for $1,400, or the whole farm for $220,000. His children became heads of families, and lived finely on the interest of these exactions. Nature demands that these families and their servants should work at something useful. This man was a professing Christian, and to ease his conscience he no doubt gave to the missionaries. These have to be fed and clothed. If these idle families were creators of what they and missionaries need, more of them can be sustained. If the 1,280 families were each to retain their money, seventy persons could be set to work at those pursuits which sustain missionaries. Wesley's "Journal" says: "Georgian Indians learned drunkenness and gluttony of Christians. Who will convert the English into honest heathens?" It is absurd to become rich to keep missionaries.

our conduct. To choose the man who has made his own riches by selfishness to make laws for us, is to choose our enemy. A very rich man has no feelings for the poor. The other day, in New York City, a carriage, containing a man worth $40,000,000, was carelessly driven over an Irish woman, and it injured her. To the policeman while arresting him, he said, "*I am Commodore Van⸺t.*" The magistrate dismissed the case with as little detention as possible. If this man had got out and lifted her into his carriage, and expressed sympathy and given her a $100, it would have done some good. A poor hackman, for driving against a woman and not injuring her, was fined $3.00.

A man in Albany, whose yearly income is $100,000, has a poor, hard-working niece, who suffers for necessary comfort, and who would be placed in a comfortable position by a single $100 yearly from her uncle. The laborer must choose men from his own class to make laws or rules—a man of frugality and plainness, not given to ostentation or show. An intelligent farmer will make the best law-maker. The earth he cultivates never cheats him; it makes him virtuous. He has no occasion to tell thumping lies to live. A farmer knows the earth will give him a support. He will not take bribes, or make riches out of the people.

The National Government seems to be an institution for taxing the people for the benefit of private interests or corporations. Many of the presidents and others get rich in the employment of the goverment. General Cass was worth $5,000,000. James Buchanan made $200,000. Mr. Fillmore is very rich. J. Q. Adams left $50,000. J. K. Polk saved $150,000. J. Tyler left $50,000. Z. Taylor, at his death, bequeathed $160,000. F. Pierce saved, while President, $50,000. Van Buren died rich. Webster spent millions, and died owing $250,000. His property was worth

$20,000. Henry Clay acquired an estate worth $100,000. Among the very many acts of peculation by Congress was the "Galphin claim." In 1773, George Galphin obtained from the Creeks a piece of land, which he gave to Georgia. After fifty years, the descendants of this man claimed compensation, which was granted to the amount of $243,871. $3,000,000 was given to the chiefs of the "Creek Nation," for restoring to Georgians fugitive slaves. The "Florida War" cost $40,000,000, it was to recover 1,500 escaped slaves. It sacrificed the lives of 4,500 soldiers. Among the items of expense was thirty bloodhounds at a cost of thirty-three dollars each. These were fed on calves, and attended by five Spaniards. To carry to the scene of operations, the bloodhounds, calves, and Spaniards were put on the backs of mules. Away they went to hunt men who wanted to be free. This was in the palmy days of Democracy. A fair lady went among "the wisdom of the nation," and got a claim allowed for $200,000, which was rejected when presented by the "sterner sex."

The room devoted to lady lobbyists is a sumptuous apartment. The carpet makes footsteps noiseless. Two windows in the thick walls, with heavy curtains hanging from cornice to floor make, cosy retreats. The chandelier is of massive bronze. The ceiling is frescoed in high colors and delicate drawing. Fascinating serpents and birds of gay plumage are blended in the design. The sofas are covered with green velvet. Here legal ladies, with snowy fingers, point to important places in papers prepared in lawyers' offices. The means to keep us from a foreign foe has made an inside enemy, and consumed a sum equal to the whole nation's wealth.

CHAPTER XIV.

THE FRENCH REVOLUTION.

Its Causes, Cruelties, and Benefits—A Contest Between Nobles and
People—The Number of its Victims—The Edict of Nantes—The
Profligacy of the Kings of France—Death of Louis Fourteenth.

"The oppressed have a right to rise against their oppressors."—Abbe Raynal.

REVOLUTIONS are painful remedies for the laborer's wrongs. They seem to be necessary to
teach kings and oppressors how far they can go
with wrong doing. They can give volumes of rules to
men, and punish for not keeping them. These rules vio-
late often men's ideas of what is right. William the Norman enacted, that whosoever killed his deer should lose his
eyes. He also had severe enactments against those who
took wood from the forests. No kind of reasoning, written
or spoken, will convince the humble that they have no share
in these things.

In the reign of Henry VIII, "72,000 rogues, great and
small, were trussed apace," that is, hung for stealing. The
number of people at this period was 1,000,000. About one
in twenty was "devoured and eaten up by the gallows." *
In the reign of George III, at one time fourteen persons
were seen by thousands suspended by their necks for political faults. During the reign of this monarch more than
100,000 persons were hung, banished, punished, and mal-

* "Chronicles of Holinshed," an historian in the reign of Elizabeth.

treated for faults that would have never happened if society had acted like the Acadians in Nova Scotia, who, for 133 years, had no case of crime or breach of public morals. It may be said that the people are made worse by being ruled by the wise.* The poor man who took home a part of a pampered horse's food, for which he was punished, would not have done it, had not the wise, or, perhaps the wicked, contrived usages and theories that exempted them from labor. Revolutions come from injustice.

"† France, from its earliest ages, had its assembly in the field of May. The king presided over the clergy, nobility, and sometimes the lower orders. The chiefs could only speak. The feudal system arose on the ruins of the empire of Charlemagne, and France had a monarch only in name. Haughty dukes, surrounded by warriors in castles, exercised over vassals the prerogatives of royalty, and often eclipsed the monarch in splendor. Their power was absolute over serfs, who tilled his acres and huddled under their castles for safety. In the language of the feudal code, the duke 'might take all they had, and imprison them when he pleased, being accountable to none.'

"France was a number of provinces, with scarcely any bond of union, dotted with castles on craggy hills, or river bluffs. These baronial fortresses were flanked by towers, pierced with loopholes, and fortified with battlements, and surrounded by a ditch. There was one large banqueting-hall where retainers and vassals met, in which was aristocratic supremacy and democratic equality. Every knight swore feality to the baron, the baron to the duke, the duke to the king, who could claim service from these and not from the serfs. Some dukes had more retainers, and were richer than the king.

* See page 100.   † This chapter is taken from Abbott's French Revolution.

"The line of the Capets became extinct on the death of Charles IV. The parliament at Paris gave the crown to Philip of Valois. The nobles, having a king to their wishes, complained that they had borrowed large sums of money of merchants and artisans, which it was not convenient to pay, and that it was inconsistent with the dignity of nobles to pay low born. A decree was passed that all debts should be cut down one-fourth, and that four months should be without interest. To reduce these plebeian creditors to a proper state of humility, the king ordered them to be imprisoned, and their property confiscated.

"He created a court at Paris of such magnificence, that the lords abandoned their castles for the city, to share its voluptuous indulgences. Neighboring kings were attracted to this court on account of its splendor. The nobles needed vast sums of money to sustain this extravagance. Overseers drove peasants to their toil, and extorted from them every farthing possible. The king, to replenish his exhausted purse, assumed the sole right of making and selling salt to each family, at an exorbitant price. Nobles were exempt from this and every kind of tax. Vincennes was then the great banqueting hall of Europe.

"In its present decay, it exhibits but very little of the grandeur it did 400 years ago, when its battlements towered above the forest of oaks—where plumed and blazoned squadrons met in joust and tournament in meteoric splendor. Hunting bands of lords and ladies swept the park. Brilliant as was this spectacle, no healthy mind can contemplate it but with indignation. To support this luxury of a few thousand nobles, 30,000,000 of people were in the extremes of ignorance, poverty, and misery.

"With the increase of centuries arose intelligence and a middle class between the peasants and nobility. Outrages became intolerable—human nature could endure no more. This middle class became leaders of the masses, and hurled them upon their foes. The conspiracy spread over the kingdom. It was a servile insurrection. The debased population, but little elevated above the brutes, were as merciless as the hyena or wolf. Frenzied with rage and despair, in howling bands they burst upon the castles, and the wrongs of centuries were avenged. Violence, torture, flame, and blood exhausted their energies. Mothers and maidens endured in terror all that mortals can endure, brutal indignities, shame, and woe. In war, even the refined and courteous often became diabolical. Those who have been degraded by ages of ignorance and oppression, when they break their fetters, become incarnate fiends.

"The nobles despised the peasants. They did not dream that the starving, cringing boors would dare even to think of emerging from their poor mud hovels, and approach the lordly castles. The insurrection of Jacques Bonhomme as it was called, was after much devastation subdued. Barbaric frenzy can seldom hold out against disciplined valor. Half of the people of France fell a prey to the sword, pestilence, and famine that ensued.

"This was the first convulsive movement made by the people. Defeated though they were, their fetters riveted anew, they obtained new ideas of power and right they did not forget. Already we begin to hear many of the phrases which, 400 years later, were upon all lips, when the feudal aristocracy were buried in the grave.

"The history of the kingdom during these dreary ages, is but the record of the intrigues of ecclesiastics, the conflicts between monarchs and nobles, and the sweep of maddened armies. The people continued to be deprived of all social and political rights. They were debarred, by ignor-

ance and depressed by intolerable burdens.   The persecutions of the Protestants had much to do with the revolutions
of Louis XIV.   In 1662, a decree was issued that no Protestant mechanic should have apprentices, and they should
be buried after sunset.   Teachers were to instruct in the
first rudiments only.   Not more than twelve were to be allowed together for worship.   In four years twenty edicts
were issued against the Protestants—none could be doctors,
lawyers, apothecaries, printers, or grocers.   Children were
often taken from their parents to be trained in the Catholic faith.   The king could insult the moral sense of the nation by traveling with the guilty Madam Montespan.   The
profligacy of the ecclesiastics, and the debauchery of the
court and nobles, was never more universal than this reign.
This was the golden age of kings.   Feudality had died and
democracy was not yet born.   The monarch was absolute.
The nobles, deprived of all political power, existed as an ap-
pendage and embellishment to the throne.

"In 1681, Louis XIV commenced his system of dra-
gooning the Protestants into the Catholic faith.   Scenes
ensued too awful to be narrated.   The brutal soldiery, free
from all restraints, committed every conceivable excess.
They scourged little children in the presence of their parents, to induce the parents to give up their faith.   They
violated the modesty of women.   They tortured and mu-
tilated their victims, till they yielded in agony.   The Protestants fled in all directions, and made desperate efforts to
escape from the kingdom.   Many died with famine by the
wayside and on the sea-shore.   Large tracts of country became nearly depopulated.   Madam de Maintenon sent her
brother a large sum of money, saying: 'I beseech you to
employ usefully the money you have.   The lands in Poictou
are sold for nothing.   The distress of the Protestants will
28

bring more into the market. You can easily establish yourself splendidly in Poictou.'

"There were about 3,000,000 of Protestants in France when dragoons were sent in every direction, by the court to compel a return to Catholicism. One of the tortures was by pricking, pulling, burning, and suffocating to deprive the victim of sleep, till he promised any thing to escape his tormentors. It was boasted that in Bordeaux 140,000 were converted in two weeks. The Duke of Noailes wrote to the court, saying: 'In his district there had been 240,000 Protestants, and at the end of the month he thought there would be none left.'

"In 1598, Henry IV, in his edict of Nantes, granted to Protestants freedom of conscience. Louis XIV revoked it in 1685. In his preamble he states: 'That the better and greater part of our subjects of the pretended reformed religion, have embraced the Catholic Church. The maintainance of the edict of Nantes remains superfluous.' It was decreed that no more exercise of the reformed religion will be tolerated. All Protestant ministers were to leave in fifteen days, and forbidden to exercise their office, under the pain of imprisonment. Protestants were punished for emigrating to other countries.

"Numbers escaped after the revocation. France lost 100,000 inhabitants, and her most flourishing manufactories. The Duke of St. Simon records that 'A fourth of the kingdom was perceptibly depopulated.' This crime against religion filled the land with infidelity, and caused remonstrances from Catholic noblemen. Montesquieu, Voltaire, Rousseau, and Mirabeau, not distinguishing between Christianity and the Papal Church have uttered cries of indignation, which thrilled upon the ears of Europe, and undermined the foundations of Christianity itself.

" M. De Sismond estimates that 500,000 persons found a refuge in foreign lands, and as many perished in the attempt to escape. 100,000 perished in the province of Languedoc, and of these 10,000 were destroyed by fire, the gallows, and the *wheel*.*

" The reign of Louis XIV was that of an oriental monarch. His authority was unlimited and unquestioned. The people had two very powerful enemies—kings and nobles. The people looked to the king to protect them against the nobles as sheep look to dogs to protect them from wolves. The king had now obtained a perfect triumph over his proud nobles, and had gathered all the political power into his own hands. He accomplished this by bribery and force.

" The acquiescence of the nobles in his supremacy was purchased by his conferring on them all the offices of honor and emolument, by exemption from all taxation, and by supporting them in luxury, indolence, and vice from the toil of the starving masses. There were now in the nation two classes, with an impassable gulf between them. On the one side, were 80,000 aristocratic families living in idleness and luxury; on the other, 24,000,000 of people, who, as a mass, were kept in the lowest poverty, who maintained by their toil the haughty nobles, from whom they received nothing but outrage and contempt.

" Nothing was done to promote the welfare of the people,

---

* In 1747, the French Parliament gave instructions how this was to be done. The executioner, when the body is stripped and stretched, with a heavy bar of iron, four feet long, will strike on the joints, then crush the shoulders with two blows on each. The executioner will commence on the feet, and strike up to the shoulder, thus breaking the feet, legs, hips, and arms. Three heavy blows are to be struck on the breast. A poor servant girl, for stealing two dresses, suffered this. Her agony lasted eleven minutes. A stream of blood issued from her mouth, drowning her cries, after her knee-joint was broken. The stealings of the ruling class cause the toiling ones to steal. The German mode of executing was to let fall a lifted wheel on the body till broken.

who were kept in the greatest ignorance. Abject misery was depopulating the provinces, when the gorgeous palaces of France exhibited scenes of voluptuousness which the wealth of the Orient had never paralleled.

"Louis XIV expended $200,000,000 on the palace of Versailles. The roofs of that vast pile would cover twenty acres. 30,000 laborers were frequently employed in embellishing the magnificent park, sixty miles in circumference. Marly, with its parks, fountains, and gardens, had also been constructed with equal extravagance. Both of these palaces exhibited scenes of profligacy, gilded by the highest fascinations of external refinement and elegance. Louis XIV left to the nation a debt of $815,000,000. For several years the expenditures had exceeded the income by $30,000,000 per year.

"Under Louis XV was that infamous Jesuit, Lavery de Tressan, Bishop of Nantes, who revived from their slumbers the most severe ordinances of Louis XIV. The royal edicts were issued sentencing to the galleys for life any man who attended auy other church than the Catholic. Protestant preachers were doomed to death; and any person who should neglect to denounce them, was consigned to the galleys.* All children were to be baptized within twenty hours of their birth. These horrible outrages upon human beings were received with transport by the clergy. When we contemplate the seed which the king and court planted, we can not wonder at the revolutionary harvest that was reaped in France.

"The Catholic Church was loathsome to the devout Christians. They preferred the philosophy of Montesquieu, the atheism of Diderot, the unbelief of Voltaire, the senti-

* Boats in the Mediterranean, propelled by triangular sails and oars. The condemned had to row these boats. They were chained often to the oar.

mentalism of Rousseau, to this merciless and bloody demon assuming the name of the Catholic Church, and swaying a scepter of despotism, which was deluging France in blood, in crime, and in woe. The sword of persecution was again drawn from its scabbard and bathed in blood.

"Many Protestant ministers were beheaded and broken on the wheel. Religious assemblies were surrounded by dragoons, and fired upon with the ferocity of savages, killing and maiming men, women, and children. Enormous sums of money were extorted by the lash, torture, dungeon, and confiscation. Fanaticism so cruel was revolting to the intelligence of the age. It is, however, worthy of note that few of the philosophers of the day ventured to plead for religious tolerance. They generally hated Christianity in all its forms, and were not disposed to shield one sect from the persecution of another. Voltaire was, however, an exception. For challenging a nobleman who had insulted him he was thrown into the Bastile. Soon after this his *Lettres Philosophique* were condemned by the Parliament to be burnt, and an order was issued for his arrest. The friendship of Frederick the Great had some influence in saving him from the punishment that his fearless opinions provoked.

"For many years he was compelled to live in concealment. He learned to sympathize with the persecuted. In his masterly treatise on toleration, and his noble appeals for the family of the murdered Protestant, Jean Calas, he spoke in clarion tones, which thrilled upon the ears of France. Franklin called on Voltaire with his grandson. He said: 'My son, fall down on your knees before this great man.' The aged poet gave the boy his blessing, with these words, ' God and freedom.'

"Louis XV ruled fifty-nine years. In boyhood his tutor taught him all the people belonged to him. At fourteen, he married Maria, the daughter of Stanislaus, the king of Poland. The king, at one of his private suppers, noticed a lady, Madam de Mailby, whose vivacity attracted him. Simply to torture his queen, he took her into the apartment, from which he excluded his lowly wife. Maria could only look to God for comfort. Madam de Mailby's sister supplanted her, and took her degrading place. She was taken away by death, and her sister, Madam Tournelle, became the king's favorite. Wherever she went, a suite of court ladies followed in her train. All were compelled to pay homage to the reigning favorite. All power was in her hands. She was the dispenser of rewards and punishments. Another sister, Mademoiselle Valois, and the Princess of Conti, became mistresses also to the king. Said a lady at this period: ' Unless God interferes, it is physically impossible that the State should not fall to pieces.'

"These died, and Madam Pompadour swayed the king's mind for twenty years. Her power became unlimited and invincible. Her heart was of iron, and she wielded all the terrors of court banishment, confiscation, exile, and the Bastile. It is said that a witticism of Frederick II of Prussia, at her expense, plunged the nation into a seven years' war. The most high born ladies in the land were her waiting women. Her steward was a knight of the order of St. Louis. A member of one of the noblest families walked by her side, with a cloak under his arm, to spread over her when she should alight from her sedan chair.

"She summoned embassadors before her and addressed them in the style of royalty. She appointed bishops and generals, and filled all the most important offices in the State and Church, with those who would do her homage. She dismissed ministers and created cardinals, declared war, and made peace. She said to the Abbe de Beris: 'I have all the nobility at my feet, and my lap dog is weary with their fawnings.' When this woman found her charms waning, she ministered to the king's appetite, by the most infamous institution ever tolerated in a civilized land. Several elegant houses were built in an inclosure, called the *Parc aux Cerfs*, near Versailles, and were used for the reception of beautiful female children, who awaited the pleasure of the king. Many years of the life of Louis XV was spent in the debauchery of girls of an unmarriageable age, and in undermining their principles of modesty and fidelity. Children were often taken by force. If the parents remonstrated they were sent to the Bastile. The cost of the *Parc aux Cerfs* was $25,000,000. It is an appalling fact, that for half a century France was governed by prostitutes.

"De Toqueville said: 'The revolution will ever remain in darkness to those who do not look beyond it. Only by the light of ages that preceded can it be judged.' This social degradation was one of the strongest incentives to the revolution. Thought was the great emancipator. Men of genius were the Titans who hove up the mountains of prejudice and oppression. They simplified political economy, and made it intelligible to the popular mind. Voltaire assailed, with the keenest sarcasm and the most piercing invectives, the corruption of the church. Montesquieu popularized and spread before the national view the policy that might render a people prosperous and happy. A seductive eloquence, in favor of the humble class, was used by Rousseau such us the world has never equaled.

"The minister that invented a new tax was applauded as a man of genius. The offices of the magistrates were sold. Judges paid enormous sums for their places, and then sold their decisions. Titles were sold, making the purchaser one of the privileged classes. All the trades and professions were sold. The number of trades and offices sold amounted to 300,000. An army of 200,000 tax-gatherers devoured every thing. To extort subsistence from a starving people, the most cruel expedients were adopted. Galleys, gibbets, dungeons, and racks were called into requisition. When the corn was all gone the cattle were taken. The ground became sterile for want of manure. Men, women, and children yoked themselves to the plow. The population died off, and beautiful France was becoming a place of graves.

"No language can describe the dismay in the homes of the peasants when the tax-gatherer darkened their doors. The seed corn was taken, the cow driven off, and the pig taken from the pen. Mothers pleaded, with tears, that food might be left for their children. The sheriff, used to scenes of misery, had a heart of rock. He went surrounded by a band of bailiffs to protect him from violence.

"The government seemed to desire to keep the people poor. These despotic kings would desolate their realms with taxation, and would excite wars that would exhaust energy and paralyze industry. The people thus impoverished and kept in ignorance might bow submissively to the yoke. The wars which, in endless monotony, are inscribed upon the pages of history, were mostly waged by princes, so as to engross the attention of their subjects. When a despot sees that public attention is likely to be directed to any of his acts, he immediately embarks in some war to divert the nation. This is the invariable source of despotism. A few hundred thousand people are slaughtered, and millions of money squandered in a senseless war. When a peace is made, it brings no repose to the people, who must toil and starve to raise money to pay the expenses of the war. In general, such has been the history of Europe for a thousand years. Despots are willing that billows of blood should surge over the land, that the cries of the oppressed may be drowned. So excessive has been the burden of taxation, that it has been calculated if the produce of an acre amounted to sixteen dollars, the king took ten, the proprietor five, leaving the cultivator one. In 1785, Thomas Jefferson, from Paris, wrote to Mrs. Trist, saying: 'Of 20,000,000 supposed to be in France, 19,000,000 are more wretched, accursed under every circumstances of human existence, than the most conspicuously wretched individual in the United States.'

"Louis XVI was an amiable young man, of morals most singularly pure for that age. He spent his leisure at lockmaking. It was upon the head of this benevolent, good king the vials of popular wrath were emptied, which had been treasured up for so many reigns. The nation was in debt, the interest could not be paid without borrowing or increasing the taxes. This the nation could not bear. The suggestion of Necker, to give the people a voice in the administration of affairs, and to tax high-born men, met with opposition.

"There were 80,000 nobles, inheriting the pride of feudal power, with thousands of dependents on their smiles. There were officers in the army, men of wealth who had purchased titles of nobility. There were 100,000 persons who had in various ways purchased immunity from the burdens of the State. These were hated by the people, and despised by the nobles. There were 200,000 priests, and 60,000 monks. There were the collectors of the revenue, and all the vast army of office-holders. The mass of the people were nearly slaves, unarmed, unorganized, and uneducated. They had been dispirited by ages of oppression, and had no means of combining or uttering a voice that could be heard.

29

"The French revolution was accelerated by a want of bread, or a short harvest, which is often short where so few are the producers. The most vigorous efforts were adopted to supply Paris with food. Nearly 1,000,000 people were within its walls. Vast numbers had crowded into the city from the country, hoping to obtain food. No law could restrain such multitudes of men, actually dying with hunger. As it was better to die with a bullet than with slow starvation, they would at all hazards break into the dwellings of the wealthy and into magazines. The sufferings of the people were so intense, that military bands had to convoy provisions through the famished districts. The peasants, who saw their children dying and gasping with hunger, would attack the convoys with the ferocity of wolves. M. Foulon, who was at one time the prime minister, said: 'If the people are hungry let them eat grass; it is good enough for them; my horses eat it. Let the people be mowed down like grass.' After awhile the people said: 'You wanted us to eat hay, you shall eat some yourself.' They tied a truss of hay around his neck, and hung him on a lamp-post.

"The morning of the fifth of October dawned stormy, damp, and cold. There were thousands in Paris who had eaten nothing that morning for thirty hours. The women of the humble classes were in an awful state of destitution and misery. The populace of Paris were actually starving. An energetic woman, half delirious with woe, seized a drum and strode through the streets beating it, occasionally shrieking 'BREAD! BREAD! bread!' She collected a number of women, which rapidly increased to 8,000. Such a strange apparition the world never saw before. Like a swelling inundation the living flood rolled through the streets, and soon a cry was heard, 'To Versailles.' A few of the most furious had pistols and guns. Gloomy winter had now commenced, and there was no money, no bread. The aristocratic party all over the realm sent across the frontiers all the funds they could collect. They wished to make France as weak as possible, so that the people might be more easily subjected again to the feudal yoke by the armies of foreign despots. In Paris alone there were 200,000 beggars. It is one of the greatest marvels that such a mass of men, literally starving, could have remained so quiet. The resources of the kingdom were exhausted during the winter in feeding the towns of France.

"The wealth of the Church was enormous. It was valued at $800,000,000. The result of all this was a cruel war in France—a struggle between the nobles and the people. It induced the nations of Europe to send their armies to force France to assume their old form of government. The people looked on the nobles and privileged classes as their enemies, among them the king and queen. Thomas Jefferson resided in Paris, and he said of Louis XVI: ' He had a queen of absolute sway over his weak mind and timid virtue, a character the reverse of his on all points. This angel, as gaudily painted in the rhapsodies of Burke, with some smartness of fancy but no sound sense, was proud, disdainful of restraint, indignant at obstacles to her will, eager in pursuit of pleasure, and firm enough to hold to her desires or perish in their wreck. Her inordinate gamblings and dissipation, with those of the *clique*, Count de Artoise, and others, had been a sensible item in the exhaustion of the treasury, which called into action the reforming hand of the nation. Her opposition to it, her inflexible perverseness and dauntless spirit, led her to the guillotine, and drew the king on with her, and plunged the world into crimes and calamities which will forever stain the pages of history. I have ever believed, had there been no queen there would have been no revolution.

The king would have gone hand in hand with the wisdom of his sound counselors, who, guided by the increased light of the age, wished only to advance the principles of their social constitution. The deed which closed the mortal career of these sovereigns I shall neither approve nor condemn.'

" Proudhomme asserts the number of the victims who were sent to the guillotine as 18,603. These, added to those who perished by civil war, make 1,022,351. The Jacobin leaders,* trembling before Europe in arms, felt that there was no safety but in annihilation of all its internal enemies. Danton, Murat, and Robespierre were not men who loved cruelty—they were resolute fanatics, who believed it to be well to cut off the heads of many thousands of aristocrats, that a nation of 30,000,000 might enjoy popular liberty. While the revolutionary tribunal was thus mercilessly plying the ax of the executioner, the National Convention, where the Jacobins ruled supremely, was enacting many laws that breathed the spirit of humanity and liberty. The taxes were equally distributed in proportion to the property. Provision was made for the instruction of youth, and the emancipation of slaves abroad.

" In the reign of Louis XV, *Lettres de Cachet* were issued. Whoever were the possessors of these could get whom they pleased into prison. All those who had influence at court could obtain them. The king could not refuse a mistress or a courtier. They were distributed as freely as postage stamps. None felt any degree of security from those who could get hold of them from being sent to the Bastile, which was a massive, cold, damp prison. Many of its cells were built in the shape of a bottle, into which the prisoner

---

* A society of revolutionists, who held secret meetings in the monastery of the Jacobine monks, to direct the proceedings of the National Convention.

was let down, and his food thrown to him.   This gloomy prison was destroyed in July, 1790.

"On the 20th of June, 1791, the king and his family left Paris for a foreign country, and were brought back, which was taken as evidence that they intended to join the enemies of France.   They were incarcerated in the Temple as prisoners.   The king was vacillating at times, making strong promises to the people, putting on their badges, and then enduring for it reproaches from his wife.   In prison he was separated from his wife and children.   In July, 1793, appears this decree: 'The Committee of Public Safety decrees that the *son of Capet shall be separated from his mother,* and committed to the charge of a tutor.'   This beautiful boy endured untold miseries, hunger, and every indignity that could be put on him.   Worn out by sickness and cruelty, in May, 1795, he died, aged ten years and two months.   On the morning of the 21st of December, 1792, Louis XVI was executed.   A few months afterward his queen suffered the same fate." *

Foreign nations interfered, which resulted in the rise of Napoleon to save France.   None can read the story of this family without being affected.   The lesson this revolution teaches us is that we can not multiply philosophers and the machinery of government without injuring the people.   To human forbearance there is a limit.   Men will not quietly die with hunger when others have more than they can consume.   The Duc d'Orleans went to a meeting of the king's cabinet with a loaf of bread made of fern leaves. He said to the king: "Sire, see the kind of bread your subjects eat."

The Americans should be thankful that they can right their wrongs without resorting to killing men by machin-

* Harper & Brothers are the publishers of Abbott's "French Revolution."

ery. They have a vote given to them, which they can use to clear away all their wrongs. The first wrong done to the American people was to let men have land who did not intend to cultivate it with their own hands. The motive was to get others to work for them. The quantity of land that Sturgis purchased of the Kansas Indians will make a State equal in area to Massachusetts. This man may not be permitted to keep this land. He bases his claim upon this: Indians can sell their own lands to whom they please. Indians, in the State of New York, living near Buffalo, have sold their claims to speculators.

"The grant of land to the Northern Pacific Railroad is 47,000,000 of acres. To the Central Pacific 35,000,000 of acres. To the Atlantic and Pacific 17,000,000 of acres. The aggregate number of acres granted by Government, for railroad purposes, is 154,201,584 acres, equal in extent, if placed in one body, to the area of the States of New York, Pennsylvania, Ohio, Indiana, and New England.*"

"There are plenty of honest men in the community who will never believe in the possibility of our law-makers lending their sanction to a profligate expenditure of the people's money. To such we commend a paragraph from the *The Stockholder*: 'Some able gentlemen have this matter [The Northern Pacific Railroad] in hand, and mean to get a *subsidy*† from the Government, which will make their scheme a rich mine,' etc. The National Government was never organized for taxing the people for private companies. As its charter of privileges now stands, at no distant day it will be worth $100,000,000, through the settlement of lands along its route. This modest corporation wants help of the United States to the amount of $60,000,000. This is certainly the most brilliant piece of railroad financiering re-

*Chicago Tribune.   † Subsidy, aid in money from governments—a tax.

cently heard of. If the United States is really going into
the railroad business to this extent, it had better go in all
over, lay out, build, equip, run the railways, and pocket the
receipts, which is something to the purpose. We do not like
this one-sided business of giving away every-thing and getting nothing. It is all outgo and no income for Samuel."*

God's earth has too long been made the sport of speculators. It was given to the people—to those who would occupy and use it. Carlyle says: "The earth belongs to
those two—to God, and to those of his children who have
worked well, or who will work well upon it." John Locke
says: "The earth was given for the use of the industrious,
and labor was to be his title to it." J. S. Mill says: "Labor
is necessary to clear, to drain, and cultivate the land and
upon this rests the sole foundation of the title to property on
the earth."

These are but the echoes of common sense; and yet the
rulers of the country are squandering the land, upon those
who do not, and will not, work upon it; to those who are
mere speculators out of the sweat of multitudes who toil on
the farms, and in the work-shops of the country! This
is the source of nearly all overgrown fortunes. It is the
chief cause of such a concentration of capital as enables a
few to monopolize breadstuffs, and thus make another terrible assessment upon the working classes. It enables others to bribe Congressmen and State Legislators to give them
abundant plunderings.

Quetalbet says: "Society *prepares* the crimes the criminals commit." Land monopoly, fostered by Legislatures,
causes crime. If all the idle lands in the States were to be
sold it would reform society. What an enormous amount
of crime the Pacific Railroad will cause! The tea and other

* Editorial from the Commercial of May, 1868.

products it will bring we can do without. Mrs. Grant says: "Before the Revolution every family had a cow." Tea was not known then. Milk and bread was one item of food. A crime was not known. Says the Commissioner of Statistics: "In 1861, among 4,000 people there was one who committed a crime against property. In 1867, there was one property crime occurred among 2,360 people."—Ohio Report.

Banks favor a few in this manner: Twenty men each possessing a house worth $1,000, as one man pledge them to the Comptroller, who gives them 20,000 beautiful pieces of paper, which are called dollar bills, for which unthinking laborers will clothe and feed a part of their number, while they are building another twenty houses. These are given to the authorities for another $20,000, under the pretense that society needs more capital. The pledger receives rents for these houses while in pledge. In this wicked manner, by pledging what is most valuable, a few fill the land with railroads, the profits of which keep men from work. The good Franklin could print $4,000,000. His rulers loaned it for $22,000, which defrayed the expenses of his colony. The result was—no poverty, no crime, no homeless men.

"Seeing to lend money at *interest*, that is to say, for *gain*, that is to say, to receive *money* for the use of *money*; seeing that to do this was contrary, and is still contrary, to the principles of the Catholic Church; and among *Christians*, or professors of *Christianity*, such a thing was never heard of before what is impudently called the Reformation.

"The ancient philosophers, the Fathers of the Church, both Testaments, the Canons of the Church, the decisions of the Popes and Councils, *all agree, all declare*, that to take money for the use of money is *sinful*. Indeed, no such thing was ever attempted to be justified until the savage Henry VIII had cast off the supremacy of the Pope. Jews

did it, but then Jews had no civil rights. They were regarded as moral monsters." *

There is one truth very certain, that labor keeps us from
perishing; and if any one will not work, he does an injustice
to him that will work. He that will not work, is no better
than a robber. Nor is it just to choose easy work, and let
another do the hard work. The generous, noble man will
resolve to do a part of the hard work. Whatever plans
make fortunes, are wicked and unscriptural. The means
whereby men become rich, are the corruptions of ages; and
when the American poor have drunk deeper from the cup
of suffering, they will overthrow the causes that make men
idle and rich. Our Savior condemned riches, and told his
disciples not to refuse to lend, and they were to take no reward for it. The opinions of the "Fathers" show that interest is sinful and unjust.

St. Basil says: "It is the highest cruelty to charge the
man who comes to borrow to preserve a wretched existence, or to seek riches from his pinching poverty."

St. Clement says: "It is wrong to charge usury [money
for the use of money] for the money which should be extended with open hearts and hands to the needy."

St. Chrysostom says: "Nothing surpasses in barbarity the
modern practice of usury; certainly the usurers † traffic on
other people's misfortunes, and seek gain through their ad-
versity. They dig for the distressed a pit of misery."

St. Augustine says: "I would not have you become usurers; it is repugnant to the law of God. Is he more cruel
who steals or purloins from a rich man, than he who grinds
a poor man with usury and becomes reprehensible?"

Leo I says: "It is true, his substance swells from unjust

---

* William Cobbett's "History of the Reformation."
† Usury, the practice of taking interest.—Lord Bacon. In this sense not used.

and fearful additions; whilst the substance of the soul decays.   Usury of money is a rope to strangle the soul."

St. Hilary says: "What is more cruel than, under pretense of relieving, to augment the borrower's distress; instead of aiding him, to add to his wretchedness?"

St. Gregory says: "Hold in abhorrence usury dealings; love your neighbor, not your money; bid farewell to surplus wealth and usury.   Excite love for the poor."

St. Ambrose says: "Rich men, poverty is a fertile field for your plentiful crops; he who has not the necessaries of life must pay you usury.   This is the height of cruelty."

St. Jerome says: "Some persons imagine usury is sinful only when received in money.   The sacred writer has proscribed *increase*,* so that you can not receive more than you gave.   Usury is prohibited among mankind in general."

St. Aquinas says: "To receive usury for money lent, is radically unjust—an inequality opposed to justice."

Aristotle says: "It is allowable for men to acquire gain by fruits and animals.   The practice of reaping money from money is repugnant to nature; its gains are base."

Plutarch says: "By giving usury and entering into contracts, we manufacture the yoke of our slavery."

Blackstone says: "In the dark ages of monkish superstition, to wit, during the prevalence of the Catholic religion, interest was laid under a total interdict."

Kent, in his "Commentaries" says: "Till the twelfth century the Jews were the only money-lenders.   Catholics did not like to engage in the business of renting money."

The rules of the Catholic Church, as given by its Councils from time to time, forbids, in the strongest language, the loaning of money on interest.   The Bulls [letters] of many pontiffs, the decrees of many emperors, forbid interest.

*INCREASE, a Bible term meaning corn, wine, oil—the produce of the earth

Time, the great changer of events, was destined to make these precepts of no effect. Catholics saw the Jews and Lombards [Italian merchants of the fourteenth century] obtaining riches, and it was a natural thought to divert these riches into other channels. In 1515, Pope Leo X invited sums of money to be contributed to be lent to the poor, or to be loaned so as to keep men from becoming poor. Indulgences were granted to those who contributed to these charitable funds, which were called *Montes Pietatis*—Mountains of Piety."*

It appears singular to us, at present, that it should have been once considered unlawful to receive interest for lent money ; but this circumstance will excite no wonder when the reason of it is fully explained. Those who borrowed money required it only for immediate use, to relieve their necessities, or to procure the conveniences of life ; and those who advanced it to such indigent persons did so either through benevolence or friendship.

Acquiring money by money was long detested, and this feeling was strengthened by severe papal laws. The people often contrive means to render the faults of legislators less hurtful. This was devised. A capital was collected, to be lent to the poor on pledges without interest. This idea was suggested by the Emperor Augustus, who sold the property of criminals, and lent the money, without interest, on pledges. Severus lent money to purchase land without interest, and took his pay in produce.

The Pope changed burdensome vows into donations to "lending-houses." The rich gave money so as to legitimate children not born in wedlock. Indulgences and holy-water created a capital. The Pope called these holy mountains of

*"Usury and Banking," by Jeremiah O'Calligan, Catholic Priest, New York. 1856. A valuable book of 550 pages, full of good teaching from the Fathers.

piety legal. In 1456, Bernardinus went around preaching against the Jews, gaming, intemperance, extravagance in dress. He founded lending houses, and collected money for them to keep people from becoming poor. A gratuity was solicited for the lending servants, which afterward became a regular assessment, to pay expenses.

These *bancos de poveri* have become mountains of misery. Half of those who use them lose their pledges. They lead men into employments that make them poor, and keep them from working in the earth. Banks are contrivances to get toiling men to build public works for idle thinking men.

The Cincinnati Suspension Bridge Co., pledge property paying interest while pledged, and get a million paper dollars, which cost but little, and rear a structure that will yield in ten or twenty years $200,000 as a yearly revenue, keeping a few in idleness. This would be a nice sum to teach children in school exercises. Those who built the bridge, fed and clothed the builders, or use the bridge, should own it, which may be done in this way: Let the State issue "bills of credit" to this community, who will pay the State interest, and devote the tolls to paying interest and principal.

The argument used for a few owning roads and bridges is that communities can not make them pay. This applies to the past when population was thin. The future will be different, when the people are numerous. The working people, through their representatives, have a right to offer to the owners of this bridge its cost in money, based on the property of the State, and say, "With this money buy farms, cultivate them, and be men. This is a sure business. Laborers are fast becoming their own merchants and employers."

CHAPTER XV.

STATESMEN AND POLITICAL ECONOMISTS.

Sketches of Washington—Livingston—Morris—Hamilton—Sedgwick—Ames—Wollcott—Burr—Adams—Jefferson—Opinions of Econo-mists—Potter—More—Smith—Malthus—Say—Ricardo—Paley.

"My son, see with how little reason the world is governed."—Chesterfield.

PRESIDENT WASHINGTON," says Mr. Jef-ferson: "entertained serious effects from the self-created 'Democratic Societies' of that day, and he believed they would destroy the government if not discon-tinued.

"Chancellor Livingston, on reaching France, was coolly received. He showed that his republicanism was unaggres-sive. His personal tastes and habits were far removed from the Jacobin standard. Few of Bonaparte's courtiers, aspiring to the dignity of the ancient regime, approached the so-cial plane of the stately Patroon. Many of them were up-starts compared with him in personal and family pretensions. His wealth was reported to be ducal. His hereditary pos-sessions were greater than half a dozen French marquisates in the days of the Bourbons. He sat in the revolutionary and pre-revolutionary congresses. A score of his family of the existing generation, and more than twice that number of kinsmen, had borne high civic and military commissions. His whole life had been spent in the highest range of office.

"Morris was one of these gigantic breed of speculators,

whom Jefferson could scarce help abhorring. He declared
for a perpetual Senate, approved by the chief magistrate, and
he must *have great personal property*. It must have *aristocratic spirit*; it must love to lord it through *pride*. It was
palace building, and buying vacant lands that consigned him
to a prison, in which he died.

"Hamilton called *Democracy* a blind and deformed *monster*. His luxury and manners exceeded those of the proud-
est English nobleman. He disliked the Constitution, and
had but little share in forming it. His plan was to obliter-
ate State sovereignties, the chief magistrate making the governors. The National Legislature was to control their laws.
Their general concerns were to be subject to the National
Courts. He called the Constitution a frail, worthless fabric,
and said that all communities divide themselves; the first
are rich and well born, the other the mass of the people. It
is quoted and believed, that the voice of the people is the
voice of God. It is not true, in fact; the people are turbulent and changeable; they seldom *judge or determine right*.
Give to the first a distinct share of the government: nothing but a permanent body can check the improvidence of
democracy. Their turbulent disposition requires checks, or
ends in despotism, and is destructive to public morality.

"Fisher Ames believed that Democracy is nothing in itself. It is a dismal passport to a more dismal hereafter.

"Theodore Sedgwick said: We have placed at the head
of government a semi-maniac [Jefferson], who, in his so-
berest senses, is the greatest marplot in nature. What think
you of a Democracy? Will it progress successfully till all
its evils are felt? This state of things can not exist long.
The enfeebling policy of Democracy will produce such intolerable evils as will necessarily destroy their cause.

"Oliver Wollcott believed our government would never

be very permanent.   He could not believe that a people, who had gone through the distresses of the Revolution, and arisen from extreme poverty, could so soon forget their sufferings, as to sport with the enjoyment of their greatest social happiness, and expose its continuance to the utmost hazard.

"Aaron Burr's plan was to divide the Union at the Alleghanies, and attack Mexico.   He embarked 300 men in fifteen boats.   He was arrested, gave bail for \$3,000, and fled to England, and was banished from there.   His expedients to keep off hunger were akin to beggary.   It was his ambition to have the manners of a Chesterfield and the morals of a Rochester.

"Mr. Jefferson said: 'Certain causes had long since produced an overcharge of the class of competitors for learned occupations and great distress among the supernumerary candidates, and the more so as their habits of life had disqualified them for re-entering among the laboring classes. The remedy he proposed was to make agriculture a scientific profession, and thus list the supernumeraries into an employment, where they would find occupation for the body and the mind.

"'The charitable schools, instead of storing the minds of pupils with a lore which the present state of society does *not call for*; which, converted into schools of agriculture, might *restore* them to that branch qualified to enrich and honor themselves, and to increase the productions of nature, *instead of consuming them*.   A gradual abolition of the *useless offices*, so much accumulated in all governments, *might also close the drain from the laborers of the fields, and lessen the burdens imposed on them*.   By these, and the better means which will occur to others, the surcharge of the learned might in time be drawn to *recruit* the laboring class of citizens. The sum of industry increased, that of misery is *diminished*. The strong desire of men to live by the labor of their *heads* rather than their hands—the allurements of large cities to those who have any turn for dissipation, threatens to make here, as in Europe, cities the sinks of voluntary misery! He held in little esteem the education that makes men helpless in the common affairs of life. This he exemplified by the example of a man who had been to Europe for an education. On a journey a saddle-strap broke, and he had to wait till some common man came along, and let out the strap at the other end.'

"Thomas Jefferson invented the best form of a moldboard for a plow. He made furniture and shod horses. He was an architect, and designed his own house. He thrashed his wheat by machinery, at the rate of 150 bushels a day. He directed the labors of his slaves in farming, mechanical pursuits, and cloth-weaving. At one time he had fifty visitors from all parts of the world. One of his slaves confessed that it took all the labor of the slaves to feed and wait on them. This was a cause of his poverty in after life. He did not believe in his grandsons attending medical colleges or living in cities.

"John Adams was classed among the believers of monarchy. The proposition that the people are the best keepers of their liberties is not true; they are the worst conceivable. They are no keepers at all, and can neither judge, think, nor will as a political body. The majority would invade the minority sooner than a monarchy." *

Madison says: "Democracies have ever been the spectacles of turbulence and contention; have ever been incompatible with personal security *or the rights of property.* A

* This is taken from H. S. Randall's "Life of Thomas Jefferson." Some sentences are omitted. The language is unchanged.

large body of men is more apt to sacrifice the rights of the minority, because it can be done with impunity. Establish it as a principle, that to give sanction to law it must be approved by a majority at the ballot-box, and you take this security and surrender these rights to the most capricious and cruel tyrants. I regret to see this growing spirit in Congress and throughout the country, to democratize our government—to submit every question, whether pertaining to organic or municipal laws, to the vote of the people. God forbid that the demagogism of this day should prevail over the philanthropic and philosophic statesmanship of our fathers. *Property is the foundation of every social fabric.* To protect, preserve, and perpetuate rights of property, society is formed and governments are framed."

Wolves become ravenous by hunger. Lions will let you pass them when not hungry. If every man had a home, he would let the homes of others alone. When a part of mankind are selfish, they must have governments to help them. Washington had land sufficient to maintain 25,000 persons. Without governments he could not collect his rents. If this land belonged to the cultivators, there would be no need of governments.

The writer was offered, in Indiana, for $300, forty acres of land. He went to see it and found a person who had purchased a tax title, and had built a cabin on it 12ft×16ft. I told him the owner was not dead. The taxes had not been paid for twelve years. He wished me to see the owner of forty acres on one side, so that he could have a road from his place, which was surrounded by abrupt and impassable banks. There was one outlet, the owner of which asked $300 for the land. I found him living in a palace, with a tessellated marble floor. The ceiling was supported by Corinthian fluted columns, having capitals exquisitely carved.

30

The ceiling was a surface of deep panels and fine carvings. This land speculator had every luxury. The man who wanted this land would have to save for six years, as he was married. His cabin contained three bedsteads, and sheltered three children and their parents. The house contained no pictures, books, or papers. The mother had never seen any of the fine arts, nor heard piano music. She told me they went in their wagon nineteen miles, to Indianapolis. When there she asked a householder if she could boil some coffee; this was refused. The two pieces of land cost $100.

The laws the "Fathers" made have caused these social distinctions. The refinement of the one was at the expense of the other. Among the Fathers not one favored the toiling classes, except Thomas Jefferson. He compared the Treasury to a huge turtle laying eggs in the sand for foul birds to eat. In 1795, Hamilton tried to get an act passed so that not less than 4,000 acres should be sold to one person. For forty years not less than 640 acres were sold at a time, at $2.50 per acre, which compelled many to purchase of others. John Adams said: "That governments were to protect the rich in their great possessions as well as the poor man in his. * * * All the officers of the Government *must be gentlemen, friends and connections of the rich and well born.*" * Most of the inequalities of life are from governments and are inventions of the avaricious and rich, to strengthen themselves and get riches. These will make half slaves of the poor, and deprive them of their birthright, the public lands—three-fourths of which get into the possession of speculators. M. Turgot, when speaking of the first-formed State constitutions, said: "They were imitations of the customs of England without any particular motives."

* John Adam's "Defense of the Constitutions," vol. i, page 373.

What domestic economy is to a family, so is political economy to a nation. Domestic economy takes the income of a family and proportions it to what it will purchase. For instance, a woman fed herself and four children on a dime a day. How it was done may be known by referring to chapter first. Political economy relates to a nation's labor, and considers how many may be taken from the laboring classes and made into soldiers and servants, so as not to have them die with hunger, or accumulate so much as to be able to revolt.

Says Bishop Potter: "We are far from denouncing the luxuries of life. We do not condemn the possessor of a handkerchief worth $50, or a $1,000 shawl. We have a greater respect for him who provides handsomely for his family. The amount of enjoyment principally depends on the number of beings enabled to obtain a comfortable subsistence, with satisfactory security for its continuance."

This writer wrote his book for the use of schools. It is strange it did not occur to him that those who create costly things are ill clad and often hungry. This man had three sons: one became an architect, one a general, another was a rector of a marble church, with $10,000 a year.

A report of a Life Insurance Co. contained this: Rt. Rev. A. Potter was insured for $5,000. He paid $3,637. What a comment on one who wrote a treatise showing how "skill and industry can be rendered most useful!"

Sir Thomas More was born in London, in 1480. He was the adviser of Henry VIII, whom he offended by telling him privately about his marriage conduct. He was sentenced to lose his head, which was done so awkwardly that several blows were struck before it was cut off.

In his book "Utopia" is described a happy society. In this book is this language: "One day I was with the king, where there happened to be a lawyer, who took occasion to run out in high condemnation of the severity in the execution of thieves, who were hanged so fast, that there were sometimes twenty on one gibbet. Said he: 'How comes it to pass that since so few have escaped, and yet so many thieves are still robbing in all places.'

"I took the boldness to speak freely before the cardinal, and said there was no room for wonder at the matter, since the way of punishing thieves was neither just in itself nor good for the public. As the severity was too great, so the remedy was not as effectual—simple theft not being so great a crime that it ought to cost a man his life. No punishment, however severe, was long able to restrain those who can find no other way of a livelihood. In this not only you in England, but in a greater part of the world, imitate some ill master, who are readier to chastise their scholars than to teach them.

"There are dreadful punishments against thieves; but it were much better to make such good provisions, by which every man ought to be put to the necessity to live, and so be preserved from the fatal necessity of stealing, and dying for it."

Said the cardinal: "There has care enough been taken for that. There is husbandry, by which they may make a shift to live."

More replied: "There are a great many nobles among you that are drones—that subsist on other men's labor—on the labor of tenants—to raise their revenues, they pare them to the quick. They have about them a great number of idle fellows, who never learned any art by which they may gain their living; and these, as soon as the lord dies, or they fall sick, are turned out of doors. Your lords are readier to feed idle people than to take care of the sick. The

heir is not able to keep together so great a family as his pre-
decessor did. Now, when the stomachs of those that are
turned out doors grow sharp, they rob no less keenly. And
what else can they do? For, when by wandering about,
they have worn out their health, their clothes, and are tat-
tered and look ghastly, men of quality will not entertain
them, and poor men dare not do it; knowing that one who
has been bred in idleness and pleasure, and who used to go
about with his sword and buckler, despising all the neighbors with an insolent scorn, as far below him. He is not
fit for the mattock or spade, nor will he serve a poor man
for so small a hire and so low a diet as he can afford to
give him."

Said the cardinal: "In them consists the force of the armies for which we have occasion. Their birth inspires
them with a nobler sense of honor than is to be found
among trades or plowmen."

More replied: "You may as well say that you must
cherish thieves on account of wars, for you will never want
the one as long as you have the other; and as robbers are
sometimes gallant soldiers, so soldiers often prove brave robbers—so near an alliance are those two sorts of life. The
maintaining of many useless and idle persons, will ever disturb you, which is ever to be considered in a time of peace.
Restrain the engrossing of the rich, who are as bad as monopolies. Let agriculture be set up again, and the manufacture of wool be regulated, so that there may be found work
for these idle people, *whom want forces to be thieves*, or who,
being vagabonds, will certainly be thieves at last. If you do
not find a remedy for these evils, it is in vain to be boast-
ing of your severity for punishing theft.

"He is an unskillful physician who can find out no other
way of healing without putting him into another disease.

So he that can find no other way for correcting the errors
of the people, but by taking from them the conveniences of
life, shows that he knows not how to govern a free nation."

"In Utopia every man has a right to every thing.   They
all know that if care is taken to keep the public stores full,
no private man *can want any thing*—no man is poor, or in
necessity.   Though no man has any thing, yet they are all
rich.   What justice is in this, that a nobleman, a goldsmith,
a banker, or any other man, that either does nothing at all
or is employed in *things that are of no use* to the public, should
live in splendor and luxury?

"A carter, a smith, or a plowman that works harder even
than the beasts, and is employed in useful labor, so that no
commonwealth could hold out a year without them, can
only earn a livelihood and lead a miserable life.   The condition of the beasts is better than theirs.   These men are
depressed by anxieties, fruitless employments, and tormented
by apparitions of want in their old age.   That which they
get by their daily toil does not maintain them at present,
and is consumed as fast as it comes in.   There is no over-
plus left for old age.

" Is not the government unjust, when it is prodigal of its
favors to goldsmiths, gentlemen, or those who are idle, or
live by flattery, contriving vain pleasures, and take no care
of plowmen, colliers, or smiths, without which it could not
subsist?   After the public has had the advantages of their
services, when they come to age, sickness, and want, their
labor is forgotten, then they are left to die in great misery.
The richer sort are often endeavoring to bring the hire of
laborers lower not only by their fraudulent practices, but by
the laws they procure to make this effect.   Though it is a
thing unjust to give so small rewards to those who deserve
so well of the public, yet they have given these hardships

the name and color of justice. * * * * They inclose all into pastures, throw down houses, pluck down towns, and leave nothing standing but the church, *to be made a sheep house*. These good and holy men turn all dwelling-places and glebe lands into a wilderness and desolation." This last clause refers to driving out the Scotch people, so as to make fleeces an article of commerce, the source of their misery from that day to this.

Plato, in the " Fourth Book of his Republic," describes a perfect commonwealth, " where kings are philosophers, and philosophers kings; where the whole city might be in the happiest condition, and not any one tribe remarkably happy beyond the rest ; where the laws govern, and justice is established; where the guardians *of the law are such in reality*, and preserve the constitution, instead of destroying it, and promote the happiness of the whole city, *and not their own particularly*; where there are no parties, of the rich and poor at war with each other," etc.

John Milton has given us a " Ready and easy way to establish a Free Commonwealth." His plan was to have an assembly of senators for life: " They must have the forces by sea and land, for the preservation of peace and liberty; must raise and manage the revenues, with inspectors to see how it was employed, with power to make laws, and treat on commerce, war, and peace, etc." Mr. Hume, in his "Idea of a Perfect Commonwealth," would have elected representatives with executive powers and the prerogatives of kings. In 1663, John Locke made a government for Carolina, in which were to be *barons, caciques, and landgraves*. The first was to have 12,000, the second 24,000, the last 80,000 acres of land.

It was to be shown in Acadia that a few thousand Catholics could live for more than a century without magistrates or crimes; and the Utopia of More was a possible and not a visionary scheme.

Adam Smith's "Wealth of Nations" all should read. It contains this: "Among civilized nations, a great many people do not labor at all, many consume the produce of ten times, frequently a hundred times, more labor than the greater part of those who work."

Rev. Mr. Malthus, in his books "On Population," says: "That if a man chooses to marry without a prospect of support to his family, it is an act which society can not justly take up, prevent, or punish. To the punishment of nature therefore, he should be left. A man who is born into a world already possessed, if he can not get subsistence from his parents, and society do not want his labor, he has no claim or right to the smallest portion of food, and, in fact, has no business to be where he is. At nature's mighty feast there is no vacant cover for him. She tells him to be-gone, and she will quickly execute her orders."

In his "Political Economy," he says: "Statesmen, sol-diers, sailors, and those who live off the national debt, con-tribute powerfully to *demand and distribution*. They insure that consummation which is necessary to *give the proper stimulus to the exertion of industry*."

Jeremy Bentham read in a coffee-house this: "The only reasonable and proper object of government is to produce the greatest happiness to the greatest number." Said he: "At the sight of it, I cried out in the greatest ecstasy." He was a lawyer, and became disgusted with law. He spent sixty years at law reforms, in putting an end to the system. His books and pamphlets number fifty. Law to him was *the offspring of a barbarous age*, the patchwork of fifteen cen-turies, a huge, shapeless, and bewildering pile. To relieve the tedium of study, he turned wooden bowls, ran in his

The rich, to keep the poor from perishing, feed them, so that they may have servants. The rich, who give to the poor, give often that which they never earned. "Thou shalt not covet other men's goods" is a command which, if observed, would prevent riches. If society possess the banks, roads, railroads, and bridges, and the merchant will tell his neighbor what is the cost of goods, and that association will distribute them at cost, then will scenes like this disappear. Inequalities will always exist while the merchant exists; and in order to attain equality he must be destroyed. Tobacco and drinking habits destroys a tenth of the nation's labor, an amount sufficient to find furnished homes for all Americans who become of age.

garden for exercise, played on a fiddle. He heated his house by steam, slept in a sack, and thought the common law the perfection of absurdity.

J. Stuart Mill, a political writer, gives us this piece of satire: "The lot of the poor, in all things, should be regulated for them, not by them. They should not be required to think for themselves. It is the duty of the higher class to think for them. This function the higher class should prepare to perform conscientiously, and their whole demeanor should impress the poor with reliance on them. The relation between rich and poor should be only partially authoritative; it should be amiable, moral, sentimental; affectionate tutelage on the one side, respectful, grateful deference on the other. The poor should be called on for nothing, but to do their day's work. Their morality should be provided for them by their superiors.

"The poor have come out of their leading strings, and can not be treated like children any more. I can not conceive how any person can persuade himself that the majority will much longer consent to hew wood and draw water all their lives in the service and for the benefit of others."

Dr. Chalmers, writing on political science, says: "Because of a fertility in the earth, by which it yields a surplus over and above the food of the direct and secondary laborers, that we command the services of a disposable population, who, in return for their maintenance, minister to the proprietors of this surplus *all the higher comforts and conveniences of life*."

Dr. Paley, in his "Political Philosophy," taught—"That the condition most favorable to population is that of a laborious, frugal people, ministering to the *demands of an opulent and luxurious nation;* because this situation, whilst it leaves them every advantage of luxury, exempts them from

31

the evils that naturally accompany its admission into any country."

Blackstone, in his "Commentaries," declares: "Among the many acts men are *daily liable* to commit, 160 are punished by death." If any should be hung through mistake, Dr. Paley kindly advises their friends: "To reflect that he who falls by a mistaken sentence may be considered as falling for his country."

Robert Owen believed that the drunkard and thief were victims of circumstances. In his "New Moral World," he maintained that money was an evil, a source of injustice, oppression, and misery to the human race—makes some the slavish producers of wealth, and others wasteful consumers. He believed that "men divided into employed and employers, masters and servants, would cause ignorance and poverty to pervade the world." Owen prepared two memorials for the Congress at Vienna, in 1815, in which were these words—"Wealth, privileges, and honors are the playthings of infants." This made some impression on it.

Mary Wollstonecraft, in her "Vindication of the rights of Women," says : "Such combustible material can not long be pent up. Getting vent in foreign wars and civil insurrections, the people acquire some power in the tumult, that obliges their rulers to gloss over their oppressions with a show of right. Agriculture, commerce, and letters expand the mind. Despots are compelled to make covert corruption hold fast the power which was formerly snatched by open force. A baneful gangrene is formed, spread by luxury and superstition, the sure dregs of ambition. The indolent puppet of a court first becomes a luxurious monster or a fastidious sensualist and an instrument of tyranny. It is the pestiferous purple, which renders *the progress of civilization a curse*, and warps the understanding, till men of sensibility doubt whether the expansion of intellect produces a greater portion of happiness or misery."

Thomas Carlyle, a "Writer of Books," said: "An earth all around, crying, come and till me;—yet we sit here enchanted! The sun shines and the earth calls; and, by the governing powers and impotences of England, we are forbidden to obey. * * * The Continental people are exporting our machinery, and beginning to spin cotton for themselves. Sad news, but irremediable. The saddest news is that we should find our national existence depends on selling cotton a farthing an ell cheaper than any other people. Cotton cloth is already twopence a yard or less; and yet bare backs were never more numerous among us. Let inventive men cease to spend their existence incessantly contriving how cotton cloth can be made cheaper, and try to invent how cotton cloth, at its present cheapness, could be divided a little more justlier among you."

Thomas Paine hated injustice and oppression. He was secretary to Congress during the Revolution. He wrote then the "Crisis" and "Common Sense," to induce the Americans to revolt. In his "Rights of Man" is found this: "We see in countries that are called civilized, youth going to the gallows and age to the workhouse. * * * To make one rich, many must be made poor; neither can the system be supported by any other means."

Rousseau, born in 1711, and dying in 1788, was hated by the authorities for his opinions. His "Emille," a treatise on education, could not be tolerated. He was banished for it. His "Social Contract" says: "Supply an administration with money, and they will supply you with chains. The very term of taxes is slavish. Foreign commerce is productive only of *a delusive utility* to the kingdom in general. It may enrich a few individuals, and perhaps some city.

The whole nation gains nothing by it, nor are any of the people any better for it. It is required that no greater quantity of land be given than is necessary for the subsistence of the occupiers."

Earl Stanhope, born in 1753, and dying in 1816, invented a printing press and a calculating machine, and was the improver of canal locks and stereotyping. He was full of enthusiasm for the improvement of the social institutions, and looked with complacency on the French Revolution as an attainment of that end. Lord Holland says of him : "He was in some senses of the word the truest Jacobin I have ever known. He not only deemed the monarchy, clergy, and nobility, but property, or at least landed property by descent, as unlawful abuses. He sometimes gave me a glimpse of his designs in proposing measures apparently preposterous, by hinting their tendency to subvert the fundamental principles of society."

His daughter, Lady Hester Stanhope, lived in Syria, and said: "Your Europe is so insipid! Leave me to my desert! What should I do in Europe? See nations worthy of their chains, and kings unworthy to reign? Wait a little, and your old continent will be shaken to its base. Every thing is worn out in Europe. The kings do not make dynasties ; they fall by their own fault. An aristocracy, soon to be effaced from the world, is giving way to a mean and ephemeral middle class, without productivity or vigor. The people, the hard-working people alone, still preserve a character and some virtues. *Tremble you, if they become aware of their strength!*"

Lord Byron despised his own class, and said: "One of the noblest sights of earth was to see a man go forth in the morning to toil for his family." In 1824, he went to fight for the Greeks, to deliver them from the Turks. He died in Missolonghi. This line denotes his humanity: "The drying up of a single tear had more of honest fame than shedding seas of gore."

Montesquieu was born in 1689, and died in 1753. His principle works are "The Spirit of the Laws," and "Persian Letters." These are some of his teachings:

"Luxury is always in proportion to the inequality of fortunes.

"Indolence and inaction is a consequence of being deprived of our labors.

"Nothing can reconcile those who have nothing to those who are in affluence.

"Commerce was only the profession of mean persons, that of knaves. It is only making those who do it dishonest.—*Aristotle.*

"So great is our luxury that people adorn with embroidery the shoes of boys and girls. The employing of so many persons in making clothes for one person *is the way to prevent others from getting clothes.* There are ten men who eat the fruits of the earth to one employed in the means of agriculture, and is the means of preventing others from getting nourishment."—*Kiavanti*

Voltaire died in 1778, after writing seventy books. From a dialogue between a man worth forty crowns and another worth five thousand, is this language:

"Whence comes this dearth of laborers?

"Because every person who has the least inclination to industry, becomes an embroiderer, watchmaker, silk weaver, lawyer, divine, beggar, or a monk. Every one as much as possible has avoided the laborious employment of husbandman, for which we were created by God.

"Our new wants are a cause of our poverty. What a cursed thing is this tax, which has reduced me to beg alms!

There are three or four hundred taxes, whose names it is impossible to remember. Was there ever a legislature, upon founding a State, that thought of creating the counselors of the king, coal measurers, gaugers of casks, assizers of wood, overseers of salt, butter, etc.—of maintaining an army of scoundrels twice as large as that which Alexander commanded by sixty generals, who laid the country under contribution? Such a legislation takes away from me one-half of my property. Upon a nice calculation, it will be found that the establishment takes away three-fourths by detail."

St. Simon was a French nobleman, and was at the siege of Yorktown. He was born in 1760, and died in 1825. He laid down this principle: "That society is composed of idlers and laborers, and that a policy should be aimed at for the moral, physical, and intellectual amelioration of the laborers, and a gradual extinction of the idlers. The means of accomplishing this was the abolition of the privileges of birth, and the classification of laborers."

Louis Blanc obtained an office under the French Government. At a party of the aristocracy he was introduced to a lady. She stood on her tiptoes, and looked over him, exclaiming, "I can not see him." He was so offended that he threw up his office, and commenced to write on the "Organization of Labor." Louis Philippe has often been heard to say, that it acted like a battering ram to royalty.

His plan was for the government "To erect social workshops to employ the idle men, and to loan them money." Tailors were set to work on clothing for the *Garde Mobile*. The King of France had to run away in 1848. He was succeeded by Louis Blanc, whose plans led to idleness and extravagance, and he, too, had to leave. A civil war was producd in which two officers, and ten thousand soldiers were killed. Both rulers found refuge in England.

Lamartine says: "Political economy ought not to be, as formerly, the science of wealth. The democratic republic ought, and will give it another character. It will make it a science by the results of which not only will labor and its fruits be increased, but by which a more general, equitable, and universal distribution will be accomplished. Ancient science tended only to render individuals wealthy, but our new science will apply itself to make the entire people rich."

Raymond, a writer on political economy, in 1823, says: "How many people do we see in each community who, instead of supporting themselves by their own industry, contrive to supply themselves with the necessaries and comforts of life from the industry of others! Some do this by fraud and overreaching, by direct violence, by the exercise of their wits, by the permission of the law, or in violation of it. What a host there would be, if all the people of the United States, who live by the labor of others, were collected together!

"The history of mankind, in all ages of the world, shows that some will never labor for subsistence if they can obtain it by plunder—that they will never labor for themselves as long as they can compel others to do it for them."

Robert Southey, the English poet, when a boy could say: "When I look at the mansions of the great, with all their splendor and magnificence; when I look at the cottage of the husbandman, and see him dividing his scanty morsel among his infants, I blush and shudder at the patience of humanity." His uncle said to him: "Robert, if you write democratic eclogues you will be poor; choose the Church and State, and you will be rich." Poverty compelled him to do this. His plan was to settle on the Ohio. The person who was to advance the money died, which compelled

him to be a pen drudge. His best poem is "Joan of Arc."
In it is described the ravages of war, and its desolating influences on the country, its besieged cities, famines, ruined
homes, and impoverished people. In one of his rural poems
is described the plow-boy, his visit to the fair, and how the
recruiting sergeant saw him and gave him punch. He portrayed to him the glory of war—"flags flying, drums beating, cannons roaring, and the French retreating." The boy
lists and "sets off for fame," then he is drilled, marched,
and countermarched. After enduring hunger and misery,
he returns home, and is robbed of his money. He com-
mits a crime, and ends his days in a penal colony. The
sufferings of England's toiling classes are told in mournful
poems by Southey.

"It was Shelley's creed, that human nature is capable of
being made perfect; that kings and priests have hindered
that glorious consummation for the attainment of their own
selfish purposes; that religion is hostile to the development of feelings of charity and fraternity; and that if the
inherent goodness of the human heart was free to work out
its mission, *the Golden Age* would be realized. There is no
doubt Shelley believed his principles to be correct, and his
views attainable. His untiring benevolence in visiting the
cottages of the poor during his residence at Marlow, stamps
with sincerity and disinterestedness his eloquent pleading
for humanity.

"'Queen Mab,' the most generally known of Shelley's
works, is a poem abounding in fine passages. He supposes
the soul of a female character, called Ianthe, to leave the
body during sleep, and to ascend, under the guidance of the
fairy Mab, to the latter's cloud-roofed palace, from whence
she contemplates the earth, and surveys the ruins of Jeru-
salem, Palmyra, Athens, and Rome. Then she beholds a

battle-field, a town destroyed in the conflict and the death-bed of a tyrant.   The poet descants upon the horrors of war, the vices engendered by *competitive commerce*, and all the social errors and evils of the present life.   The spirit describes the *auto-de-fé* of an atheist.   Mab, after defending materialism, summons the wandering Jew, who relates the crimes, abuses, and consequent misery, which are alleged to have resulted from Christianity.   Having thus passed in review the past and present, the fairy queen favors Ianthe with a glimpse of the future, when all the moral and material beauty of the Golden Age, and all the prophetic anticipations of the millennium are realized and fulfilled.   The earth, in the language of St. Simon, is re-habilitated, and no longer produces rank weeds and poisonous fungi, but everywhere flowers and fruits.   Fens and marshes, which had exhaled malaria, are covered with waving grain; the whirlwind and the storm are known no more; the burning deserts of Arabia are rendered cultivatable; the polar ice is dissolved; and the wild denizens of the forest have forgotten their thirst for blood—the lion sports with the kid.   The nature of man has experienced a change corresponding with this beautiful picture of the external universe.   War, slavery, commerce, and all the evils of the present society are no longer known; his passions are tempered and harmonized; temperance has banished disease from his frame, and prolonged his life, and his existence has become a long midsummer's day—a dream of Arcadia or Paradise realized.

"'The revolt of Islam' is of a different cast.   The poet arises from slumber visited by unquiet dreams, and meets on the sea-shore a beautiful female form, by whom the story is related.   She is beloved by a spirit, who conducts her to the glorious senate of the departed friends of the human race, where she meets Laon, a patriot of Argolis, who re-

23

lates the story of the revolt of his countryman against the tyrant of Islam. This poem is far superior to Queen Mab, and is replete with passages of extreme beauty. The hymn in the fifth canto of the nations who have liberated themselves by revolt, is a complete exposition of Shelley's views and opinions. It declares fear to be the cause of man's misery and degradation, proclaims the moral beauty of equality, and announces the advent of peace, love, freedom, and universal brotherhood.

"'Prometheus Unbound,' is as metaphysical and mystical as are most of Shelley's poems. The atheistic tenets of the poet are boldly proclaimed. The idea of the perfectibility of human nature is here reproduced. The overthrow of Jupiter, and the unbinding of Prometheus harbinger the restoration of the Golden Age. These three poems present us with a complete view of Shelley's social philosophy, and the whole tenor of his life."—*Chambers's Works.*

Extract from Shelley's Queen Mab.

> "——Those gilded flies,
> That, basking in the sunshine of a court,
> Fatten on its corruption! What are they?
> The drones of the community: they feed
> On the mechanic's labor. The starved hind
> For them compels the stubborn glebe to yield
> Its unshared harvests; and yon squalid form,
> Leaner than fleshless misery, that wastes
> A sunless life in the unwholesome mine,
> Drags out in labor a protracted death,
> To glut their grandeur; many faint with toil,
> That few may know the cares and woe of sloth."

Hugh Miller's "School and Schoolmasters" teaches us to escape poverty by working directly on the soil, which will give us plenty of food, fleeces, and candles. He says: "I found myself standing before a life of labor and restraint,

The prospect appeared dreary in the extreme—the necessity of toiling from morning to night, and all for a little coarse food and homely raiment; and I fain would have avoided it.   * * * In less than a fortnight I succeeded in obtaining a very considerable mastery over the mallet.   I astonished Uncle David [his teacher in stone-cutting] by setting myself to compete with him, and by hewing nearly two feet of pavement to his one.   * * * We found twenty-four workmen in a corn-kiln, open at the gable ends, and a row of beds on the sides.   Over each bed hung a sack of oatmeal, which was their summer's food, without milk or meat.

"The oatmeal was boiled in water, and made into cakes, which were baked before the fire.   The uncle grumbled because the meal went so fast; he laid it down as a law that only two cakes a week should be eaten.   I mixed up a peck of meal.   During the baking the uncle came in, and exclaimed, 'What's this, laddie, are ye baking for a wadding?' 'Just baking one of the two cakes, master,' was the answer. This raised a laugh, and cured uncle of two cakes a week. There was a diversity of opinion how much salt should be put in the porridge, and how long it should boil.   A cook contrived, in the same pot, to make half of the porridge without salt, the other half very salt.   When the two men sat down to eat, one exclaimed, 'He has given me porridge without salt.'   The other exclaimed, 'He has given me porridge as salt as brine.'

"Candle-light indulgences could not be afforded.   To pass fifteen hours in darkness was no easy task.   Exploits were told.   A stone-cutter, on his night journey home, fell into a grave.   On getting out, he was pursued by some body-stealers, who wanted him for a 'subject.'   Another time he was attacked by robbers, from whom he escaped, and was lost in a mist.   To keep warm he went among some sheep."

Mr. Miller tells us he "had all his fingers oozing blood at once; and labor was torture handling dirty stanes. My poor master suffered more than I did. The wall went up painfully with his chopped and bleeding hands, which made him fretful."

Mr Miller became editor of a paper, and his best essays are made into a book of 500 pages, called "Literary and Political Essays," in which he describes a farm laborer's cottage as no better than a shed—no window frames, the roof lets in the rain, which makes the floor quite soft, and keeps the beds damp. It does no good to keep fire, as this abode is so open. It is owned by the land-owner for a yearly tenant, and contains a father and mother, four daughters, and two sons. These have only one room.

Mr. Miller worked on "hanging stone-steps with *torus* and *mouldings* formed on them," and also on stone columns. It seems not to have ever occurred to him, that were men to work less on stone-carving, and more on homes for those who support men by useful toil, human happiness would be promoted. He chose rather to flatter the vulgar rich. In his essays, he speaks well of Wellington, and gives us an amusing account of a Burns' festival in a shower of rain. He heaped ridicule on the Chartists, whose plans were well meant, and were trials to mitigate human misery. He seems to have no remedy for the social ills of life.

This author writes beautifully on "*Ptericthys, Anadontas,* and *Unionidæ.*" This kind of knowledge would be well if no misery were to be found. If this writer had told the gentlemen to do something useful, as a means of lessening the burdens of the poor, he would have been of more utility to men.

CHAPTER XVI.

SOCIAL AND MORAL INNOVATORS.

THE OPINIONS OF VOLNEY—FRANKLIN—FENELON—CAREY—FOURIER—HAR-
RIET MARTINEAU—JOSEPH KAY—DR. PRICE—JAQUES TURGOT—FORTES-
QUE—WILLIAM GODWIN—JOHN WESLEY—WILLIAM WICKLIFFE.

"Let tyrants know there exists a place on the earth, where oppressed men
may escape from their chains."—ABBE RAYNAL's address to Americans.

OUNT VOLNEY, in his "Ruins of Empires,"
says: "I perceived in the extremity of the Mediterranean, in one of the nations of Europe, a prodigious movement, such as when a violent sedition arises
in a vast city—a numberless people rushing in all directions
to the public places. My ear, struck with the cries that
resounded to the heavens, distinguished these words: 'What
is this new prodigy? What cruel and mysterious scourge
is this? We are a numerous people, and we want hands!
We have an excellent soil, and we are in want of subsistence! We are active and laborious, and we live in indigence! We pay enormous tributes, and we are told they
are not sufficient! We are at peace without, and our property and persons are not safe within! What is the secret
enemy that devours us?'

"Some voices, from the midst of the multitude, replied:
'Raise a discriminating standard, and let all those who maintain and nourish mankind by useful labors gather around
it, and you will discover the enemy that preys upon you.'

"The standard being raised, the nation divided itself into two unequal bodies, of a contrasted appearance—one with sunburnt faces, the marks of misery and labor; the other, a little group, an imperceptible fraction, in rich attire covered with gold and silver, and in sleek and ruddy faces, presenting the signs of leisure and abundance.

"Considering these men more attentively, I found that the great body was composed of farmers, artificers, merchants, and all the professions useful to society. The little group was made up of the ministers of worship of every order, financiers, nobles, men in livery, commanders of troops, and other hireling agents of governments.

"These two bodies being assembled face to face, they regarded each other with astonishment. I saw indignation and rage arising on one side, and a sort of a panic on the other. The larger body said to the smaller one:

"'Why are you separated from us; are you not of our number?' 'No,' replied the smaller group, 'you are the people; we are the privileged class, who have our laws, customs, and rights peculiar to ourselves.'

"*People.*—'And what labor do you perform in society?'

"*Privileged Class.*—'None; we were not made to work.'

"*People.*—'How, then, have you acquired these riches?'

"*Privileged Class.*—'By taking pains to govern you.'

"*People.*—'What! we toil and you enjoy! we produce and you dissipate! Wealth proceeds from us, you absorb it; you call this governing! Privileged class, a distinct body not belonging to us! Form your nation apart, and we shall see how you will subsist!'

"Then the smaller group deliberated on this state of things. Some just and generous men said: 'We must join the people, and bear a *part of their burdens*, for they are like ourselves, and our riches come from them.' Others, arro-

gantly, exclaimed : 'It would be a shame, an infamy for us
to mingle with the crowd; they are born to serve us. Are
we not the noble and pure descendants of the conquerors of
this empire? This multitude must be reminded of our own
rights and of their origin.'

"*The Nobles.*—'People! know you not that our ancestors conquered this land, and your race was only spared on
condition of serving us? This is our social compact, the
government is constituted by custom, and prescribed by
time!'

"*People.*—'O conquerors, pure of blood, show us your
genealogies! we shall then see if the robbery and plunder
that is in an individual, can be virtuous in a nation.'

"And forthwith voices were heard in every quarter, calling out the nobles by their names; and they related their
origin, parentage, how their great-grandfather, grandfather,
or even father, were born traders and mechanics. After
acquiring wealth in every way, they then purchased their
nobility with money, so that very few families were of the
original stock. Said these voices : 'See those purse-proud
commoners, who deny their parents! See those plebeian re-
cruits who look on themselves as illustrious veterans!'

"To stifle them, audacious men cried out: 'Mild and
faithful people acknowledge the legitimate authority, the
king's will. The law ordains.'

"*People.*—'Privileged classes, explain the word legitimate!
if it means conforming to the law, say who made the law?
Can the law ordain any thing else than our preservation?'

"Then the military governor said : 'The multitude will
only submit to force. We must chastise them. Soldiers,
strike this rebellious people!'

"*People.*—'Soldiers! you are of our blood, will you strike
your brothers, your relations? If the people perish, who

will nourish the army?' And the soldiers grounded their arms, and said : 'We are likewise the people, show us the enemy!'

Then the ecclesiastical governors said : 'There is but one resource left, the people are superstitious; we must frighten them with the names of God and religion.'

" 'Our dear brethren! our children! God has ordained us to govern you!'

"*People.*—'Show us your power from God!'

"*Priests.*—'You must have faith ; reason leads astray.'

"*People.*—'Do you govern without reason?'

"*Priests.*—'God commands peace. Religion prescribes obedience.'

"*People.*—' Peace supposes justice. Obedience implies conviction of duty.'

"*Priests.*—' Suffering is the business of this world.'

"*People.*—'Show us an example.'

"*Priests.*—'Would you live without gods and kings?'

"*People.*—'We would live without oppressors.'

"*Priests.*—'You must have mediators, intercessors.'

"*People.*—' Mediators with God, kings, courtiers, and priests! Your services are too expensive, we will manage our own affairs.'

" Then the little group said : 'All is lost—the multitude are enlightened.'

" The people answered : 'All is safe. Since we are enlightened, we will commit no violence; we only claim our rights. We feel resentments, but we must forget them. We were slaves, we must command, we only wish to be free, and liberty is but justice.' "

Volney, a French nobleman, was born in 1753, and died in 1797. He maintained that the force of the State was in proportion to those who tilled the soil and owned it.

Dr. Franklin wrote this on a margin of one of Jefferson's pamplets: "Happiness is more generally diffused among savages than in civilized societies. No European, who has once tasted savage life, can ever afterward bear to live in our societies. The care of providing for artifical wants—the sight of so many rich wallowing in superfluous plenty, whereby many are kept poor and distressed by want—the insolence of office—the snares and plague of law, and the restraints of custom, all contribute to disgust them with what we call civilized society."

Archbishop Fenelon, a Catholic divine, offended the king of France by his " Telemachus," which reproved him for his misrule. The morals in this book are sublime. Its political maxims are for the happiness of mankind. This good man died in 1715. These are extracts from his book:

" If he is qualified to govern in peace, it must follow that he should be governed by the wisest laws. He must restrain pride and luxury, and suppress all arts which can only gratify vice. He must only encourage those which supply the necessaries of life, especially agriculture, to which the principal attention of the people should be turned.

"Whatever is necessary will become abundant. The people being inured to labor, simple in their manners, habituated to live upon a little, and therefore easily gaining a subsistence from the fields, will multiply without end. The people will be healthy and vigorous, not effeminated by luxury, veterans in virtue, not slavishly attached to a life of voluptuous idleness.

"When they [savages] were told of nations who have the art of erecting superb buildings, and making splendid furniture of silver and gold, stuffs adorned with embroidery and jewels, exquisite perfumes, costly meats, and instruments of music, they replied that the people of such nations are ex-

32

tremely unhappy in employing so much labor and ingenuity to render themselves at once corrupt and wretched. Superfluities effeminate, intoxicate, and torment those who possess them. They tempt those who do not possess them to acquire them by *fraud* and *violence*. Can that superfluity be good which tends only to make men evil? Are people of these countries more healthy or more robust than we are? Do they live longer, agree better with each other. Are not their hearts corroded with envy, and agitated with ambition and terror? Are they not incapable of pleasures that are pure and simple? And is not this incapacity the unavoidable consequence of the innumerable artificial wants to which they are enslaved, and upon which they make all their happiness depend.

"These were the sentiments of a people who acquired wisdom by the study of nature. They considered refinements with abhorrence, and it must be confessed that, in their simplicity, they were great. They lived in common, having no partnership in the land. The head of every family is a king."

Helvetius, in his "Essay on Man," says: "A small fortune will suffice a busy man. The largest will not supply him that has no employ. A hundred villages must be laid in waste to amuse an idle wretch. The greatest princes have not sufficient riches to supply the avidity of a woman, an idle courtier, or a prelate. It is not the poor, but the idle rich that feel the want of immense riches, for which nations are loaded with taxes and ruined. How many citizens are deprived of necessaries, merely to support the expense of a few discontented mortals! When riches have stupefied the faculty in man, he gives himself up to idleness. He feels at once a pain in serving himself. If a man were truly noble and honest he would spend his time in tears."

Douglas Jerrold, in his "St. Giles and St. James," contrasts the condition of the rich and poor. "In the streets of London an infant is found on a door step. The by-standers exclaim 'God help it,' and with this easy adjuration we consign thousands and tens of thousands of human beings to want and ignorance; doom, when yet sleeping the sleep of guiltlessness, to future devils—their own misguided passions. We make them outcasts, wretches, and punish them in their wickedness for our own selfishness and neglect.

"The child is before us. May we not see about it, contending for it, the principles of good and evil? a contest between the angels and the fiends? Come hither, statesmen; you who live within a party circle; you, who fight some miserable fight; continually strive in some selfish struggle for *power* and *place*, considering men only as *tools*, the merest instruments of your aggrandizement; come here, in the wintry street, and look upon God's image in its babyhood! Consider this little man. Are not creatures such as these the noblest, grandest things of earth? Have they not solemn natures—are they not subtly touched for the highest purposes of human life? Come they not into this world to grace and dignify it? There is no spot, no coarser stuff in the pauper flesh before you, that indicates a lower nature. There is no felon mark upon it—no natural formation indicating the thief in its baby fingers—no inevitable blasphemy upon its lips. It lies before you a fair and unsullied thing, fresh from the hand of God. Will you, without an effort, let the great fiend stamp his fiery brand upon it? Shall it, even in its sleeping innocence, be made a trading thing by misery and vice? a creature borne from street to street, a piece of living merchandise for mingling beggary and crime? Say; what, with its awakening soul, shall it learn? What lessons whereby to pass through life, making an item in the social sum? Why, cunning will be wisdom; hypocrisy its truth; theft its natural law of self-preservation. To this child, so nurtured, so taught, your whole code of morals, nay, your brief right and wrong, are writ in stranger figures than Egyptian hieroglyphics, and—time passes—and you scourge the creature never taught, for the heinous guilt of knowing nought but ill! The good has been a sealed book to him, and the dunce is punished with the jail."

Rev. Sidney Smith, in 1820, said: "In what four quarters of the globe, who reads an American book?" H. C. Carey, of Philadelphia, has written 3,000 pages on political economy. His books, for truth and clearness, exceed all that has been written on this subject. His books are, an "Essay on Wages," "Past, Present, and Future," in two volumes, and "Social Science," in three volumes. He teaches earnestly that the farmer and mechanic should be together, so as to save the middleman. In his "Social Science" is this language: "Why does misery and crime exist? Why, when so large a portion of the earth is yet unoccupied? Human beings are suffering for food, and crowded together in unwholesome dens, to the sacrifice of comfort, decency, and health. Why does one nation export food, of which its own members are in need, while another nation sends its manufactures throughout the world, although hundreds of thousands at home are scarcely clothed? In short, what is the cause of the measureless woe that exists on the earth? * * * * * Seeing the great disparity there is between the different conditions of human life, we ought to raise each lower class to a class above it. This is the true equalization of mankind—not to pull down those who are exalted and reduce all to a naked equality, but to raise those who are abased, to communicate to every man genuine pleasures, to elevate every man to all true wisdom, and to make men participators of a comprehensive benevolence. This is the path which the reformers of mankind ought to travel. This is the path they should pursue. Do you tell me that society can never arrive at this improvement? I tell you we can come nearer and nearer yet."

Charles Fourier was born in 1772, and died in 183–. He was, at five years of age, punished for telling the truth in his father's shop, which he never forgot. It led to this truth, that agricultural association and wholesale dealings were the only means of neutralizing fraud and falsehood in commercial dealings. His father left him $20,000, which he invested in rice, sugar, tea and coffee. This was taken from him for the use of the hospital troops of the Convention. A vessel laden with goods, belonging to him, was wrecked, which made him poor. Being fond of fruit, he was obliged to pay sevenpence for an apple in a town, which were sold for three farthings a dozen in the country. These and some other causes led him to frame his system of "phalanstery, social husbandry, and attractive industry." He waited for a large capitalist to carry out his plans; none offered himself to put them in practice.

His ideas were based on reasoning like this: A piece of ground takes one person twenty-four hours to dig it. If twelve men are put at it they will be "joyous and happy, and do it in an hour and a half." Groups were to take care of the poultry, others to work in the kitchen, workshops, and gardens, "under movable canvas canopies." All these groups have made free choice of the functions they are engaged at. If a shower of rain came up, those who worked in the house were to go to the fields with carriages after the distant laborers.

Says the translator of Fourier's book: "Large cities engulf

vast masses of men in a kind of a living death, and doom
them to wear away their lives in a wilderness of brick and
mortar, amid the tumult and traffic of crowded streets, while
all nature is robing herself in magnificence, as it were, to
regale the senses of her lord, and raising her glad anthems
to Him who arrays the earth in loveliness. The artisan is
a stranger to scenes like these. The trees may be clothed
in beauty unknown to him, the groves may be resonant with
music that sounds unheeded by ears attuned only to the dis-
cord of creaking machinery.

"I do not call mere wages an index to the happiness of
man. He may vote for a representative unbiased by threats,
and yet be a slave in soul, ground to the dust. If he suc-
ceeds in getting a little capital, it is at the expense of worn
limbs and an aching brow. Something must be wrong in
our political schemes, to reduce men so low in the scale of
happiness. Man was undoubtedly placed on the earth to cultivate and embellish it. He is invited, by its infinite variety,
to satisfy his ever-multiplying wants, and encircle himself
with its choicest beauties and costliest varieties. The
earth, with all its boundless riches, is a waste, a wilderness,
an unreclaimed desert.

"Labor is the lot of man. Without toil he could not support his body. That vast multitudes of men should be
doomed to the soul-deadening drudgery of beasts of burden,
is a libel on humanity. No agrarian scheme of division and
anarchy is proposed to rob the rich and aggrandize the
poor. The system now introduced seeks to show how
multitudes may be released from heart-wearing toil, and the
rich from corrupting and corroding idleness. The poverty-
stricken may be raised to opulence, while the rich may be
surrounded with additional magnificence."

Harriet Martineau has shown what a woman can do, in

grappling with this difficult subject, which few men understand, nor do two men understand it alike. This lady treats political science in the same way as Ricardo and others. She believed that there should be distinct classes to receive rents and create capital. Her books are called "Illustrations of Political Economy," in which are interwoven the incidents of domestic life, with its cares and struggles, its hopes and fears. She has given to this dry, tedious science the novelty of fiction and the pleasures of romance. Her "Tales and Sketches" show that women can think as well as men. Her "Manchester Strike" describes the distress of families, and how the factory children enjoyed their long holiday at first to be succeeded by pinching want. She very clearly points out that employers lose the rents of their shop, and how their capital yields no profits; or, if the capital was partially borrowed, how the interest diminished the fund of the employer. This book shows how the work they might have done was made in other countries,* and how other people became skilled at the same work, and their competitors. When the workmen are ready to go to work, after losing their wages, the employer can not give work to as many as he did, his capital, stock, and machinery have wasted.

Her books teach that laborers receive wages, capitalists profits, and land owners rents. What mankind want is a plan whereby they can all alike receive wages, profits, and rents. For useless labor this talented woman had no condemnation. These two examples, or others like them, should afford satire for the pens of philosophers. The pal-

---

* There was a strike among Paris hatters. English workmen gave to them money for their support. During this strike English hatters were supplying Paris with hats. If a hatter strikes and makes a $2.00 hat worth $2,25; if the shoemaker strikes, and make shoes at $2,00, worth $2,25 a pair, what will the hatter gain? Nothing. When one class strikes all should strike.

ace of Versailles was repaired at a cost of $200,000,000, for the accommodation of 100,000 philosophers, pensioners, nobility, and statesmen, who were to surround the king. A single monument cost $10,000,000. The utility of these may be shown by the conversation of two weavers in the streets of Hull. One said to the other: "There is Wilberforce's monument, it has given work to a great many mechanics." Said the other: "If the labor on it were in implements of industry, or on cottages for the poor, the labor would be of some utility, and promote the happiness of the human race."

Wayland has given to us "The Elements of Political Economy" in three divisions—on "Production," "Distribution," and "Consumption," which, when analyzed, say to laborers: You are an inferior class; it is your duty to produce and distribute, to be consumed by a superior class, clothing, food, and other things. This is from his book: "Consumption is the destruction of values. By this is not meant the annihilation of the *material*, but only of a particular form *of utility*. Thus, if gunpowder be burned, if bread be eaten, if a tree be felled, the particular utility each originally possessed is destroyed forever. And the destruction of value takes place altogether independently of the result which may in different cases ensue, because that destruction is as truly effected in one case as in another. A load of wood that has been burned, as truly loses its utility—its power of creating heat—when it is destroyed by a conflagration as when it is consumed under a steam-boiler, or in a fireplace, though the result in the two cases may be very dissimilar. If bread be thrown into the sea, its utility is destroyed just as much as if it were eaten; though, in the one case, there is no result from the consumption, in the other, it is the means of creating the vigor necessary for labor."

It is self-evident, that if a person spends his day-time in learning this, he will be poor or make some one else poor. It will bring about the result mentioned by Say—the laborer will get none of the comforts of life. Thousands have been taught out of these books, yet they can not prevent the increase of want and crime.

The Rev. Mr. Blake, author of "Political Economy for the use of American Schools," "thinks it very improper to teach the poor the nature of political economy. * * * The rich and the poor are necessary to each other; because, without the rich, the poor would starve, and without the poor the rich would have to work. * * * If, besides furnishing subsistence for himself, the wages of the laborer do not enable him to maintain a wife and bring up a family, the laborers will gradually diminish, and the scarcity of laborers will raise their own wages, which will enable them to live with more comfort and rear a family; but, as the capitalist will always keep wages as low as he can, the laborer and his family can seldom command more than the necessaries of life."

Bulwer, in his writings, seems to plead for the poor criminals, and to blame society for their many crimes. In his "Eugene Aram," he puts this complaint in the mouth of one of them: "Why is this? The world is my treasury; I live upon my kind; society is my foe; laws order me to starve: but self-preservation is an instinct more sacred than society, more imperious than laws."

Bulwer seems to look upon the governing powers as no better than thieves. His "Paul Clifford," the tenth chapter reads as follows: "'Listen to me, Paul,' answered Augustus; 'all crime and excellence depend upon a choice of words. I see you look puzzled. I will explain. If you take money from the public and say you have been robbed,

33

you have undoubtedly committed a great crime; but if you say you have been *relieving the necessities of the poor*, you have done an excellent action. If, afterward when dividing this money with your companions, you say you have been sharing booty, you have committed an offense against the laws of your country. But if you observe that you have been *sharing with your friends the gains of your industry*, you have performed one of the noblest actions of humanity. To knock a man on the head is neither virtuous nor guilty, but it depends upon the language applied to the action to make it *murder* or *glory*. Why not say, then, that you have shown *the courage of a hero*, rather than *the atrocity of a ruffian?* This is perfectly clear, is it not?'

"'It seems so,' answered Paul.

"'It is so self-evident, it is the way all governments are carried on. If you want to rectify an abuse those in power call you *disaffected*. Oppression is *law* and *order*. Extortion is a *religious establishment;* and the taxes are the *blessed constitution*. Therefore, my good Paul, we only do what all other legislators do. We are never rogues so long as we call ourselves honest fellows, and we never commit a crime so long as we can call it a virtue! What say you now?'

"'My dear Tomlinson, there is very little doubt but that you are *wrong;* yet if you are, so are all the *rest of the world*. It is to no use to be the only white sheep in the flock. Wherefore, I will in future be an excellent citizen, by relieving the *necessities* of the *poor*, and sharing the gains of my *industry* with my friends.'"

This same author, in this book, says: "The learned professions are masks to your pauper rogues; they give respectability to cheating, and a diploma to feed on others."

Joseph Kay, in his "Social Condition of England," tells

us of scenes that no benevolent mind can bear to read of, a father and mother and six children in one bed. In a room in Church Lane were found two widows with four children, three single women and one man, two husbands and their wives. These were respectable people. Houses are so offensive that persons can not visit them with medicines or consolation. There are scenes so depraved that they can not occur in savage life."

Chateaubriand, in his "American Travels," says: "The mercantile spirit is beginning to carry them away; interest is fast becoming with them a great national vice. A gold-bearing aristocracy is ready to spring up, with a love of distinctions and a passion for titles. People imagine there is a universal level in the United States; it is a complete error. There are circles that disdain each other, and between them there is not any connection. The enormous inequality of fortune threatens still more seriously to destroy the spirit of equality. A cold and hard selfishness reigns in the large towns."

Fortesque, Lord High Chancellor under Henry VI, says: "Every inhabitant is at liberty to fully use and enjoy the fruits of the earth, products of the farm, and the increase of his flocks. All the improvement he makes by his own personal industry, or of those he retains in his service, are his own, to use and enjoy, without the let, interruption, or denial of any man. If he be injured, he shall have satisfaction against the party offending. Hence it is that the inhabitants are rich in silver and gold, and in all the necessaries of life. They drink no water unless at certain times, by the way of doing penance; they are fed in great abundance with all sorts of flesh and fish; they are clothed in good woolens; their bedding is of wool, and that in great store; they are all well provided with household goods and implements for husbandry. Every one, according to his rank, has all things to make life easy and happy."

"Evidence before the House of Commons, in 1824, stated that the laboring classes of Suffolk were robbers too deeply corrupted to be ever reclaimed. The sheriff of Wiltshire stated the food of the field laborers to be potatoes. The judges of the King's Court declared the general food of the laborers to be bread and water, and that some had eaten horse-flesh and brewer's grains.

"A law recently published tells the world that this nation, once the greatest and the most moral in the world, is now a nation of incorrigible thieves, the most impoverished, fallen, and degraded that ever saw the sunlight."—*Cobbett.*

Such a condition of life is caused by selling the food of laborers abroad for useless things. It is converting men, who should be farmers, into sailors, custom-house officers, life-insurers, and other pursuits that cause the misery of the nation.

Burke, in his writings, said : "Religion is for the man in humble life, to raise his nature, and to put him in mind of a state in which *the privileges of opulence will cease*, where he will be equal by nature and more than equal by virtue."

Reasoning like this will not make the toiling man contented, when earth has such an abundance. Burns has said :

> "If I'm designed yon lordling's slave,—
>   By nature's law designed,
> Why was ever an independent wish
>   E'er implanted in my mind?
> If not, why am I subject to
>   His cruelty or scorn?
> Or why has man the will, the power,
>   To make his fellow mourn?
>
> See yonder poor o'erlabor'd wight,   Who begs a brother of the earth
>   So abject, mean, and vile,   To give him leave to toil."

Dr. Channing says: "The fruits of modern civilization are, a contempt for other's rights, fraud, oppression, a gambling disposition in trade, reckless adventure, and commercial revulsions tending to impoverish the laborer, and to render insecure every condition of life. Relief is to come from the new application of Christian principles, and of universal justice to men."

M. Sismondi says: "There is spoliation. The rich man robs the poor, when he draws from his fertile and easily cultivated soil his opulence. Whilst he who has raised this income, who with his sweat has bathed every production, dies with hunger."

"The great living mass, who are the creators of wealth, are trampled down with as much indifference as if they were weeds."—*London Times, December 8th*, 1844.

John Ball, a priest, in 1378, went up and down England, inculcating on the minds of the common people that mankind were all derived from one common stock; and he explained to them that it was to support a few in riotous luxury, in extravagance and debauchery, that many were reduced to starvation. He tried in vain to find out the right a few had to bind the mass of their fellow-beings to their will, because they happened to be born in a palace. He also informed them all had an equal right to liberty and the goods of nature, from which they had been deprived by the ambition of the insolent few. Three years after this the Wat Tyler rebellion broke out, caused by these circumstances: The French wars of Edward III caused much expense, to meet which a tax was put on every person fifteen years of age and upward. A collector of this tax went to the house of Tyler, and demanded the tax for the mother and her daughter. A dispute arose with the mother about the age of her child. The ruffian resorted to his usual brutal method of deciding the difficulty. The indignation of the mother and the terror of the daughter caused such an outcry that a multitude was quickly assembled, which hastened the father, who came with his blacksmith hammer, and laid the agent of oppression dead at his feet with a single blow. Tyler soon had 100,000 armed men. The king fled to the Tower for safety. Tyler demanded an audience. He told the king his people were perishing on account of taxation, and his father did not treat them so. The young king said: "He did not know the people suffered." The attendants gathered around to hear Tyler tell his story, which caused him unthinkingly to lay his hand on his sword. This offended Wm. Walworth, Lord Mayor of London, and he struck him with his spear. Another thrust him in the side. The arrows of the angry insurgents were about to be sent among the royal retainers. The king, with great presence of mind, threw himself among them, and said: "I grant all your demands ; follow me, I will be your leader." The concessions made were afterward revoked, and the leaders were executed. This rebellion loosened the chains of the people and taught kings a lesson.

The demands were—*first*, freedom from the condition of serfs ; *second.* the reduction of the lands to a moderate price ; *third*, that they be charged with no more taxes than their forefathers paid ; *fourth*, the right to sell in all the fairs in the kingdom; *fifth*, a field rent instead of villanage services; *sixth*, the right to hunt and fish.

Wm. Godwin, a philosophical recluse, during the storm of the French Revolution, sent forth out of his retreat arousing thoughts and burning words, that gave vigor and life to the heaving mass of minds around him. In his "Political Justice" is this: "Kings are the most unfortunate and the most misled of all human beings. Royalty allies itself to vice. Kings debauched from their birth, and ruined by their situation, can not endure intercourse with virtue. Monarchy is so unnatural an institution, that mankind have, at all times, strongly suspected it was unfriendly to their happiness. The man who, with difficulty, earns his scanty subsistence, can not behold the ostentatious splendor of a king without being visited by some sense of injustice. He inevitably questions, in his mind, the utility of an officer whose services are hired at so enormous a price.

"These reflections are so unavoidable, that kings themselves have often been aware of the danger of their imaginary happiness. They have sometimes been alarmed at the progress of thinking, and have often regarded the prosperity of their subjects as a source of terror and apprehension. Hence, the well known maxims of monarchical governments, that it is necessary to keep the people in a state of poverty and endurance, in order to render them submissive, and ease is the parent of rebellion. Hence, this lesson is perpetually read to monarchs: 'Render your subjects prosperous, and they will speedily refuse to labor; they will become stubborn, proud, unsubmissive to the yoke, and ripe for revolt. It is *impotence* and *penury* alone that will render them supple, and prevent them from rebelling against the dictates of authority.'—*Fenelon's Telemachus.*

"A second source of destructive passions, by which the peace of society is interrupted, is to be found in the luxury, pageantry, and magnificence with which enormous wealth is usually accompanied. Human beings are capable of encountering, with cheerfulness, hardships when they are impartially shared by the rest of society The *rich* are, in all such countries directly or indirectly the legislators of a *State;* and are perpetually reducing oppression into a *system.* Legislation, in almost every country, is in favor of the rich."

Let no one think that if we mitigate human misery the earth will be too populous. It has been computed that the 20,000,000 of acres in Ireland, will support 100,000,000 of persons in potatoes. Sharon Turner tells us that the rice that can be grown in China will maintain 900,000,000 of people. Let no one harden their hearts with Malthusian doctrines, or think the earth will be too populous, and look on little children with pain, and imagine they will increase faster than food. Hugh Miller tells us that pampered animals do not increase as fast as those in an opposite condition. If universal luxury should prevail, it will no doubt put a "check on population."

Wm. Godwin has given us an "Essay on Population," in which he asserts that three-fourths of the earth is a wilderness. This book was to show how absurd were the teachings of Malthus. Godwin, by these quotations, taken from Montesquieu's "Persian Letters," proves that our world is not as populous as it was:

"Italy, though its present population is confined to the towns, is a mere vacancy and a desert. It seems they exist for no other purpose than to mark the spot where those magnificent cites stood, with whose policy and wars history is filled.

"Rome contained a greater population than any one of the most powerful kingdoms of Europe does at present. There were single Roman citizens, who possessed 20,000 slaves for rustic purposes.

"Sicily, in times of old, contained within its shores powerful kingdoms and flourishing states, which have entirely disappeared.

"Greece is so wholly deserted as not to contain the one-hundreth part of the number of its former inhabitants.

"Spain, formerly so abundant in men, exhibits nothing at

the present day, but a variety of provinces, almost without inhabitants ; and France is an unpeopled region compared with the ancient Gaul that Cæsar described to us.

" The North of Europe is in a manner stripped of its people. The times are no more when she is obliged to separate her people into portions, and to send them forth in swarms and colonies, to seek some new spot where they might dwell at large.

" Poland and Turkey in Europe are almost without inhabitants.

"Asia is not in a much better condition. Asia Minor, which boasted of so many powerful monarchies, and so prodigious a number of great cities in her limits, with Greater Asia, or the part subject to Turkey, is in no better condition.

" Persia, if we compare it with its former condition, we shall see it contains but a very small residue of the population which anciently furnished the innumerable hosts of Xerxes and Darien.

"As to the smaller states, which were placed in the vicinity of these great empires, they are literally unpeopled, such as Circassia, Guriel, and Imiretta. The princes over the extent of the country in which they now preside have scarcely under their subjection as many as 50,000 beings.

"Africa has always been so unpenetrated that we can not speak of it with the same precision as of the other parts of the globe ; but, if we only turn our attention to the coast of the Mediterranean—the portions which are known—we see how wretched it has sunk since the period in which it first formed a Roman province of the highest kind. Its princes are now so feeble, that they are strictly the smallest powers in existence.

" Egypt has not suffered less than the countries I have mentioned.

"In a word, I review the different nations of the earth, and I find nothing but destruction. I seem to see a race of beings who have escaped from the ravages of a universal plague or a universal famine.

"Upon a calculation, I am led to think that the earth does not contain the fiftieth part of the population that inhabited it in the time of Cæsar. What is more astonishing, that its population grows thinner every day; and if it goes on at this rate, in one thousand years the human race will become extinct.

" Here, then, my friends, we are presented with the most fearful catastrophe that imagination can conceive of, yet it is hardly attended too, because it proceeds by insensible degrees, and spreads itself over such a series of ages. This very thing incontestibly proves, that there is an innate vice, a concealed and inaccessible poison, a wasting disease, which clings to our nature and can not be removed."

David Hume wrote an " Essay on Population," which contradicts the author of *Lettres Persannes*. The strange doctrines of Malthus found an opponent in Sharon Turner, a legal gentleman, whose life begun in 1761, and ended in 1847. By improving his leisure hours he has left a pleasing, enlightening, and enduring monument in his " History of the Anglo-Saxons " and "Sacred History of the World." Each is in three volumes. The last begins with man in his creation, brings him through the deluge, and down the disturbed stream of time to the present age. Malthus, in the last books, gets some hard blows for asserting his incongruous, contemptible ideas that man's increase lessens his food. Turner's books contain this : "When the work is indispensable we can only take such laborers as we can get. As the working population *increases*, selection becomes possible." This applies to the idle. He treats on the "food supplies."

Mr. Wesley wrote on almost every subject. He did not write on political subjects. The code of rules he gave to his people will make any nation rich. His rules forbid ornaments on dress, houses, or equipages. His rules make him a Christian philosopher of the highest order. No one in modern times has exceeded him in benefiting mankind. He said: "The early Christians made no account of perishable goods. They despised all that luxury had introduced, all the idle expense in magnificent buildings, costly apparel, sumptuous furniture, and vessels of gold. As to their dress, they wore no glaring colors, mostly white, the emblem of purity. They used no costly stuffs, rings, jewelry, or perfumes; nothing fine or delicate. Plainness, modesty, gravity, and a contempt for ornament was visible in their whole exterior."

In his "Sermon on Money," it is thus written: "Do not waste any part, merely in gratifying the eye, by superfluous or expensive apparel, or by needless ornaments. Waste no part of it in curiously adorning your houses; in superfluous ornaments or expensive furniture, costly pictures, gildings, books, paintings; in elegant rather than useful gardens.

"Who would expend any thing in gratifying these desires, if he considered that to gratify them is to increase them? Nothing can be more certain than this: daily experience shows, the more they are indulged they increase the more. Whenever, therefore, you expend any thing to please your taste or other senses, you pay so much for sensuality. If you lay out money to please your eye, you give so much for an increase of curiosity—for a stronger attachment to the pleasures that perish from the using. While you are purchasing any thing that men applaud, you are purchasing more vanity. Had you not, then, enough vanity, sensuality, and curiosity before? Was there need of any such addition?

And would you pay for it, too ? What manner of wisdom is this ? Would not the literally throwing your money into the sea be a less mischievous folly ? "

Mr Paley, in his "Evidences of Christianity," said, you can tell Methodists by their plainness, they resembled the early Christians. Rev. Mr. Paley would not say that now. If Mr. Wesley could see now the costly female colleges that are erected, he could say, in the language of Mary Wollstonecraft: "A few brilliant minds at the expense of all the rest." He could also say: The costly wood and stone carvings, frescoed ceiling, glass stained, effigied, mullioned windows, carpeted floors, and easy sofas that the pupils enjoy, are at the expense of the comforts of some one else. To demonstrate this is easy : The parents of these pupils became Christians, which made them thoughtful and money saving. These savings, instead of being invested in lands and looms, cultivated by the investor, are put in bridges, roads, stocks, corner lots, and wild lands, the profits of which keep them in learned, splendid idleness.

These investing Christians are conscious that their gains through the State's care can go into the people's pockets. If these pupils, the children of light and grace, would work at farm work two hours a day, during the planting and reaping time, and two hours daily in winter spinning and weaving, they would have created their own food and clothing, which would make them feel happier and better, and relieve others from the burden of keeping them, who would find time for home learning. Mr. Wesley, when young, made a vow that he never would be rich. He said: "If I am worth more than fifty pounds at my death, call me a thief and a robber."

CHAPTER XVII.

REASONS FOR REFORMS.

> " Seize upon truth wherever found,
>   On Christian or on heathen ground;
>   Among your friends, among your foes,
>   The plant's divine where'er it grows."—Cowper.

R. WILLIAM PALEY, D. D., Archdeacon of Carlisle, in his "Principles. of Moral and Political Philosophy," says: "If you should see a flock of pigeons in a field of corn, and if (instead of each picking where and what it liked, taking just as much as it wanted, and no more) you should see ninety-nine of them gathering all they got into a heap, reserving nothing for themselves but the chaff and the refuse; keeping this heap for one, and that the weakest, perhaps worst, pigeon of the flock; sitting around, and looking on all the winter whilst this one was devouring, throwing about, and wasting it; and if a pigeon more hardy or hungry than the rest, touched a grain of the hoard, all the others instantly flying upon it, and tearing it to pieces; if you should see this, you would see nothing more than what is every day practiced and established among men.

"Among men, you see the ninety and nine toiling and

(385)

scraping together a heap of superfluities for one (and this one, too, oftentimes the feeblest aud worst of the whole set, a child, a woman, a madman, or a fool); getting nothing for themselves all the while but a little of the coarsest provision which their own industry produces; looking quietly on, while they see all the fruits of their labor spent or spoiled; and if one of the number take or touch a particle of the hoard, the others joining against him, and hanging him for the theft."

This is found in "Littell's Living Age:" "At a meeting of the King's Council, at which a bishop was to have been appointed, a member proposed Dr. Paley. At the mention of his name, the king cried out: 'What! what! what! Pigeon Paley!—make Pigeon Paley a bishop? No, no, no; never!'"

In society we often see men, who toil hard all day for others, and scarcely get a sufficiency of good food, or a decent suit of Sunday clothing in which to go to church and learn the moral duties of life.* The reason why this is so, men work at unprofitable employments. To illustrate this, if you visit a cabinet wareroom in the principal street of this city [Cincinnati], you will see book-cases worth $2,000, bedsteads worth $1,000, and chairs $100 each. It will excite wonder at the delicate carving, fine polished woods, inlaid with silver, satin and ebony wood from Brazil, mother

* "Brethren, you have in your city as much misery as there is anywhere. I have seen more than one family in a room. I am often called to bury their dead. I invite these poor to church. Then I call and inquire, if they had been to church. The reply was: 'We looked in and saw the merchants and bankers, and could not overcome the difficulties.' I said they are a good sort of people, and want to do you good."—A part of a sermon preached in Wesley Chapel, Cincinnati, Nov. 30th, 1868. By the Rev. Charles Ferguson. Plainness of dress, as recommended by Mr. Wesley, cures these "difficulties" and invites people to church.

of pearl, ivory, and tortoise shell, forming beautiful mosaic, a landscape, or a bird of brilliant plumage.   Often a bedstead has on it a carved hunting scene.   The head-board is a carved mass of festoons and foliage, surrounding a bird's nest with the bird on the edge of it cut in high relief.   We often see a marble-topped table, with its whimsical-carved frame, covered with gold.   If laboring men turn reformers they are often taunted with being idle, drunken, worthless vagabonds, and if they had any energy they would rise above their condition.   Those making this assertion are well off, and generally think others can become so.   The money that pays for this finery is often ill-gotten, and those from whom it is taken should be making comforts for themselves.   It is impossible, from the nature of things, that the maker of these articles should be in any other condition than that of poverty, because some people use a thousand times more labor than others do.

A Candidate's Home.—"The mansion is a most magnificent one, with a finish such as is seldom seen this side of the water.   At every turn, evidences of European travel meet the eye, while the floors of the principal apartments are laid in marble mosaic of elaborate patterns.   Attached to the main building is an elegant floral conservatory, in the style of a grotto, filled with all the choicest exotics, peeping out from every little cave, in every variety and color.   At a little distance from this there is a succession of hot-houses, in which I noticed, growing most luxuriantly, bananas and pine-apples, and other tropical fruits.   The grounds, which are seventy-three acres in extent, are most charmingly diversified, and in all the highest state of ornamental cultivation.   The views from the front and rear verandas of the main building are wonderfully grand and beautiful."*

* Cincinnati Commercial, July 15, 1868.

In addition to this he has no doubt velvet carpets, and his seats are covered with soft shaggy plush, or satin damask. Laborers, sitting on them not knowing their softness, would be frightened at the sinking sensation.   A truthful epitaph.

To keep from

falling into oblivion the name of

GEO. II PENDLEDON,

simple-minded and homeless men dug, polished,

carved, lettered, and sculptured this marble.

" He rose in the morning and went to bed at night,"

for———years.

He could say with Watts, " There are a number of us born

Merely to eat up the corn."

His plans to pay a nation's debt was an inundation of

paper money.

He was an imitator of Charles XII, of Sweden,

who paid his debts with copper that was by his decree

made to be of the same value as silver.

He had no plans to ameliorate the condition of

impoverished, suffering men.

His "Escort," numbering, perhaps, 200 men, left this city, and went to the city of New York, to name this man to be the chief ruler.   They took with them fifteen barrels of beer, and five of whisky.*   Said a paper of that city, "Their

* I asked a printer, an eye-witness to this carousal, if these things were so. He said: The amount of liquor was, perhaps, twice as much.   At their quarters in the city, these " commissary stores " were put in a corner and given away.

procession had a woe-stricken and dilapidated look." What
pain this scene must have given the moral Democrats, to see
their delegates under the power of bad drink, while naming
a chief ruler! The result of such conduct is, that very bad
men get promoted. What a reproach it is that New York
City, filled with book and Bible printing-houses, the source
of those noble charities that are felt over this land and the
earth, should elect a John Morrissey, a pugilist, to Congress,
to make rules for the moral part of community, who has the
ability more than others, to knock a person down.

This Pendeldon who lives so finely in his sister's home, has
splendid wealth, a father's patrimony. His biographer tells
us he has traveled among the ruins of Thebes, and gazed
upon the Pyramids of Egypt. The money taken from the
dwellers on the banks of the Ohio, was given to the Arabs
on the Nile. In his life, sent out to prove that he was a proper person to be the " standard bearer of Democracy," nothing is said of his visiting the afflicted, and helping to dry up
their tears; nor is any thing said about founding asylums
for the unfortunate.

The food of this man is the finest and the best. There is
no doubt that some part of it is coated with white sugar,
and covered with sugar angels, cupids, birds, and flowers,
at a great cost. It is self-evident that this costly food, during its preparation took much labor which should be better employed. The luxury of this man is misery to some
one else. Says one, Does not this give employment? It
does; it is unnecessary employment. The wages that are
paid should be employed in creating comforts for those who
bought his lots and farms, to get which they suffered pain.

We can very justly question the fitness of such a man
to be above the humble ones, to make rules for them, or to
rule them. In the first place, he has no sympathy for them,
34

no feelings in unison with theirs, nor been a partaker of their sufferings. He has never been rudely repulsed when he asked for work, or reproached for not doing it well, or having the quantity deficient. He has never experienced the painful feelings of begging for work, or those when discharged. This man receives prompt obedience from submissive servants, pleasing adulation from compliant merchants, and good wishes from kind friends, who enjoy his grapes and pine-apples, his conversation, books, gardens, conservatories, elegant pictures, luxurious seats, and abundant dinners. A man thus surrounded with all that heart can wish or desire, and continually greeted with the smiles of friends, his wishes gratified, and plans carried out, will insensibly lead him into the opinion that he is a superior person, which will be increased by seeing his well fed, comfortably clad appearance of his servants. He will give his money to mechanics for his grottoes and other fancies, which will procure for him the title of benefactor from flattering friends, who ignore the fact that these benefits are from his tenants that eat butterless bread, from interest-paying men whose houses are unadorned.

This man's person in his baby-hood and boy-hood, was covered with fine linen, and costly velvets. The world to him was full of playthings to destroy. He could roll on the grass in ecstacy, gather flowers, or chase butterflies. His youthful back never ached with gathering potatoes; his little fingers never were numbed with cold, gathering apples; he never shivered in the cold, feeding cattle, or groaned at chopping wood. Servants did his bidding, which taught him to command. To improve his faculty of observation, to give his education a finish, to give him a lofty mien among men, parental fondness sent him on a tour of foreign travel.

A person thus nurtured and trained becomes effeminate, indolent, luxurious, and selfish. This class, not knowing how to labor, when they are made statesmen will make the laws so that they need not work. That legislators get bribes is well known. Lobbyists have received $20,000 for getting bills through legislatures. If a man applies for a bank charter, or a life and fire insurance permit, he gets a mine of wealth. The member who gets these granted by the legislature receives a reward of him who is the recipient of these privileges. Hence it is often said that legislators make fortunes.

The Romans erected a temple of honor, and those who trod its courts were pure and unsullied. If this luxurious man, whom we have described, should present himself at the door of the temple, this conversation might ensue with the door-keeper:

"Upon what do you base your right to tread these courts?"

"I have got the learning of the colleges."

"How do you spend your time?"

"After I rise in the morning I go into the grottoes and inhale the perfume of the flowers. I also go into the grapery and eat grapes."

"Do you not know that the laborer goes forth to till the soil; he returns in the evening with aching bones, and without his labor you will soon perish? Why do you not assist him?"

"My education forbids it."

"The laborers strangely believe that legislatures can shorten the hours of labor; your reason teaches you that if you assist them it will shorten their laboring hours."

"I do head work."

"Your head work makes some people slaves; do you not see some part of the female community poor and thinly clad, whilst another part are richly and gorgeously clothed, the fashion of which is often grotesque, wavy, inordinate in quantity and length, dragging over the walks, gathering up brush, cabbage leaves, cigar stumps, etc? Have you ever expostulated with the vain female, who shows her want of humanity and sense, by covering her person with spangles, ribbons, tags, and feathers, and shown how absurd it was to follow the frivolous fashions when so many can be made happy by the excess of labor they demand and consume?"*

"No."

"Then the gates of the temple of honor are closed against you. Its courts are easy of access. Have only a few habits, and supply them with the labor of your own hands. In this temple is the door of the temple of fame, and in it are some vacant niches; you can get one if you will vindicate the laborer's cause. How painful is the thought that he who performs the hardest toil gets the poorest pay! It is time he should have more of the comforts of life. Teach him that it is not paper or gold money that will benefit him, but universal labor at something useful."

Says the Commercial: "Dr. Price, Abbe Mably, and M. Turgot gave the framers of this government some good advice." It is a source of sorrow it has not been observed. These men, judging from their acts, believed they had no moral right to riches. Abbe Mably was born in 1709. He displayed sound moral principles, and a regard for the good of mankind. He was fond of applying ancient, political maxims to modern States, which gave great offense.

Jaques Robert Turgot was born in Paris, in 1727, and

*Chaucer, in his "Persone's Tale," has some keen satire on woman's dress. " The cost of embroidering, endenting, ounding, paling, bending, and cost-lewe furring on the gounes, their moche superfluitee in length, trailing in the dong and myre, wastes, consumes, wears threadbare and are rotton with dirt, all to the damage of the poor folk who might be clothed out of the flounces and draggle-tailes of these children of vanitee."—In the time of Richard II.

died in 1781. When a boy, he determined to sacrifice all advantages to liberty and conscience. He wrote on the goodness of religion for mankind. He was a disciple of Quesnay,* the head of a political sect called "Economists." In 1761, he was appointed Intendant of Liomoges. He was made Comptroller of the finances in 1774. In a time of scarcity he distributed food, and introduced the cultivation of potatoes. He made new roads without burdening the people, established charitable workshops, opened schools of instruction for women in the art of midwifery, moderated the duties on articles of first necessity, freed commerce of its fetters, enlarging the rights of men to follow industry, abated the rigor of direct imposition on the profits of contributors, and promoted an equal distribution of the taxes. He made salt free, reformed the royal household, and made many reforms in political economy.

His plans were turned into ridicule, by making little snuff-boxes, and calling them "Turgentines." The good Louis said of him: "No one loves the people but M. Turgot and I." La Harpe says of him: "He was a man of strong mind; nothing could divert him from doing justice. He had only two passions, science and public good." During the few years he was occupied as minister of finance, he bent all his views to the relief of the people. Attached to the doctrines of the Economists,† he developed them in edicts that tended to their encouragement and improvement.

* Francis Quesnay, physician of Louis XV, taught that only those who cultivate the earth, or otherwise bring into use the natural powers of the mineral, animal, and vegetable kingdom, can be regarded as really increasing the wealth of the community.

† Those who analyzed the frame of civil society, gathered light from those who lived before them, and tried to form a more liberal social system than those that were known. One of them, M. De Gournay, attacked a system which compelled a man to get a privilege to sell a commodity.

He changed acts of sovereign authority into works of reasoning and persuasion. His reforms created him many enemies. He lies under the stigma of promoting the French Revolution, and he is charged with making innovations in favor of the people. He died at forty-nine.

Dr. Price, a Welsh Protestant minister, was born in 1728, and died in 1791. In 1785, he gave to the world "Observations on the American Revolution, and the means of making it useful to the world." He gave us plans how to pay the national debt, to preserve and perpetuate this nation. He showed that absence from *foreign commerce* would make us virtuous and happy. He said: "No man can be raised to an elevation above others without danger. They who trust their rights to others trust to enemies."

After a lapse of ninety years, this people have degenerated, and we can not now be called a free nation. The revolutionary sires would not pay to Britain threepence a pound duty on tea, or use their stamped paper. The usages of our society are so contrived that millions can live and not work at any thing useful, and become very rich. Jay Cooke is supposed to be worth $10,000,000 ; William B. Astor, $60,000,000; Com. Vanderbilt, $50,000,000 ; Dan. Drew, $15,000,000. The interest on these sums is $10,000,000, and will keep from useful labors 25,000 persons. This is only a small part of those who live on the labor of others who obtain it without reflection on the part of those who create it. These distinctions were introduced in this way : Our fathers were a plain people, and were content with the productions of home. Franklin's wife used to boil his milk, and pour it on bread for his breakfast. Merchants have taken away cloth, blankets, leather, etc., and exchanged them for tea leaves, which are re-sold to the poor, who are injured by this exchange. Were this to cease blankets and clothing would be more abundant among us. The Pacific Railroad is an example of what Mr. Price said, to prove the danger to us in delegating civil power to others. Our representatives have given away to a company of men land sufficient to make four States as large as South Carolina, which contains 19,000,000 of acres. This transaction, in the future, will make hundreds of thousands of Americans slaves. The "N. Y. Ledger" says "the Pacific Railroad will make such private fortunes as the world never saw." James Rothschild died, in 1868, worth $400,000,000. This sum will find homes, implements, and land sufficient for 40,000 families. This paper means the time may come when some men will have the maintenance of eighty, perhaps 100,000 families. The benefits of this road are to him who works doubtful. It is not improbable we pay for what China sells us $100,000,000 worth of our most useful goods. $150,000,000 of products will go over this road to buy gold. These two amounts, if saved, will give half of our people, who are without homes, at the end of ten years, a home worth $850. This calculation supposes the nation to number 6,000,000 families, and that five persons form a family. These two sums are a year's traffic.

This road will introduce luxury, the desire to be covered with laces, ribbons, and fine cloths, Near the city of New York a farmer gets a dollar for a bushel of corn. The farmer on the Pacific road will sell five bushels of corn for a dollar. When this distant farmer spends his dollar, he can not get as much for it as the New York farmer. It is the duty of every one to obtain all the comfort he can in exange for his labor. Hence it is the duty of poorly-paid mechanics to go among the distant farmers and exercise his trade where provisions are cheap, where his labor will sell for a higher value. It is not the duty of either of these two classes to give any part of their earnings to enrich railroad men who live in magnificent style. These wealthy railroad owners were once merchants, became land speculators, and issuers of paper money. If the laborers will sweep the merchants away, they will become the owners of railroads.

Were the cost of the Pacific Railroad spent along its route in all kinds of manufactories, the people would become rich and happy. This merchants will prevent, as it will send them to the plow and workshop.

Merchants have a way of taking the subsistence of our people to Europe and exchanging it for trifles, to the injury of the poor of those countries, who, to make silks, laces, and fine shawls cheap, must live and work in cellars and attics. Says a Commissioner: "Their chambers look like caves, in which the air is never renewed. The poor man is in rags, his children are lean and puny, with emaciated limbs, ulcerated fingers, and crooked, softened bones." The director of the Prussian king's factories, M. Mayet, in 1796, said: "The cessation of work causes some to steal, others to emigrate. Their vices are the offspring of others' luxury, which are produced by some acquiring riches. Workmen must not be suffered to enrich themselves. In becoming so he is difficult and exacting, enters into combinations, imposes laws, and becomes dissipated. The rich stuffs he makes should be watered with his tears." Were Americans to do without foreign goods, their makers would emigrate to other lands—to cultivate them.

John Adams took great offense at the advice and plainness of Mably, Price, and Turgot. He wrote as a reply, "The Defense of the State Constitutions." M. Turgot said: "The Americans have imitated the English Government without any motives." Mr. Adams wrote more than 1,500 pages showing that mankind should be governed by the

superior classes.   He wrote in favor of three powers ruling
this people : a Governor, Senate, and House of Representatives.   The Senate were "to be rich and high born," so
that they could protect their property from the aggressive
poor. The House of Representatives was to be composed of
the poor, who would be a check on the oppressiveness of
the rich.   It is a beautiful fiction, two houses a check on
each other.   Both are rich now and plunder toiling men.

Mr. Adams said : "They [the rich] have rights as well as the others. They
have as clear and sacred rights to their large possessions as others have to theirs,
which are smaller.   Oppression is to them as possible, and as wicked as to
others.   The rich, therefore, ought to have as an effectual barrier in the constitution against being robbed as the poor."

This acknowledges that the rich are not just to laboring
men.   That we have degenerated from happiness, virtue,
and freedom, may be inferred by reading Mrs. Grant's book
on America in 1760: "Every one in town or country had
a garden, with all kinds of vegetables.   After it was dug no
man intruded.   I have often seen a minister's wife with a
basket of seeds and a rake over her shoulder.   A woman
in easy circumstances would plant, sow, and rake.

"Each family had a cow.   Nothing could be more pleasing to a benevolent mind than to see the inhabitants of a
town containing not one very poor or very rich, very ignorant or very knowing, very rude or very polished individual; to see all these children of nature enjoying themselves
in easy indolence, or social intercourse.

"Fraud and avarice are the vices of society, and do not
thrive in the forest."

Mr. Winterbottom, in his "History of America," printed
in 1797, says much on the happy condition of the people.
The Americans should feel shame at having lost so much
liberty, which comes from delegating political power to men

35

of wealth.   In Vol. III is this : "The American States furnish a smaller proportion of rich and poor than any other district in the known world.   In Connecticut the distribution
of wealth is more equal than elsewhere, and will apply to
all New England.   The great body of the land-holders are
cultivators of the soil.   They are removed from temptations
of luxury.   Their industry and frugality exempt them from
want.   The people of New England obtain their estates by
hard labor, and none are better furnished with the conveniences of life.   Idleness with those of independent fortune
is disreputable."

The writer has read much to find out if any crime existed in the beginning of this nation.   Mr. Winterbottom tells
us, in 1792, Boston had seventy-seven convicts making nails,
on a small island guarded by sixty soldiers.   This city then
contained 35,000 persons.   New York City had a greater
proportion of bad people than this.   It was caused by this :
" The Governors of this [N. Y.] State were many of them
land-jobbers, bent on making their fortunes ; and being invested with power, they engrossed for themselves, or patented away to their favorites, a great part of this province.
The genius of this State still favors large monopolies of
land."—*Winterbottom*.

This same author tells us : " That young people marry
early without obstacles, and are not tempted to dishonor
themselves.   Disgusting disease was almost unknown before the Revolution.   Foreign armies naturalized it. * * *A
grandmother at twenty-seven is often seen.

"Georgia gave away her land on condition of cultivation,
residence, and defense.   When the male line expired, the
land was to go back to the government, so as to prevent one
person having more land than another.   This was null and
void if it did not make the female heir's possession too large.

" In Kentucky, in 1780, if a man staid a year in that State, and raised a crop of corn in it, he was entitled to 400 acres of land. In this State towns were laid out, the minister, schoolmaster, tavern-keeper, and magistrate had each a building lot given them. Judges and Congressmen had more than one given them."

Why should social distinctions exist in human life? Is not the laborer who prepares the fuel to keep us warm, the bricks and mortar that constructs the home which shelters us from the pitiless storm, as good as they are, and just as useful? Is not the mechanic who makes the leather that protects the feet, and he who makes the clothing that keeps us warm, entitled to lots as well as Judges and Congressmen who corrupt human society, and live by its corruptions.*

"John Locke was forced by the proprietors of Carolina to make them a government. He gave to each county a landgrave and two caciques, who could only own two-fifths of it. The three-fifths were to belong to the people. Virginia gave to settlers 1,000 acres, who were to pay a penny an acre rent."—*Winterbottom's American History.*

---

* Hon. B. F. Wade seems to be an exception. These are his sayings: "That system of labor which degrades the poor man and elevates the rich; which drags the very soul out of him for a pitiful existence, is wrong. We must elevate the laborer and give him a share in the proceeds of his labor. The shadow of a great struggle is upon us, and we must meet it. There is a deep discontent, a feverish excitement, a restlessness with their lot among the poorer classes we can not disregard. The people want more recreation, enjoyment, and relief from their monotonous, half-starved condition, and they will have it."

This philanthropist made attacks on slavery, when our religious people were dormant. He battled with prejudice in high places, and made a part of the colored people of the District of Columbia men—by obtaining for them the privilege of voting. He caused laws to be made that the wild lands should be free to those who would settle them. This he might have done sooner had he not been surrounded with Southern Senators, whose rule of action was to suppress all plans that would ameliorate the condition of Northern laborers, because the contrast with their slaves would be too great.

If this author could collect this information, so could the Fathers of this nation do the same. Their conscience and reason should have taught them that they should have given building lots to mechanics, and limited farms to laborers. The Fathers seemed to think that the toiling part of community should pay the nation's expenses. To illustrate this: The Fathers gave 160 acres of land to a church, if the members should rent this land and pay the pastor his salary out of these rents. Where is the justice in making a few tenants pay for the preaching that many enjoy? To a school district is given 160 acres, and it is sold to two persons for $1,600. This sum, when at interest, will pay the teacher. Why should injustice be practiced on these two men, and they paying the teacher's salary exempting the parents who get the benefits, and are able to pay the teacher. The Revolution benefited all, who should equally pay its expenses. To make laborers pay for land was unjust. The uncultivated land is God's gift to man, and no body of men have the right to sell lands, on which there has been no human labor, nor has any one a right to more than he can cultivate. Selling the wild lands to pay for past wars to exempt "the rich and well-born" from taxation, has filled this country with woe and crimes.

John Adams, in his "Defense," says: "The people of Bilboa [in Italy] arose and killed the officers appointed to collect the duty on salt. They defeated 3,000 soldiers sent against them, and drove them into the sea.

"In the Swiss republic of Grisons, the inhabitants live together in a perfect equality, exempt from the refinements of luxury. There are none so rich as to gain an ascendency. There are noble families who live by cultivating the earth."

Mr. Adams gives us a sketch of more than fifty republics and states, which he thought were not suitable for us to

imitate.   He also wrote much to ridicule the opinions of
Plato, Milton, Sidney, Locke, and Franklin, who thought
men would be happier without cumbersome governments.
John Adams while in England, from 1784 to 1787, wrote
to prove that we needed such a government as now exists,
which has brought this people from innocence to crime,
from a period when all had homes, to now when half of the
nation have none.   It has introduced crime and a state of
insecurity that is alarming.   It was not so once.   The Marquis Beccaria, a French political writer, in his book, says:
"Criminals in the English colonies become honest people.
We are astonished at the change, yet nothing can be more
natural.   The condemned are forced to continued labor;
opportunities to vice are wanting.   *They marry and multiply.*
Oblige men to work, and you make them honest."

John Adams and his friends got plenty of land, and the institutions of the nation were so framed that the people would
be poor and work their land.   The first method was to destroy "The Penn. Loan Office," where poor men could
borrow money to begin farming with on land rented at one
cent per acre.   The second method was to cause them to
buy land of a speculator at a high rate.

The theory of government is, men wanting happiness
must find it in society, useful industry, and assisting each
other.   At a public meeting, one says: If we build a railroad to the coal-mines it will save our time.   A majority voting for it, the expense is met by the people pledging their
property to the State for the money, or it can be built by an
annual contribution for ten years.   Suppose a tribe, numbering thirty, want to have a war.   They debate and conclude that seven soldiers can be fed, clothed, and equipped,
out of their number.

One says I will lend to you the money.   After awhile a

thinking mind sees that it is unnecessary to keep a paper money lender. This little community, by making its own paper money, will compel the lender to become a soldier or a producer. This applies to 30,000,000. Future generations can not give back this generation the food and clothes which they have paid to soldiers. It is very simple to give the cost of the war, two or three times over, in the form of interest, with the hope of getting in the future that which has been spent in the past. It is the duty of a people to maintain as many soldiers as they can, and when the war is over end the expense. War is one of these occasions that enables many to attach themselves to society, and obtain a permanent support.

Senator Chase, at the beginning of the war, found this nation with a currency of $300,000,000, which he increased to $700,000,000. It caused the commodities of life to be twice as high. To those who furnished supplies, he paid in paper, earning interest. Those who had saved money could only purchase half as much as they did. Many statesmen are in favor of bringing paper money to the value of gold. This will cause misery to those who are in debt. It will take more labor to pay the nation's interest. Issuing paper was an injury to the working people.*

If I were to stand on a highway and take ten cents from a man I should be punished. If I put a bar across a road, and say to a traveler you must pay me ten cents to travel on this road, as I built it, the traveler could say, laborers built this road, mechanics and farmers clothed and fed them. You have only used cunning to obtain this road, which has cost you paper money, the making of which did not take a day. It is the duty of society to purchase this road by is-

---

* The writer believes this nation's debts should be paid as agreed on. Taxes might have supplied the soldier's wants. The debt is a scheme to live easily.

suing paper money and offering it to the unnatural owner for
it. This money will buy him farms and tools, then he can
go to work like the rest of mankind. Working people do
themselves an injustice to allow others to live in idleness
from the profits of the roads and bridges. The pike between Piqua and Troy, O., receives one-third of its value
annually in tolls. The American people are getting to be
numerous, and it is just that these tolls should be theirs.

Society saves a fourth of its time having money. The issues of money from a State would give us a currency. A
good man never seeks an office. A farmer, having always
good crops, well-fed cattle, obedient, well-behaved children,
neatness on his farm, not overrun with weeds, one not given
to kid gloves or fashionable clothing, who speaks kindly to
his neighbor, and assists the orphans—such a one will be
a good public officer. Having learned to live from the soil,
he will not favor paper or credit schemes that will make
coats, hats, shoes, food, etc., twice the value of the usual
price, and then buy large quantities of them on credit for
the use of soldiers, which are to be paid for by future generations. Common minds know these things are in the
country, and that the tax-gatherer can collect the money to
purchase them, and that the operation can be renewed till
the war is ended. The mind of such a man can not see,
after feeding and clothing a number of soldiers, how the
cost is to be got back again twenty or thirty years from now,
and we still keep on feeding and clothing a number of persons. When a person fills an office well, and is not given
to peculation, how absurd it is to remove him.

There are a number of persons who meet to discuss
"Social Science;" this may give them some light. In the
beginning of this century, Botany Bay had 5,000 criminals.
To reform them, they were set to work on public fountains,

making fine columns for public buildings, and to work on the governor's stables. In addition to this, add the maintenance of ladies learning Latin, in cells with carpeted floors and papered walls, officers of government, policemen with clubs, professors of colleges, and other persons too numerous to mention, and you make them poor, abject, and envious. One inquires, Why am I made to differ from others? Why are others fed on turkeys, eggs, and fowls, while I am in rags, and have the coarsest fare?* To get the superfluities of life, I will not trample on others! To gain riches, I will not push others down! I will try and bear my burdens! Society has made me what I am!†

It must be self-evident if you relieve the poor convicts of these burdens, you make them virtuous and happy. The more you pile scholars, philosophers, statesmen, and others on toiling men, the more hungry, vicious, and ignorant they become. It is the duty of all to spend a part of their time in the field and shop. The people of Acadia and uncivilized Paraguay show us that security, order, and virtue can be attained without our usages. A display of virtue like this can never happen in highly civilized countries. Columbus writes to his king and queen thus: "When the Pinto was wrecked, the natives swam about and collected every thing on the beach. The property could not have been better taken care of in Spain. Nothing was stolen."-*Winterbottom.*

A great source of intemperance is from the idle sons of rich men, who, having no occupation, learn habits of dissipation. Many, who work, having poor homes, are attracted

---

Bishop Potter, in his "Arts and Sciences," tells us that sawdust can be made into palatable puddings.—Harper's Family Library.

† Bishop Potter, in his "Political Economy," gives us the Chaplain's "Report of the Conn. State Prison." "Thieves and robbers attempt to justify their course, on the ground that one man has no right to hold property more than another, and they take from the rich only."

to the gay drinking saloons.   It is not improbable that this
nation spends annually $300,000,000 on tobacco and strong
drink, which in ten years will buy every five persons a good
house having four rooms.   A mechanic, when buying a
drink, saw an open door, and heard a female voice, saying :
"Where did you get this fine furniture?"   The reply was :
"The fool's pence bought it."   The man repented?   During a rain-shower a woman took refuge in his house, and
said : "I know you, sir: where did you get your fine furniture?"   He replied: "The fool's pence bought it."   He
told her what she had said, and its effect.

A tobacco-using and liquor-drinking person can cure his
faults by visiting "The Children's Home" or an "Asylum
for Orphans," and see good women clothing and feeding
poor outcasts.   The effect will be—money foolishly spent
will be used doing good.   Another method to cure an afflicted
drinking man is to try and send a poor boy to an industrial
school.   This will give him a sincere mourner at his grave,
who will inscribe on his tombstone this affectionate record.

MR. ——— MADE ME A GOOD AND USEFUL MAN.

If a person persists in smoking and drinking, he is liable
to be poor, to be put in a mean coffin, and carried to his
grave in an express wagon as if he was a brute.

To escape the miseries of war caused some pious men to
go to new countries to create homes.   They were very systematic, as will be seen by this account:

They were governed by *abbots* and *priors*, who had charge
of the *abbey*.   The next officer was the *almoner*, who distributed alms at the gate for the poor, and gave home relief.

The *sacrist* took care of the communion vessels, provided
the bread and wine, kept the altar-cloths clean, furnished
wax-candles, and rung the bell at service and burials.

The *chamberlain* had the care of the dormitory, and the providing of beds, razors, scissors, towels, clothes, and shoes for the monks, and tools for shoeing the abbot's horses.

The *cellarer* provided flesh, fish, fowl, wine, wheat, fire wood, malt, and kitchen utensils for monks and visitors.

The *hospitaller*, gave entertainment to guests and travellers. He was to have beds, seats, tables, napkins, basins, plates, and spoons for the guests, and bring them food.

The *master of the infirmary* took care of the aged and sick, and prepared food and comfort for their infirm condition.

The *head-chanter* had the care of the choir service, the organist, and chorister, and provided them with books. He had charge of the abbey-seal, chapter-book, records of the public business, and furnished parchment, pens and ink for the writers, and colors for the painters of missals.

The rules of St. Benedict directed that six hours daily were to be given to manual labor in shops in the monastery. Some were tailors, shoemakers, jewelers, cabinet-makers, book-binders, sculptors, carvers, painters, and writers.

The *cursitor's* business was to visit the shops, and notice who were absent, idle, and talking. It was his duty to go about during prayers and see that none were asleep.

Institutions like these were wanted to refine and teach industry to the rude Saxons. They accomplished this, and became corrupt. These monks got the greatest part of the land as gifts. They contrived to have the abbey on a running stream, so as to have a mill. The garden and bakehouse were on the place, so as not to go abroad for supplies. This made them rich. Then their labor was done by servants. Wicliff brought some charges against them. His opinions became universal, and these institutions were absorbed by the men of wealth, who set the poor man to work for their benefit. A change is coming that will help the poor.

The farmers and mechanics create a pile of food and useful things, annually, amounting to $3,000,000,000. These various classes of consumers destroy the greatest quantity.

Lawyers, physicians, and clergymen...............	$83,000,000.
Merchants and clerks.................................	73,000,000.
National and State governments....................	700,000,000.
Those who insure lives and houses.................	30,000,000.
Tea makers and gold seekers........................	200,000,000.
Cost of tobacco and drinking........................	300,000,000.
Earnings of railroads, bridges, and pikes............	100,000,000.
Interest paid on railroad and private debts.........	100,000,000.
House rents from 3,000,000 of families............	90,000,000.
Profits to bankers and brokers......................	25,000,000.
Amount consumed by non-producers..........	$1,701,000,000.

In our Senate it was said : "Your manual laborers are but slaves ; and if they knew their power, your government would be reconstructed." Laborers working for a rich man give him an easy abundance. Were they philosophers, they would say: "We want not your money ! Go work, add to a world's wealth !" To make a store front a mass of statues, eyeless faces, and fine stone-carvings, in which to put our hats and shoes, is unnecessary and wasted labor?

Pious "Aunt Effie" expected to die with hunger. "The Shepherd of the Plain," for his Sunday dinner had potatoes and salt. The family, in the "First of the Week," were thankful for gravy on their Sunday food. The meat was eaten next day. On Wednesday the bones were stewed. The diet, the rest of the week, was bread and potatoes. "The Happy Waterman" was a frugal Christian, which enabled him to buy a boat, and comforts for home. This was taken as evidence that he had found a lost purse of gold. It cost him much to get acquitted. These sorrowful tales, and others, are found in a Methodist book-store in this city, which is as beautiful as can be seen anywhere. The two entrances are arched. The window top is a quarter of a circle in each corner, joined by a straight line. Six delicate columns, with foliated capitals ornament the doors. On the arches are oblique openings, and carved leaves and scrolls. The upper windows are columned in the corners. The highest windows have between them as brackets a smiling female face, and two male faces with sheep's horns. The cornice has four gargoyle likenesses in it. The imposing cornice has on it two large globes. Poverty comes from ill-spent labor.

A book printer sets up "Notes on the Revelations," or "On the Infallibility of the Pope." He then has to wait till another work comes in, which is "The Prairie Boy," or "The Fisherman's Son." While waiting for work, the printer often loses six months in the year. There are so many new titled books made in a year, that their names can not be read or remembered. This printer is an involuntary idler.

Laborers would be happier if they would leave those, who draw such large supplies of their toil for frivolous uses, and go into the wilderness and found new homes. Skilled laborers, by exchanging labor, can have, in two years, houses and mills to make life happy. They need not labor more than four hours in a day, and live free from painful fears and cares.

The earth has an abundance. Labor has multiplied forty times by machinery since we have become a nation. Most of our people are poor. We are further from freedom now after a national existence of a century. The cause is delegating power to rich men, who use it to benefit themselves.

CHAPTER XVIII.

CONCLUSION.

A WASHINGTON LETTER—THE PACIFIC RAILROAD A MEANS OF ACQUIRING
TERRITORY WITHOUT WAR—HOW THE KING OF PRUSSIA OBTAINED REVE-
NUE FROM A CANAL—GENERAL DEARBORN'S TESTIMONY ON MERCHANTS.

" Love mercy, do justice, and walk humbly with thy God.".—BIBLE PRECEPT.

COMMON sense should be the guide of the laborer
on the subject of political economy.   The political
economists, whose books are used in the colleges,
mislead the laboring men so as to have ease. They flatter the
follies of the rich, that they may gain their money.   Statesmen at Washington will not ameliorate the laborer's condition, as it would doom them to toil, and put an end to the
extravagant dressing, feasts, and parties of their wives and
daughters. If you remonstrate with these people on the
sin of destroying what has cost so much toil, they will tell
you it is good for trade, it gives work to mechanics. If you
tell them it is cruel to keep servants so long on their feet, to
wait on them and prepare their food, it will awaken no pite-
ous feelings, or a desire to share their toils.

A Washington letter tells us of a poor boy in its jail, who
writes to his sister thus: "'I have a nice, warm room, good
bed, and plenty to eat.   I believe I will be sent to the penitentiary, where I will be clothed, fed, and taught a trade,
and be able to obtain my living.' His companions in the
street shouted to him, and hoped soon to be with him.

"How many of these rogues in punishing do we make? The rich grow richer, and the poor poorer. What will be our proportion after a time? What are the terrors of the penitentiary to a half-starved boy?

"I think we have succeeded in catching the most harmless of our criminals; the weak alone are detected. The cold, cautious, calculating scoundrel goes unpunished. On the floor of the Senate or House note the faces of the men who have stolen their *thousands*, and see their clear, intellectual countenances. These are the larger and more dangerous rogues, who have not only escaped conviction, but are honored among men. They move in the best society, their wives are admired, and daughters sought after."*

This will ever be the condition of society while the men of wealth make the laws. The laborers should leave their farms and shops, to attend primary meetings, and send to rule their own classes, those who are free from selfishness and avarice. All power only should be vested in those who toil; without their labor we would all soon perish. A good man will resolve not to be rich. He will labor with his own hands, and will tell, if he knows, what is the cost price of goods. He wants no profits, and will invite others to become his partners. A man, to be rich, is evidence that he is wanting in benevolence, and is not fit to make laws. To prove which, take the example of a man in Illinois, who owns 40,000 acres, or eight miles square, which are cultivated by 3,500 persons. He is richer than all of them.

Our rulers knew that conquest is attended with danger, and that legislation is the same as conquest. For instance, beyond Missouri are large tracts of land, stretching to the Pacific Ocean, which, at the proper time, would have been filled with a laboring people, who would rely upon their own

* Cincinnati Commercial, January 29, 1869.

resources; they would surround themselves with all kinds of factories, and be strangers to luxury, having ease and leisure. Our rulers wish to make the people slaves, the victims of merchants, and a prey to land speculators. This was done by making a decree, that an area equal to three times Great Britain shall belong to a few, who shall build a railroad to the Pacific. These share the plunder with the rulers, and will be a means of gaining enormous tribute out of the settlers. The design is to compel them to send wool and get clothing from a distance.

Once the king of Prussia built a canal at the State's expense, and rented it to the highest bidder. If the people will use the herb which East India merchants introduced among us, it would have been wise had Congress printed $100,000,000, which would have cost $200,000, and built the road, and then rented it to the highest bidder every ten years; it would give an increasing revenue. Franklin said: "Silks and satins put out the kitchen fires. Tea can not be called a necessary. Were all men scholars, we would want bread."

A fearful retribution seems to overtake traders. Gen. Dearborn, a collector of the port of Boston, said: "He was satisfied that, among 100 merchants, not more than three ever attained independence." This is the testimony of others. Woes are pronounced against riches in the world to come.

John Adams kept an account how he spent his time from 1763 to 1795. This is an entry: "This day my men have made hay, and I have read Plutarch." Would it not have been more humane if he had said, I have this day made my hay, and read Plutarch in the evening? It would have relieved his drudges, who would have had an opportunity to obtain some learning also. How natural it was for Messrs.

Adams, Hamilton, and Morris, when sent to frame the usages of society, so to do it that they could have easy lives.

To society belongs the roads and bridges. Private individuals owning these have obtained them through the baseness of rulers. Common roads in England are owned by the community, and their earnings are devoted to keeping the poor. A king does not like to hear the murmurings of his people. He contrives to have as few as possible to eat up his people's subsistence. The Prussian king wears his coat so long, it would not sell for a dollar. He is frugal, to save his people from being absorbed by other nations.

In republics are many tyrants, who fatten on the people, eat up their food, and consume their clothing. Their plan is to fill an office, make all they can, and retire at the end of two or four years. Americans would be very wise if they would keep the revenue and post-officers in their places for life, if honest. It is so in England, where losses are rare. The king's courier was solicited to take private messages with his king's, which was the means of a post-office being owned by a nation. Congressmen send their clothes, and even bags of potatoes to their homes, which is a cause why the post-office is deficient in means to pay expenses.

A great source of revenue to rulers is to receive bribes from those to whom they grant privileges, such as bankers, life-insurers, and others. The time was when men went about telling fortunes, practicing palmistry, or telling where gold was hidden. These have taken to life-insurance, with permission of "the collected wisdom of the nation," causing men, in this case as in the others, to live without doing any thing of utility. Says a Massachusetts Report, by John E. Sanford: "There are in this State, in 1867, forty-seven life-insurance companies. The number of policies issued, in fourteen months, was 145,000, and the amount insured

If persons would hang up in their rooms a copy of the ten commandments, a list of the insurance rules, and keep houses apart, fires would not often happen. If taxes were abolished, the State would derive nearly enough revenue to pay its expenses, if it would insure the property of its citizens. Many patriotic people would like to serve society insuring, at a small salary for life. If those who insure men's lives, and those who subsist from the profits of insurance, were to work at cultivating the earth, they could feed 10,000,000 of persons. Life insuring persons are supposed to prevent poverty; they cause more poverty than they prevent. Nothing will end the ills of life but universal, useful labors; it will make earth a paradise.

8

for was $420,000,000. The number of policies dropped *for want of persistency was* 40,000, which called for the sum of $100,000,000. To satisfy the claims of those who were bereaved $9,000,000 was paid. Twenty-seven insurance companies had a surplus of $7,595,675. The sum paid to the companies during the year, was $62,000,000, and it was paid by 430,000 policy holders, to whose friends the companies owe $1,200,000,000."*

These facts may be made out of this report, for every eighteen dollars paid out, fifteen accumulates in the treasuries, and their accumulations are $100,000,000. The great States of New York and Pennsylvania also insure as much as Massachusetts, and it is not improbable that their gains are the same, which will hire 54,000 laborers, whose productive powers, with machinery on good farms, will maintain 3,000,000 of persons.

This nation has machinery equal to 150,000,000 of people. Every one has working for him five inanimate slaves, fed with fire, that want no food or clothes. Modern science and skill has taught us to make the earth yield twice as much as it did fifty years ago. Why do fathers resort to life-insurance companies to provide for their children? The money thus acquired may be lost in business or soon spent, then there has to be a return to toil at last, which finds the person unskilled, unused to labor, with perhaps, no strength. Parents should very early inure their children to plainness in dress and diet, to toil and discipline. Children, strangers to costly food and apparel, will not wish for them, and, being taught industry, will not be feeble and helpless. One who *insures lives* is a person who is determined to get the products

* Let no one accuse me of wanting human feelings, because I attack these institutions. The ruler of the Universe has done his part well in giving us a beautiful earth to cultivate, and we suffer refusing to do it.

36

of others without giving any hard labor for them. He is one who gets as much as he can for as little as he can.

The shoemakers of this city [Cincinnati] have had their wages increased by a strike, which will be the means of increasing the difficulties of the other laborers, to purchase their shoes. If these, in retaliation, increase their wages, the shoemakers will have gained nothing. For many generations strikes have been made without any benefit.

If the shoemakers were to carry their factory into the country, instead of paying $180 rent for four rooms, they need only pay $60. Do these shoemakers pay a quarter of a dollar a pound for their lard and hams? These, by preparing and curing for themselves, need only cost one-eight of a dollar per pound. A society of shoemakers, purchasing potatoes at wholesale prices, and distributing them to the members, will save a third of the price. Two acres of tile-drained soil will give a family of six half their food, and the winter's food of a cow and chickens. If the *tour de ordure* be made the receptacle of chips, weeds, ashes, and straw, and these put on the acre for the cow, it will make cabbages so large that they will be the diameter of a barrel. Of corn, 125 bushels can be obtained on the acre, sixty of which will feed the cow 120 days, and the remainder will fatten 780 lbs. of pork. There will be a fatted calf to kill. The cow will eat up the corn-stalks, beet-tops, cabbage leaves, and a load of hay during the winter, and will give a pound of butter every day. The milk will make tea not wanted.

A cow has been taught to drag a plow and rake between rows. It helping, the garden can be cultivated very easily in one hour each day during the summer. It will do a woman no harm to work an hour daily in the garden. Apples are $2.25 a bushel, which sum can be saved in a country home.

The English laborer seems in a fair way of gaining independence. There are 700,000 members belonging to the "Trades Unions," who have millions in their treasuries. In their "Benefit Societies" and "Savings Banks" they have $500,000,000. Many thousands of them are partners with their employers. They purchase fat cattle and divide their beef. They own mills, buy grain, and have cheap flour.

The N.Y. Tribune says: "Within sight of our steeples 200,000 persons are unemployed." The cause of which is, farmers cultivate all they can, make their houses and clothing as much as they can by machinery, which makes the laborer unnecessary, and enables them to have for foreign lands $400,000,000 worth of their products for luxuries, the greatest bulk of which is absorbed by the exchangers? "The Agricultural Bureau," in 1866, said: "The value of farm products was $1,563,184,134."

Mechanics create values to the amount of 1,000,000,000, half of which is wasted, or put in the wrong place. To illustrate: A President's inauguration is described in a thousand little papers around this city. If the "Commercial," "Gazette," "Times," and "Chronicle," only contained this, it could be circulated all over Ohio in twenty-four hours, as they have steam-power sufficient to print millions of papers, having in them five times more news than a country paper. Many will say, How can merchants advertise? Every farmer knows where his store is. It is only necessary to know where things are made, who sells them at wholesale, and what are their cost, which can be told best in a book.

We have many encyclopedias on various subjects, many books of travels and history, on natural, mental, and moral philosophy, and annotations on the Bible, more than we can read. Plato's Dissertation on Government seems better for the universal happiness of men than Adams' "Defense." Plato's cause of crime is as clear as any modern jurist can

give us. He said: "A youth, having spent his patrimony,
and knowing no pursuit, resorts to plundering." The Eu-
ropeon travels of Mrs. Stowe and Mr. Greeley will instruct
and please for a generation. The sermons of Wesley are
still able to teach men eternal life. Why should new authors arise to impoverish themselves and their compositors?
Printers would like to own embellished homes with carpeted
floors and frescoed walls. Three-fourths of the printers
have no homes, nor will this number ever be able to acquire
any. It is only by going at those pursuits that make the
home and its inner articles. Were three-quarters of the
printers to change work, books would be still as cheap and
abundant. Book-makers in England and America have
the stereotyped plates of 150,000 books.*

An selfish man, to gain his neighbor's custom, enriches
his store front with stone-carved *scrolls* and *leaves*, sur-
mounts it with *pinnacles*, and little *gables* ending in *finials*.
In the center is a *canopy* over a *statue* clad in a Roman toga.
The windows are *gothic*, and filled with delicate *tracery*. Is
not this wasted labor? Would it not make the outcasts of our
earth happy to have this for a home, and keep them from
the haunts of vice? All this labor is for a temporary resting
place for our shoes or hats, or something else.

An agricultural report tells us: "The yearly value of
the tobacco is $52,000,000." The after-working adds as
much more. It has been computed that this nation uses
100,000,000 gallons of whisky in a year. One-fourth of
this nation are boys under twenty-one; a third of these are
over fourteen, and number 1,250,000. It will be found by

* The writing and type-setting on this book has cost me fifteen month's
time, which would have made me a good furnished home. This labor is sure,
book making is uncertain. Conscience impelled me to do it, to try and enlighten my fellow toilers. This book contains nine sheets of paper, and they
are worth eighteen cents. The printing is two cents, and binding twenty-five.

calculation that the amount spent on tobacco, and drinking, will give each boy $125, to pay for teaching him handicrafts, and how to cultivate land. Users of tobacco and drink, you should feel shame wasting so much labor. I asked a man, who was polishing a tomb-stone worth $40,000, if he was not doing himself an injustice at such labor, which deprived him or others of some comforts. He said, "He was paid to do it." I told him to trace the source of the pay, and he would find it was obtained by oppression, such as buying land cheap and selling dear, or in pursuits without labor.

A beaver gnaws a tree with his teeth, which falls across a stream. He makes holes in the bottom ; aided by the weight of other beavers,the ends of short logs are sunk in the holes, the other ends rest on the fallen tree. Branches and mud fill up the crevices. On the top they build their cells. The efforts of these industrious animals should put to shame the idlers of society, who have abundant implements.

The Swiss remove the dirt around a tree's roots, and then chop them away. Two men turn a cog wheel, which extends a cogged beam and pushes it over.* This way a person can clear an acre in two months, which has been known to yield support to four persons. A person, having a spade and a hoe, can, with them, in a single month, obtain food for a year. With machinery he can create it in a week, which is six bushels of wheat, six of potatoes and three of beans. Twenty-five bushels of corn will give a sufficiency of bacon, and sixty plenty of milk and butter. Our home machinery will enable him to make three suits of clothing in two weeks. H. Thoreau, with six weeks' hand laboring, could live a year.

* I have no faith that I can chop down a tree with horizontal blows. I have a strong belief I can strike vertical blows at the roots, and with a rope and pullies bring it down. I have known an employer order a workman to be turned away for attending an Odd Fellow's funeral. Why are we subject to others' scorn when a home can be made so easily? Then we are independent.

We owe persons for supplying our nation with war materials who never did a day's work in their lives. Our laborers, who made these materials, are supplying the wants of those who did no work. An economy of this nation's labor will cut off these supplies. France, in 1759, had an exhausted treasury; its minister, M. Silhouette, did not believe in borrowing but in taxing. His plans of economy were ridiculed by wearing short coats without sleeves, using wooden snuff-boxes to save gold ones, making black faces in place of portraits that were formed by throwing the shadow of the face on paper, with a candle-light, and marking the outlines. This likeness, drawn by a pivot rod, became A SILHOUETTE. This manner of making a picture may have suggested sunlight paintings.

The labor on gold, tea, tobacco, whisky, beer, and foreign luxuries is annually $650,000,000, which would pay our national debt in four years. The users of these articles will not give them up. Luxury is nearly as bad as drunkenness. If a person, having no house and garden, uses unnecessaries, when loss of employment and sickness comes, he often becomes a burden on the saving and industrious. Having a war debt gives us a plea to tax luxuries to death, which will relieve our farmers and useful mechanics of half their burdens, and add laborers to their number. The people who have suffered so much during the late war should be willing to have the State insure property against fire. The authorities should issue paper money and purchase the principal railroads in New York, Pennsylvania, and New Jersey, and devote their revenues, with insurance profits, to the principal of the national debt. The reasons for this are, it will add to the laborers men to produce the comforts of life. Who has the right to live and do no work? None! These road builders used no real capital, only cunning. La-

borers, who fed and clothed the workmen, were the real
capitalists. Society should own these roads. Their usurping
owners can feed and clothe 3,000,000 of persons. Governments are assemblies of rich men to shift the burdens of a
State on the laborers, to save themselves from them, to give
privileges and monopolies, so that they can live without doing any work. For instance, it was a nation's duty to tax
every family to give Washington a reward; to give him for
his services 200,000 acres of land was to oppress a few laborers. A great State resorting to selling lands to poor people, to found an agricultural school, is contemptible. Taxation is a just plan to pay public debts, it is equal on all.*

In feudal times men exacted tolls for traveling on roads;
this custom still exists. As population increases it will be a
great source of oppression. Roman history tells us that Ti-
berius Gracchus resolved to improve the condition of the
common people. He saw indigent freemen working for aristocratic nobles. To emancipate them he had laws passed,
limiting the nobles to 500 acres of land, and their minor children to 250. To slaves he gave land. We need some president or statesman who will gain for our laborers more of
the comforts and conveniences of life.

When Catholic missionaries visited England, it was filled

*Many will say it will not do for governments to own, or do so much, there
will be cheating. Abolish taxes and derive revenue from public works, give
the managers their places for life, a salary, a percentage, and a pension in age.
You will find more fidelity among the humble than the rich. Persons living
plainly will be the most honest. I reason from my own feelings. I do not
wish to burden my mind with any wrong act to torment my dying hour.

My book-making task is ended. It is painful to oppose what men call established truths. I have done it reluctantly, impelled by the trials and privations
of some of my own class. I regret I have not given them a better book, free
from grammatical errors. I am sincere in the belief that the robberies of the
government, the acquisitions and luxury of the rich, cause a part of society to
be vicious and vindictive, filling this nation with lewdness, crime, and poverty.

with the remains of Roman barbarism, Saxon rudeness, ignorance of the rites of marriage, and Druidical cruelty that required the sacrifice of human beings. These priests made a mighty change, by a division of labor and frugal living. They have erected beautiful, architectural piles that are the admiration of men, which became to the rude people schools of learning, refinement, music and arts, hiding-places to the down-trodden, refuges to the poor slave, homes to the hungry wanderer, an asylum to the friendless, a resting place to heavenly pilgrims from the follies of a wicked world.

Within those religious houses was the *scriptory* of the patient monk, whose busy pen filled the library of his *monastery*, and has given us glimpses into the past. The ornamenting of the church with paintings and sculpture also occupied the recluses' time. Nuns taught needle-work, embroidery, and the adorning of the altar with linens and laces.

This period was to the English laborers their best days. No commerce to take away food for diamonds, no paupers, or national debts. The Pope, to obtain a larger *Peter-pence*, sent Italian priests, whose exactions made enemies, and was a cause of breaking up this system. The arts introduced, the culture taught, were not lost. Rich men, having lands, appropriated these arts to their pleasures. Changes are yet to take place in society. The power of rich men, like that of the monks, must pass away. The laborer must become a laboring capitalist, and not a capitalist's laborer. He must become moral, sober, and intellectual, to obtain this position.

FINIS.

Date Due
